Lexicography and the *OED*

The Oxford English Dictionary.

A NEW

ENGLISH DICTIONARY

ON HISTORICAL PRINCIPLES;

FOUNDED MAINLY ON THE MATERIALS COLLECTED BY

The Philological Society.

EDITED BY

Dr. JAMES A. H. MURRAY,

WITH THE ASSISTANCE OF MANY SCHOLARS AND MEN OF SCIENCE.

N — NICHE
(Volume VI)

By W. A. CRAIGIE, M.A.

OXFORD:
AT THE CLARENDON PRESS.
LONDON, EDINBURGH, GLASGOW, NEW YORK, AND TORONTO:
HENRY FROWDE.

The cover from the fascicle *N-Niche* edited by W. A. Craigie and published in
September 1906.

Lexicography and the *OED*

Pioneers in the Untrodden Forest

Edited by

LYNDA MUGGLESTONE

OXFORD

UNIVERSITY PRESS

OXFORD
UNIVERSITY PRESS

Great Clarendon Street, Oxford OX2 6DP

Oxford University Press is a department of the University of Oxford.
It furthers the University's objective of excellence in research, scholarship,
and education by publishing worldwide in

Oxford New York

Athens Auckland Bangkok Bogotá Buenos Aires Calcutta
Cape Town Chennai Dar es Salaam Delhi Florence Hong Kong Istanbul
Karachi Kuala Lumpur Madrid Melbourne Mexico City Mumbai
Nairobi Paris São Paulo Singapore Taipei Tokyo Toronto Warsaw

with associated companies in Berlin Ibadan

Oxford is a registered trade mark of Oxford University Press
in the UK and in certain other countries

Published in the United States
by Oxford University Press Inc., New York

British Library Cataloguing in Publication Data

Data available

Library of Congress Cataloging in Publication Data

Data applied for

ISBN 0–19–823784–7

1 3 5 7 9 10 8 6 4 2

Typeset in Minion
by Graphicraft Limited, Hong Kong
Printed in Great Britain
on acid-free paper by
Biddles Ltd., Guildford & King's Lynn

Preface

Lexicography and the OED was written with the main intent of examining the first edition of the *Oxford English Dictionary*, originally published by the Clarendon Press in Oxford between 1884 and 1928 under the title *A New English Dictionary on a Historical Basis*. Though *OED*, the title by which it is now known, gradually crept into use over these years (see further Chapter 1, n. 1), first on the covers and wrappers of the individual parts and on the binding-cases of the quarter-persian edition, and, in the edition of 1933, on the title-page too, it is the original title of *A New English Dictionary* (*NED*) which perhaps most clearly signals the departures which were, in a variety of ways, deliberately being made in terms of English lexicography in the course of its formation. As the relevant entry in the fascicle *N–Niche* (edited by W. A. Craigie and published in September 1906) indicates, *new* can be taken to signify that which is 'first invented or introduced; novel' as well as that 'different from that previously existing, known, or used': 'now made, or brought into existence, for the first time'. The new dictionary of the Philological Society was intentionally to be all these things, not least since, as Murray himself stressed, it was a venture in which the lexicographer must almost necessarily assume the role of pioneer, exploring—and charting—the hitherto unknown territories of the English language in both past and present.

Adopting a range of lexicographical and linguistic perspectives, the chapters in this volume, many using previously unpublished archive material, examine the results and processes of the pioneering endeavours which thus informed the origins, and the realization, of the *OED*. The dictionary is, however, a complex and by no means static construct. As a result, though the central focus remains on the first edition of the *OED*, the 1933 *Supplement* edited by W. A. Craigie and C. T. Onions, Robert Burchfield's four-volume *Supplement* of 1972–86, the publication of the integrated edition of *OED2* in 1989, edited by Edmund Weiner and John Simpson (and especially the appearance of the latter on CD-ROM in 1992 which has, in itself, immeasurably facilitated much of the research in this volume) also feature where relevant, if to a lesser extent. As revision of the dictionary continues towards the publication of *OED3*, it is moreover clear that the pioneering ventures which Murray saw as integral to the art of lexicography are by no means restricted to the past.

Acknowledgements are primarily due to the staff of Room 132 in the Bodleian Library for their unfailing courtesy and help with the archives of the Murray Papers and, in equal measure, to Jenny McMorris from the Archives of Oxford University Press for her help and advice on the OUP archive materials connected with the dictionary. Thanks should also go to John Simpson and Edmund Weiner at the *OED*, to John Davey and Sarah Dobson at OUP, and to Pembroke College, Oxford, and the University of Oxford for the period of leave which enabled the volume to assume final shape much more swiftly than would otherwise have been the case.

LCM

Contents

Notes on Contributors

Richard W. Bailey is Professor of English Language and Literature at the University of Michigan. He is the author of *Images of English. A Cultural History of the English Language* (1991) and *Nineteenth-Century English* (1996).

Charlotte Brewer is a Fellow of Hertford College, Oxford, and is the author and editor of books and articles on the textual history and analysis of *Piers Plowman*. She is working with Lynda Mugglestone on a book on the history and development of the *OED*.

Anne Curzan is an Assistant Professor of English at the University of Washington in Seattle. She has published articles on the history of gender in English and the use of historical corpora in linguistic research.

Peter Gilliver is an Associate Editor of the *Oxford English Dictionary*.

Michael Rand Hoare was Reader in Theoretical Physics at the former Bedford College, London. Since early retirement in 1983, he has worked primarily on aspects of the cultural history of science, recently completing a two-volume work, *Weighing Fire: Literary Science 1700–1900 in European perspective*.

Dieter Kastovsky is Professor of English Philology at the University of Vienna. His publications and research interests cover English inflectional morphology and word-formation (synchronic and diachronic), semantics, morphological typology, and the history of linguistics.

Elizabeth Knowles has been Managing Editor of Oxford Quotations Dictionaries since 1993, and has edited the *Oxford Dictionary of Phrase, Saying, and Quotation* (1997) and the *Oxford Dictionary of Twentieth-Century Quotations* (1998). An experienced historical lexicographer, she co-edited the *Oxford Dictionary of New Words* (2nd edn., 1997), and previously worked for ten years on the *New Shorter Oxford English Dictionary*.

Michael K. C. MacMahon is Professor of Phonetics in the Department of English Language at the University of Glasgow. His publications and research focus particularly on the history of phonetics in Britain and Europe.

Jenny McMorris is Assistant Archivist at Oxford University Press, responsible for the archives of the *OED* and the smaller dictionaries since 1985.

Lynda Mugglestone is Fellow in English Language and Literature at Pembroke College, Oxford, and News International Lecturer in Language and Communication. She is the author of *'Talking Proper': The Rise of Accent as Social Symbol* (Oxford: Clarendon Press, 1995), and has written widely on nineteenth-century language and associated issues.

Noel Osselton has divided his academic career equally between universities in Holland and England, and has held chairs of English Language in both countries. His publications have been mainly in the field of post-Renaissance vernacular lexicography. A founder member, and later President, of the European Association for Lexicography, he now lives in retirement in Durham.

Vivian Salmon has taught in the Universities of London (Bedford College), Edinburgh, and Oxford. Her publications include *Francis Lodwick: A Study of his Writings in the Intellectual Context of the 17th Century* (1972), *The Study of Language in 17th-century England* (1988 [1979]), and *Language and Society in Early Modern England* (1996). She has also written on Elizabethan English, with special reference to Shakespearian drama, and is currently engaged on research into the history of ideas on language especially in 17th- and 19th-century England.

Penny Silva is Deputy Chief Editor of the *Oxford English Dictionary*. She was Director of the Dictionary Unit for South African English, Rhodes University, from 1991–8, and managing editor of the *Dictionary of South African English on Historical Principles* (1996). She was consultant on South African English to the *Oxford English Dictionary* (3rd edn., in preparation) and the *New Oxford Dictionary of English* (forthcoming).

Eric Stanley is the Rawlinson and Bosworth Professor of Anglo-Saxon in the University of Oxford. He has written on Old and Middle English language and literature and on English lexicography of all periods. He is on the International Advisory Committee at the Dictionary of Old English at Toronto, and was one of the small team of 'Critical Proof Readers' on the *Supplement* II edited by R. W. Burchfield (Oxford, 1976).

Abbreviations

CWW K. M. E. Murray, *Caught in the Web of Words. James A. H. Murray and the* Oxford English Dictionary (New Haven and London: Yale University Press, 1977).

EDD J. Wright (ed.), *The English Dialect Dictionary* (London and Oxford: Froude, 1898–1905).

EETS Early English Text Society.

MEU3 R. W. Burchfield (ed.), *The New* Fowler's *Modern English Usage*, 3rd edn. (Oxford: Clarendon Press, 1996).

MP Murray Papers, Bodleian Library, Oxford.

OED2 J. A. Simpson and E. S. C. Weiner (eds.), *The Oxford English Dictionary First Edited by James A. H. Murray, Henry Bradley, W. A. Craigie, and C. T. Onions combined with A Supplement to the Oxford English Dictionary edited by R. W. Burchfield and Reset with Corrections, Revisions, and Additional Vocabulary*, 20 vols. (Oxford: Clarendon Press, 1989).

1

'Pioneers in the Untrodden Forest': The *New* English Dictionary

LYNDA MUGGLESTONE

> I feel that in many respects I and my assistants are simply pioneers, pushing our way experimentally through an untrodden forest, where no . . . man's axe has been before us.
>
> (Murray 1884: 509)

Pioneer, in the figurative sense selected by James Murray in his account of the complex demands which the making of the *New English Dictionary*[1] was to place upon the lexicographer, receives its formal definition in the fascicle *Ph* to *Piper*, edited by Murray himself, and published in June 1906: 'One who goes before to prepare or open up the way for others to follow; one who begins, or takes part in beginning, some enterprise, course of action, etc.; an original investigator, explorer, or worker, in any department of knowledge or activity.' With its emphasis on both original exploration and new beginnings, on opening up new territories rather than following already established paths, the image of the pioneer as thus defined was one which, in a number of ways, was to be seen as particularly appropriate for those engaged upon the task of writing, and researching, the *OED*. Though Florio in *A Worlde of Wordes* (1598), Blount in his *Glossographia* (1656), and, most explicitly, Phillips in his *New World of English Words* (1658), had long since depicted the lexicographer as an explorer in a universe of words (an image later also

---

[1] *OED1* first appeared, in parts or sections (see Appendix I) from 1884 to 1928, under the title of *A New English Dictionary on Historical Principles, Founded Mainly on Materials Collected by the Philological Society* (*NED*), its name a clear signifier of the departures intended in terms of English lexicography. Though *NED* continued to be 'official use with the Oxford University Press' (Onions 1928: 1), *OED* as an alternative title was established from 1895 (see Preface) although *NED* continued to hold pride of place on the title-pages of the individual parts. In the 'corrected re-issue' of 1933 (which includes an 'introduction, supplement, and bibliography'), the work as a whole appeared as the *Oxford English Dictionary*. The abbreviation *OED* is used throughout the volume to denote references to the first edition; the *Supplements* (1972, 1976, 1982, 1986) edited by R. W. Burchfield, and the second 'integrated' edition of the *OED* (*OED2*) ed. J. Simpson and E. Weiner (Oxford, Clarendon Press: 1989) are specified separately.

deployed by Murray),[2] the *OED* was to represent a new level in such enquiries, explicitly rejecting in many cases the precedents offered by the past. 'The notion that a Dictionary ought to contain the whole world of English words' was, Murray stated, entirely new (MP/[1910]: 13). Moreover, as he elaborated, in all aspects of lexicography, from the history and development of senses 'in which simply nothing whatever has been done in English' (1884: 509), to questions of etymology, meaning, pronunciation (and the modes of transcription to be employed), there was necessarily to be a return to first principles, and a commitment to new points of departure. 'I am absolutely a pioneer', he wrote to Henry Sweet; 'nobody exc[ept] my predecessors in specimens of the Dicty. has yet *tried* to trace out historically the sense-development of English words . . . I shall have to do the best I can at defining probably 80,000 words that I never *knew* or *used* or *saw* before' (MP/29/3/1882).

Conceptions of the pioneering acts of lexicography integral to the *OED* in fact considerably predate Murray's own involvement with the project. Trench's seminal 'On some Deficiencies in our English Dictionaries', originally presented as two papers to the Philological Society in November 1857, engages, for example, upon a detailed redefinition of both dictionary and lexicographer as they might appear in their ideal manifestations. In the mid-nineteenth century existing English dictionaries, as Trench observed, manifested a number of problems, frequently being unsystematic in modes of inclusion and exclusion, in the kinds of data deployed, in their treatment of obsolete words and of word families, as well as in features such as the accurate dating of words and the distinguishing of synonyms. In their place Trench offers a vision of 'an entirely new Dictionary; no patch upon old garments, but a new garment throughout' (1860: 1). Since previous dictionaries uniformly betrayed an 'imperfect registration . . . of the words of our language' (1860: 2), this was to be remedied by the full 'inventory' of the language which a new dictionary could and should provide. Inadequacies in the recording of both historical development and sense division were likewise pervasive, but these too could be transcended in a new, and perfected, work founded on the joint precepts of empirical investigation and historical principle. As Murray was later to write of the promised fulfilment of these ideals in the *OED*: 'It is because the present work starts anew from the beginning, collects and exhibits its own materials, founds on these its own explanations, deduces from them the logical order of the senses, and in its entire construction and arrangement follows modern scientific and historical principles, that it claims to be in a distinctive sense A NEW ENGLISH DICTIONARY' (MP/[n.d.]/1883: 4). Though this paean disappears from the final version of the Preface to Part I, its validity was to remain unquestioned in terms of the distinctively fresh start which the *OED* was seen to represent in all aspects of lexicographical endeavour.

---

[2] See Murray's lecture 'The World of Words and its Explorers' given on board the RNS Saxon on 8 Aug 1905, and to the Hawick Archaeological Society in 1906.

The role of the lexicographer was likewise to be subject to considerable revision. Whereas Johnson had expounded upon the problems caused by a lexicographical practice in which 'modes of expression were to be rejected or received' and 'choice . . . to be made out of boundless variety' (1755: A1^v), such subjective partialities were, Trench stressed, no longer deemed tenable. 'It is no task of the maker [of the dictionary] to select the *good* words of the language', he affirmed; 'If he fancies that it is so, and begins to pick and choose, to leave this and to take that, he will at once go astray' (1860: 4–5). In a role as historian rather than critic, the maker of dictionaries was henceforth to act as prime linguistic witness to the shifting nuances of speech, divorced alike from fallible notions of its needful 'fixing' and from the conceptualization of change as inevitable decline.[3]

As these precepts indicate, the theoretical model espoused by Trench formalizes above all a commitment to descriptivism above prescriptivism, and to empiricism above the ipse dixit, setting up, in effect, a new agenda for both principles and practice in English lexicography. It was this that Herbert Coleridge, as the first editor of the proposed new work, inherited and endeavoured to implement, establishing, together with Trench and Frederick Furnivall, a reading programme by which the all important primary data would be collected by members of the Philological Society and by the general public. The *Proposal for the Publication of a New English Dictionary* duly stresses the pioneering efforts which were to be required: 'we shall endeavour to show more clearly and fully than has hitherto been done, or even attempted, the development of the sense or various senses of each word from its etymology and from each other' ([Philological Society]1859: 4). Though the dictionary as then conceived was, in a number of respects, different from that which was later to be published,[4] this clearly stands as the first point of departure for a work which, in spite of Coleridge's confident protestations ('in about two years we shall be able to give our first number to the world. Indeed were it not for the dilatoriness of many contributors . . . I should not hesitate to name an earlier period' (1860: 77)), was not to appear until 1884 when Part I, *A–Ant*, was published, and not to be completed in its entirety until 1928.

Furnivall and Coleridge, as W. A. Craigie and C. T. Onions later comment, 'were embarking on an uncharted sea, quite unwitting of the long course which had to be sailed before the farther shore could even come into sight' (1933: p. viii). The image of the unknown is an apt one; within a year Coleridge was dead,[5] and Furnivall had succeeded him as editor; within another decade the project had declined (though Furnivall and a few others continued to work assiduously towards its

---

[3] See further Chapter 11.

[4] It was conceived at this point as tripartite in structure with a main dictionary, separate vocabularies of technical and scientific words, as well as of proper names and places, and provided with an etymological appendix. A full account of the early history of the *OED*, and Murray's involvement with it, can be found in Murray (1977), henceforth referred to as *CWW*.

[5] See Appendix II: Personalia.

realization), and by 1879 the project had been born anew, with a new editor, James Murray, a new reading programme, and a new commitment to do justice to the complex vision first articulated by Trench. Patriotism and philology combined to give fresh zeal to the making of what was thus, fundamentally, to be a *new* English dictionary. As Murray commented in the course of the annual Dictionary Evening at the Philological Society in 1884, though he 'had often sighed to think that [Coleridge] and others were not spared to see the fruits of their labours', nevertheless there was a sense in which 'it was better for the Dictionary that it was not done then'. Philology, especially in England and France, 'had been positively *made* during the last fifteen years'. In consequence, had the dictionary project come to fruition at the time of its first formulation, 'it was certain that by this time they would all have been ashamed of it, and agitating to do it all over again' ([Philological Society] 1884: p. vi). The state of lexicography on the Continent made such comments still more pertinent. Just as Johnson's dictionary had been seen as providing England with a work which equalled, if not surpassed, that produced by the Académie Française ('Johnson, well-arm'd like a hero of yore Has beat forty French, and will beat forty more!', as Garrick declaimed in celebration of this dual contribution to national honour and English lexicography (Boswell 1791: i. 301)), so too was the *OED* to assume a similar significance, though this time in terms which encompassed philological science, the historical method, and the deficits hitherto perceptible in English lexicography in comparison with that achieved elsewhere.

The reputation of English philology was a recurrent preoccupation of the Philological Society. 'For the last sixty years, a period which embraces the beginning as well as the growth and development of linguistic science', the English have done 'little to advance the study of comparative philology by independent research', lamented Richard Morris in his Presidential Address for 1875. They were instead content to look to Germany for nearly all scientific knowledge (1875: 1–2). Succeeding him as President, Henry Sweet made the same point, stressing the 'vague ideas of philological method', the dilletantism, as well as the absence of 'a thorough knowledge of the earlier periods of [the] native language' which continued to hamper English achievements in this context (1877: 11–12). In comparison with Jacob and Wilhelm Grimm in Germany, and Emile Littré in France, all of whom strove to implement the philological advances of the nineteenth century in terms of lexicography, England seemed even more lacking.[6] Dictionaries such as Johnson's represented only 'the pre-scientific stage' of philology, 'when real analogies were overlooked, and superficial resemblances too easily seized; when anything was thought possible, and *a priori* reasoning applied to problems which could only be solved by patient induction' (MP/17/9/1883: 2). The proposed dictionary was, in this respect, to assume particular importance, offering the means by which such disparities (and deficiencies) might be transcended, and national

---

[6] See further Chapter 4.

honour restored. It was, for example, in precisely these terms in which Max Müller stressed its potential import in 1878 to the Delegates of Oxford University Press:

In an undertaking of such magnitude, in which one might almost say that the national honour of England is engaged, no effort should be spared to make the work as perfect as possible, and at all events no unworthy rival of the French Dictionary lately published by Littré, or the German Dictionary undertaken by the Brothers Grimm.   (Müller 1878)

Sweet's earlier letter to the Press, formally proposing publication of what was envisaged at this stage as a four-volume work, enforced the same idea. 'The great advance of Philology of late years has completely changed the conditions of a good dictionary', he declared, likewise making reference to the work of Littré in France. Nevertheless, 'no such dictionary exists of the English language' (MP/20/4/1877). Patriotism and the new philology assume joint prominence in the dictionary as thus proposed; it was above all to stand as 'a new Dictionary worthy of the English Language and of the present state of Philological Science' (Murray 1879: 1), an 'English Littré' which, while explicitly acknowledging the inspiration provided by its Continental counterparts, was, in a number of ways (and true to the pioneering spirit in which it was conceived) to seek to go beyond established precedent even here. Larger, more wide-ranging, implementing the historical method in a diachronic scale which dwarfed that adopted in both the *Deutches Wörterbuch* and the *Dictionnaire de la langue française*, making more exhaustive use of citations, as well as incorporating, as Trench had intended, extremely liberal criteria for inclusion,[7] the *OED* was, Murray proclaimed in 1912, ultimately to take first rank within the echelons of lexicographical scholarship, not only nationally but internationally too: 'No literary or scientific work of any value, has ever in human history been produced as quickly, & lexicographers in all languages regard it as simply marvellous', he averred; 'the marvel of scholars is the *amazing rapidity* with which it is done. Grimm's great German Dictionary was begun about 1840. The first fasiculus was published in 1852. It will take 25 or perh[aps] 30 years still to finish. Our first part one came out in 1883; we have already overtaken Grimm & left it behind' (MP/8/12/1912).[8]

Even if not always agreeing with these convictions about the speed of progress being made, reviewers readily recognized and praised the results achieved by a dictionary which served to bring England into line with international standards of scholarship. It is 'the most complete and authoritative lexicon of our time, leaving as it does all rivals behind, especially in its philological treatment

---

[7] An early version of the 'Notice of Publication of Part I of a New English Dictionary on a Historical Basis' makes these claims explicit: 'it was thought that the time had arrived when materials should be collected for a new and more complete English Dictionary which, in fullness of detail, and critical accuracy, might bear a comparison with the *Deutsches Wörterbuch* of Jacob and Wilhelm Grimm' (MP/18/10/1883a: 1).

[8] A–Ant, the first part of the *OED*, in fact appeared in March 1884, not 1883 as Murray states here, though, from Murray's point of view as editor, work on it had been completed by late 1883.

of words and their historical growth and usage', stated the *National Observer* (29 December 1894). Other reviewers concurred: it is 'a new start in English lexicography on scientific principles and by systematic methods' (*The Athenaeum* 1884: 177), 'an achievement without parallel in the lexicography of our living languages' (*The Academy* 1884: 105).

In such commendations, it seems clear that the innovations which this deliberately 'new' dictionary endeavoured to implement were, at least at times, received with due appreciation. Stressing innovation above tradition does nevertheless bring its own problems. As Henry Bradley commented, 'the morality of dictionary-making involves many difficult questions', not least since 'the traditional practice has been to copy shamelessly from one dictionary to another' (MP/18/10/1889). While the original formulation of the *OED* often rendered such traditional practices unsustainable, bringing undoubted benefits in, for example, the identification of countless ghost words hitherto recorded as if they had a real existence in the language (see, for example, Murray's entry for *abacot*), the return to first principles was, however, not always to prove easy. Lexicography, as Béjoint (1994) rightly stresses, is typically a discipline rooted in tradition rather than innovation, one founded in continuities rather than a deliberate separation from what has gone before. As a result, though on one hand the idea of the pioneering efforts required was to inspire those who worked on the *OED* ('it pleases me, at any practicable amount of work, to get at the facts, and force them to yield their secret', as Murray wrote to Edward Arber of the many hours expended on this necessarily original research (MP/24/12/1904)), it was, on the other, to mean that the 'Dictionary Ideal' was, in a number of ways, translated only with considerable difficulty into the realities of research, writing, and publication.

Trench had, of course, already warned of the imperfections inevitable in the attempt to realize a vision of this kind (1860: 29). Henry Sweet gave an even more timely reminder in the early days of Murray's editorship: 'Even the most insignificant enterprizes [*sic*]—editing the smallest texts—have the sense of an unattained ideal, and you are engaged in one of unexampled magnitude, on very insufficient foundations' (MP/3/4/1882). Just how insufficient these foundations were, at least in the beginnings of the project, was rapidly enforced on Murray. Assuming the role of editor in 1879, he embarked, as he thought, upon a task of which the foundations had already been laid. The first reading programme had generated some two million slips and these, he was assured, had largely been arranged and copy-edited. As Walter Skeat confidently asserted, 'it has taken 10 to 15 years to get the results together: & they only want arranging in some places. There are *gaps*, I firmly believe; I believe that perhaps even a whole letter may be missing: but *what there is is of the highest value*' (MP/6/4/1876). Forming the corpus of evidence on which the dictionary was to be based, such materials were salient to its projected success, not least since the gathering of original data in the form of precisely dated and located citations was to be one of the cornerstones of its distinctiveness. Though the principle of their value remained true ('the perfection of the Dictionary in its *data*' is, for example, given as axiomatic in Murray's Presidential Address to the Philological Society (1880: 129)), their reality, in spite of Skeat's (and Furnivall's) optimism, was often sadly lacking.

'When I took the first survey of my undertaking, I found our speech copious without order, and energetick without rules: wherever I turned my view there was perplexity to be disentangled, and confusion to be regulated', wrote Johnson of the beginnings of his own lexicographical labours (1755: A1ᵛ). His words might well have been applied with more truth to Murray as he surveyed the materials from which he was intended to construct the dictionary of the Philological Society. As he berated Furnivall, 'There are some cruel jokes in your reports G "done", "nearly done", "will be done in 1872"—a mass of utter confusion, which will take many months to put even in alphabetical order' (MP/10/5/1879*a*). Far from taking over a corpus which, as he had been led to believe, was in a state of some completion, it was instead at times to require a feat of pioneering ingenuity even to locate its necessary components. 'We have been trying to take stock of materials, and think that we either *have* or know of the existence of all, except H, Q, Pa', he continued, expressing considerable uncertainties nevertheless about the precise nature of such location. Furnivall's reply further illuminates the disorganisation and lack of system with which Murray was initially faced; '*W*: I forget'; '*Pa* I forget altogether'; '*X*, I now recollect is in my Dict. cupboard. I'll get it out, & will send it by Monday's post'; 'H is, perhaps, with the Am[erican] G. P. Marsh'—'I think, certainly' he adds above the line (MP/10/5/1879*b*).

Pa was long to prove a puzzle, eventually being traced to Ireland and needing, in the event, to be done entirely again (see *CWW*: 177). The slips for H, as Furnivall remembered three days later, were in Florence, from where they were retrieved. Even once tracked down, however, further problems often remained in the quality of such materials (a topic dealt with in more detail in Chapter 2), The Continental precedents looked to in the formulation of the *OED* provided telling precedents here too. Only six of the eighty-three volunteer readers who had provided material for the writing of the *Deutsches Wörterbuch* had proved satisfactory; only one of them could truly be seen as ideal. It was clear that, for the *OED*, the only solution was to generate a second reading programme to supplement the first. Keeping the volunteer principle as the only method by which, in spite of its potential inadequacies, the necessary material could be elicited, Murray appealed in 1879 for a thousand new readers to help to complete the corpus within three years. Many duly responded, and Murray's Presidential Address of 1880 announces the existence of 754 readers, who have undertaken 1,568 books, finished 924, and returned 361,670 quotations. One year later, the readers number over 800 (though the fact that some had finished their allotted books meant that only 510 were continuing to gather the evidence vital to the project). Some measure of quality control had also been instituted, some readers being asked to redo the work of other readers suspected of being inadequate.[9]

---

[9] See further Chapter 2.

Though such achievements were considerable, they were not entirely to overcome the problems of assembling the corpus essential for a dictionary on scientific as well as historical principles. Copious in some respects, it was markedly inadequate in others; in 1884, for example, Murray notes that for more than 80 per cent of the words new quotations must be found to enable their history to be completed in a satisfactory manner. Similarly general searches had to be undertaken for all words in the attempt to determine the existence of other senses or possible antedatings. Even then, as Murray pointed out, 'we cannot exhaust the ground, or attain to absolute certainty' (1884: 516). For some senses, no citations existed at all, as for *aged* ('of such an age'), though this particular difficulty was resolved by Mrs Murray who 'after a long search', located it on a seventeenth-century brass in Kendal Church ([Philological Society] 1883: pp. v–vi). The indeterminacy of the vocabulary (the 'nebulous mass' described by Murray in his celebrated 'General Explanations') of course remains the major theoretical problem with which the lexicographer is faced. If the ideal articulated by Trench was to give a complete inventory of the language and its history, the compromises which were instead necessitated by 'the imperfect record of our language' were rapidly brought home to Murray. The necessary reliance on written data meant that even considerations of a word's first use were inevitably an approximation. 'The word was *spoken* before it was *written*', he stressed. In consequence, 'the written instance is, in most cases, evidence, not that the word was then coming into use, but that it was already established and known to readers generally' (Murray 1884: 517). It could, he recognized, thus already have been current in conversation or letters for ten or twenty years. Elicited data displayed other problems too, often betraying, as Chapter 3 explores, a significant imbalance in the kinds of sources used (or not used). Other imbalances were perceptible in the evidence itself so that, for example, over fifty citations existed for *abusion,* fewer than five for *abuse.* This, as Murray acknowledged, could have been countered by a somewhat different set of instructions from those actually supplied for the second reading programme. 'Make a quotation for *every* word that strikes you as rare, obsolete, old-fashioned, new, peculiar, or used in a peculiar way', the latter noted, only afterwards specifying the need for information on ordinary words too. It would in fact have been better (though impracticable) to start again with one which instead directed 'Take out quotations for all words that do *not* strike you as rare, peculiar, or peculiarly used' (1884: 516).

By the very methods used for its elicitation, the materials assembled for the *OED* were thus regularly—and inevitably—to prove deficient. Only the provision of 'complete verbal indexes to all books' could surmount such problems and, in the late nineteenth century, this was 'not only impossible, but the results would themselves be unmanageable' (Murray 1884: 516). The emphasis was on pragmatic solutions, the method selected being 'the only practicable one' in spite of the fact that it could not, and contrary to the original plan of the *OED*, be exhaustive in the results obtained. If Murray began as an idealist ('I wanted to see an ideal Dictionary & to show what I meant by one' (MP/15/12/1903)), his conversion to realism was an early one. The pioneering endeavours involved in the making of the *OED* frequently took on the nature not of glorious conquests, but of laborious quests for unknown senses and unknown words, elusive meanings and lost constructions, all necessary to supplement a record of the language where material was indeed often conspicuous by its absence (a phrase for which, like so many others, the *OED* received adequate documentation only after the event).[10] Murray's letters record a series of time-consuming searches as he attempted to establish patterns of usage and word history which had hitherto remained undocumented: 'We know nothing of the origin of the phrase "Pilgrim Fathers"'; '*Life-boat* is, I fear, one of the words, on which nearly all the work is yet to be done' where the quotations 'throw no light on the origin of the word'; 'I want as early as possible an instance of the phrase "Old Age Pensions" . . . The Dictionary ought to show the history of a word which has such a future' (MP/[n.d]/1900, 23/6/1900, 16/12/1904). Many such quests were to prove unsuccessful, as the extant correspondence also makes plain: 'I am sorry to say that I cannot help you with the word "divisural"—I never saw it before'; 'I am sorry to say I can offer no suggestion as to the origin of the word *Purree*. I have never met with the term' or, similarly, 'I regret to say that I have never met with the word "Diorism". I will endeavour to look in likely places and will let you know the results of my search, if successful' (MP/25/1/1896, 2/7/1909, 25/6/1895).[11] As already indicated with reference to the phrase *conspicuous by his absence*, however, even where successful in finding what was required, the information could come too late for the purposes of printing. Henry Bradley is explicit on the frustrations this could impose:

I am vexed to find that the expression *flaunting Fabian* occurs in Nash's *Lenten Stuff*, a book that is supposed to have been read for the Dictionary. It is I suppose now too late to insert the quotations. I wish I knew absolutely what books one might feel sure had been exhaustively read.   (MP/1/7/1893)[12]

For some words or senses, the requisite information might, on the other hand, never appear at all, leading to the use of made-up examples, a practice which, as Murray commented in the context of *about* and *above*, was far from the desired ideal: 'I have been painfully disappointed to find how poorly the meanings and constructions of these words are illustrated from modern English writers.' He was, in the end, compelled to invent his own citations as evidence 'after spending

[10] 'I wrote 12 letters to journalists, critics, and literary men, such as Prof. Pollock, Mr Sala, the Editor of the Times, &c. in the effort to find out the original use of "conspicuous by his absence", and I had long since passed the word "Absence" before I found the clue' (MP/18/10/1883*b*).

[11] *Divisural* does not appear in the *OED* though *Purree* ('A yellow colouring matter imported from India and China, from which the pigment Indian *yellow* is prepared. It is essentially the magnesium salt of purreic or euxanthic acid') is included with citations from 1852. The search for *diorism* ('The act of defining; distinction, definition') was also successful.

[12] In this instance, the relevant page had not been printed off and the Nashe quotation was inserted.

hours of precious time—when I really had not moments to spare—in trying to find them . . . This is very unsatisfactory' (Murray 1882: 6–7). Such problems were of course intrinsic to the complex task which the editors of the *OED* were trying to accomplish. As Murray later lectured his audience at the London Institute, 'Verily a wonderful world, when we survey it, is the *World of Words:* but how impossible is its exact census, how laborious the work of its exploration!' (MP/[1910]).

Similar difficulties attended questions of inclusiveness within the dictionary. Trench's original ideals in this context were clear. As Murray affirmed in the first draft of the Publication Notice for Part I, 'The DICTIONARY aims at being *exhaustive*. Not every one who consults it will require all the information supplied; every one, it is hoped, will find what he actually wants' (MP/[n.d.]/1883: 3). The same draft also indicates the problematic nature of this claim. 'This *exhaustive* must be limited somehow', Furnivall notes in the margin. Further annotations by Alexander Ellis reinforce this contention: 'You omit "slang" & perhaps obscenities thus are by no means exhaustive'. In the proof of 17 October this section has disappeared, the ideal of total exhaustiveness already being seen as far too open to question for it to be included in this explicit and categorical form. A variety of problems (linguistic, ideological, pragmatic) would in fact combine to curtail the possibilities of including all words within the dictionary.

From the standpoint of linguistic theory, for example, the indeterminacy of the vocabulary rendered such total documentation impossible, a point which Murray himself was frequently to iterate. The ideological considerations raised by Ellis present problems of a different order. Questions of linguistic propriety, as least as concern word inclusion, should in theory have no place within a dictionary founded on the pioneering principles of objectivity and empiricism, of impartial documentation, and the implementation of descriptive rather than prescriptive tenets. 'Though disagreeable', Ellis reminded Murray, putting the case for a rejection of this form of linguistic censorship, 'obscene words are part of the life of a language' (MP/[n.d.]/1883: 3, marginal annotation). Slang, contrary to Ellis's preconceptions here, was (though with exceptions) included in the dictionary.[13] A restricted group of obscenities was not, deference to Victorian sensibilities here having presumably led to their polite omission from the published record if not from the data files themselves, in a curious compromise by which the impartial record is maintained, but not submitted to the public gaze.

Selective presentation of this kind did not go unnoticed, not least in terms of the expressed aims of the *OED* and its avowed historical principles. 'I venture

---

[13] *Bounder*, was, for example, originally excluded on precisely these grounds. Regarded as 'undergraduate slang' and first encountered by Murray in Oxford in 1876–7, 'the opinion was that it ought not to be recognized in the Dictionary'. As Murray noted, 'much of undergraduate slang is very evanescent. It flourishes luxuriantly for a term or year, or for three years, & then often disappears, buried beneath a later growth. We shall see what its fate is, when we consider the question of a Supplem[en]t.' If found in literature then 'it will demand a niche', he conceded (MP/22/4/1903). Provided with citations from 1889, *bounder* was included in the first volume of the *Supplement* in 1972.

to send you a word that is not found [in the dictionary] . . . omitted perhaps by an oversight or perhaps under the mistaken impression that it is slangy', John Hamilton informed Murray. While carefully avoiding its use in the substance of his letter, he went on to provide a stalwart defence of the reasons why it should in fact have appeared:

It is an old English word of Teutonic origin, & is just as good English (though by the nature of things not so much used in polite society) as the words, leg, arm, heart, stomach, & other parts of the body . . . It has cognates in French, German, & Dutch . . . The mere fact of its being used in a vulgar way, does not ban it from the English language & its absence from your Dictionary is brought forcibly before one's eyes—as it was before mine in rapidly turning over its pages—by the presence of the *same syllable* in big letters as a contraction of *Contra.* In reality it is no more vulgar than bowels or womb, & hardly so vulgar as a certain word inserted in your Dictionary to indicate the posterior under letter B.   (MP/1/9/1899)

Murray drafted a reply a few days later. 'It was not without regret that any word of historical standing was omitted', he wrote, confirming the conscious compromises which had been made in this 'generally satisfactory' decision (MP/4/9/1899). One of the regular (and most trustworthy) contributors to the dictionary, James Dixon, had, however, advised otherwise. 'It will look cowardly to shirk it', he pointed out with some justice, though compromise was not entirely avoided in his own proposed solution: 'I think it might be curtly dismissed, of course without a quotation, a thing presque introuvable. I think print the word, and say "An obscure term applied to the private parts of a woman". The thing itself is not obscene' (MP/17/2/1891).[14]

Omission here was, of course, the result of carefully deliberated decision (see also Burchfield 1973). More problematic were absences which resulted from the unsystematic implementation of editorial policies. For adjectives on the model of *African, Canadian,* for example, the general principle had been to exclude such forms on the grounds that, as Murray noted 'it was seen to be impracticable to include *all* adj[ective]s of this kind'. In the event, however, principle and practice failed to agree. *American* and *German* were included since both, at the time of compilation, had given rise to transferred senses (*Americanist, Americanization, German measles*). In the absence of such transferred senses (at least in the data files of the dictionary), *African* and *Cuban,* among others, were omitted. With the benefit of hindsight, Murray was forced to acknowledge that this policy would have been different had the dictionary been written again, such anomalies being untenable in terms of its professed aims: 'people who found *American* included & *African* not, might think that there was inconsistency, and that to avoid this, it might have been expedient to include *African* also, which, if every thing could have been foreseen, would perhaps have been done' (MP/24/12/1906).

---

[14] The term to which Dixon refers is *cunt,* though misidentified in *CWW* (195) as *pudendum,* presumably in a further instance of linguistic delicacy. It was later included in the 1972 *Supplement.*

Of course, as Ladislav Zgusta contends (1971: 191), the ideal lexicographer is a prophet as well as linguist, foretelling the difficulties which would be encountered as well as their needful resolution. The unprecedented scale—and complexity—of what was being attempted in the *OED* (together with the real difficulty of sustaining formal policies, with absolute rigour, over a work which spans forty-four years in publication, and considerably more in execution) made such apparent inconsistencies unavoidable in many respects. They represent in effect further instances of the compromises which practical lexicography enforced upon the lexicological ideals with which the project started out. On the whole, however, and to its great credit, the *OED* was to prove steadfastly resistant to pressures for the exclusion of words and uses which, for a variety of reasons, were deemed unsuitable for a dictionary of this kind. Loanwords, discussed further in Chapter 6, were particularly interesting from this point of view. Words of science and technology, discussed in Chapter 9, provide a further case in point, not least since they were marginalized by both Trench and Coleridge in their original conceptualizations of the dictionary. The proof sheets of the *OED*, especially in the early fascicles, likewise record a number of attempts at their attempted elimination. 'Rubbish', writes Skeat by the side of *anencephaloid* and *anerithmoscope*. 'Mere tradesman's make-up', he adds dismissively by the side of the latter. Murray carefully reasserts the descriptive principles on which the dictionary is founded; 'so is the name of every new article' he inscribes in response. In the published fascicle both words are retained, as are *aneurysmal, aneurysmatic, aneurysmatical, aneurysmous, abiogenetic, abiogenetically, abirritant* (and derivatives), for all of which Skeat had also advised deletion. Editorial principles tended to remain firm on this issue, contrary at times to the expressed wishes of the Delegates of Oxford University Press (and the opinions of reviewers),[15] and in spite of the added complexity which the recording of such scientific vocabulary was, in practice, to add to the making of the *OED*. 'I find a good deal of embarassment with the technical words', Bradley commented, for example: 'The quot[ations] from scientific books seem to have been made in many cases by readers who cannot have been well acquainted with the subjects' (MP/15/6/1886). Entry words here were often to form a completely unknown territory. 'Even in quite modern words, no one seems to know how they were formed or what, as words, they mean', Murray lamented to the Philological Society (1881: 263). Scientists themselves were moreover not necessarily ideal in resolving such difficulties. As F. Mott noted in attempted clarification of the word *chrysophyll*, it could indeed safely be included as 'one name for the yellow colouring matter of plants'. However, he added, 'for the last 50 years the colouring matter of plants has been under investigation by various chemists, who

---

[15] See the review of *E–Every* in *The Athenaeum*: 'Seeing that a complete record of technical terms is not aimed at, nothing is gained by the insertion of such items of scientific jargon as eclampsy, edriopthalmian, ekbergite, ekmannite enostosis, entellus' (OED/MISC/59/1/13). See also Chapter 9.

have mostly agreed that there are at least two distinct substances, but have *not* agreed to call them by the same names' (MP/10/3/1889). The recording of such words was nevertheless vital for the historical record of the language, not least in the nineteenth century itself. As Murray comments in the Prefatory Note to *Team-Tezkere*, only *telegraph* and *telescope* (and derivatives) appear in Johnson's *Dictionary* of 1755 where, in the *OED*, words with *tele-* occupy sixteen columns, 'an example of how scientific discovery and innovation have enlarged the vocabulary'.

The appropriateness of various forms of data as lexicographical evidence proves in fact to be a recurrent topic, and not only in terms of the language of science. The *OED* has of course been criticized on a number of occasions for its evident privileging of literary data (see McConchie 1997, Schäfer 1980, Willinsky 1994, as well as Chapter 3 in the present volume). Nineteenth-century criticism, however, often instead tended to stress the unacceptability (and unauthoritative nature) of sources outside this particular sphere for the purposes of citation. Henry Hucks Gibbs, a valued contributor to (and subeditor of) the *OED*, offered clear precepts on this head: 'we should always get the best authority we can for a word or phrase . . . hasty writing in newspapers is not the best authority, except when it is the *only* authority, and . . . then it must be used' (MP/14/6/1882). The Delegates of the Press concurred in the *Suggestions for Guidance in Preparing Copy for the Press* (*CWW*: 221–4), likewise arguing that quotations illustrative of modern literary words should be taken from 'great authors', and certainly in preference to any which might be drawn from newspapers. Such comments attempt to impose a hierarchical order on citational evidence, in contrast to the descriptive imperatives intentionally endorsed by the dictionary itself. 'Fling our doors wide! all, all, not one, but all must enter' as Furnivall had exclaimed (*CWW*: 137), matching principle with practice in the thousands of citations he provided from various daily newspapers. If Furnivall here provided ample evidence of norms of usage more akin to the quantitative norms isolated by Béjoint as salient components of a descriptive dictionary (those 'based on the observation of all the reasonably fluent members of a speech community. Any form is good so long as it is used by a certain number of speakers' (1994: 100)), comments such as those made by the Delegates and Gibbs instead assert the precedence of norms more qualitative (and prescriptive) in nature 'based on the usage and on the opinion of the "best" language users'. Ironically, newspapers themselves tended to agree. 'It certainly seems to us . . . that in some cases a little too much use has been made . . . of ephemeral and anonymous publications of the present day', averred *The Times* (26 January 1884: 6): 'the value of recording contemporary usage is obvious, but though a scientific dictionary should be by no means Della Cruscan in its selection of words, it should surely maintain as far as possible a classical standard in its selection of authors cited.'

The departures in English lexicography made by the *OED* could, as here, prove distinctly problematic for a public well versed in older traditions of prescriptive lexicography.[16] Murray's responses to such misconceptions simply asserted the linguistic priorities that must be maintained: 'To the philologist & historian of language—newspaper quotations are the *most valuable* of current instances—they show how the language grows—they make visible to us the actual steps which for earlier stages we must reconstruct by inference' (MP/9/6/1882). Like the Observer's Paradox which must be overcome by the modern sociolinguist in order to examine the realities of speech, so too was the language of the popular press to take on a quality unimagined by Gibbs in his censure of their 'hasty forms'. Here, as Murray concluded, 'I shall have all English scholarship of the world on my side.'

Such patterns of qualitative (if erroneous) discrimination prove remarkably persistent in assumptions about the data 'properly' to be used by the *OED*. Considerations of the validity of some literary texts above others indicate, for example, another form of compromise within the impartial record intentionally to be presented, leading to the suggested privileging of some forms of evidence above others. Women writers come in for especial mention in this context. 'Furnivall has a fancy that it is good to quote women, because the writings of women are a characteristic of the Age' wrote Gibbs (MP/3/5/1883), here rightly stressing the fact that the dictionary should operate no fixed agenda: '[it] is not meant to be a record of the progress of the Emancipation of women but of the birth and life and death of words'. This adherence to descriptive principle is tempered, however, by the censure subsequently directed at writers such as Mary Elizabeth Braddon as 'authoritative' sources of evidence within the dictionary. 'She is a hasty writer', Gibbs admonishes Murray: 'grinds out novels by the yard, and does not give herself time to think whether she is writing good English or not' (MP/3/5/1883). Rhoda Broughton comes in for similar condemnation. 'Such solecisms should not find entrance without a note of reprobation', Gibbs advised with reference to her use of the word *accentedest*: 'when Miss Broughton writes English I should quote her, but else . . .' (MP/14/7/1882). Murray clearly took a different view, forcing Gibbs to acknowledge that *accentedest* 'was as you say *formed* legitimately enough—as "chained" is' (MP/30/7/1882). His defence takes a practical form too; Broughton's *Nancy* (1873) provides the first, unmarked, citation for the word in its inclusion in the dictionary (' "Algy!" repeat I, in a tone of profoundest, accentedest surprise'). It was a policy maintained without dispute by the other editors of the dictionary; Broughton is cited on 443 occasions over its length. Braddon appears with even greater frequency, appearing as the source of 1,515 citations.

Constructions of acceptability (and its converse) in terms of the evidence ideally to be used within the dictionary do nevertheless serve to attest a level of popular resistance to the purely descriptive terms on which the *OED* was founded.[17] In a dictionary which, as we have seen, was deliberately conceived as 'a new

---

[16] See further Chapter 11.   [17] See further Chapter 11.

garment throughout', this was, predictably, not the only aspect of lexicographical practice to present the lexicographer with new challenges. In terms of etymology, for example, Richardson (1836–7) had stated as axiomatic that the precedents set by Johnson in this context must be cast aside by the lexicographer in favour of the principles of philosophic etymology adopted by John Horne Tooke. Though Murray can be seen to concur with Richardson in his statement that 'one does not look in Johnson for Etymology, any more than in 18th c. writers for biology or electricity' (MP/20/12/1906), the speculative etymologies of Horne Tooke were, if anything, still more remote from the philological rigour at which he aimed (see further Chapter 5). 'Etymology began in England about 1850', Murray stressed. Here too there was to be an emphatic return to first principles. 'In dealing with any previous etymological treatment of a word, I always go predisposed to find it wrong', he noted of his practice in this respect; 'I fasten on the weakest point, & if that fails, the thing is done; if it stands, try the next' (MP/13/3/1892). Distinguishing rigorously between facts, which are henceforth to be the true province of the dictionary, and ' "etymological" phantasms, which are pleasant enough in Wonderland or on the other side of the Looking-glass', the direction to be taken by the *OED* was clear, if somewhat more complex in practice. The facts required could, for example, prove markedly elusive. *Bullion* is 'a hopeless case', wrote Bradley in dismay (MP/3/5/1886); 'I must confess defeat', he admitted in a similar mode on *beat* and *bait* (MP/8/10/1885). Other words too proved initially resistant to the resolution of etymological cruces; *catsup*, he conjectured, 'must probably be more original' than *Catchup*, but 'why should any one want to change *tch* into *ts*' especially 'with such an absurd quasi-etymological result as *cat-sup*?' (MP/20/3/1888). Murray too was perplexed by the seeming impossibility of arriving at the necessary information. Even among words in daily use 'many thousands of difficulties still remain unsolved' (1884: 10), fundamental points about word origin and development often remaining obscure along with the evidence necessary for their resolution. If the image of the pioneer engaging with the unknown was one to which Murray had recourse on a number of occasions, it is perhaps nowhere more pertinent than in the etymological explorations of Murray, Bradley, Craigie, and Onions, as they sought to solve the many puzzles of linguistic history which had, hitherto, been left in obscurity.

Other perplexities beset the lexicographer in terms of explanations needed for the words themselves. The scale of the *OED*, as well as its diachronic range, meant that inevitably words were encountered which were to prove remarkably resistant to analysis and adequate elucidation. This, Murray stressed, was where the 'real work' of the dictionary lay, 'the power of seeing the sense of quotations, of formulating the senses of words, of writing good definitions, or revising the defective ones of imperfect helpers' (MP/15/6/1897). A letter on *hay-cratch*, a particularly elusive form, illuminates some of the difficulties faced. 'I have been asking wildly about it', he notes; 'I should be glad to be told what it is', not least since its meaning is, so far, 'quite unknown' (MP/26/11/1892). The *OED* was not in the end to contain an entry for this term, though the letter goes on to detail Murray's valiant attempts to conjecture its true interpretation:

> Is it the sparred place over a horse's head in a stall, through which he pulls out the hay?
> Is it the sparred arrangement on or near the ground in a cow-house through which the cows pull out hay ?
> Is it a particular thing I have seen in fields, through the spars of which . . . beasts pull out hay in winter . . . Is it all or any of these, or something else?

Dearborn posed a similar puzzle. 'Could you send me a short definition', he requested Liddell: 'Never hav[ing] seen the vehicle or its picture, I do not know what is a convenient description—cart, carriage, wagon, etc.' (MP/29/11/1893).[18]

Still worse was the semantic resolution of certain aspects of poetic and literary usage. Where possible, and constituting a particularly clear instance of the emphatic return to first principles, Murray often resorted to direct communication with the writer concerned. Results here could be variable. 'Can you tell us anything of the meaning and source' of *brean*, he asked Robert Louis Stevenson, only to find that it was, in fact, a typographical error for *ocean* (MP/19/2/1887).[19] Though Tennyson provided a satisfactory explanation of *balm-cricket* (see *CWW*: 201 and n. 48), other writers were less forthcoming. Swinburne provides a case in point:

> I have no idea where I may have used the word 'harvestry'. I suppose I must have done, if lexicographers say so; but when or how I cannot guess. I only seem to remember—& that vaguely—some older authority for a word which without such authority I do not think I should have used.   (MP/7/6/1897)

Murray was scathing about such authorial incompetence as in his reply to a query about the meaning of Rossetti's *voidee cup*:

> One cannot take the language of poets too seriously . . . if I may infer from the results of appealing to other poets for explanation of their cruces, [Rossetti] would probably say 'I have really forgotten; I was under the impression that I had seen or heard it somewhere; can I have been under a misapprehension? what terrible people you dictionary fellows are, hunting us up about every word . . . That is the general sort of answer one gets, which means 'we write for amusement, & not to be studied as texts; if you will make school-texts of us, yours be the responsibility!'   (MP/8/3/1901)

Voidee cup does not appear in the dictionary.

Even once the requisite information had been obtained, the art of definition remained a complex and demanding one. The proofs bear witness to many last

---

[18] Presumably on Liddell's advice, the preferred term was 'wagon': 'A vehicle, a kind of light four-wheeled wagon used in country districts in the United States.'

[19] As Murray commented in a later lecture to the London Institute (MP/[1910]: 33], 'if we had been less careful *Brean* would have been duly recorded in the Dictionary as a word used by R. L. Stephenson [*sic*]: and it was perhaps lucky that the context did not suggest any particular sense'.

minute changes of phrasing and expression in the attempt to convey the precise nuances required.[20] At other times, help was requested from outside, as individual editors confessed their inability to come to a satisfactory result. This was the case with *high-churchman,* for which Murray sent the proof with his 'not very successful attempt' to Fairburn, adding 'It would be a charitable deed if you would try to help me frame such a definition . . . as would be accepted by High and Low, or at least wd. not give them reasonable cause of offence' (MP/19/4/1898). Arriving at a form acceptable to all seemed, at times, impossible; Murray's drafts could be rephrased by Gibbs, Bradley received suggested emendations from Murray. 'Do you think the treatment of *Gladstonian* is quite adequate, and such as to be satisfactory to people generally?', he queried with reference to Bradley's original sense (a) in proof: 'Belonging to or characteristic of W. E. Gladstone' (*OED*/MISC/464/1). Though adjectives derived from proper names 'stand on the frontier of our territory and cannot be expected to receive very full treatment', nevertheless, Murray argued, 'for the last 10 or 12 years' the dominant sense had clearly been 'Adhering to Mr Gladstone in his effort to give Home Rule to Ireland'. Something, if possible, in the dictionary thus 'ought to be done to supply this striking void'. In the published fascicle the sense has duly changed: 'after 1886 used *spec.* (chiefly by opponents) as the designation of the party which supported Gladstone's proposals for establishing Home Rule in Ireland'.

Defining words hitherto undefined was of course merely part of the role assumed by the *OED,* and Chapter 5 will examine in more detail the multifarious difficulties faced by a dictionary which, in terms of semantic analysis as all else, was intentionally to move beyond that which had already been established. The letters of Murray and Bradley detail the tremendous burden which this particular aspect imposed. 'The terrible word *Black* and its derivatives' took one of the volunteer helpers on the dictionary three months to arrange; even then it required a further three weeks' work from one of the Scriptorium assistants, and another week from Murray himself (MP/24/6/1886). Still worse was *pass* which 'tortured my brain for nearly 150 hours', Murray told Furnivall in the certain knowledge that much of it would still have to be pulled to pieces again (MP/31/3/1904). Even with the most scrupulous attention to detail in this context, definitions could still go awry, sometimes spectacularly. 'I don't know who can have given you the definition of "Howitzer"', one correspondent exclaimed; 'Horizontal is the exact contrary. It is essentially a high-angle firing weapon, and would never, *under any circumstances,* be fired horizontally' (MP/9/10/1913).

Difficulties of this order prolonged the making of the dictionary beyond all expectations. The Delegates of Oxford University Press, originally committed to

---

[20] *Aphanozygous,* originally defined as 'Having the bony arches of the cheeks invisible from the outside' is corrected in proof by Murray to read 'Having the cheek-bones invisible when the skull is viewed from above'. *Temple* sense 1 ('An edifice dedicated to the worship of a deity or deities') is likewise remodelled in early August 1910: 'An edifice or place regarded primarily as the dwelling-place or "house" of a deity or deities; hence, an edifice devoted to divine worship.'

a four-volume work to be finished in ten years,[21] instead found themselves faced with one which, at times, seemed to have no end in sight. 'It would be in vain if . . . the pursuit of an unattainable standard in particular minutiae were to end in the non completion of the Dictionary', they reminded Murray, urging greater progress and more rapid publication (MP/31/1/1887). The tension between scholarly and commercial, especially in the early days, appeared irreconcilable. Murray's bitterness at the situation in which he found himself as editor-in-chief of the *OED* can be palpable. 'If this original work is not to be done, it is a different matter', he wrote to the Secretary of the Delegates (MP/24/6/1886). 'I cannot, I am sorry to say, put more work or effort in to it, than I am doing.'

The very point of the *OED* was, however, its originality, and this was, as Murray, Bradley, Craigie (and, later, Onions) were all to find, both the root of its problems and its salvation. It was, at heart, an attempt to realize an ideal in scientific and lexicographical terms. Often working eighty or ninety hours a week, it was this which, ultimately, sustained Murray: 'the feeling that the best has been done to realize, within the narrowest limits possible, the ideal of a dictionary on historical bases'. As he added, 'if circumstances make this an impossible and too costly task, then I have nothing to sustain me amid the arduous toil of the work' (MP/5/3/1896). Its arduousness was indeed undeniable. The dictionary is imaged as an 'abyss' that 'will never cry "Enough!"' (MP/25/2/1882), 'the work of a machine & not of human beings struggling with some of the most difficult problems of human history'; it is a relentless journey and 'tremendous struggle', a laborious path to the 'mountain-top' of midway through the alphabet from which point those who work on it may 'advance each year down-hill-ward to the end' (MP/14/1/1900). It was, in addition, a venture of which Murray would not see the conclusion, though his commitment to the pioneering spirit in which it was conceived never wavered. Three years before his death, he gives a careful picture of the way in which the parts of the dictionary, under their several editors, were gradually assuming their final places:

I am half through T, which I began on 1 Jan. 1910, $2\frac{1}{2}$ yrs. ago. In another $2\frac{1}{2}$ or less, I may hope to be at V. Before that time Bradley will have finished SH & overtaken Craigie, & the latter ought to have finished S and overtaken T, so that all will be done from A to Tz, and all three editors will be working at the last half vol[ume] U to Z, of which W is the only considerable letter. This I think we ought easily to do in 2 years more; so that we may, I think now, reckon that the end of 1916 will see the Dictionary finished. If I live to then, I shall be 80, and it will also be my Golden Wedding; let us hope that the Grand Conjunction of all these cycles will really take place.   (MP/22/7/1912)

---

[21] It is, however, clear as early as 1882 that Murray was aware of the unfeasibility of the project as thus construed. As he admitted to Gibbs (MP/12/2/1882), the 'now patent' fact was that 'the work *cannot* be done in anything approaching to the time which we first named . . . it is certain that the very shortest period which the work will still take is 13 or 14 years, i.e. added to the 3 years already spent, 16 or 17 years practically it may be a good deal more, for there are still certain unknown quantities to consider'.

It was instead the spring of 1928 which saw the dictionary completed, Murray having died in 1915 and Bradley in 1923. W. A. Craigie (appointed as co-editor in 1901), and C. T. Onions, appointed in 1914, guided the project to its end, productivity hampered by the war (which saw both Scriptorium and the press depleted of assistants) and by other commitments (Craigie was, for example, also working on the *Dictionary of the Older Scottish Tongue* from 1921, as well as (from 1925) editing the *Dictionary of American English* in Chicago). The final publication of *Wise–Wyzen* on 19 April, *X–Zyxt* having been published seven years previously in October 1921, was not, however, to conclude the lexicographical endeavours required. Onions in June of the same year stresses the need to 'fill up the gaps unavoidable in a dictionary compiled on historical principles' (1928: 4), asking, like Murray in 1879, and Coleridge before him, for volunteer readers for a Supplement rendered necessary by the lexical shifts which had taken place since the dictionary was first compiled, as well as by the antedatings, omissions, and inevitable imperfections which had since come to light. A new stage of the pioneering venture had begun.

REFERENCES

Murray Papers

MP/6/4/1876. W. Skeat to J. A. H. Murray.
MP/20/4/1877. H. Sweet to J. A. H. Murray.
MP/10/5/1879*a*. J. A. H. Murray to F. Furnivall.
MP/10/5/1879*b*. F. Furnivall to J. A. H. Murray.
MP/12/2/1882. J. A. H. Murray to H. H. Gibbs.
MP/25/2/1882. J. A. H. Murray to H. H. Gibbs (draft).
MP/29/3/1882. J. A. H. Murray to H. Sweet.
MP/3/4/1882. H. Sweet to J. A. H. Murray.
MP/14/6/1882. H. H. Gibbs to J. A. H. Murray.
MP/9/6/1882. J. A. H. Murray to B. Price.
MP/14/7/1882. H. H. Gibbs to J. A. H. Murray.
MP/30/7/1882. H. H. Gibbs to J. A. H. Murray.
MP/[n.d.]/1883. Proof of first draft of 'Preface' to *NED* Part I. *A–APO*.
MP/3/5/1883. H. H. Gibbs to J. A. H. Murray.
MP/17/9/1883. Proof of *Notice of Publication of a New English Dictionary on a Historical Basis*. Part I. *A–Ant*.
MP/18/10/1883*a*. 3rd Proof of *Notice of Publication of a New English Dictionary on a Historical Basis*. Part I. *A–Ant*.
MP/18/10/1883*b*. J. A. H. Murray to B. Price.
MP/8/10/1885. H. Bradley to J. A. H. Murray.
MP/3/5/1886. H. Bradley to J. A. H. Murray.
MP/15/6/1886. H. Bradley to J. A. H. Murray.
MP/24/6/1886. J. A. H. Murray to L. Gell.
MP/31/1/1887. L. Gell to J. A. H. Murray.
MP/19/2/1887. J. A. H. Murray to R. L. Stevenson.

MP/20/3/1888. H. Bradley to J. A. H. Murray.
MP/10/3/1889. F. T. Mott to J. A. H Murray.
MP/18/10/1889. H. Bradley to J. A. H. Murray.
MP/17/2/1891. J. Dixon to J. A. H. Murray.
MP/13/3/1892. J. A. H. Murray to unnamed correspondent (draft).
MP/26/11/1892. J. A. H. Murray to Mr Darlington.
MP/1/7/1893. H. Bradley to J. A. H. Murray.
MP/29/11/1893. J. A .H. Murray to Mr Liddell.
MP/25/6/1895. H. Yeomans to J. A. H. Murray.
MP/25/1/1896. S. H. Vines to J. A. H. Murray.
MP/5/3/1896. J. A. H. Murray to C. E. Doble.
MP/7/6/1897. A. Swinburne to J. A. H. Murray.
MP/15/6/1897. J. A. H. Murray to L. Gell.
MP/19/4/1898. J. A. H. Murray to A. Fairburn.
MP/1/9/1899. J. Hamilton to J. A. H. Murray.
MP/4/9/1899. J. A. H. Murray to J. Hamilton.
MP/[n.d.]/1900. J. A. H. Murray to Mr Matthews.
MP/14/1/1900. J. A. H. Murray to E. Arber.
MP/23/6/1900. J. A. H. Murray to H. Warren.
MP/8/3/1901. J. A. H. Murray to Miss Hastings.
MP/22/4/1903. J. A. H. Murray to Revd G. P. Taylor.
MP/15/12/1903. J. A. H. Murray to Dr Bryce.
MP/31/3/1904. J. A. H. Murray to F. Furnivall.
MP/16/12/1904. J. A. H. Murray to Canon W. L. Blackley.
MP/24/12/1904. J. A. H. Murray to E. Arber.
MP/20/12/1906. J. A. H. Murray to Mr Jenkinson.
MP/24/12/1906. J. A. H. Murray to unnamed correspondent.
MP/2/7/1909. G. Ranking to J. A. H. Murray.
MP/[1910]. J. A. H. Murray. Ms of 'Lecture to London Institute'.
MP/22/7/1912. J. A. H. Murray to W. Skeat.
MP/8/12/1912. J. A. H. Murray to Revd W. Stathers.
MP/9/10/1913. Major J. H. Leslie to J. A. H. Murray.

OED *Archives at OUP*

OED/MISC/59/1/13. Review of *NED* Vol. III, Part 1 *E–Every*. *The Athenaeum* (1891).
OED/MISC/464/1. J. A. H. Murray to H. Bradley, 20 December 1898.

Published works

Béjoint, H. (1994). *Tradition and Innovation in Modern English Dictionaries*. Oxford: Clarendon Press.
Boswell, J. (1791). *The Life of Samuel Johnson LL D*. ed. L. F. Powell (1934). 4 vols. Oxford: Clarendon Press.
Burchfield, R. W. (ed.). (1972–86). *A Supplement to the Oxford English Dictionary*. 4 vols. Oxford: Clarendon Press.
Burchfield, R. W. (1973). 'The Treatment of Controversial Vocabulary in the *OED*'. *TPS*: 1–28.

Coleridge, H. (1860). 'A Letter to the Very Rev. The Dean of Westminster'. Appended to Trench (1860): 71–8.

Craigie, W. A. and Onions, C. T. (1933). 'Historical Introduction'. *A New English Dictionary on Historical Principles*. Introduction, Supplement, and Bibliography. Vol. I. A–B. Oxford: Clarendon Press, pp. vii–xxxiv.

Johnson, S. (1755). *A Dictionary of the English Language*. London: W. Strahan.

McConchie, R. W. (1997). *Lexicography and Physicke. The Recording of Sixteenth-Century Medical Terminology*. Oxford: Clarendon Press.

Morris, R. (1875). 'Fourth Annual Address of the President to the Philological Society. Introduction'. *TPS*, 1875–6: 1–18.

Müller, F. M. (1878). *Observations by Professor Max Müller on the Lists of Readers and Books Read for the Proposed English Dictionary*. Oxford: Clarendon Press.

Murray, J. A. H. (1879). *An Appeal to the English-Speaking and English-Reading Public to Read Books and Make Extracts for the Philological Society's New Dictionary*. Oxford: Clarendon Press.

—— (1880). 'Ninth Annual Address of the President to the Philological Society'. *TPS*, 1880–1: 117–74.

—— (1881). 'Report on the Dictionary of the Philological Society'. *TPS*, 1880–1: 260–9.

—— (1882). 'Report on the Present State of the Dictionary of the Philological Society', *TPS*, 1882–4: 5–7.

—— (1884). 'Thirteenth Annual Address of the President to the Philological Society'. *TPS*, 1882–4: 501–31.

Murray, K. M. E. (1977). *Caught in the Web of Words: James Murray and the* Oxford English Dictionary. New Haven and London: Yale University Press.

Onions, C. T. (1928). 'Report on the Society's Dictionary'. *TPS*, 1925–30: 1–5.

[Philological Society]. (1859). *Proposal for the Publication of a New English Dictionary by the Philological Society*. London: Trübner and Co.

—— (1883). Monthly Abstract of Proceedings. *Proc. Philol. Soc.*: iii–vi.

—— (1884). Monthly Abstract of Proceedings: 'Annual Dictionary Evening'. *Proc. Philol. Soc.*: v–vi.

Richardson, C. (1836–7). *A New Dictionary of the English Language*. London: William Pickering.

Schäfer, J. (1980). *Documentation in the* OED: *Shakespeare and Nashe as Test Cases*. Oxford: Oxford University Press.

Sweet, H. (1877). 'Sixth Annual Address of the President to the Philological Society'. *TPS*, 1877–9: 1–109.

Trench, R. C. (1860). *On Some Deficiencies in Our English Dictionaries*. 2nd rev. edn. London: John W. Parker & Son.

Willinsky, J. (1994). *Empire of Words. The Reign of the OED*. Princeton: Princeton University Press.

Zgusta, L. (1971). *Manual of Lexicography*. Prague: Academia.

2

Making the *OED*: Readers and Editors. A Critical Survey

Elizabeth Knowles

If there is one single image associated with the dictionary, it is that of the elderly James Murray in his Scriptorium, standing in front of shelves overflowing with slips. In one sense this is regrettable; while it properly represents Murray's enormous individual contribution, it obscures the significant part played by a large number of people who may never have visited the Scriptorium, or even met Murray face-to-face. It is the intention in this chapter to look more closely at the way in which their work was done, and the implications which this has for the project as a whole.

In considering the question of readers, subeditors, and editors there is one key fact to be borne in mind: the typical contributor was an unpaid volunteer who was not only working 'out-of-house', but was in fact often living at a considerable geographical distance, with instruction and comment being supplied largely through the written word. In this context, it is worth noting the final sentence of Henry Bradley's Prefatory Note to Volume IV:

My removal to Oxford, which took place in the middle of 1896, has, by enabling me to confer with my assistants personally instead of by correspondence, materially facilitated my work, and the results are already visible in the greatly increased rapidity with which the copy has been produced.   (1901: p. viii)

What was involved in the initial work? To begin with, there was a mass of raw material with which those engaged in the editorial process had to deal. The reading programme for the dictionary produced boxes and bundles of 5 × 3 slips of paper, each slip bearing an illustrative quotation for a word or phrase, together with the citation details of the source from which it was taken. The word or phrase illustrated (the 'catchword') was written in the top left-hand corner of the slip. When Murray took over in 1879 he continued and extended the collection of material, and in years to come he was clear that it was largely the material collected under his direction which had been of real value to the dictionary. A letter of 1899 looks back to the early years of the reading programme:

There are numberless puzzles about the early history of the Philological Society's materials which I have long despaired of unravelling, contenting myself with doing the best possible with the materials since they came into my custody . . . the original materials are bad enough, and rarely to be trusted, and, in point of fact, 5/6 of the quotations that we print, are taken from those collected under my supervision since 1879 . . . A very small proportion of the Dictionary is composed of 'materials collected by the Phil. Soc.' . . . I often wish I had made a bonfire of the old and begun anew.   (OED/MISC/13/24)

Some allowance must be made for Murray's tendency to doubt the probity of systems other than his own, but it seems likely that his estimate was a just one. The original readers, once assigned their tasks, had little or no supervision or feedback on results. In consequence it is inevitable that even those who did not fall by the wayside would have developed considerable variance in the material they produced. Murray's often cited anxiety to control and oversee the whole work may well thus have sprung from his awareness of the necessity to correct 'stylistic drift' by constantly reiterating essential principles. He was also aware of how common it was to lose readers and subeditors; an enthusiastic beginning was not necessarily followed by sustained progress.

In the essential structure of the project, Murray was at the centre, accompanied (at first in Mill Hill and later in Oxford) by a small number of assistants who worked with him preparing text for the press and revising proofs. Volunteer readers sent in batches of slips for various vocabulary items; these had to be alphabetized, and ranges of work made up for the initial work ('subediting'). Batches of slips were sent out for the first editorial work, and in due course drafted entries came back. These were stored until it was time for the next round when they were sent out again, together with all the new material for the range which had been amassed in the meantime. From 1896, when Bradley arrived in Oxford, a second centre for the dictionary was established at the Old Ashmolean; there was then necessarily a degree of communication between the two groups, as well as between each group and its outside workers.

The material would be revised by the 're-subeditor', and once more the finished work would come back. Finally the point would be reached at which it was necessary for a range to be prepared for the Press, and it was only then that the editor himself (i.e. Murray, Bradley, or later, Onions and Craigie) was likely to inspect the work. There was, moreover, a considerable time-lag between material arriving at Oxford and its being worked on by in-house subeditors; another disadvantage when dealing with those who were geographically remote. It was in fact not unusual for the same subeditor to work twice through the same material before it reached the editor's hands. For example, James Bartlett subedited the material for G twice, first in 1888 (and the immediately following years) and again in 1897–8, a great many additional quotations having accumulated in the interim. It was also quite possible that by the time the text had reached the proof stage the original subeditors would no longer be alive. A paragraph from Bradley's

Preface to M shows that four out of six named subeditors had died before the volume appeared. Similarly, in his Preface to Volume VII (1909), Murray paid tribute to 'the generous and, in many cases, long-continued services of these voluntary contributors, so few of whom, alas! survive'.

The respective roles of subeditors and re-subeditors, especially in relation to Murray himself, are clearly indicated in the Prefatory Note to Part II, *Ant–Batten*. As well as assistants in the Scriptorium, Murray had the help of several voluntary outside workers. Alfred Erlebach (before becoming an in-house assistant) had subedited *Au–Az*. The Revd Arthur P. Fayers, of Rawdon, near Leeds, had subedited part of *Bap–* as well as the section from *Bath–* onwards. G. A. Schrumpf had spent several weeks on the first draft of the word *At*, and W. J. Ashley, of Lincoln College, Oxford, had subedited *Bar* and its derivatives. From *As–* onwards the remainder of the material, having first been put into shape by in-house assistants, had been 'carefully revised, amended, and extended' by C. B. Mount of Oxford, Dr Brackebusch of London, and E. Gunthorpe of Sheffield. These three volunteers were singled out for special praise:

[They] have kindly brought the experience gained in sub-editing other portions of the materials to the task of taking those already sub-edited, incorporating therewith the latest additions, revising the subeditors' discrimination and arrangement of the senses, and contributing generally to the ultimate form of the articles, immediately in advance of my own final work for the press.   (Murray 1885: p. v)

It was of course of crucial importance that the written instructions supplied should be as detailed as possible. There are various manuscript copies of 'Directions to SubEditors', which set out what was to be done with the material, beginning with the essential task of arranging the slips in alphabetical order of catchword. Even this was not necessarily straightforward. The catchword should be ordered in accordance with the 'typical form' (that is, what was recognized as the dominant spelling) of the word, rather than with the actual spelling on the slip. It was thus necessary, after the first sort, to look again for any catchwords representing an obsolete form, and to resort these slips to their proper place. While doing this, the subeditor was also expected to make cross-references from the obsolete to the typical form: 'Insert blank slips bearing the obsolete form as a catchword, in the places whence you remove the others, with a cross-reference to the "Typical Form"', state the instructions (OED/MISC/91/9); 'thus, in the place whence you have removed the slips for *Abricock*, insert a blank slip, bearing "*Abricock* obs. f. *Apricot*"'. Once this had been done, the real work could begin. 'Your slips are now in homographic groups', the editor encouraged; 'i.e. groups of words identical in spelling, but perhaps really consisting of several distinct parts of speech, or even of words having no connexion' (OED/MISC/91/9). It was, however, possibly less than helpful that this use of *homographic* to mean 'of, belonging to, or consisting of homographs' was apparently Murray's own coinage: this remains the first and only illustrative quotation for this sense in the *OED*.

Division into parts of speech was the next step; slips for *pale*, for example, had to be divided according to whether they illustrated noun, adjective, or verb. Afterwards the slips were arranged by date for each word, although there was at this point a specific warning against attempting to clarify the meanings. Each word was given an initial blank slip on which was to be written the typical form of the catchword, and a list of historical forms of the word in chronological order. Semantic analysis now began, with quotations for each word being classified according to meaning and construction. Subeditors were to make these divisions as precisely as possible, with the help of whatever dictionaries they might have to hand. The subeditor had then to arrange, in chronological order, all the slips illustrating each meaning and construction. It is clear that here the purpose of the work was to prepare the material for more expert hands: 'Write . . . a provisional definition, at least, for the Editor's revisal; arrange their meanings in logical order—your earliest quotations will generally, but not always, contain the original English meaning' (OED/MISC/91/9).

All slips for phrases were to be placed after the word or sense to which the phrase was assigned. Slips for compounds or combinations of a word, however, were placed in a batch at the end of that word, where the editor could most readily find them. This outline is in principle the pattern familiar from the printed text of the *OED*, although at this stage it was still being assumed that phrases would be assignable to individual senses. In practice, this did not always prove possible; some words therefore required separate paragraphs in which phrases could be grouped as a set. Subeditors were to make every effort to complete the illustrative quotations for each sense, although it was recognized that at times the material might be lacking. 'You may not be able to accomplish all these steps', the directions acknowledge (OED/MISC/91/9). Nevertheless 'kindly pursue them in order, and do as much as you can, endeavouring to return the work to the Editor in as advanced a state as possible, and above all, *in complete order as far as it has gone.*'

The 'Directions to Editors' chronicle the initial stage of editing. It is notable that each stage involves work with slips, but evidence from the *OED* archives suggests (unsurprisingly) that subeditors were also likely to draw up plans for the semantic divisions of longer words. Thus Miss J. E. A. Brown, who subedited *Bel–Betrust*, drew up a plan on a sheet of foolscap paper dividing the verb *bereave* into eight main senses with six further subsenses. As eventually published it had three main senses and three subsenses, the remainder of Miss Brown's divisions being taken as contextual examples of a broader sense. Similarly, Dr Brackebusch, working on the adjective *bad*, drew up a plan requiring twenty-six senses (the final article had eight). As this illustrates, it was a danger for subeditors working in isolation that they would see semantic divisions in what were actually only contextual uses. This could of course be corrected at the next stage, or by the in-house subeditor, but at the cost of some time spent on rearrangement. It is in the light of the frustration occasioned by this that we may consider some tart comments made by Henry Bradley on notes by James Bartlett.

[BARTLETT] I prefer to leave these to a more skilled hand.
[BRADLEY] You should have left it *all*. (OED/OS/168/6/4)

[BARTLETT on *monad*] I have tried very hard to grapple with this difficult word, but have found so many of its uses too obscure to discriminate and discuss that I very reluctantly let them *severely* alone.
[BRADLEY] good! (OED/OS/168/6/2)

The verb *shake* presented particular difficulties:

[BARTLETT] I feel quite incompetent to tackle the formidable early forms of the word, and so leave them alone. Also the numbering off.
[BRADLEY] I move to delete all after 'incompetent'. (OED/OS/242/9/2)

The second, or revision, stage (similarly laid out in 'Directions to Re-subeditors') also took place out-of-house and at a distance, although at this point there was more expectation that the editor would soon be looking at the material. The first priority here was to deal with new slips, which had to be arranged and treated according to the rules laid down for the first editing stage. It was now that the impact of the new material on the primary editing had to be assessed, and any necessary modifications made to the list of historical forms and dates. It was also possible that a new form might emerge which was alphabetically widely separated from the typical form. In such cases, a cross-reference was to be made on a blank slip and, if this fell outside the range being dealt with, it was to be returned to the editor for insertion in the proper place. (It is noted explicitly that cross-referencing for forms already recorded would have been done by the previous subeditor.) The re-subeditor now embarked on subediting proper with the instruction, 'Read through the subeditor's definitions, and master his plan of the word.' Having done so, the new material was incorporated, with new slips being inserted at the appropriate semantic and chronological points. Further alterations and emendations might also be necessary if, for example, the new evidence (or the re-subeditor's own observation) suggested that definitions should be modified or senses rearranged; suggestions for changes were to be written on the blank slips left by the previous subeditor in front of each section.

The directions at this stage give us a picture of second-stage editing in which re-subeditors might alter what the original subeditor had done. They were, however, explicitly not encouraged to do anything which would hinder the editor's seeing the original plan. Materials for the entry could be assembled in as up-to-date a manner as possible, but where defining is concerned, there is a clear implication that the final version was to be the responsibility of the editor. This stage-by-stage sifting may well have ensured that each word received the most thoughtful consideration. It is nevertheless clearly not a procedure geared to speed. It is also worth noting that there is no suggestion that when new quotations were added, older quotations should be removed.

We may at this point give some consideration to the actual numbers involved. In the Preface to Volume I, Murray gave some significant figures. More than 800 readers had responded to the new appeal made in 1879; while most of them were from Great Britain, a large number were from the United States, and there were also volunteer readers in British colonies and foreign countries. Over three years, their efforts provided a million additional quotations. As far as the editing was concerned, over the course of the volume Murray had a total of twelve in-house editorial assistants: Alfred Erlebach, John Mitchell, James B. Johnston, G. F. H. Sykes, F. E. Bumby, Walter Worrall, A. T. Maling, R. H. Lord, C. G. Balk, H. F. P. Ruthven, C. G. Crump, and G. Parker. As well as these there were 'about thirty subeditors (including a few who had never ceased to work for the Dictionary)' who 'offered their gratuitous services in arranging quotations, preparing definitions, and otherwise contributing to the execution of the work' (Murray 1888: p. vi).

The numbers involved illuminate what were to be two constant factors: the essential support provided by (in the main voluntary) outside workers, and the considerable input of editorial time required to train them in the requisite skills and to establish and maintain an acceptable quality in their output. Instructions to subeditors and re-subeditors assume an orderly progression (although it is clear from the outset that the requirement for the editor to make all final decisions was likely to result in a serious bottleneck). However, some subeditors were less reliable than might have been hoped. An early letter from Murray to a dilatory contributor (MP/25/10/1881) notes, for instance, that failure to send material in as agreed had been a serious hindrance. Arrangements had been made for its receipt and a letter of remonstrance had been ignored. The contributor was firmly requested to send off the slips immediately, without further waste of the editor's time.

There could also be friction between the editors themselves. In November 1901 Bradley wrote to Murray requesting that the Scriptorium staff be asked not to make unauthorized alterations in his copy, and pointing out that remedying such unwanted contributions resulted in expenditure of time. On 21 November he wrote again. He began by apologizing for not having realized that the particular alteration of which he had complained was made according to a general rule rather than having been an arbitrary decision on the part of Murray's assistant, Mr Sewell. However, he was still unhappy with the general situation:

My assistants have often called my attention to instances in which the text of a quotation has been altered at the Scriptorium to a form in which the word illustrated did not occur at all. Mr Worrall says that this has happened with quotes from 1611 Bible which have been put back to Wyclif.   (MP/21/11/1901)

Bradley went on to give details of the way in which he preferred to work, his comments indicative of the manner in which the work of readers, and perhaps also of primary subeditors, was regarded: 'Whenever I do a word from the beginning I always (barring oversight) look up the passage, as the sense is seldom securely established by the quot[ation]s as sent by our readers'. As he admitted, there were nevertheless a number of texts for which this was impossible:

As we have no b-text Chaucer, and our means of verifying quots. from Gavin Douglas are inferior to yours, we must continue to rely on the Scriptorium for corrections of text in quots. from these two authors. But in the case of the Bible, Shaks., Milton, Malory, Cursor, Langland, etc., my assistants ought to be responsible for the text of quots., leaving only the references to the Scriptorium staff. (MP/21/11/1901)

Murray had evidently raised another question about the material sent to the Scriptorium since Bradley moved on to defend his numbering of the slips, a practice adopted, he stressed, 'because portions of copy were constantly getting lost at the Scriptorium'. Murray's reply accepted Bradley's suggestions for dealing with sources. The notion of even one missing slip, however, was another matter:

We are surprised to be told that 'portions of copy were constantly getting lost at the Scriptorium'. So far as any one here can remember, this is the first time we ever heard of such an irregularity, and, frankly, *we believe it impossible*. There are no holes in the Scriptorium floor through which such portions could slip, and as every table is cleared from time to time, and every stray slip found put into its place . . . it is to us so inconceivable as to be utterly impossible, that even a single slip could be permanently lost. I believe I have lost or mislaid only *two* slips since the Dictionary began in 1879; one of those which I mourned for years and years, and spent hours in looking for, turned up a few weeks ago under *ocean* to which it had been sent from *charnel*, when not used there. (MP/?22/11/1901)

The question of disappearing copy caused something of a storm since, according to Bradley's letter of 25 November, the Scriptorium assistant C. G. Balk assumed that Bradley was suggesting that copy had been 'deliberately caused to disappear'. Balk evidently apologized for this assertion in a courteous and friendly letter; however, he 'unfortunately followed it . . . with another letter which I much regret, as I think the writer himself probably will when in a calmer mood'. Bradley sensibly did not allow himself to be drawn into a discussion of Scriptorium methods of text-management; he did, however, allow himself a bland comment on Murray's claim: 'A system of arrangements so perfect in method that accidental disappearance of slips is *impossible* is unfortunately so far out of my experience that it did not occur to me to regard the alleged fact as proving even gross carelessness, far less anything worse' (MP/25/11/1901).

This exchange is one of particular interest in the light it throws on relations between the two groups of lexicographers, each struggling to deal with a flood of slips and galley proofs, and each somewhat doubtful of the accuracy and carefulness of the other. It also highlights another constant: the desire to recheck for oneself the work done by another. Over the years this constituted one of the major obstacles to progress.

In the Preface to Volume I, Murray took occasion to render particular thanks to those contributors whose work was the systematic and continuous critical reading of proofs 'to improve the work as a whole by criticism, or to enrich it by additions' (1888: p. xiii). Pre-eminent among these gentlemen (who included Henry Hucks Gibbs, later Lord Aldenham, and Murray's one-time editorial assistant James

B. Johnston), was 'Mr. Fitzedward Hall, DCL, who, as a voluntary and gratuitous service to the history of the English Language, has devoted four hours daily to a critical examination of the proof-sheets'. Unlike, for instance, the Broadmoor patient Dr Minor, who began and remained as a reader supplying quotations from chosen texts (see Knowles 1990), Hall's crucial role was that of a critical reader of the proofs; he was thus able to contribute to any part of an entry. The long and detailed correspondence between Murray and Hall hence serves to shed light on many of the staples of the editing process. (It should be remembered that while the main connection was with Murray, Hall also read proofs for Bradley: his work is acknowledged in Bradley's Prefatory Note to *E–Every*.)

In the last quarter of the nineteenth century, the American-born Fitzedward Hall was living a semi-reclusive life in Wickham Market, Norfolk. He had originally come to London from India, but in 1869 he was dismissed from the India Office, by his own account on the (unfounded) charge of being both a hopeless drunkard and a foreign spy. He was and remained convinced that his nationality opened him to the enmity with which he believed Americans were regarded by the English. Hall had sufficient private means on which to live, and he and his family left London for East Anglia. A few years later his marriage broke up, and after this he effectively lived the life of a recluse. His life, in fact, largely became his work for the dictionary. Four hours a day were spent on proofs; for much of the rest of time, he was reading for vocabulary. 'You may depend upon me to the last gasp', he had written in 1897, and this seems to have been literally true; according to his son, the last time Hall held a pen was when, on the day before his death, he signed a dictated postcard to accompany the proof sheets he was returning. Although they never actually met, through their letters he and Murray became friends; 'I grieve more than ever that I never saw him face to face nor grasped his honoured hand', Murray lamented when Hall died in 1901 (OED/MISC/13/31).

Though it is a matter of regret that while Murray's letters to Hall focus on lexicographical matters, Hall's surviving letters in the Murray Papers are largely those which deal with personal health and circumstances, the material which is preserved in this correspondence, and the information we have about Hall's work for the dictionary does serve to provide unique details about the kind of work done by long-time contributors. Murray's appreciation of Hall's work was clear. He warmly praised 'the daily and never-to-be-forgotten labours which you have so generously and splendidly performed for the Dictionary'. This 'rises before me as one of the most splendid records of disinterested work in the annals of literature', he added, 'not its least wonderful feature being the sustainment of interest and work for long years' (OED/MISC/13/4). When in December 1893 he heard that Hall was ill, he was concerned both personally and professionally:

The everyday wish which I have from visitors to the Scriptorium, or correspondents on the subject of the Dictionary is 'May you live to see Zymotic': that wish, I most heartily transfer to you, for I really dread to think of the falling-off in our work, which the failure of your help would mean. It is true that you have spoken of leaving materials at my disposal, but alas! how little worth are the best materials without the master-mind that knows how to use them, and make them useful!   (OED/MISC/13/4)

The friendship between them moreover meant that Hall was treated as a confidant, to whom accounts of general anxieties and worries could be addressed. The autumn of 1895 was, for instance, a time of particular pressure:

For the last 12 months, since Mr Mitchell lost his life in Wales in the end of Augt. 1894, I have lived in a kind of chronic fever of excitement arising from anxiety to go on, & the constantly retarding & chafing influence of insufficient and inefficient help. Every day has found me short of what I hoped to do, & nearly every day has brought unforeseen and worrying causes of delay, from the omissions & inaccuracies of new assistants not observed in their initial stage.   (OED/MISC/13/12)

When such errors were observed, it often took longer to correct the mistakes; another reason, Murray explained, why he had not personally written to Hall for some time. At other times Murray wrote of the difficulties he experienced in writing the dictionary, though he was equally appreciative of Hall's own labours towards this work. 'I have been reduced almost to the state of a machine, grinding out "copy", & have hardly had an instant for thought, or any brain-power to entertain it', he commented on the strain of finishing D, adding: 'I am afraid the 3 proofs a week must have a terrible strain on *you*; it was so, for some of my "readers" who do not bestow on the pages a little of the labour & time that you do . . . I have to record with deepest gratitude our obligations to you for your superb help, which has so enriched the 3 volumes now finished, and to express with trembling the earnest desire that you will be able to give us your help for a long time to come' (OED/MISC/13/16).

Hall's main function was that of providing critical comment at proof stage, and a number of the letters record detailed discussions about individual words. In November 1894, for example, Murray wrote to thank him for the 'wealth of material sent for Develop'—a word which had already 'cost a great deal of trouble in MS'. Hall had obviously supplied a good many further quotations which were of particular value for semantic analysis as well as linguistic history:

What is printed represents a fourth or fifth of the quots. merely; but those left out were mostly of this century, while yours carry several shades of meaning back to last century. The essential meaning of those you pin together seems to me to be 'unfold', but it certainly approaches or quite comes to 'discover, detect' in some cases. Of course 'discover' is *literally* the same thing, except that in *discovering* you may have simply to *lift* a cover, whereas in *developing* the cover has to be *unrolled* or *unwound*—but the result is the same, the contents lie bare—and hence in fig. senses the two words coincide. (OED/MISC/13/7)

Hall regularly dealt with items of core vocabulary such as *develop*, though his contributions could be equally useful for loanwords too. Murray, for example, thanked him for his assistance with *Devanagari*, the name of the alphabet used for Sanskrit, Hindi, and other Indian languages, and 'on the very *verge* of the province of an English Dictionary' (OED/MISC/13/7). Hall's comments on the entry for *devilry* were significant in other ways, here presumably causing a new entry to be introduced. 'I took *deviltre* to be a misprint for *devilrie*. The interchange of *r* and *t* is very frequent: we have had series of instances since we began', Murray admitted in response to Hall's corrections: 'I think your suggestion as to deviltry being East Anglian is very likely correct' (OED/MISC/13/9). Hall's comments on spelling could also be of influence: 'My old assistant Mr Erlebach who came to give me a little help in my pressure at Xmas, has an article I believe in type for some magazine in some points of spelling, where these words are touched on', Murray wrote: 'I have told him that you rather doubted *diagraming*, and he asked today for your address that he may submit his article to your kindly criticism' (OED/MISC/13/10). Here Hall was presumably persuaded by the arguments; the entry for *diagram* gives the inflections as *diagramed* and *diagraming*. Advice on pronunciation was also requested, as on *diaskeuast* for which Murray set out the various possibilities for Hall's opinion in 1895 (OED/MISC/13/11).

By the spring Murray was well launched on H, writing to Hall in early April about the entry for *hand*, and asking him to send only what struck him as needed to supply omissions or correct error. *Handsome* was also presenting difficulties, and the suggestion was made that Hall might draft and send a definition. By the summer, they had reached *He–*. A letter of 28 July, dealing with the pronoun *he*, provides an interesting example of detailed requests for illustrative quotations:

We want good instances
1 Of *he* applied to mountains, rivers, rocks, &c personified.
2 Of *he* pleonastic in ballad style—the noble Percy he—and in modern illiterate use 'my father he is called Billy'
3 Of *he that* and *he who*, so as to date the appearance of the latter
4 Of *he* with prep.l phrase, as 'he of Macedon', 'he of the sevenfold shield', 'he with the wooden leg'. Cf 'there stood *she* of Medici, the stateliest of the line'
5 Of *He who* meaning *one who, any one who*. (I think we have enough of *he* meaning man, male, and *he-* in *he-goat, he-saint, he-fellow*.)   (OED/MISC/13/18)

Hall continued to supply quotations as well as reading proofs, as a letter of October 1897 confirms (while also throwing an interesting light on the 'perfect system' of whose existence Henry Bradley had been so doubtful): 'In some mysterious way we have lost the enclosed quots. which you appear to have sent with the accompanying Proof . . . I thought our systematic method rendered any such vanishing impossible' (OED/MISC/13/20). H, like D, represented final editing, but further down the alphabet the first subediting stages were still in progress; here too Hall was involved. On 22 September 1898 Murray wrote to say that he had got the *photo-* words for the volunteer subeditor dealing with that part of P, and was sending Hall particulars of what would be useful. He was particularly appreciative that Hall should be prepared to do this while still embroiled with H; *how* especially had been difficult for both of them. It was, of course, said Murray, a difficult article, and one in which perfection lay far off.

Hall's work could also bring to light the problem of inadequately-read sources, and the need to supplement them. 'You have doubtless observed of late that you have had to supply numerous references to quots. from Davies *Athenae Brit[annicae]*', Murray wrote, for example: 'our own quots. from the work seem to have stopped' (OED/MISC/13/23). The letter went on to describe and castigate 'the silly practice' encouraged by Furnivall, by which volunteers had been encouraged to collect vocabulary only for the letters on which they were themselves engaged, being 'urged to get their friends to read books for *their own letters* only—so as to provoke a rivalry of good works between them, the fatal result being that *I* never know whether a book reported as read was read as a whole or not, until some accident recalls the fact that of late we have not seen any quots. from the book in question'. This letter is particularly significant because it not only sets out the problem but also (with due regard to constraints of time and budget) proposes a solution. If, Murray suggested, Hall's references to the relevant work were to hand in accessible form, they could be copied out onto blank slips, and someone could be employed to copy out the actual quotations in the Bodleian Library in Oxford. This 'would be much cheaper than turning them up once or twice a week during the next 10 or 12 years, necessitating a journey every time, the ordering of the book, etc.' (OED/MISC/13/23). The initial copying out, he suggested, should be done by someone found by Hall (though paid by Murray). It is especially noteworthy here that Murray was confident that Hall's choice of words would be acceptable— a marked contrast to his views of the wordlists supplied by the Broadmoor patient Dr Minor. When, a few years later, Murray was getting quotations from books indexed by Minor, he warned the chosen reader, John J. Thompson, that Minor's lists were more numerous than was needed; he even suggested that it might be easier for Thompson simply to reread the book for himself.

By 1900 Hall was in fact nearing the end of his life, and it is evident from Murray's last letters to him that Hall's physical capabilities were weakening. Murray wrote to ask 'whether we can do anything to help you, whether there is any mechanical work, copying, or combining lists, which could be done for you *here*, or under your superintendence by young people there; if there is, we could afford to pay for it as clerkly work, & should be glad to do so' (OED/MISC/13/28). The letter also suggests, however, that Hall was becoming less conscious of the publishing schedule, and of the necessity to restrict the number of corrections in proof. 'I am not able to use nearly all the quots. that you so kindly send: perhaps you could restrict the number sent to those which you think absolutely needed as being earlier or later than, or different from those we have', Murray suggested: 'The fact, that a quotation is *better* than one we have, cannot always be taken advantage of to substitute it. We send to printer the *best we have*, and to these in the main we must stick, except where the superiority of others that come in later is very great indeed.'

Murray's last letters to his long-time contributor were written in this year; Hall died in February 1901. The aim was then to make use of the materials left behind, a process recorded in an exchange of letters between Murray and Hall's son, Richard. What becomes clear from this correspondence is that whatever instructions he may have received from Murray, Hall had in fact worked to his own system, rather than to one directed from Oxford. Those dealing with his papers had not only to find the material they believed to exist but also, if possible, to reconstruct the system by which he had worked. The problem was one only too likely to arise in the case of a long-time contributor who had always worked at a distance, and who had in the main been treated as a collaborator rather than as a subordinate.

The first difficulty related to missing material. Murray wrote to thank the younger Hall for a package of quotations, but pointed out that there should be more to be found. There should have been a 'mass' of material from the end of J; evidence from Hall's favourite books and authors were also missing from K and L. 'We have little doubt that there is somewhere another series of slips, or if not, a series of note-books containing references from which he used to get his quotations, turning up the actual passages, & copying them out probably from his library', Murray concluded (OED/MISC/13/32). Additional information appeared the next day: 'We have just found among the L materials sent us, these Index-lists of words, which seem to belong to some book or collection of quotations' (OED/MISC/13/33); 'I send them', said Murray, 'in the hope that they may suggest something to you.'

This provided an outline of Hall's method: the systematic indexing of chosen books whereby words and page references were recorded in vocabulary lists. There were also unexplained annotations: references to unidentifiable sources indicated by '*My 1*' and '*My 2*' against particular items in the wordlists. While it was clear that such annotations formed an integral part of Hall's system, it was and remains impossible to deduce their meaning. Hall's index lists, or 'analyses of books', turned out to be much more extensive than Murray had expected: 'When we remember that they would probably have taken him, had he lived, 4 hrs a day during the next 10 years, or some 12,000 hours, it is evident we shall in some way have to expend *more* than that number of hours upon putting them in order, & taking out the quotations' (OED/MISC/13/37).

The solution, Murray thought, was a general appeal for volunteers on the lines of the 1879 'Appeal to the English-speaking World'. This was in fact done, as Murray later informed Hall's son:

In accordance with a paragraph which the Sec[retar]y of the Philological Society inserted in some of the London papers, a large number of persons have written to me offering to copy out the passages to which your father left references in the papers which you sent us, providing I can send the books to them to be excerpted. You kindly offered to lend us such of the books as we might wish to have for the purpose; I send you accordingly a list of the books which I should at present like to borrow to be thus excerpted. (OED/MISC/13/37)

Correspondence about Fitzedward Hall's books continued between Murray and Richard Hall throughout the summer. In Oxford, going through Hall's papers, they were effectively reconstructing a list of Hall's major sources, and if possible identifying the actual edition from which Hall had worked. This was not always easy. Richard Hall's surmise of 'the vol. of La Primaudaye's *French Academy*' was correct for one source, for example, but 'it is not the part wanted, which is part III of date 1618. We do not know that Dr Hall had it, but there is a pencil list for it. Apparently it is bound up with something else, prob. a later edn. of the whole work' (OED/MISC/13/43). Only thirteen citations appear in the *OED* for the third part of *French Academy*, so it is possible that here Hall's copy was not traced and his index not used.

Another mystery, however, was at least partly solved. 'The mysterious references to *My 1*, *My 2*, etc., on which we could get no light before, receive some illumination', Murray wrote in the same letter; 'On the list belonging to W. Watson's *Decacordon* there is a note "See also my Vol 4 of words." Hence it is evident that there is somewhere a (MS.) book of words in 4 volumes at least, whence those in *My 1* etc. were extracted.' These would, he concluded optimistically, 'certainly come to light somewhere, & somewhen'. (There is regrettably no record of whether this happened.)

At this point examination of another archive source is relevant; a collection of letters written by Murray to John J. Thompson, one of the volunteer readers who was to help with excerpting Hall's books. This correspondence moreover provides an excellent illustration of Murray's preference for keeping things in his own hands rather than delegating the work to an assistant. Despite the enormous pressure under which he was working, Murray provided the initial brief, continued to conduct the correspondence, and to supervise the work.

In June 1901 he wrote to Thompson, enclosing a book of Hall's together with blank quotation slips. His instructions were explicit: Thompson was to take quotations for all the words after J in the enclosed pencil list, being careful to ensure that references were accurately given, and that quotations were long enough to be clear and grammatical. Murray also offered, if more slips were needed, to send blanks which could be filled up with date and title. The excerpting was a success, Murray thanking him in early July for the 'excellent' material, and adding that he would gladly send another book as soon as he got one. As he explained, Richard Hall had difficulty identifying the particular edition wanted so the necessary books tended to reach him piecemeal. Murray suggested another source, asking whether Thompson had used Dr Williams's Library [which] 'contains many books for which Dr F. Hall made indices, tho' he had not the book of his own' (OED/MISC/11/9). He recommended a specific title (Richard Montagu's *Diatribae upon the first part of the late History of Tithes*, 1621), which he wanted read for words in K–Z. He would get the slips printed and send Hall's wordlist.

Arrangements for access to Dr Williams's Library initially proved more difficult than Murray had hoped, but in the meantime another book came to light: Richard Brathwait's *Strappado* (1615). Murray said that he was ordering 500 slips to be printed which would 'give approximately 2 quots. to a page although it would of course have been capable of yielding many more' (OED/MISC/11/13). Thompson also had another suggestion: he would read parts of the *Encyclopaedia Britannica*, an idea which delighted Murray although there were obviously problems in dealing with so large a piece of work. His solution was for Thompson to look for what were likely to be new or rare words in the scientific articles. With his blend of the *Encyclopaedia Britannica* and Hall's books, Thompson in this way became a valued reader, praised by Murray for his accuracy in choice of vocabulary ('Your notions as to the kind of words to be included in the Dictionary are precisely & exactly those set forth in the *Preface*' (OED/MISC/11/16)). Murray sent him a number of further sets of printed slips, and Thompson duly worked on the *Diatribae* and *Strappado*. Murray also asked him to acquire Donne's *Pseudo-Martyr* from Dr Williams's Library, while waiting for Hall's son to produce a fresh batch of books from Hall's library. After this (which Thompson completed in early September) he was asked to obtain the 1612 edition of Thomas Beard's *Theatre of God's Judgements*. He was also requested to add quotations for any other words which were not given on Hall's list, but which he thought might be useful. The next letter from Murray is dated 4 October; in it for the first time is a suggestion that Fitzedward Hall's work might not always be conclusive. Indeed the additional quotations suggested by Thompson appeared to be quite as important as those originally noted by Hall. Murray could only suggest that the omissions were caused by inadvertence, adding that as Hall had done so much, he must have done some of it very rapidly.

Thompson continued to work through the autumn of that year, dealing with L'Estrange's *God's Sabbath* (1641), King's *Lectures on Jonas* (1594), and Raynold's *Byrth Mankynde* (1634). Various linguistic, as well as technical, questions evidently came up in the course of work such as the meaning of *pro-selenique* in *God's Sabbath*. Murray, admitting that it was initially mysterious, explained that it stood for the Greek word meaning older than the moon or, as might now be said, older than the hills. *Proselenic* is labelled *rare* in *OED*; *God's Sabbath* is and remains the sole instance of usage. Thompson went on to read Sclater's *Key to the Key of Scripture* (1629) and Hales's *Golden Remains* (1673). Both were completed by December when Murray sent a copy of Lydgate's *Minor Poems*, another book for which Hall had prepared a list:

The writings of Lydgate are of great importance; he was in some respects the Dr Johnson of his century, in his free use of words from Latin (directly or through French), and being immensely read in the 16th c (far more than Chaucer—thus is he constantly followed by Spenser, who perh[aps] had not read Chaucer at all), his vocabulary is very important. I should therefore be very glad if you would go through the book extracting not merely F. H.'s words, but examples of every word L–Z of Latin derivation—all those in *-ation*, *-ture*, *-ive*, *-ence*, *-ment*, etc.   (OED/MISC/11/26)

The native English words were of less interest since they could be covered by earlier and later writers; although it was possible that Lydgate might provide a late example of a word which was becoming rare, it was not practicable to try to identify such items. A bundle of 500 slips, again allowing for a rate of about two quotations to a page, was enclosed. Thompson, like Hall, worked rapidly and on New Year's Day Murray wrote acknowledging his 'exhaustive' work on Lydgate. He was hopeful that, as Thompson proceeded through the book, quotations for the more common words would diminish. Nevertheless 'wherever you think it doubtful give us the benefit of the doubt and extract the quotation. Such a full exhibition of Lydgate's language will be of very great consequence to the Dictionary' (OED/MISC/11/27).

The work on Lydgate having proved such a success, Murray produced another important source: 'two volumes of the 15ᵗʰ c. translations of Higden' for which he asked Thompson 'to extract . . . the same kind of words as you did from Lydgate, viz. the Latinized terms. These characterize the Harleian transl. more than that of John de Trevisa, and have yielded many of our first instances of these words— sometimes indeed the only instances' (OED/MISC/11/29). Work here, however, did not require to be as fully done as on Lydgate; only longer words and such as had not come through French were to be noted. If a Latinized word occurred also in Trevisa, then it was to be taken from there by preference. The slips were printed to suit both or either.

Thompson began with Volume II as Volume I had already been extensively read. In just under three weeks he was ready to move on to Volume III, which was accordingly sent, with advice on steps to avoid repetition of extraction:

We think it would help you if you had beside you those quotations you have already taken out—this would prevent your taking out several quotations for the same word. If you agree with this we will arrange the quots. you have sent in alphabetical order, take out those for the letters we are working at (L, O, & Q) and send back to you the remainder. When you have read vol. III perhaps you would only send to us any more quots. you may have for L, O, & Q and keep all the others to compare in reading the later volumes. These quotations you are sending us will prove very useful—we find that several you have now sent are *two hundred* years earlier than we already have.   (OED/MISC/11/30)

As the dictionary progressed, requirements had inevitably to be modified. In mid-March 1902 Thompson is being updated on current progress:

The five volumes of the Dictionary now out go down as far as the end of the letter K. Of the later letters L has been finally prepared as far as *Light*, O as far as *Of*, the whole of Q. Quotations need not be sent for any of these parts—although some you have been sending us recently for those portions we shall be glad to use in the *Supplement* as being earlier than what we have given.   (OED/MISC/11/33)

His work continued to facilitate the editing process by remedying gaps. This year was moreover that in which Dr Minor, the Broadmoor patient who had for long contributed quotations to the dictionary, finally gave up his work. Thompson's success in dealing with the Hall material must have made him the obvious choice for assistance in this case too. As Murray wrote:

Dr Minor, who has so long sent us extracts for each letter as we reached it, from rare books in his own collection, is obliged by failing health to relax his efforts, & has sent us some of the most important books, in order that we may get the work done for the remaining letters. If you could take one of these, I shall be very glad to send you one with slips & instructions. Dr Minor has made out verbal indexes for the words he meant to extract (more numerous than were needed). You can either use these, or read the book independently, & afterwards compare what you have extracted with his List, and tick off those that are in yours, adding any that his list may suggest.   (OED/MISC/11/38)

Thompson evidently agreed, and Fryer's *Voyage to the East Indies and Persia* duly arrived. The 'main thing', Murray stressed, was 'to get the words connected with the countries visited for which Fryer is often of the earliest witnesses, adding to these any other antiquated, novel, or peculiar words & phrases that strike you'. As he added, 'we should hardly quote him for ordinary literary words at the time, since we have so many literary writers of the same date' (OED/MISC/11/39). First uses from Fryer cited in the *OED* include not only *maharajah*, *Marathi*, and *Parsee*, but also (in the 'antiquated' or 'novel' categories) senses of *moil*, *mould*, and *outland*. Reading was completed successfully by the end of October, and work continued on Dr Minor's books. The pattern appears to have been that slips were printed for the wordlists (despite the admitted view that 'Dr Minor's List [*sic*] are nearly always excessive'), and then book, slips, and wordlist were sent off to Thompson, who by this time was a valuable and experienced reader.

His ability to cope with scientific vocabulary was also a distinct advantage. In April 1903 this resulted in a specific request to go through the work of John Barclay (the anatomist, 1758–1826). Barclay had published in 1803 a small book entitled *A New Anatomical Nomenclature*; although this was now very rare, with no copy in Oxford or Cambridge, it seemed likely that any important new terms would also have appeared in the more accessible *Muscular Motions* (1808). And, concluded Murray, in case of special words they could get the University Librarian in Edinburgh to refer to the earlier work. The work was particularly important, Murray stressed: 'After considerable neglect, Barclay's notions as to nomenclature were resuscitated some 15–20 years ago, and his terminology is now largely adopted—notably his words in *-ad*, some of which we in ignorance missed in our earlier letters. Kindly extract for all words A to Z' (OED/MISC/11/45).

The letters between Murray and Thompson grow fewer in the last two years of the correspondence; Thompson clearly had other responsibilities, and after Dr Minor's books no further cache of work presented itself. The letters as they stand, however, throw valuable light on the contribution made by outside workers, and on the kind of support by letter which was needed and supplied. They also illuminate vividly the degree to which detailed guidance was provided and controlled by Murray himself: as has been seen, it does not appear to have been in question that the work should have been delegated by the editor to one of the in-house editorial assistants. And this is perhaps the central point: the relationship of each outside worker was directly with the chief editor. This had enormous benefits in terms of the quality of the direction given; it must also have had a substantial negative impact on the editor's own rate for final editing. It is none the less one of the most remarkable features of the dictionary that so much was achieved by a widely disparate and dispersed body of readers and editors working far from the centre of production, and yet somehow holding with remarkable consistency to the central tenets of the work.

ACKNOWLEDGEMENTS

In researching this paper I have been most grateful for the help given by Jenny McMorris of Oxford University Press Archives, and by the staff of Room 132 in the Bodleian Library. Thanks are also due to a number of my colleagues, in particular Yvonne Warburton, who read and commented on earlier versions; to the Editor of the present volume, Lynda Mugglestone; and to the memory of K. M. Elisabeth Murray, who first gave me generous access to the Murray papers in her Sussex scriptorium. Lesley Blake has been an expert and patient typist.

REFERENCES

Murray Papers

MP/25/10/1881. J. A. H. Murray to W. J. E. Cranesley.
MP/21/11/1901. H. Bradley to J. A. H. Murray.
MP/?22/11/1901. J. A. H. Murray to H. Bradley.
MP/25/11/1901. H. Bradley to J. A. H. Murray.

OED *Archives at OUP*

OED/MISC/11/9. J. A. H. Murray to J. J. Thompson, 2 July 1901.
OED/MISC/11/13. J. A. H. Murray to J. J. Thompson, 5 July 1901.
OED/MISC/11/16. J. A. H. Murray to J. J. Thompson, 25 July 1901.
OED/MISC/11/26. J. A. H. Murray to J. J. Thompson, 18 December 1901.
OED/MISC/11/27. J. A. H. Murray to J. J. Thompson, 1 January 1902.
OED/MISC/11/29. J. A. H. Murray to J. J. Thompson, 3 July 1902.
OED/MISC/11/30. J. A. H. Murray to J. J. Thompson, 22 February 1902.
OED/MISC/11/33. J. A. H. Murray to J. J. Thompson, 20 March 1902.
OED/MISC/11/38. J. A. H. Murray to J. J. Thompson, 3 October 1902.
OED/MISC/11/39. J. A. H. Murray to J. J. Thompson, 4 October 1902.
OED/MISC/11/45. J. A. H. Murray to J. J. Thompson, 21 April 1903.
OED/MISC/13/4. J. A. H. Murray to F. Hall, 7 December 1893.
OED/MISC/13/7. J. A. H. Murray to F. Hall, 27 November 1894.
OED/MISC/13/9. J. A. H. Murray to F. Hall, ? December 1894.
OED/MISC/13/10. J. A. H. Murray to F. Hall, 8 February 1895.
OED/MISC/13/11. J. A. H. Murray to F. Hall, 22 April 1895.
OED/MISC/13/12. J. A. H. Murray to F. Hall, 26 September 1895.
OED/MISC/13/16. J. A. H. Murray to F. Hall, 30 December 1896.
OED/MISC/13/18. J. A. H. Murray to F. Hall, 28 July 1897.

OED/MISC/13/20. J. A. H. Murray to F. Hall, 20 October 1897.
OED/MISC/13/23. J. A. H. Murray to F. Hall, 10 February 1899.
OED/MISC/13/24. J. A. H. Murray to F. Hall, 11 April 1899.
OED/MISC/13/28. J. A. H. Murray to F. Hall, 2 February 1900.
OED/MISC/13/31. J. A. H. Murray to R. Hall, 17 February 1901.
OED/MISC/13/32. J. A. H. Murray to R. Hall, 21 February 1901.
OED/MISC/13/33. J. A. H. Murray to R. Hall, 22 February 1901.
OED/MISC/13/37. J. A. H. Murray to R. Hall, 24 April 1901.
OED/MISC/13/43. J. A. H. Murray to R. Hall, 4 July 1901.
OED/MISC/91/9. Directions to Subeditors, manuscript copy in *OED* papers.
OED/OS/168/6/2. Ms notes in *OED* papers.
OED/OS/168/6/4. Ms notes in *OED* papers.
OED/OS/242/9/2. Ms notes in *OED* papers.

Published works

Bradley, H. (1901). 'Prefatory Note to F', *NED* Vol. IV: F and G. Oxford: Clarendon Press, pp. vii–viii.

Knowles, E. M. (1990). 'Dr Minor and the Oxford English Dictionary'. *Dictionaries*, 12: 27–42.

Murray, J. A. H. (1885). 'Prefatory Note to Part II', *NED*, Part II: *Ant–Batten*. Oxford: Clarendon Press, pp. v–vi.

—— (1888). 'Preface to Volume I'. *NED* Vol. I: A and B. Oxford: Clarendon Press, pp. v–xvi.

—— (1909). 'Preface to Volume VII'. *NED* Vol. VII: O, P. Oxford: Clarendon Press.

3

OED Sources[1]

CHARLOTTE BREWER

One of the many ways in which the *OED* differed from its predecessors was in the attitude it took towards its sources, both in selecting and in recording them. The earliest English monolingual dictionaries, from Cawdrey (1604) onwards, had taken lists of words and of definitions, without acknowledgement, from preceding dictionaries (mono- and bilingual) and from glossaries to printed works (see Starnes and Noyes (1946) and Schäfer (1989)). But no hint of this was to be found in their texts, which printed definitions only, without supporting quotations. It is clear from both the title-pages and the prefaces to these works that they were initially conceived as 'hard-word' dictionaries, designed to help women, boys, and less-well educated men to improve their use and understanding of the English language; consequently the range of words was limited. By the early eighteenth century, dictionaries had become far more comprehensive works, vying with each other in their boasts of including vast numbers of words which were drawn from a much wider range of registers. But not until Johnson's dictionary of 1755 did a lexicographer substantiate definitions with quotations from (mostly) documented sources, and this development brought about a profound change in lexicographical principle and practice.

Johnson's 'chief intent', as stated in his *Plan of a Dictionary* (1747), was to 'preserve the purity and ascertain the meaning of our English idiom' by registering the usage of writers from the golden age of Elizabeth to the best usage of his own day. But scrutinizing real usage in order to establish meaning opened Johnson's eyes to the indeterminacy both of language itself and of the way it is used. Thus his Preface to his dictionary, written after its compilation, expresses in a number of different ways his sense of the difficulty of pinning meaning down: 'words are hourly shifting their relations, and can no more be ascertained in a dictionary, than a grove, in the agitation of a storm, can be accurately delineated from its picture in the water' (Johnson 1755: Preface). This understanding, proceeding from his use of quotations, is absent from his predecessors' dictionaries, and might seem to imply, indeed necessitate, a descriptive rather than a normative

[1] I am grateful to Lynda Mugglestone, John Simpson, and Jenny McMorris for help and advice on aspects of this chapter.

approach to language. Despite it, however, Johnson's dictionary is imbued with prescriptivism, both in his choice of sources and in his judgement on the usages his sources illustrated. He censored usage in choosing his quotation sources from a clearly defined and limited range of literary giants and of writers of established stature in selected other fields, for example, theological or philosophical, and he censured these writers' usage even while recording it in his dictionary.

One of the ways in which the early *OED* lexicographers sought to be pioneering was in breaking free from the prescriptivism of Johnson and the other lexicographers who had followed him. Unquestioning inclusion of all words from all printed (or written) sources was stated as the starting-point of the dictionary in the Philological Society's *Proposal for the Publication of a New English Dictionary*:

the first requirement of every lexicon is, that it should contain *every word in the literature of the language it professes to illustrate* [original italics]. We entirely repudiate the theory, which converts the lexicographer into an arbiter of style, and leaves it in his discretion to accept or reject words according to his private notion of their elegance or inelegance. ([Philological Society] 1859: 2–3)

But this was an ideal impossible to realize. As described in the Introduction, linguistic, ideological, and pragmatic factors all severely curtailed both the extent of the sources which the lexicographers drew upon and the nature of the vocabulary which they eventually documented. The gradual erosion of the ideal of inclusiveness—and the consequent shift from descriptiveness to prescriptiveness, since every decision to exclude a word is a departure from the purist ideal of descriptive lexicography so confidently stated by Trench and the others—is a fascinating feature of the early stages of *OED*. The process of selection (for selection it had inevitably to be) of sources involved two theoretically distinct stages: first, the choice of the printed or written works from which to cull material for inclusion; and second, the choice of the particular words and quotations from these sources which were to be included in the dictionary. In this chapter it is the first of these processes that will come under investigation (to the extent that such an investigation is possible given the limited evidence available): how in practice the lexicographers determined on the range and nature of the sources evidenced in the final publication, and, in turn, what conclusions about language and writers it is legitimate to draw from the *OED* source data.

One of the first tasks of Coleridge, Furnivall, and Trench was to make out a list of books and assign volumes to individual readers. The Society's *Proposal* described how, within two years of Trench's first delineation of the project, 'upwards of 100 collectors have voluntarily given their services, and more than 160 works and parts of works have been submitted to examination upon a uniform system' ([Philological Society] 1859: 1). As for what works these should be, it declared, 'We admit as authorities all English books, except such as are devoted to purely scientific subjects, as treatises on electricity, mathematics, &c., and works written subsequently to the Reformation for the purpose of illustrating provincial dialects'.[2] The Society also stated the proposed time-range of the dictionary and divided this into three periods: I: 1250–1526 (the date of the 'first printed English New Testament'—namely, Tyndal's); II: 1526–1674 (Milton's death); and III: 1674 to the present.[3] The Society aimed shortly to issue an

> alphabetical list of all A.D. 1250–1300 words. We shall then ask our contributors to read among them all the printed books of the remainder of the first period, viz. 1300–1526, the fourteenth-century literature being taken first; each contributor giving us extracts containing both the new and the obsolete words . . .
>
> For the period 1526 to Milton, we shall ask each contributor for a quotation for every word, phrase, idiom, &c., in his book that does not occur in the Concordances to the Bible and Shakspere, or that to the Bible only, if the Shakspere Concordance be unprocurable . . . For the period from Milton to the present day, we shall after a time issue a list of Burke's words, and ask for a quotation from the modern writers for all words, &c. not in the list.
>
> ([Philological Society] 1859: 5–6)

The *Proposal* acknowledged that the use of the two concordances as a way of identifying which words were worth recording was not ideal, and indeed it was to cause a good deal of trouble as it dissuaded the original readers from recording usual words, whose subsequent documentation consumed vast amounts of valuable editorial time. 'In the mean time', the Society asked for contributors who preferred to work on eighteenth- and nineteenth-century literature to analyse carefully 'the works of any of the principal writers, extracting all remarkable words, and all passages which contain definitions or explanations . . . We have not given a list of these writers, as their names must be familiar to all; but Wordsworth, Scott, Coleridge, Southey, Tennyson, Ruskin, Macaulay, and Froude may be mentioned as pre-eminently important' ([Philological Society] 1859: 6).

It has been said that 'it is a lexicographical truism that . . . the *OED*'s reliance on literary quotations is problematic because it skews the representative character of the sampling' (Taylor 1993: 6). The line-up of nineteenth-century writers specified by the *Proposal* directs prospective dictionary readers to sources then commonly recognized by the educated middle classes, without defensiveness, embarrassment, or anxiety, as canonical—not just for English literature, but for the English language in its entirety (the distinction was not recognized as a meaningful one).[4]

---

[2] With what we can recognize as an inevitable partial contradiction of this generous principle, the *Proposal* continued ' . . . At the same time we reserve to ourselves a discretion of deciding, in doubtful cases, what shall or shall not be deemed a Dictionary authority . . .' ([Philological Society] 1859: 2–3).

[3] According to Murray, Furnivall said that 'he never believed in these divisions, and thought that Coleridge attributed far too much importance to the influence on the language of the Scripture versions; but that no one then knew really how language could best be divided into periods, so he accepted this as a provisional order' (Munro 1911: 126).

[4] See *OED* s.v. *literature* 3a: ' . . . the body of writings produced in a particular country or period . . .'.

This collection of names also makes it clear that writers who use language in markedly idiosyncratic ways are not to be excluded (here Scott is the egregious example; in the event he was quoted by *OED* nearly four times more than any of the other named authors, coming overall second only to Shakespeare).[5] It seems certainly to be the case that *OED* overrepresents such writers, partly because of external pressures to record their usage (such as that from the OUP Delegates in 1883, and the more general expectation that the *OED* should particularly bear witness to the usage of 'great writers'; cf. *CWW*: 223–4), but also because the lexicographers from the start encouraged their volunteers to concentrate on these rather than on more general sources.

The *Proposal* is followed by a 'List of the Printed Literature of England Belonging to the Period 1250–1526' (1859: 17–29). This detailed a total of 170 works for the first period designated by the *Proposal*, of which 86 were in the process of being read.[6] The list of works and authors from the second period, all of which had been taken up by readers, is strikingly large—190 in all. By contrast, only five works or authors (again all undertaken) are named for the third period: the *Annual Register* (the periodical founded by Dodsley and Burke in 1758) 1758–88, the works of Burke, Tennyson, and Coleridge, and Ruskin's *Modern Painters*.

Over the next few years this document was reissued and revised, apparently by Furnivall, and several different recensions of it, recording different numbers of texts and readers, survive in the *OED* archives, often covered with Furnivall's handwritten annotations to take account of additions and changes. One of the striking features of the various lists is the consistently small number of books in the pre-1500 period. It was in part in an attempt to rectify this that Furnivall made one of his most important contributions to the *OED* project, his foundation of the Early English Text Society. This published an extensive range of Old and Middle English works over the next decades and provided dictionary readers with much

---

[5] Scott is quoted 16,628 times in the *OED* (often for archaic or dialectal words and senses), Tennyson 6,972 times, Macaulay 5,575, Southey 4,741, Coleridge 3,702, Ruskin 3,323, Wordsworth 2,055, and Froude 2,006. Burke is quoted 3,576 times; given that his vocabulary was specially treated in the early period of list-making, it is surprising that this comparatively high figure is not higher still. These figures (and others in the remainder of the chapter) are taken from the *OED2* on CD Rom; quotations evidently added in *OED2* are discounted (it is my experience that they are anyway so few as to be negligible, and this judgement is confirmed by John Simpson, editor of *OED3*). It is tricky to draw conclusions from such comparisons. By one yardstick, Coleridge is the most heavily quoted of the named writers since the number of words in the works consulted by *OED* is the fewest, and hence his work is proportionally more heavily excerpted than that of any of the others (contrast the treatment of Wordsworth). Taylor (1993: 124 ff.) and Willinsky (1994: Appendix of tables) also give some figures for *OED*'s relative quotation of writers; I assume my results are often different from theirs (usually higher) because I have used the superior searching powers of the *OED2* CD Rom (published 1994; on problems with using the *OED1* CD Rom to search for author citations see Gray (1988: 73 nn. 1, 3)). I have also tried to identify each of the various different forms under which an author's name is listed.

[6] These figures are necessarily approximate, as distinctions between different works are not always clear and as full references are not always given. I have counted item by item according to the original list, and kept to the dating divisions of the list also.

more of the material they needed to extend the treatment of the language of the earlier period (on Furnivall and the EETS, see Brewer (1996: 65–90)). Nevertheless, the *OED*'s treatment of medieval words and senses is patchy and unreliable, and the *Middle English Dictionary* was one of the major dictionaries to be embarked upon as a necessary supplement to the treatment of certain periods in the *OED* (see Craigie (1919), Kurath *et al.* (1954)). Another obvious feature of these early lists is the comparatively slight coverage given to nineteenth-century works. By contrast, this period turned out to be the one with the greatest wealth of quotation given in *OED*, probably because volunteer readers could cover contemporaneous writings far more easily and readily than those of earlier periods, but also because Murray subsequently asked for many more works from this period to be read than from earlier periods. These two contrasting examples illustrate how difficult it is to infer much from the proportions, variations, and contents of the pre-1879 lists as regards the final choice of sources quoted by *OED*.[7] Indeed, it is virtually certain that the most profitable reading was done in the years following 1879, when Murray took over the leadership of the dictionary; in the intervening period the project flagged owing to a lack of resources and of direction from Furnivall. Murray's own judgement was that 'In the end less than a sixth —probably only a tenth—of the quotations used came from the old material' (*CWW*: 169).

Murray was appointed editor of the Society's dictionary on 1 March 1879. K. M. E. Murray (*CWW*: 173–7) gives a graphic account of her grandfather's shock and dismay when he received the dictionary material (in dribs and drabs) from Furnivall: he was appalled at the condition of many of the slips and at the unsystematic way in which tabs had been kept on the various subeditors (responsible for individual letters and sections of letters). Slips arrived unsorted in sacks, or in one instance in a baby's bassinet, a dead rat was found in one and a live mouse and her family in another, various readers had died and their work proved extraordinarily difficult or impossible to recover. Not surprisingly, Murray immediately instituted extensive changes in the management of the project. In April 1879 he issued through the Society *An Appeal to the English-speaking and English-reading Public in Great Britain, America and the Colonies*, an important document informing the public of the history of the dictionary so far, and beating the drum for more volunteers. Two thousand copies of the *Appeal* were published in three editions in less than a year, and had a major galvanizing effect on the reading of sources, bringing in 'some eight hundred readers in Great Britain and four or five hundred in the United States . . . between them they added a million slips to those already in the Scriptorium' (*CWW*: 177–8).

---

[7] R. W. McConchie (1997: 189–90) attempts to make some inferences from medical books listed in one of the documents as being read for the dictionary; however, a check of the titles and authors against *OED2* on CD Rom indicates that very few of these texts were eventually quoted in the *OED*. It is impossible to know whether this means that the reading was never done, or that the slips were lost, or that it was decided (for whatever reason) to exclude words and quotations from these sources.

The *Appeal* repeated the *Proposal*'s earlier declaration on comprehensive coverage of the language: 'We admit as authorities all English books, except such as are devoted to purely scientific subjects', and described in fairly buoyant, and probably over-optimistic, terms the reading so far carried out:

In the Early English period up to the invention of Printing so much has been done and is being done that little outside help is needed. But few of the earliest printed books—those of Caxton and his successors—have yet been read . . . The later sixteenth-century literature is fairly done; yet here several books remain to be read. The seventeenth century, with so many more writers, naturally shows still more unexplored territory. The nineteenth century books, being within the reach of every one, have been read widely; but a large number remain unrepresented, not only of those published during the last ten years, while the Dictionary has been in abeyance, but also of earlier date. But it is in the eighteenth century above all that help is urgently needed. The American scholars promised to get the eighteenth-century literature taken up in the United States, a promise which they appear not to have to any extent fulfilled, and we must now appeal to English readers to share the task, for nearly the whole of that century's books, with the exception of Burke's works, have still to be gone through.[8] Special attention must be paid to the dramatic literature of the early eighteenth and late seventeenth century, as in this will be found the earliest occurrence of much of our modern phraseology, which is now good and stately English, but was familiar or colloquial a century and a half ago.   (1879*a*: 3)

The *Appeal* was accompanied by a 'List of Books for which Readers are Wanted', which was twice updated in successive editions. The first version names only fourteen works or authors for the fifteenth century and earlier, but many of these are major ones, and eventually furnished substantial number of quotations for *OED*: Lydgate (5,217 quotations), Gower (4,066), Trevisa's translations of Higden (2,944), Mandeville (2,547), Malory (1,653), and Wycliffe (11,971—the figure is so large because it includes quotations from the Wycliffite Bible, which the use of Cruden's concordance had ensured was heavily quoted). Chaucer's major works had presumably been read as only his 'Minor Poems' are listed (quotations from Chaucer's works in the *OED* were eventually to total 11,902, making him according to Willinsky's list the fifth most quoted author after Shakespeare, Walter Scott, Milton, and Wycliffe). Thirty works are named for the sixteenth century and thirty-seven for the seventeenth; these are overwhelmingly literary in character, with a smattering of theological and historical titles.

The section for the eighteenth century begins with a note that 'the literature of this century has hardly been touched. Readers are safe with almost any eighteenth-century book they can lay their hands on'. Forty-six works or authors are named as 'books that *ought* to be read'; they are again overwhelmingly literary. The

---

[8] This remark seems to be the ultimate source of Schäfer's statement (1980: 53) that 'because of a breakdown in organization', the eighteenth-century slips assigned to American readers 'never reached Murray's scriptorium'. Schäfer's implication is that the slips had been lost; rather it appears that they had never been written in the first place. (American readers, particularly university academics, were subsequently enormously productive of slips; see Murray (1880: 123–4)).

nineteenth-century section is now the longest, reflecting the eventual proportion of quotations devoted to this period, with one hundred works or authors named with the note that 'more of this is done than of the eighteenth century, but much remains to do . . . slips from any current book, review, or other work are acceptable'.[9] As with the other sections, literary works dominate, with theological, historical, and philosophical ones close behind; but there is also a small number of completely different titles: Tyndall's *Alpine Glaciers*, Lyell's 'Geological Works', the works of Faraday and Darwin, and Grove's *Correlation of Physical Forces*. This must indicate a wish on Murray's part to widen the range of the recorded lexicon. J. Tyndall's various works were eventually to yield a substantial 2,451 quotations (for a comparison with some major literary sources see n. 5), of which the two-volume *Alpine Glaciers* (1860) accounted for 1,589.[10] Many of the words cited from this writer are not specifically scientific or otherwise technical (as may be observed by scrolling through the lemmas on the *OED* CD Rom). Darwin's works, by contrast, yielded 1,784 quotations, Lyell's 1,303, Faraday's 482, and the volume by W. R. Grove just 171. The lemmas quoted from the works of these four writers appear to include many more specifically technical terms.[11]

One may speculate as to why Murray appeared more open, at this stage, to such publications for the nineteenth century than he does for earlier centuries.[12] The answer may be that he was more keenly aware of the special importance of science for his own period, that this recognition was shared by the educated public and more especially by the *OED* readers, that nineteenth-century scientific works were more available than those from earlier periods. (It should be noted that the names of Darwin, Lyell, Faraday, and Grove reappear on each of the two subsequent editions of the *Appeal*'s list of authors to be read, suggesting that their works were not enthusiastically snatched up by readers.)

The second edition of the *Appeal* was published on 24 June 1879, and its revised lists indicate a good, though various, rate of take-up for the different periods. Eight works or authors (including Gower and Wycliffe) had been removed from the pre-1500 list, and the remaining six were supplemented with seven more (including *Gesta Romanorum* and *Cursor Mundi*; the latter (variously dated) was to provide

---

[9] The mention of reviews significantly directs readers towards contemporary periodical literature, which was to receive extensive treatment in *OED* (see Willinsky 1994: 118–27); a note to readers at the end of the third edition of the *Appeal* asks particularly for new words from 'contemporary magazines, reviews, literary and scientific journals', suggesting that Murray regarded such literature as the best source for neologisms.

[10] Professor John Tyndall (1820–93) was an eminent physicist and became a friend of Carlyle in the latter's old age; see *DNB*.

[11] Though all four are cited for non-technical lemmas also—often supported by very well-chosen quotations; cf. that of Darwin s.v. *struggle*. Sixty-one of Darwin's total quotations are from the 1880 edition of his *Movements and Habits of Climbing Plants*, and these lemmas appear to be almost entirely technical.

[12] A note at the end of the list, hence applying apparently to all periods, welcomes 'offers to read any other book . . . especially early treatises on any of the sciences'. Although this was repeated in the second and third editions of the *Appeal*, the number of scientific works listed for the earlier periods is small.

Table 1. Successive editions of 1879 *Appeal* and numbers of authors/works to be read listed per century

Century	First edition	Second edition	Third edition
Fifteenth and earlier	14	13	17
Sixteenth	30	19	16
Seventeenth	37	31	48
Eighteenth	46	48	52
Nineteenth	100	124	112

the enormous figure of 12,772 quotations for the published dictionary, the second most heavily quoted work after the Bible). Many more works had been taken up for the sixteenth century—nineteen of the original thirty, and the remaining eleven supplemented with eight new titles. Eighteen of the thirty-seven seventeenth-century works and authors had been taken up, and twelve new ones added; twenty-two of the eighteenth-century ones had been taken up, and twenty-four new ones added; while for the nineteenth century, forty-one authors had been taken up, and sixty-five added, to produce a total of 124 now on offer to readers, still by far the largest for any century. In his Presidential Address to the Philological Society for that year, Murray reported that he had so far printed 1,500 copies of the *Appeal*, that 165 readers had volunteered their services, of whom 128 had chosen their books and were at work. 'The number of books actually undertaken and entered against readers is 234; arrangements are in progress for perhaps half as many more' (1879*b*: 570).

The third edition of the list, published on 1 January 1880, again indicates a smart rate of progress in the reading and assigning of books. The pre-1500 section had expanded to seventeen items, though this included one, Mandeville's *Travels*, that had been on the first but not the second list—perhaps the reader who had originally taken it up had handed it back again, or perhaps the list-making had been at fault. Nine works had apparently been taken on by new readers since July, and Murray had added twelve new titles to the list, including *Ayenbite of Inwyt*, which was to yield 2,552 quotations. Ten titles had been taken up from the sixteenth-century list, and seven new ones added, resulting in a total of sixteen works now offered to readers; fourteen items had been taken up from the seventeenth-century list, and thirty-one added—suggesting that Murray felt this period needed more attention (it now contained forty-eight items). For the eighteenth century, twenty-one items had been taken up by readers, and a further twenty-five added to the list by Murray, making a total of fifty-two now on offer to readers. The take-up rate for the nineteenth-century works was again the best, with forty-six items disappearing from the July 1879 list by the time the January 1880 list was drawn up. Murray added a further thirty-four to the list, to bring it to the substantial total of 112.

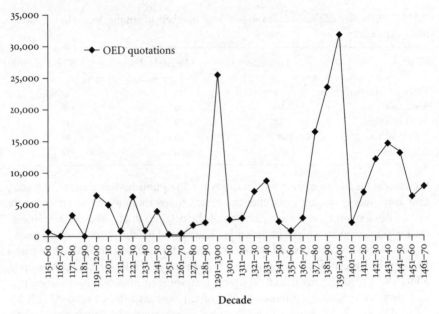

Figure 1. *OED* Quotations 1151–1470

All this suggests a considerable amount of activity on the part of both lexico-graphers and readers, and the swift substitution of one set of books for another indicates that some thought was being devoted to the selection of appropriate source material. Murray himself commented that 'The formation of the list of books was a long and arduous work; and it is no matter of wonder, if it has been found to contain the names of books which we have since discovered to have been read years ago, and to omit many which ought to have been included, and must be included in a supplemental list' (1879*b*: 570). Interestingly enough, the proportions of books listed per century correspond only partially to the propor-tions of quotations per century found in the eventual *OED*. The period before 1580 is indeed illustrated with comparatively few quotations (not surprisingly, given the comparatively small number of sources). By contrast, the years *c*.1581–1610 are heavily quoted, as much as the early decades of the nineteenth century. The eighteenth century has far fewer quotations, while the number for the nineteenth century rises steadily decade by decade (see Figures 1 and 2 and the Appendix to this chapter).

This discrepancy warns us that although the lists accompanying the *Appeal* might seem to invite analysis, it is once again not clear how much we can infer from them. Assigning a book to a reader did not necessarily result in a sheaf of usable quotations. The reader might have returned very few slips, or the slips returned might not have been deemed useful by the lexicographers when it came to the point of choosing which quotations to print in the dictionary. Thus Defoe's works,

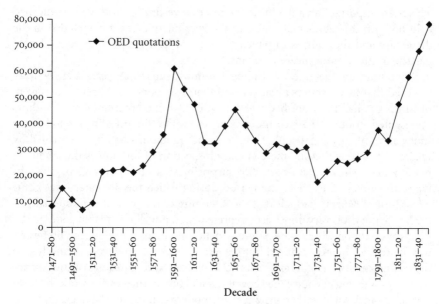

Figure 2. *OED* Quotations 1471–1850

apparently taken up between the first and second lists, produced a massive 4,715 quotations, while Whittock's *Complete Book of Trades* (1842), which was put on the July 1879 list and presumably taken up by a reader as it did not appear on the January 1880 list, is cited only once in *OED* (for the word *quannet*, a type of file).

The three editions of the 1879 *Appeal* are therefore best thought of as snapshots of Murray's reading list at an early stage in his work on *OED*, giving us only an indication of the sorts of works he thought valuable to read. The reasons why some of the listed works proved extraordinarily productive in terms of eventual quotation yield, while others did not, cannot be pre-judged in advance of further research. It is tempting to assume, though, that inconsistencies of the sort that Schäfer (1989) and McConchie (1997) identify in both reading practice and lexicographical processing may well have played an important part (see further below). The general domination of the reading lists by major writers and poets, including a host of historical, philosophical, and theological authors (only a handful of them female), must have decisively shaped the character of the lexicon eventually displayed by the *OED*. However, it would be wrong to suppose that Murray was uninterested in widening the range of sources. The second and third editions of the *Appeal* successively added to the proportion of non-literary works—though the total number of such publications remained very small and their subsequent documentation in the dictionary highly variable (they include a variety of publications on such areas as horticulture and other practical crafts, financial and business studies, and the natural sciences; as already mentioned, the number of scientific sources is significant only for the nineteenth century).

This is an important area for future research, investigation into which will shed light both on the representativeness of the vocabulary eventually included in the dictionary and the sources to which the Oxford lexicographers need to devote particular attention in future revisions.

From now on the rate of reading continued apace. A year later, Murray reported that there were 754 readers, and that 1,568 books had been undertaken, of which 924 had been finished (1880: 121); in 1881, the 'total number of authors represented in our Reference Index is 2,700', while 'the titles in our Reference Index amount to some 4,500'. About 656,900 quotations had been returned by readers: 'it is clear that the mere cursory inspection of the slips is the labour of many years' (Murray 1881: 261). Not surprisingly, relative coverage of different types of sources varied over the period during which the dictionary was compiled. In 1879 Murray had felt that the 'literature of the present and especially of the last century was very imperfectly represented in our slips, and that good quotations for common words were painfully deficient'; by 1880 the 'general literature' was, he felt, adequately covered but readers were asked 'to devote themselves to the examination of scientific and technical books, and special treatises of any description, not forgetting of course the general examination of such earlier works hitherto unread as may yield earlier instances of modern words and later examples of obsolete . . .' (Murray 1880: 125); the plea was repeated the following year (Murray (1881: 269). This confidence in the adequate representation of contemporary sources had disappeared by 1892, when he called for 'Dr. Furnivall, or some other competent person, [to] draw up from Mudie's catalogue or other source, a list of works published since 1875' to enable them to represent literature of the last quarter of the nineteenth century (Murray 1893: 275).

Before proceeding to an examination of the range and nature of the sources eventually printed in *OED*, we should consider some of the problems encountered by and with the readers. There is no doubt that many readers perceived their task as being to record unusual words and senses rather than common ones, and this resulted in partial reading and uneven representation of sources (see Chapter 1). As Knowles observes (p. 32), Furnivall's encouragement of 'the silly practice by which sub-editors were urged to get their friends to read books for *their own letter* only—so as to provoke a rivalry of good works between them', resulted in uneven source coverage, which Murray had no means of identifying 'until [and, one might add, unless] some accident reveals the fact that of late we have not seen any quotes from the book in question'; Murray complained at a dictionary evening in 1892 that this was 'a most pernicious and deceptive practice' (1893: 275).[13]

---

[13] In the past he had sometimes been less despairing about the variable standard of reading, and his ability to correct oversights; cf. for instance Murray (1880: 122): 'As a whole the books have been satisfactorily read; and when, as has occasionally happened, the work of a reader of an important book has appeared to us inadequate, we have not hesitated to ask another reader to go through it again. This plan we have found it desirable to take with many of the books undertaken in former years, as to the completion of which we had no satisfactory evidence.'

But even when readers were conscientiously trying to register all relevant words, there would be a natural tendency for the eye to slide over familiar words and pick up unfamiliar ones, and in addition it would sometimes be very difficult to identify unusual uses of words where there was no corresponding peculiarity of morphology. An example is the verb *mirror*, which is found in Nashe, but its first occurrence dated by *OED* 227 years later in Keats's *Lamia*.[14] Murray's mention of the theoretical desirability but practical impossibility of 'complete verbal indexes' (see above, p. 8; Murray 1884: 516) is highly significant, for—not surprisingly—the works or authors for which concordances were available (Shakespeare, the Bible, Milton, Pope) receive exceptionally full treatment in the *OED*. Any inferences drawn from the *OED* coverage about the significance of these writers for the development and illustration of the English lexicon are flawed ones: the exceptionally full representation of their language in the dictionary is due at least as much to the lexicographers' consultation of the concordances as to the intrinsic qualities of these writers' diction.[15]

Further problems arose because of the vagaries of individual readers. Material in the *OED* archives shows that some readers were phenomenally productive of slips, others not, so that it would have been impossible for Murray to regulate strictly the proportions of material coming in from one period rather than another, or one type of source rather than another. It may also be that Murray was susceptible to strong pressure from individual readers to include certain sources. The letters in Bodley's Murray archive from his old friend Robinson Ellis (the distinguished editor and translator of Catullus) indicate that he read every fascicle through as it appeared, counting up the instances his translation was cited and reporting his views on the wisdom of Murray's choice of sources (Ellis is quoted 574 times altogether, 542 times from his Catullus translation). This rapt interest in the successive editions of the dictionary was shared by a number of logophiles; Arnold Bennett described *OED* as 'the longest sensational serial ever written!' (*The Periodical* 1928: 25).

All of these factors would have influenced the thoroughness with which sources were read and the choice by lexicographers from the material that the readers supplied. Murray was well aware of the problems: for example, on the difficulty of picking up the first occurrence of a word, he declared, 'Earlier instances will, I doubt not, be found of three-fourths of all the words recorded, above all, of the words introduced from Latin since the Renascence' (1884: 517). In addition, he knew that his reading programme of sources could not but be deficient: 'It is true that *all* books have not been read, not by a long long way' (1884: 522–3).

---

[14] See Schäfer (1980: 58). P. J. Wexler (1981) comments that 'It is a commonplace that a diction-ary often records long gaps between the appearance of a root-form and its derivative—say between an adjective and an adverb; but is this a fact about language, or about lexicographers?' (I also quote this example in Brewer (1993: 321).)

[15] See Schäfer (1980: 39–40).

Turning to the *OED* itself, how can we examine the dictionary to come up with a reliable account of the nature of its quotation sources and the ways in which these were used? There are two major bibliographic aids: the printed bibliography, which lists over 13,000 authors in over 22,000 books;[16] and the CD Rom, which allows one to search the quotations by date and by name of author. Published work on sources is so far sparse. Up to 1997 the only major quantitative and analytic work on sources was that of Jürgen Schäfer (1980, 1989), whose investigations (the last tranche of which was posthumously published) were necessarily limited by the fact that the *OED* was not then in electronic form.[17] In *Documentation in the OED*, Schäfer analysed the *OED*'s treatment of Shakespeare's vocabulary relative to its treatment of several other authors, whose works had also been read by *OED* readers, and found 'astonishing divergencies in authorial reliability and period coverage' (1980: 69). While almost every single word of Shakespeare's texts had been registered in *OED* in one way or another, the words and usages of less popular authors like Nashe or Wyatt had been both inconsistently and imperfectly recorded (Schäfer found that the 'reliability rate' for recording Shakespeare's works was 93.1 per cent, compared with 63.1 per cent for Nashe, 50 per cent for Malory, and 42.3 per cent for Wyatt).[18] This meant that basing any hypotheses about the linguistic creativity of individual authors, or of individual periods in the English language, on *OED* data was a risky enterprise. Besides demonstrating the variations in *OED* coverage of individual writers, Schäfer also looked at the variations in *OED* coverage of different periods in the language, to discover that two periods in particular were vastly better represented in the dictionary than others—the late-sixteenth century and the nineteenth century. His analysis was provisional, based as it was on representative sampling of the dictionary citations, but it appears to have been strikingly accurate (see Figures 1 and 2, compiled from the CD Rom data, which confirm his findings).

Schäfer's 1989 work, *Early Modern English Lexicography*, examines around 130 sixteenth- and early seventeenth-century monolingual printed glossaries, some 90 of which were also sources for *OED* quotations and/or listed in the *OED* bibliography, to show that *OED* again recorded their words and senses partially and inconsistently (of the total of around 18,400 lemmas listed by Schäfer, about 3,850— a fifth or so—were omitted by *OED*). These words cannot be dismissed as 'dictionary' words unsuitable for treatment by *OED*, partly because *OED* cites many dictionary words from other sources (and also, occasionally, from these sources),

---

[16] These figures are taken from Taylor (1993: 173). Schäfer (1980: 50 n. 13) found on the basis of sample-checking that the bibliography recorded more than 97 per cent of the titles mentioned in first citations in *OED*, but John Simpson believes that its overall accuracy in recording titles cited in the dictionary is significantly lower.

[17] References to previous work, for various reasons unsatisfactory, can be found in Schäfer (1980, 1989).

[18] The reference made by Bradley to one of Nashe's works indicates, extraordinarily, that as late as 1893 he thought that Nashe had (or should have) been thoroughly excerpted; see Chapter 1, p. 9 and n. 12.

but mostly because many of the hard words in these early glossaries were taken from examples of real usage, not from other dictionaries.

The interesting thing about this is that it indicates that *OED*'s treatment of sixteenth-century English is in some respects defective, despite its wealth of word- and quotation-citation relative to that of other periods.[19] Schäfer also makes the important point that the *OED* lexicographers were influenced by the teleological or evolutionary notion of language prevailing at the end of the nineteenth century: 'The English language of the early modern period is not documented [by *OED*] in its own right . . . but only glanced at askance from a limited perspective with survival into the present as an important criterion for registration' (1989 ii: 3). The bulk of new words in this period may well have seemed indistinguishably bizarre and exotic to contemporaneous eyes, so that little difference would appear to a sixteenth-century reader to exist between Cockeram's *autonomy* ('Libertie to liue after ones owne law') and his *aurigation* ('A driuing of a Coach'). As Schäfer comments,

When the historical lexicographer, fully aware of this peculiar situation, discriminates between lemmas worthy and not worthy of registration, he inevitably reverts to a prescriptivism difficult to reconcile with the principles of modern linguistics. In addition, the resulting truncated view of the lexical situation of the English Renaissance precludes any further studies as to which, or how many, of the new formations survived and for what reasons. (1989: ii. 3)

Not the least remarkable of the characteristics of these two pioneering works is the enormous industry required to compile Schäfer's *OED* data. The subsequent publication of the dictionary in CD Rom form has transformed our ability to interrogate the *OED* and ascertain its practice in many areas, in particular in its use of sources. This electronic aid was available at a late stage in the writing of Dennis Taylor's outstanding study of Thomas Hardy (1993), which is the first extensive examination of the relationship between a creative writer and the *OED*. Murray constantly consulted Hardy about individual words and usages (their correspondence is preserved in the *OED* archives), and 'while Hardy snatched up the volumes of the dictionary as they appeared, Murray's readers snatched up the volumes of Hardy as they appeared, in order to incorporate their distinctive words in the dictionary' (Taylor 1993: 117).

Taylor understands that the CD Rom 'has opened up the map of Victorian vocabulary' (1993: 124). However, his statement that 'We can now gauge the canonical status of a given author for the OED and for the standard printed language' is incautious, as is his quotation of Schäfer (1980: 60): 'The number of the *OED*'s

[19] The inadequacy of *OED*'s coverage of sixteenth-century English was recognized as early as 1919, when W. A. Craigie (1919) first advanced the argument for a dictionary of Early Modern English. See also Bailey (1980). Bailey (1978) has produced a list of *c.*4,400 citations of words and senses (taken from articles in *Notes and Queries* and other printed sources) in the early modern English period which are untreated by *OED*.

first citations taken from an author's work has been a favourite yardstick for measuring his linguistic creativity.' This implies that *OED*'s choice of quotation sources may be assumed to give a representative picture of how language was actually used. But Schäfer's point, by contrast, was that such a yardstick is highly unreliable: *OED* documentation says more about the literary and linguistic pre-dilections of the readers and lexicographers than about the 'standard printed language' *per se*. Taylor is aware of many of the problems of *OED*'s documentation of sources but takes the (reasonable) view that the treatment of the nineteenth-century period is likely to be the most accurate since it was based on the largest number of quotations (1993: 131). He gives a range of fascinating figures for *OED*'s relative coverage of major nineteenth-century authors,[20] looks also at Hardy's relative use of unique words (i.e. those cited by *OED* as unique), and forms the judgement that '*Hardy is a leader in using unique words, one of the last in using first words, and low to moderate on the scale for using revivals* [original italics]. What this means is that unlike most writers, Hardy's first words were not picked up and used by later writers but remained unique words' (1993: 126–7).

This is a striking and attractive conclusion to draw from the *OED* data. It may well be true, but Taylor's method of establishing it is essentially flawed: the data is only as good as the job done by the lexicographers. Or, to put it another way, it tells us about the lexicographers and the process of compiling the dictionary, rather than about the language itself. The important questions are, how thoroughly did the lexicographers read Hardy's works? How did their treatment of Hardy compare with that of other authors? How sound were their criteria for exclud-ing or including his vocabulary (and what were those criteria)? It is rash to rely on inferences from the quotation data alone; equally, it is very difficult to answer these questions from other sources.[21]

Two more recent works have also dealt with *OED*'s use of sources, although in very different ways. Willinsky (1994) attempted an ambitious account of the dictionary as 'a selective representation reflecting certain elusive ideas about the nature of the English language and people'. The book is based on a broad survey of sources and is bursting with good ideas (for example, on how 'a century's worth

[20] Hardy is less often cited than Blackmore, Robert Browning, Elizabeth Browning, Carlyle, Darwin, Dickens, Disraeli, George Eliot, Thomas Huxley, Kingsley, Meredith, Morris, Newman, Thackeray; he is more often cited than Arnold, William Barnes (the poet and dialectician), Charlotte Brontë, Emily Brontë, Lewis Carroll, Clough, Darley, Dobson, Edward Fitzgerald, Gaskell, Hemans, Henley, Hous-man, Hughes, Henry James, Kipling, Mill, Pater, Patmore, Reade, Christina Rossetti, D. G. Rossetti, Swinburne, Francis Thompson, Trollope (Taylor 1993: 125). The quotation figures given by Taylor for each of these writers do not correspond with those obtainable from *OED2* on CD Rom; cf. n. 5 above.

[21] Taylor (1993: 128) reports that *OED* 'listed as standard 243 unique Hardy words, but did not list 1,276 other unique Hardy words'; he appears unduly unsuspicious as to the reasons why, suggesting that Murray applied an 'elusive' criterion for inclusion in these instances, namely, that if a word 'survives as a possibility' it is to be treated in the dictionary. This criterion is elusive indeed, as I think it derives from a misreading by Taylor of the *OED* 'General Explanations' (p. xviii). I also think that the variable treatment of Hardy's words is at least as likely to reflect variable recording by readers as it is to be the result of considered lexicographical judgement.

of editors at Oxford has constructed the history, the scope and range, of the English language' (1994: 93), or on the problems of using poetic sources for evidence as to what words mean (1994: 59 ff.)). However, it is also characterized by careless and partial analyses and by error.[22] It contains an exceptionally interesting Appendix of tables that provides valuable (though not reliable) data on the *OED*'s use of sources; for example, the top five authors by citation in Johnson's *Dictionary* and in *OED*, the top twenty authors by citation in *OED*, the top twenty books by citation in *OED*.[23]

McConchie (1997) offers a thorough investigation of the *OED*'s treatment of sixteenth-century medical words and senses. The core of the study is 3,985 items of new data for the *OED* (1997: 6), which McConchie came across in an analysis of thirteen sixteenth-century medical works. Of this data 27 per cent takes the form of words unrecorded by *OED* (1997: 135), and many of the words, whether unrecorded by *OED*, or antedatings, or new senses, are 'now familiar'—i.e. part of the general lexicon (1997: 7). McConchie argues that the *OED* readers in neglecting medical sources overlooked another important area of lexis, which is significant both in its own right and also because it contains a reasonable proportion of words or usages which were (or have since become) part of the more general lexicon.

McConchie thus reinforces Schäfer's two main points: first that the sixteenth-century lexicon is not adequately represented in *OED* despite receiving so much attention, and second that the *OED* is mistaken in its view of the English lexicon as 'an artefact whose creation was largely in the hands of literary authors' (1997: 9–10)—a view reflected and in turn fostered by the lexicographers' choice of sources. McConchie's study also gives further evidence of the precariousness of the assumption that *OED* sources were on the whole reliably and consistently examined and excerpted, showing time and again that 'sources already scrutinized, and even relatively thoroughly excerpted, may nevertheless be productive of much more material' (1997: 155).[24]

It is obvious that a good deal of further work on *OED*'s use of sources is still to be done. There are a number of different directions in which this could go. One is investigation, on the model of Taylor (1993), of a writer's reciprocal relationship with the dictionary, for which obvious future candidates are Hopkins, Joyce, and Auden, all of whose work was extensively quoted in the second *Supplement*. Such interdependence—writers reading the *OED*, putting dictionary words into

---

[22] See the devastating review by E. G. Stanley (1997).

[23] Willinsky (1994: 209–21). There are various inconsistencies between these lists; e.g. Palsgrave appears as one of the top twenty authors cited, yet *Lesclarcissement de la langue françoyse* (1532) is wrongly omitted from the list of top twenty works cited (with 5,418 quotations, this work would come no. 7 on Willinsky's list).

[24] Thus 'the fact of a book's having already been read is simply no guide to what useful data might still be found in it, unless it can be shown to have been exhaustively excerpted as in the case of Shakespeare' (1997: 177–8).

their poetry, and then having these in turn recorded by *OED*—raises complex issues about the nature and function of the dictionary.[25]

Research also cries out to be done on the *OED*'s representation and treatment of the language of both its most and least favourite writers and sources. The usage of Dickens (about 8,550 quotations), Browning (3,070 quotations), Tennyson (6,970 quotations), Carlyle (6,620 quotations), or Ruskin (3,315 quotations), sometimes highly idiosyncratic, is minutely attended to, for example, while that of Wilkie Collins (something under 30 quotations), Christina Rossetti (134 quotations), or Blake (112 quotations) is by contrast minimally quoted (see note 5). Investigation of non-literary sources—domestic, horticultural, commercial, sporting, etc.— is another major desideratum. More information on all these areas would shed light on one of the most important questions hanging over both the original *OED* and its future editions: the extent to which its choice of quotation sources, and the highly variable thoroughness with these were read, give a fair representation of the general lexicon.

REFERENCES

Bailey, R. W. (1978). *Early Modern English: Additions and Antedatings to the Record of English Vocabulary, 1475–1700*. Hildesheim, NY: Olms.

—— (1980). 'Progress Towards a Dictionary of Early Modern English', in W. Pijnenburg and F. De Tollenaere (eds.), *Proceedings of the Second International Round Table Conference on Historical Lexicography*. Dordrecht, Holland; Cinnaminson, NJ, USA: Foris Publications, 199–226.

Brewer, C. (1993). 'The Second Edition of the *Oxford English Dictionary*'. *Review of English Studies*, n.s. 44: 313–42.

—— (1996). *Editing Piers Plowman: The Evolution of the Text*. Cambridge: Cambridge University Press.

Burchfield, R. W. (ed.) (1972–86). *A Supplement to the Oxford English Dictionary*. 4 vols. Oxford: Clarendon Press.

Cawdrey, R. (1604). *A Table Alphabeticall*. London: I.R.

Craigie, W. A. (1919). 'New Dictionary Schemes Presented to the Philological Society, 4th April 1919'. *TPS*, 1925–30 (1931): 6–11.

Gray, J. (1988). 'Milton and the *OED* Electronic Database.' *Milton Quarterly*, 23: 66–73.

Johnson, S. (1747). *Plan of a Dictionary of the English Language*. London: Knapton, Longman *et al.*

—— (1755). *A Dictionary of the English Language*. London: W. Strahan.

Kurath, H. *et al.* (1954). *The Middle English Dictionary: Plan and Bibliography*. Ann Arbor: University of Michigan Press; London: Oxford University Press.

McConchie, R. W. (1997). *Lexicography and Physicke: The Record of Sixteenth-Century English Medical Terminology*. Oxford: Clarendon Press.

---

[25] In Brewer (1993: 328–9) I gave examples of such a lexicographical loop in the case of Auden. Taylor (1993, for example: 143–4) discusses the treatment of Hopkins's vocabulary in Burchfield's *Supplement*; his remarks should again be treated with caution (e.g. 'the *OED* can be used as a profitable measure of how Hopkins has or has not influenced the language').

Munro, J. (ed.) (1911). *Frederick James Furnivall: A Volume of Personal Record*. London: Oxford University Press.

Murray, J. A. H. (1879a). *An Appeal to the English-speaking and English-reading Public in Great Britain, America and the Colonies*. Oxford: Clarendon Press. 3 eds.

—— (1879b). 'Eighth Annual Address of the President to the Philological Society'. *TPS*, 1877–9: 561–6 21.

—— (1880). 'Ninth Annual Address of the President to the Philological Society'. *TPS*, 1880–1: 117–74.

—— (1881). 'Report on the Dictionary of the Philological Society'. *TPS*, 1880–1: 260–9.

—— (1884). 'Thirteenth Annual Address of the President to the Philological Society'. *TPS*, 1882–4: 501–31.

—— (1893). 'Report on the Progress of the Philological Society's New English Dictionary'. *TPS*, 1891–4: 268–78 (delivered 1892).

Murray, K. M. E. (1977). *Caught in the Web of Words: James Murray and the* Oxford English Dictionary. New Haven and London: Yale University Press.

Oxford English Dictionary, 1884–1928: Speeches Delivered in the Goldsmiths' Hall (1928). Oxford: Oxford University Press.

Periodical, The (1928). 'The Oxford English Dictionary Completed'. 13/143. 15 February.

[Philological Society]. (1859). *Proposal for a Publication of a New English Dictionary by the Philological Society*. London: Trübner & Co.

Schäfer, J. (1980). *Documentation in the OED: Shakespeare and Nashe as Test Cases*. Oxford: Clarendon Press.

—— (1989). *Early Modern English Lexicography*. Oxford: Clarendon Press. 2 vols.

Stanley, E. G. (1997). Review of Willinsky (1994). *Review of English Studies*, n.s. 48: 218–20.

Starnes, De Witt T., and Noyes, G. E. (1946). *The English Dictionary from Cawdrey to Johnson, 1604–1755*. Chapel Hill: University of North Carolina Press. 2nd edn. (1991), Amsterdam: John Benjamins.

Taylor, D. (1993). *Hardy's Literary Language and Victorian Philology*. Oxford: Clarendon Press.

Trench, R. C. (1860). *On Some Deficiencies in our English Dictionaries*. 2nd rev. edn. London: John W. Parker & Son.

Wexler, P. J. (1981). 'Supplementing the *Supplement*'. *Linguistica Computazionale*, 7: 293–9.

Willinsky, John (1994). *Empire of Words: The Reign of the OED*. Princeton: Princeton University Press.

APPENDIX

Figures 1 and 2 show the number of quotations per decade, 1151–1470 and 1471–1850 respectively (there is a difference of scale between the two tables to accommodate the fact that so many more quotations were gathered per decade for the post-1470 period).[1] The striking feature for both periods (1151–1470 and 1471–1850) is the amount of variation in the number of quotations. For the earlier period, this is partly explained by the fact that there was less available printed material for the readers to read, inevitably resulting in an uneven treatment of periods. The difficulties of dating works produced before printing tended also to encourage a cluster of dates at a round number—the middle or end of a century.

The two striking peaks in Figure 1, at 1291–1300 and 1391–1400, are in part the result of such a cluster. They are also due to the intensive mining of a few specific sources: for example, Robert of Gloucester, dated 1297 (3,222 quotations), *Cursor Mundi*, dated 1300 (10,771), Trevisa, dated 1387/1398 (6,750).

The post-1471 period is more interesting to analyse, and the results are more significant for future research, since there is at present no dictionary other than *OED* which covers this period. The general picture is clear: a slight dip between 1481–90 and 1521–30, a striking peak in the years around 1600, a staggered decline to a trough at 1731–40, and then a more-or-less steady, steep rise into the nineteenth century. (This rise continues post-1850 to a peak of 119,880 quotations in the decade 1881–90, then falls sharply during the early twentieth century to 30,770 quotations in 1911–20, rising again to 89,990 quotations in 1961–70.)

As before, abrupt rises in the line can often be explained by the intensive excerpting of one or more particular authors or works. Thus the rise between 1511–20 and 1521–1530, from 9,652 to 21,576 quotations, is almost half accounted for by a single text, Palsgrave's *Lesclarcissement* (5,418 quotations). The next sharp rise, between 1581–90 and 1591–1600, is in large measure to be explained by the massive documentation of Shakespeare's vocabulary over this period (33,304 quotations in all), while that between 1631–40 and 1651–60 is probably due to the extensive excerpting of pamphlets printed during the period of civil unrest. Various sorts of methodological problems surround the interpretation of this material and further research on it is underway.

Note

[1] Following Schäfer (1980), I have analysed decades as beginning in years 01 and ending in 00. *OED* sets out to record the English language from 1150 (see 'General Explanations': p. xviii), hence I have taken 1151 as the starting point for analysis; collection of dictionary materials began roughly at the time of Trench's paper 'On Some Deficiencies' (1860; delivered 1857), hence I have closed the analysis at 1850.

4

Murray and his European Counterparts

NOEL OSSELTON

Most (but not all) historical dictionaries are hybrids. They combine two functions: (1) to provide a full description of the vocabulary of their own day—words in use, their meanings, their status, pronunciation, and so on; but (2) at the same time to order and present all kinds of information about its past. Such historical information may be seen as directly relevant to the purposes of present-day description (as when the reader is shown how different senses of a word have intermingled in earlier writings, leaving semantic traces today), but very often it will clearly not be so (as when words included in the dictionary have gone forever from the current language, and occur nowhere in books now commonly read).

The *OED* is one such hybrid, along with three other notable multi-volume works which were planned and began publication in western Europe in the middle of the nineteenth century: the *Deutsches Wörterbuch* of the Grimm brothers (*DWB*), Emile Littré's *Dictionnaire de la langue française*, and the *Woordenboek der Nederlandsche Taal* (*WNT*) of Matthias de Vries. The historical orientation of these great works is unsurprising. This was a time when the scholarly study of the vernacular had come to be dominated by the achievements of Danish and German scholars such as Rask, Bopp, and Grimm in establishing their comparative-historical model. Schleicher wrote in 1863 on Darwinianism and *Sprachwissenschaft*: if linguistic studies were to aspire to the intellectual cachet of the natural sciences they needed to be based on historical observation and analysis. The *OED* may then be seen as one part of a common endeavour to interpret modern language in terms of its history.

Other major scholarly works of historical lexicography such as Bosworth's *Anglo-Saxon Dictionary* (1882–98) and the *Middelnederlandsch Woordenboek* (1885–1929) belong to the same period but need not be considered here. These are not hybrids: they are devoted solely to the purposes of historical description within a defined (and closed) period of time, and they have no concern for the

Table 1. Four historical dictionaries: chronology and size

	DWB	Littré	WNT	OED
Initial impulse	1838	1841	1851	1858
First fascicle/volume	1852	1863	1864	1884
Final fascicle/volume	1961	1873	1998	1928
Number of pages	33 872	4 646	45 805	15 490
OED-size pages (equivalent number)	22 421	4 646	25 038	15 490

language of their own day. On such period dictionaries in general see Aitken (1987) and Bailey (1990).

Within the English dictionary tradition it was no new thing to include historical information. Etymologies had been included in monolingual dictionaries from Thomas Blount's *Glossographia* (1656) onwards. Even for the restricted period he had chosen, Dr Johnson set out his quotations and arranged the senses in chronological order (without dates) 'to mark the progress of meaning', and Charles Richardson assembled a mass of early documentation for his *New Dictionary of the English Language* (1836–7), though with the primary design of demonstrating the original meanings of existing words rather than that of illustrating current usage.

For the *OED* and the other monumental national dictionaries of the nineteenth century, historical information was, however, not simply a cultural extra. They all saw it as their mission to describe the present vocabulary in terms of the past; all were founded on 'historical principles' (though only *OED* proclaimed this on the title-page). Yet even a cursory look at entries in them will show how sharply they differed in the choice of historical information for inclusion, in the style in which it was presented, and in the purpose which it was felt to serve. Notions about what such a dictionary should be evolved slowly, leaving room for local preference, and each of the great national dictionaries for German, French, Dutch, and English adopted distinctive tactics for marrying up historical record and modern language description.

In part the differences between these works have to do with sheer size and the vagaries of their publishing history. Table 1 gives an overview of the four dictionaries: how long they took to produce, and how big they are (here expressed in *OED*-size page equivalents). Comprehensiveness exacts a price: the bigger a dictionary is and the tardier its production, the more difficult it will be to exert editorial control and maintain consistency throughout the whole text, and the long gestation of *WNT* and *DWB* was to lead to disturbing internal shifts in style and method. The French scholar Quemada (1972: 430) has argued with some force that in dictionary making the necessary unity of conception and method can hardly be sustained for more than twenty-five or thirty years.

JACOB AND WILHELM GRIMM, *DEUTSCHES WÖRTERBUCH* (1852–1960)

The brothers Jacob and Wilhelm Grimm turned lexicographer late in life and they survived to edit only the letters A to E (plus part of F) in the great German historical dictionary which still carries their name. Indeed the subsequent parts of 'Grimm' produced up to a century later may be seen as having diverged so far in method and intention as to have little in common with the founding volumes apart from the name (Reichmann 1991: 300). There was also a great expansion of material as work on the dictionary progressed: the entry for the verb *essen* 'eat' (1862) takes up eight columns, as against *trinken* 'drink' (1950) with thirty-seven columns; the three colours *blau*, *rot*, and *grün* (1860, 1893, and 1935—production of the dictionary did not proceed in an entirely orderly way through the alphabet) occupy two, thirteen, and twenty-six columns respectively. But it was, of course, the initial work by the Grimms that Littré, De Vries, and Murray all knew—Littré refers to the 'deux célèbres frères' in his Preface (Littré 1862: p. v); De Vries first met Jacob in 1846, and their correspondence lasted until Grimm's death in 1863 (Van Sterkenburg 1992: 158, 229); Trench refers as early as 1857 to the Grimm brothers, who were indeed honorary members of the Philological Society of London, and whose idea of recruiting volunteers to collect quotations served as an operational tactic for the *OED*.

The early volumes of the Grimms may then be seen, if not as the model, then at least as the inspiration for the historical dictionary as we have known it since the mid-nineteenth century. The two short entries shown in Figure 1—one Germanic, and one a loanword—may serve to illustrate some of its characteristic features.

BARBAR, m. *homo peregrinus, incondita lingua loquens, humanitatis expers, noch nicht bei* LUTHER, DASYPODIUS *und* MAALER, *zuerst bei* HENISCH. *doch haftet im* 17 *jh. und später die griechische und lateinische betonung :*

    wer sind wir! sind wir die,
    vor den der bárbar oft voll zittern auf die knie
    gesunken ?   GRYPHIUS 1, 7 ;
    verrathen durch den freund. den, den der bárbar ehret,
    erwürgt der blutfürst, ach.   1, 22 ;
    der bárbarn liebe. LOHENSTEIN *Cleop.* 22 ;
    bis du der bárbarn stolz voll gröszern stolzes dämpfest.
        Uz 1, 142 ;
    von verschwornen bárbarn überfallen. RAMLER 1, 75.

man schrieb und sprach auch um 1700 *im* pl. bárbern. *Allmählich aber drang die französische aussprache* barbare *wie* Tartare *durch :* bárbàr, barbàr, Tártàr, Tartár, *pl.* barbaren, Tartaren:

    sie liefen mit zerstreuten haaren,
    und warfen schon vor angst halb todt
    sich vor den feldherrn der barbaren. GELLERT 1, 139;
    so hart als auch der feldherr war,
    so konnt er doch dem zauberischen flehen
    der weiber nicht ganz widerstehen.

    denn welchen mann, er sei auch zehnmal ein barbar,
    weisz nicht ein weib durch thränen zu bewegen ? *allda ;*
    der morgen kömmt, und Lucia
    ergibt sich thränend dem barbaren. 1, 240.

der frauenname Barbara (*verkürzt* Bärbel), *gr.* Βαρβάρα, *behält den ton auf erster silbe, desgleichen* bárbar, bárber, *ein pferd aus Africa.*

BAUMGARTE, m. *pomarium, pometum,* ahd. poumgarto (GRAFF 4, 251), mhd. boumgarte (BEN. 1, 483ᵇ), nnl. boomgaard, *dessen nom., wie bei dem einfachen* garte, *gewöhnlich schon das* N *zuläszt* (garten = *franz.* jardin) baumgarten *z. b.* Galmy 25. GÖTHE 24, 246 ; *Saadis* persianischer baumgarten. *nicht nur der unorganische* gen. baumgartens, *sondern auch der umlautende* pl. baumgärten : strasze, die sanft auf hügel mit ofnen baumgärten und in gelbblühende gründe stieg. J. PAUL *Tit.* 2, 49. *vgl.* bangart.

Figure 1. Entries from the *Deutsches Wörterbuch* (1854)
Source: Durham University Library

Definition

The absence of any German explanation of meaning is striking. In his Preface Grimm poured scorn upon earlier lexicographers who had wasted time and effort in tedious definitions of well-known objects such as 'table' (where the single word *mensa* would be just as effective); it is an argument which would apply well enough to the self-explanatory compound *baumgarte* ('tree' + 'garden' = orchard), though the non-Latined dictionary user might well expect some help with *barbar* 'barbarian'. Grimm opted openly for Latin in his definitions as being the best-known and most enduring of all languages ('die bekannteste und sicherste aller sprachen', *Preface*: p. xl) and wrote a spirited defence of his practice when criticized for it. Alongside Latin equivalents he regularly throws in a Dutch cognate, and sometimes a French term too ('*auslegen, exponere, pandere, étaler*, nnl. uitleggen'); occasionally, there is even an English phrase ('a pair of eyes' for *augenpaar*); he does, however, commonly turn to his vernacular German for the purpose of clarifying subsenses in longer entries. The entries for many words (especially compounds and derivations) contain nothing more than an indication of gender, with *ad hoc* jottings of a style familiar to us from the earliest renaissance lexicographers ('**bibelstelle**, *f.*'; '**bibelstück**, *n. was* bibelabschnitt'; '**bibelstunde**, *f. in schule und kirche*'). In general it is fair to say that Grimm's heart was simply not in the business of providing a consistent and logical record of meanings: his dictionary entries contain at best only the rudiments of a definition (Reichmann 1991: 316).

Dating and historical coverage

There are no dates anywhere in the articles for *baumgarte* and *barbar*, though Grimm does sometimes provide useful guidance (the French derivative *alamodisch* had a currency 'from around 1600 to 1720'). The existence of *baumgarte* in Old and Middle High German is indeed noted from the dictionaries of Graff and Beneke, but for the further chronology the reader has to rely on private knowledge of when Gryphius, Ramler, and others cited were actually living. Dating of quotations was, however, to become a normal feature in the later volumes of *DWB*. All the citations above are drawn from sixteenth-, seventeenth-, and eighteenth-century writers, even in the case of *baumgarte*, where the word had existed from the very earliest stages of the language. Throughout the early volumes, the usual range of literary quotation runs from Luther to Goethe; Grimm was criticized by his contemporary Sanders for failing to do justice to the language of his own day (Kirkness 1980: 186) and admitted that he had neglected nineteenth-century usage.

Linguistic commentary

In the more substantial entries for common Germanic words the focus of linguistic interest is on origins. Nearly half of the lemma *buch*, for instance, is taken up with a discussion of the terms for 'book' in the various branches of Germanic, and in Latin, Greek, Hungarian, Lithuanian as well as the Slav and Celtic languages, showing its probable connections in meaning with 'beech'. The first of two columns for the noun 'bear' is largely given over to the matter of early beast fable. It was to be expected of the founder and greatest exponent of comparative-historical Germanic philology that he should beat the track of etymology wherever it could most interestingly lead. For Grimm, the motive for including expansive and sometimes speculative etymological comment was that of tracing a basic, primitive meaning (*Urbegriff*) in which later semantic developments were rooted. This is not etymology for etymology's sake: Grimm seeks to interpret the language of his day from its past history and its position in relation to other Germanic languages (Bahr 1991: 19–20). With the transparent compound *baumgarte* clearly no account of origin was needed, and over two-thirds of the entry is devoted to a single morphological detail: *baumgarte* could also take a final *-n*, and this had led historically to the creation of new 'inorganic' genitive and to mutated plural inflections, which are then duly illustrated in the quotations chosen. With the other word, *barbar*, it is not morphology but the stress-pattern which engages the lexicographer's attention. We are shown (with verse quotations chosen to suit) how the classical accent on the first syllable was long retained in German until the typically French accentuation took over in the eighteenth century. For each of these words Grimm thus battens on that single point in historical development which he judges to be most interesting—in the one case, morphology, in the other, syllable stress. A similar eclecticism is manifested in other ways: for instance, no consistent record of variant spellings is attempted, but under *brot* 'bread' he notes that the spelling *brod* is *unhochdeutsch* (i.e. Low German), that *brodt* is 'even worse', and then provides a list of spellings preferred in earlier dictionaries; modern pronunciation is not regularly given in the dictionary, though incidental details are put in where help might be needed (the final *-t* of the French loanword *credit* is to be pronounced distinctly in German, he says, as also in *habit* and *bandit*); notes on synonymy also occur—Trench (1860: 47) praised the Grimms for this, citing *becher-kelch* and *degen-schwert*, though it must be said that other opportunities for the elucidation of semantic distinctions are missed, as when the cluster of terms *mahl*, *bild*, *art*, *sitte*, and *gepräge* are listed (but not differentiated) in the entry for *character*.

Nomenclature

In the matter of foreign (especially French) loanwords Grimm took a more puristic stance than later editors of the dictionary, often adding cautionary or justificatory comments on those that were included (*bataille*, *effect*, *égal*). Understandably, items from dialect mattered to him especially where the known record (for example, from the Bavarian, Swabian, and Swiss varieties of German) could shed light on etymologies (*Preface*: pp. xvi–xvii). Compounds and derivations were a particular problem because of the enormous number of them (both actual and potential) in the German language. They are lemmatized separately in Grimm, who hopefully proposes (*Preface*: pp. xli–xliii) to include only the common and current ones. Under *altar*, he refers to the inexhaustible variety of compounds to which this foreign ecclesiastical word has given rise, with the revealing comment that 'nothing could be learned from them about the language' ('aus welchen für die sprache nichts zu lernen ist'). Even so, twenty-five *altar-* compounds are then entered in the main alphabetical list.

Readership

In a memorable passage in his Preface Grimm has a vision of his dictionary finding a place in every household not unlike that of the Family Bible: he sees the *paterfamilias* presiding in the evening over the family circle, picking out and discussing words from it for the (linguistic) betterment of his sons, while the mother listens attentively. His volumes were to be a shrine preserving the riches of the German language for the whole nation—'what have we in common but our own speech and literature?' (*Preface*: p. iii). Yet the Latin definitions and the learned etymologies hardly fit in with this cosy domestic scene. Every page he edited reveals Grimm as a scholar addressing scholars, and an initial print run of 5,000 reducing to 2,000 (Horlitz 1991: 410, quoting Dückert) in itself shows (if evidence were needed) that his dictionary never became the staple reading of the family circle. Nevertheless, Grimm's idyllic domestic scene tells us something about his lexicographical style. It goes well with the more practical notes on usage (*allesam* 'for which *allesam(m)t* is better and more usual'; see Kühn 1991) and with the structure of his entries, in which etymological, historical and word-explanatory information are all woven into a single narrative. Grimm *talks* to his readers—his lemmata may be typographically unsophisticated but his verse is set out as verse, and his eclecticism, the technique of picking on interesting bits of information about the language and its past, do make his work more *readable* than that of his fellow historical lexicographers: who would ever have recommended *reading* OED entries to the family circle?

ÉMILE LITTRÉ, *DICTIONNAIRE DE LA LANGUE FRANÇAISE* (1863–73)

Littré's dictionary took thirty years to complete (the first contract with Hachette was in 1841) and it was virtually a one-man job—in the end he agreed only reluctantly to the appointment of three assistants (Hamburger 1988: 151). With 4,646 pages—something under one-third of the length of the *OED*—the dictionary is aimed not at the professional scholar, nor the common man, but at *l'homme cultivé*, and its commercial success (which surprised Littré) may be thought to have owed something to his notoriety as a republican and a positivist philosopher (Rey 1970: 20, 177). He is firm in his belief that the modern language—'l'usage contemporain'—must be the prime concern of the lexicographer (even of the historical lexicographer) but opts to take *contemporain* in the extended sense of everything from Malherbe (1555–1628) down to his own day, drawing his 'modern' examples from classical French authors (plus others 'qui méritent pourtant d'être

SERMONNEUR (sèr-mo-neur), *s. m.* || 1° Celui qui fait des sermons; n'est guère usité en ce sens qu'avec ur sens de dépréciation. En un mot, le sermonneur est plus tôt évêque que le plus solide écrivain n'est revêtu d'un prieuré simple, LA BRUY. XV. || 2° *S. m.* et *f.* Sermonneur, sermonneuse, celui, celle qui fait des remontrances, des discours ennuyeux et hors de propos. La voix manquant à notre sermonneuse, LA FONT. *Psaut.* Toujours sermonneurs, toujours pédants, J. J. ROUSS. *Ém.* II. Un sermonneur politique aura beau leur dire que la force du peuple est la leur, ID. *Contr.* III, 6.

— HIST. XIIIᵉ s. Mes li chetif sermonneor Et li fol large donneor Si forment les enorguillissent [les femmes], Que lor roses lor enchierissent, *la Rose*, 7655. || XVIᵉ s. Les danses sans instrumens ou sans chansons, seroient les gens en un lieu d'audience sans sermonneur, DESPER. *Contes*, XL.

— ÉTYM. *Sermonner;* prov. *sermonaire;* ital. *sermonatore.* L'ancienne langue a dit aussi *sermonier.*

Figure 2. Entry from Littré, *Dictionnaire de la langue française* (1863)
Source: Durham University Library

consultés') over a period of some two and a half centuries. In this view of the lexicographer's target language, Littré might usefully be compared to Dr Johnson, whose dictionary of 1755 (while not even claiming to be historical) effectively covered the English language from Sidney to his own time: had he been a Frenchman, Johnson might also fittingly have referred to the authors favoured for excerption as 'nos classiques'.

Through his earlier studies of Old French authors, Littré had come to see how their language could illuminate modern usage; he was convinced that even a modern dictionary needed a historical base, and refers approvingly to the great work then being undertaken by the Grimms in Germany. The written records of French went back 700 years, and to embrace this linguistic heritage within the dictionary would enrich it greatly, and also serve to lend authority to the account of the language. It is this perception of two stages in the development of the language—a more or less static classical phase now to be described in detail, and an earlier growth phase which may shed light upon it—which determines the characteristic shape of Littré's dictionary entries.

The short entry for the word *sermonneur* (see Figure 2) can be taken as fairly typical: the first twelve lines of the lemma set out the modern meanings of the word, and the remaining eight lines, under the headings HIST[*oire*] and ÉTYM[*ologie*] supply the historical background to it. The entry begins with the current pronunciation; the literal meaning backed up by a quotation from the seventeenth-century writer La Bruyère; then (with masculine and feminine forms) the derived sense of 'sermonizer', with a quotation from La Fontaine and two from Rousseau. Under *Hist.* there are lists of quotations ordered by centuries (here only the thirteenth and sixteenth) with sources but no further linguistic apparatus. Older spellings (*sermonneor*) are preserved here, though elsewhere in the lemma 'classic' authors (even seventeenth-century ones) appear in modern dress. Placed last, as throughout the dictionary, there is a brief comment on etymology, here with Provençal and Italian forms and a reference to 'l'ancienne langue'.

The basic structure outlined above, with all the modern material in each entry given first with careful and methodical definitions, means that his dictionary suited the needs of those whose interests did not seriously extend beyond the current language: historical matter does not obtrude, since it is relegated to the end of each lemma.

Dating

Beyond the broad separation of the current from the historical, the dating of linguistic material was not one of Littré's main concerns. Citations from early works such as the *Chanson de Roland* or Froissart's *Chronicles* are indeed arranged in blocks by centuries, but for common words as many as forty may thus be lumped together. In the modern section, for current French from 1600 onwards, quotations are not dated at all, though they are presented in chronological order: no doubt *l'homme cultivé* could be assumed to know when La Fontaine wrote his Fables, and the date of Rousseau's *Contrat Social*. It is as if dating did not matter greatly anyway, since all these classical authors were to be regarded as in some sense contemporary. Littré is sparing in his quotations where the sense is not in doubt; the entry for the word *anguille* 'eel', for instance, has five numbered divisions and numerous idioms and collocations, but there is only one quotation (from Molière) to back it all up.

Sense-development

Apart from incidental remarks in his sections on etymology, Littré shows little concern for semantic development before 1600: early quotations are merely listed, without meanings, and it is up to the enquiring user to disentangle the sense-patterns represented. In the modern section he rejects the Academy dictionary practice of putting the most usual sense first, and adopts the principle of logical order, starting from the basic meaning in classic writers of the seventeenth century. The carefully constructed 'logical' order of senses is inevitably often at variance with the sequence in which the words entered the language. Littré is content that it should bring out what he calls an *enchainement historique*, but the longer entries are complex and may be found confusing (Matoré 1968: 121); *feu*, for instance, takes up ten densely packed columns with its forty-four distinct senses, and Littré's bleak typography does anything but help.

Pronunciation

Unlike the Grimms, Littré gives the current pronunciation of all words, adding guidance on phonetic liaisons, rhyming words, etc. and occasional notes on provincial forms (*doit:* 'en Normandie on prononce *douè*'). Modern pronunciations are sometimes roundly condemned, as under *orgueilleux, or-gheu-lleû*: 'quelques-uns prononcent *or-ghè-lleû*; ce qui n'est pas bon'. In the Preface Littré acknowledges that a historical dictionary ought properly to deal with the matter of pronunciation historically. But in the present state of scholarship he could promise no more than to provide incidental information on older pronunciation whenever this was to hand; thus we are told, for instance, that Molière sometimes makes *biais* a monosyllable, sometimes a disyllable, and that the word *satisfaire* might lose its second -*s*- in seventeenth-century speech.

Synonymy

Littré goes further than the Grimms in institutionalizing synonymy, and under a separate section heading *SYN*[*onimie*] we are given compact and elegantly contrived notes on related terms (for example, *cataracte–cascade, orgueil–vanité*) for about one in every fifty entries—curiously without cross-references from the paired items. Littré saw these notes as a means of avoiding circular definitions (*Preface*: p. xix); the treatment is synchronic, and at times his radical views come through, as when he observes (*république–démocratie*) that the United States may be called a democracy, but that to apply the word to France is to take it in a wrong sense.

Usage

Lexicographical strictures are not limited to pronunciation. Under another (rather commoner) section heading *REM*[*arques*], Littré presents linguistic information from grammarians and earlier lexicographers, takes on knotty points of usage ('Doit on dire . . . ?'), and indulges in a whole array of authoritarian pronouncements. Voltaire, he notes, had no aspirate in *harengère*, 'ce qui est une faute'; the word *casuel* had come to be used in the sense of 'fragile', though nothing in the etymology or the history of the word could justify that; he similarly deplores *vis à vis* for *au lieu de, envers*, a fault said to have been introduced into France by Rousseau, who is elsewhere (s.v. *causer*) characterized as 'pas toujours très-pur'.

Archaism and neologism

By adopting a two-and-a-half-century catchment area for modern French Littré landed himself with serious problems of obsolescence, and he fully acknowledges these in his Preface: the classical language had not been sheltered from change, and many innovations of the eighteenth and nineteenth century had been injudicious. His entries are then littered with temporal usage labels (*inusité, peu usité, ancien mot, vieux, cette locution vieillit*, etc.). Neologisms are similarly noted, sometimes with further detail (*méticuleux* 'un néologisme du XVIIIe siècle'; *seméiologie* and *seméiotique* 'mots mal faits'; *railroute* 'mot qu'on a proposé pour remplacer railway'). The heritage of somewhat obsolescent words in the modern section is seen by the compiler as a counterweight to recent and often undesirable changes in the language: it is respect for the past which will save us from current errors. No wonder that he expresses a preference for quotations from older writers ('Pour citations, les plus anciens exemples doivent être préférés aux nouveaux', *Preface*: p. xvii) and stays true to that principle throughout his dictionary.

Littré confesses a debt to the Academy dictionary. He takes over all items in it, and even sets a distinctive mark against those words he has added. But he sees his own dictionary as radically different because it is historical. Data from the past are the equivalent in lexicography to discoveries by experiment in the natural sciences. There is in Littré no Trench-like insistence on providing a neutral chronological record of all the words of the language, past and present. He claims that in his work it is the witness and example of history which supplants the rational or merely subjective judgements of his predecessors, and for him the useful part of history began with Malherbe in the late sixteenth century.

THE *WOORDENBOEK DER NEDERLANDSCHE TAAL* (1864–1998)

One motive for setting up the *Woordenboek der Nederlandsche Taal* was an urge to promote uniformity of language between the northern and the southern (Flemish-speaking) Netherlands after the period of French hegemony, and the decisive impulse for its creation came at the third *Nederlandsch Taal- en Letterkundig Congres* held (significantly) in Brussels in 1851 (Van Sterkenburg 1992: 15–19). The *WNT* thus precedes the *OED* in its inception; and now, after 147 years in which successive generations of editors have been chipping away at the alphabet, it has ended up with its 45,805 pages as the biggest (but also, both in method and in content, as the least coherent) of the four historical dictionaries considered here.

Under a motto proclaiming that 'language is the soul of the nation, it is the very nation itself' the original editor Matthias de Vries (1820–92) saw it as his task to provide a record of the cultivated literary language of his day, while at the same time doing proper justice to the past (*Preface*: p. xli). The entry for the word *abdij* 'abbey, monastery, convent' in Figure 3 may serve to show how he set about the task. This consists of

(1) information on word-class, gender, plural form;
(2) ten lines of compact historical information; De Vries held the view that a dictionary—even a historical dictionary—was no place for etymological research or speculation; with scholarly care he cites secondary sources for Germanic cognates, gives the Latin etymon *abbatia* and adds a comment on the irregular 'etymological' spelling *abtdij* (which crops up in one of his quotations);
(3) the main part of the entry (fourteen lines) with two defined senses supported by eight illustrative phrases and two identified verse quotations;
(4) a sub-section **Samenst**[ellingen] for the two (self-explanatory) *abdij-* compounds that are listed.

Definitions are in the vernacular, here as throughout the dictionary. We know that De Vries discussed his whole project with the Grimms (*Preface*: p. lvi), and agreed to differ on this point: Latin may be fine for plant names, he says, but not for the words in a dictionary intended for educated people in general ('de geheele

ABDIJ, znw. vr., mv. *abdijen*. Ohd. *abbateia*, *apteia* (GRAFF 1 , 92); mhd. *abbeteie* , *aptei* (BEN. 1 , 2); nhd. *abtei*; eng. *abbey*; deensch *abbedi*; mnl. *abedie*, *abdie*; alle meer of min verbasterde vormen van mlat. *abbatia*. Voorheen schreef men ook wel *abtdij*, als ware het woord gevormd van *abt* met een zekeren uitgang *dij*. Doch de mnl. vorm *abedie* toont overtuigend, dat de *d* uit de *t* van *abbatia* is ontstaan, evenals in *abdis* uit die van *abbatissa*; verg. ook *Proosdij* nevens *Proost*.

1) Mannen- of vrouwenklooster, door eenen abt of door eene abdis bestuurd. || De abdij te Aduard. De abdij van Rijnsburg was een vrouwenklooster. Eene abdij van Benedictijnen. De monniken dier abdij hebben steeds door geleerdheid uitgemunt.

> 't Was in de abdij niet doodsch en naar,
> Noch stil en eenzaam dag en nacht.
> **TOLLENS** 12, 132.

> Tot de kerkklok van de abtdij
> Mij in 't mijmren stoort.   6, 44.

2) De gebouwen eener abdij. || De abdij te Middelburg. De puinhoopen der abdij van Egmond. De abdij van Rijnsburg was „een gebouw, dat in Holland geene wedergade had."

Samenst. *Abdijgoederen* (mv.), *abdijkerk*.

Figure 3. Entry from the Woordenboek der Nederlandsche Taal (1864)
Source: Brotherton Library, University of Leeds

beschaafde natie', *Preface*: p. lxiv). The pronunciation of *abdij* is not given, though there are occasional notes elsewhere, mainly on foreign loans (for instance, how *artillerie* is pronounced by military men), but also on some native Dutch words, for example, homographs with variable stress. The typography here is more pleasing than that of the *DWB* or Littré: quotations are in a distinctive smaller type and set out as verse, the numbered definitions are indented, and bold face with spaced letters is introduced for the sub-section heading. Elsewhere the compiler uses a dozen or more different sub-section headings under which he appends *ad hoc* comments (both diachronic and synchronic) on morphology, pronunciation, and also synonymy (rather more frequently than in Littré). The use of this device was, however, much reduced in later volumes. As in the early Grimm, quotations here have no dates—readers could in any case find further details in the bibliography, consisting initially in 1882 of some thousand titles (Moerdijk 1994: 276).

Quotations, historical coverage

According to De Vries, quotations in a historical dictionary were not to be regarded as documentary evidence (*bewijsplaatsen*) but rather as appropriate examples of a word in a living context, to be chosen 'with judgement and good taste' (*Preface*: pp. lxiv–lxv)—here, for *abdij*, both of them are from the popular nineteenth-century poet Hendrik Tollens (1780–1856). The starting-point for the full range of literary quotation in the *WNT* was initially the Bible translation of

1637 (*Statenbijbel*), though De Vries later came to realize that this should be moved back to 1580 so as to include major writers such as Hooft (1547–1626), who could hardly be ignored in a national dictionary. The lemma for *abdij* illustrates the gap in the *WNT* between the historical, philological section (with fully documented forms from Old High German, etc.) and the account of 'modern' usage. The early spellings *abedie, abdie* are referred to, but usage in Middle Dutch with its remarkable literature and copious records is simply left out, even for this word from monastic times. In his Preface (pp. xxxvii–xxxviii) De Vries mused on the ideal of recording the whole history of his language over a period of seven centuries; but feared that the inclusion of Middle Dutch words in all their regional varieties and spellings would simply swamp the modern language in a mass of obsolete and unrecognizable forms. In the outcome, coverage of the Middle Dutch period was left to the great *Middelnederlandsch Woordenboek*, which may indeed be regarded as chronologically supplementary to the *WNT*. For De Vries the lexicographical task was thus rendered easier, in as far as he could focus on the living language and literary usage of recent centuries.

Compounds

Compound words give rise to the same lexicographical difficulties in Dutch as they do in German (and in part, in English): there are too many of them, freely-formed, an open-ended category. De Vries argued strongly in his Preface against the pointless inclusion of self-explanatory ones in the main alphabetical list of the dictionary, but the problems remain. Long lists (sixty or more under *avond-*) are given under the first element, and the user is referred forward for those accorded separate alphabetical treatment. But these lists are often subdivided according to semantic category, so that the enquiring reader needs to know the meaning of the word before he can look it up. Sometimes De Vries cuts short the problem by saying 'the commonest ones are . . .' (*Alpenbloem, Alpendal*, etc. under *Alpen-*); other compounds are categorized as unusual, archaic, or poetic.

Spelling

Because of long-standing uncertainties between rival orthographies for the Dutch language, De Vries needed to set up a modern spelling system of his own—an unusual requirement for the maker of a historical dictionary, though Noah Webster would have understood. Details of the scheme were published by his fellow editor Te Winkel in 1863, and this was later to become the official basis of the modern Dutch spelling system, though there have been many modifications since. In the dictionary there is no systematic historical account of spellings for each word, but comments occur quite frequently on the most acceptable form for French loanwords in Dutch (for example, *akkoord, apart* for the French *accord, à part*)—a topic of impassioned public and scholarly debate in Holland even today.

Collocation, idiom

Under *aar* 'ear (of corn)' the definition of the word in the *WNT* is followed immediately (and before the first quotation) by a list of nine typical adjective collocates—*rijpe, volle, welige, gele, goudgele, gouden, ledige, schrale, dorre aren*—and for the word *avond* 'evening' we are given some thirty common idiomatic phrases. Quotations in a historical dictionary (if there are plenty of them) may chance to illustrate such characteristic phrases as 'golden corn', but De Vries (as the Grimms and Littré before him) makes extensive use of made-up or unattributed constructions or sentences, and the coverage of idiom is all the richer for it. Such carefully contrived sentences may also supplement definition by filling in historical background information, as in 'the monks of this abbey always excelled in learning' (under *abdij*, above), or (for the next entry) 'the abbesses of Rijnsburg were always of noble birth'.

Authoritarian comments

De Vries is less forthright than Grimm in offering normative advice. 'Contrary to usage . . .' ('*tegen het gebruik*') is a typically mild warning against offending items and it occurs, rather strangely, even in reference to established eighteenth-century writers. Dialect is excluded on principle (*Preface*: p. xxxviii), and so he needs no stick to beat it with. Foreign loanwords were, however, a particular problem in Dutch at that time: under *arts* 'medical doctor' the popular term *semi-arts* (for one not yet fully qualified) is dismissed as barbarous, and in general De Vries keeps out the more blatant Gallicisms; in the Preface he even goes so far as to set out linguistic conditions (stress pattern, derivational productivity in Dutch, shift from original meaning) which must be fulfilled before foreign loans might qualify for inclusion in the dictionary.

The later volumes

The first volume of the *WNT* (*A–Ajuin*) appeared in 1882, and in the Preface (p. xxxv) De Vries announced that the collection of source-material for A to Z (which had by then lasted thirty years) had been completed. After his death ten years later no new chief editor was appointed, and those already working on the project tended to go on their own way, each on his own patch of the alphabet. The catchment area of the dictionary became greatly expanded to include non-literary material, far more foreign loans, archaisms, and (for their historical value) dialect terms. Almost a century after the first fascicle, a series of *canones lexico-graphici* was drawn up (in 1962), but the dictionary as a whole has undergone numerous shifts in style and method: a perceived neglect of eighteenth-century Dutch literature was for instance remedied only later in the alphabet, and significant innovations reflecting word-field theory and componential analysis are to be detected in the editing of more recent entries (Van Sterkenburg 1978: 94–6). The later volumes tend to have fuller entries (fifty-eight columns for *voet* 'foot',

as against twelve columns for *arm*) and to provide a more tightly organized—
and very impressive—descriptive historical inventory of the lexicon.

There have been changes in the documentation too. As we have seen, De Vries
attached no dates to his quotations. Later editors tended to date minor sources
(for example, legal documents), but it was only in 1942 that a policy of consistent dating was adopted (Moerdijk 1994: 111). Far more important are the switches
in historical coverage. The *terminus a quo*, originally 1637, then 1580, was later
(but not until 1892) shunted back to 1500 so as to link on to the Middle Dutch
dictionary. Meantime the *terminus ad quem* of the *WNT* edged forward with
successive volumes—as is the way with historical dictionaries *de longue haleine*—
to 1971 (in Volume XXI), only to be cut back again and fixed irrevocably at the
year 1921 for all remaining volumes. This draconian decision, taken (and taken
successfully) in 1975 to ensure completion within another twenty-five years,
meant that the *WNT* in the end surrendered all pretence of covering contemporary usage.

MURRAY AND HIS CONTEMPORARIES

Though James Murray (born in 1837) was much the junior, he and Jacob Grimm
(1785–1863), Emile Littré (1801–81), and Matthias de Vries (1820–92) were at least
in part contemporaries, and each was committed to the task of creating an
authoritative dictionary for the language of his day, authority being conferred not
merely by weight of documentation and sheer size, but by taking the record of
each word as far back as it could usefully go and by anchoring usage in quotations from an accepted canon of earlier and modern writers.

It is not surprising then that, sharing the philological preoccupations of their
age, they produced largely similar answers to a number of common problems.
As might be expected, given their historical focus, information on **etymology** was
common to all. In the *OED* (and sometimes in the early De Vries) etymologies
are typographically segregated, and Littré's rather brief notes come as something
of an afterthought at the end of the lemma; but for the Grimms the more complex (and sometimes speculative) details of word origin are typically woven into
the account of its meaning so as to bring out the natural sense development. Foreign
loanwords were no great problem for Littré; both in *DWB* and *WNT* there was
a shift away from an initial purism as the dictionary progressed, but the *OED* has
been the most accommodating throughout (with Murray's useful distinction of
denizens, aliens, and casuals—see further Chapter 6). The *OED* also appears
to be the most receptive of the four dictionaries in respect of **nonce-words** (the
principle of 'every word in literature' opened the gates here), ghost words, and
other ephemera. The problem of **technical terms** is discussed in every preface, and
every editor knew the risk of being overwhelmed by the number clamouring
for inclusion; despite his literary preferences, Grimm managed a fair coverage of

vernacular ('muttersprachliche') technical terms (Schiewe 1991), and De Vries like-wise favoured native terms, giving a special place to the language of seafaring and hydraulic engineering on the grounds of particular national expertise. In the Germanic languages **compound words** are a similarly open-ended group, though the lexicographical difficulties are more acute in German and Dutch than in English (with its more clearly built-in notion of established compounds). Through its more sophisticated typography the *OED* was able both to do without the long strings of self-explanatory main-entry compounds (*Buchbinderlohn*, *Buchbinderjunge*, etc.) such as occur in the early Grimm, and to avoid the over-complex semantic classifications of the *WNT*. For minor **derivations** such as *buddingness* the *OED* also copes well by means of lemma-internal bold face in smaller type, generally finding room for definitions of them too. Unlike the other dictionaries the *OED* does not set out lists of common **collocational patterns**, and it is alone in not backing up definition by set studies of **synonymy**. Each of the four editors faced up to the problem of how to arrange the **sequence of meanings** in polysemous words: whether to set them out in a supposed 'logical' order, or to keep to a chrono-logical order as dictated by available documentary evidence. Zgusta's analysis (1989) shows how Murray's compromise solution sought to make the best of both systems. As examples above will have shown, Littré and (in the early volumes) Grimm and the *WNT* all tend to indulge in **authoritarian comments** on usage, and the *OED* must be counted the least prescriptive of the four.

One of the more striking differences of which the regular user of the four dic-tionaries must be constantly aware is that the *OED* maintains so remarkable a consistency throughout the alphabet. Look up *wasp*, or *yellow* (edited in the 1920s) and you find that the entry is ordered in the same way, and gives the same kind of information as you will find under entries such as *bee* and *brown* from the 1880s. Compare *brother* (1888) with *sister* (1911) and you find that each ranks just over four columns. The more rapidly produced and single-handed work of Littré is similarly all of a piece, but (as we have seen above) the same certainly cannot be said of the *DWB* or of the *WNT*, both of which suffered serious changes in editorial style and scope during their much longer period of gestation.

The one feature which most of all marks out the *OED* among its rivals is the sheer length of its continuous documentation from the earliest records of English down to the very latest (with only the regrettable though understandable omis-sion of items in the vocabulary of Old English which had disappeared before 1150). For common words such as *book* or *sheep* the reader is provided with a string of quotations all treated *ex aequo* and illustrating English usage for a thousand years back. None of the other dictionaries discussed here attempts anything so ambi-tious. For Jacob Grimm it was from Luther to Goethe; that is, from about 1550 to what were for him modern times—and even then he was criticized for skimp-ing the nineteenth century. Littré's ordered description begins at 1600, and Matthias de Vries initially took the Dutch authorized version of the Bible in 1637 as his boundary, though this was moved back to 1500 in the course of publication.

To record a thousand years of continuous word history is one thing. To focus on and characterize a more or less homogeneous 'modern' phase lasting some three hundred years is quite another, even when the earlier record of a word may be separately represented as in the sections marked *Hist.* in Littré or in Grimm's extended etymological discussions. Total national chronological coverage, as a lexicographical option, has perhaps left the *OED* with less room for other matters (idiom, for instance, collocation, and synonymy), and has seemingly led to other features in which editorial practice has differed sharply from that of the European homologues.

One of these is the treatment of spelling. The *OED* is unique in presenting as a fixed feature within the lemma a structured chronological overview of the known spelt forms of the word. The other dictionaries go no further than incidental comments on variant (and sometimes older) forms, though Littré does retain Old French spellings in the quotations given in his historical sections. The remarkable lists of spellings in the *OED* (a godsend to editors of older texts) are often very long (24 variants for *emperor*; a combinatorial possibility of 429 spellings for *neighbour*) and usefully they include even scribal oddities such as *esssse* 'ash' from the *Ayenbite of Inwyt*. The other dictionaries were in any case focusing on a phase in the language in which spelling was more settled: De Vries specifically declined to include Middle Dutch because he felt the multitude of dialect forms might crowd out the modern language. By devising the highly compact spelling analyses Murray produced a neat solution to what could have been a similar problem in English.

In the matter of pronunciation the *OED* (perhaps rather oddly) operates much as any modern dictionary. It provides the reader with a careful record of contemporary spoken forms (these now in turn constitute quite a useful record of mid-nineteenth-century pronunciation, drifting gradually into early twentieth-century renderings as you go through the alphabet) and the stress patterns in compounds and derivations are also most faithfully given. Is this a task for the historical dictionary? Grimm and De Vries did not think so; Littré did include the modern pronunciation of French, though probably mainly to get in his pretty frequent prescriptive comments. Given that pronunciation is to be treated at all in a historical dictionary, one might expect to find a discussion of historical changes alongside modern forms in a regular slot. As it is, the occasional comments on former pronunciations, such as that *balcony* was stressed on the middle syllable until *c.*1825, occur elsewhere in the lemma.

Brevity in quotation is another characteristic feature of the *OED*. Murray's citations from Shakespeare, for instance, are whittled down to eight or nine words on average, often mere snippets—no room there for anything like the readable chunks of Schiller's poetry that brighten up the pages of Grimm, or Littré's lengthy philosophical passages from Voltaire. This disciplined functional use of quotation goes with the practice (from the start, in the *OED*) of authenticating each and every sense and subsense of a word, and doing it if needed for a thousand years.

The *OED* is unique also in providing from the very beginning—and in bold face too—dates for all the quotations that are taken up: in the *DWB* and *WNT* this happens only in the later volumes. The urge to do this may be seen to arise naturally from the strikingly heterogeneous character of writings drawn on (not only 'nos classiques'), and especially from the inclusion of writers from the remotest ages. But precise dating also promotes a sharper definition of the contemporary. It is a legitimate ideal for the historical lexicographer to cover the whole reach of each word's history, with evidence of the earliest possible instance and of the latest possible instance as well: zero antedating, zero postdating. Murray clearly achieves this more fully than his rivals: where he pinpointed the contemporary, they aspired rather to define the modern. He also (along with up-to-date pronunciation) allowed for a somewhat inflated illustration of modern-day English, with clusters of very recent quotations which go beyond the needs of mere historical record: the verb *to branch*, for instance, with quotations going back to the year 1400, has *five* illustrations for the nineteenth century, including two from the 1870s and one from 1884 (the fascicle was published in 1886).

But the alphabet is a hard taskmaster. Though the editors of the *OED* (partly no doubt through Trench's vision and the early establishment of satisfactory *canones lexicographici*) were able to avoid regrettable methodological changes, the long passage of editorial years from A to Z is revealed starkly in the text because of their sharper focus on the contemporary. If you have a closed corpus from the start the material at the end of the alphabet may be out of date when you get there. But if (as in the *OED*) you have a kind of creeping corpus, the language you are describing at Z is very different from the one which seemed so brand-new when you were busied about A, and the more up to date you wish to be, the more it will show. For Littré (who finished quickly), as well as for the Grimms and De Vries, this editorial problem of the hybrid modern and historical dictionary was less acute because they took a more relaxed view of what 'modern' meant.

REFERENCES

Aitken, A. J. (1987). 'The Period Dictionaries', in R. W. Burchfield (ed.), *Studies in Lexicography*. Oxford: Clarendon Press, 94–116.
Bahr, J. (1991). 'Periodik der Wörterbuchbearbeitung: Veränderungen von Wörter-buchkonzeptionen und -praxis', in Kirkness *et al.* (eds.), 1–50.
Bailey, R. W. (1990). 'The period dictionary. III: English', in F. J. Hausmann, O. Reichmann, and H. E. Wiegand (eds.), *Wörterbücher/Dictionaries/Dictionnaires. Ein internationales Handbuch zur Lexikographie*. Berlin: De Gruyter, 2, 1436–56.
Hamburger, J. (1988). *Monsieur Littré*. Paris: Flammarion.
Horlitz, B. (1991). 'Deutsches Wörterbuch—Hausbuch der Nation? Probleme der Benutzung und Benutzungsmöglichkeiten', in Kirkness *et al.* (eds.), 407–33.
Kirkness, A. (1980). *Geschichte des Deutschen Wörterbuchs 1838–1863. Dokumente zu den Lexikographen Grimm*. Stuttgart: Hirzel.

Kirkness, A., Kühn, P. and Wiegand, H. E. (eds.) (1991). *Studien zum Deutschen Wörterbuch von Jacob Grimm und Wilhelm Grimm*. Tübingen: Niemeyer.

Kühn, P. (1991). ' " . . . wir wollen kein Gesetzbuch machen". Die normativen Kommentare Jacob Grimms im Deutschen Wörterbuch', in Kirkness *et al.* (eds.), 105–68.

Matoré, G. (1968). *Histoire des Dictionnaires Français*. Paris: Larousse.

Moerdijk, A. (1994). *Handleiding bij het Woordenboek der Nederlandsche Taal (WNT)*. The Hague: Sdu.

Quemada, B. (1972). 'Lexicology and lexicography', in T. A. Sebeok (ed.). *Current Trends in Linguistics*, 9, 395–475.

Reichmann, O. (1991). 'Zum Urbegriff in den Bedeutungserläuterungen Jacob Grimms (auch im Unterschied zur Bedeutungsdefinition bei Daniel Sanders)', in Kirkness *et al.* (eds.), 299–352.

Rey, A. (1970). *Littré, l'Humaniste et les Mots*. Paris: Gallimard.

Schiewe, J. (1991). 'Fach- und Wissenschaftssprachen im Deutschen Wörterbuch', in Kirkness *et al.* (eds.), 225–61.

Schleicher, A. (1863). *Die Darwinische Theorie und die Sprachwissenschaft*. Weimar: Böhlau.

Sterkenburg, P. G. J. van (1978). 'Nederlandse lexicografie en taalwetenschap', in B. P. F. Al and P. G. J. van Sterkenburg (eds.), *Wetenschap en Woordenschat*. Muiderberg: Coutinho, 86–104.

—— (1992). *Het Woordenboek der Nederlandsche Taal. Portret van een taalmonument*. The Hague: Sdu.

Trench, R. C. (1860). *On Some Deficiencies in our English Dictionaries* (2nd rev. edn.). London: John W. Parker & Son.

Zgusta, L. (1989). 'The Oxford English Dictionary and other Dictionaries (Aikakošyam)', *International Journal of Lexicography*, 2: 188–230.

5

Time and Meaning: Sense and Definition in the *OED*

PENNY SILVA

Eighteenth-century theories of meaning, philosophical and a priori in nature, 'began with the mental categories and sought their exemplification in language, as in universal grammar, and based etymology on conjectures about the origin of language' (Aarsleff 1967: 127). The source of the 'true' or 'original' meaning of words lay in their etymologies—but in this philosophical approach, etymological work was 'a matter of discovery through skill, rather than knowledge through study' (Aarsleff 1967: 248). John Horne Tooke, the master of what Dugald Stewart termed 'etymological metaphysics' (Aarsleff 1967: 107), exercised a powerful influence in late eighteenth- and early nineteenth-century thinking about language in Britain. For Horne Tooke, the etymology—that is, the 'primordial meaning revealed by it'—comprised 'all the senses of the word and those of all its derivations' (Zgusta 1991: 599). Yet the meaning of words was also the basic tool by which etymologies could be discovered, and imaginative postulations—'a fabric of conjectures' (Murray 1900: 118)—sometimes resulted:

A *bar* in all its uses, is a defence: that by which any thing is fortified, strengthened, or defended. A *barn* (*bar-en*, *bar'n*) is a covered inclosure, in which the grain &c. is protected or defended from the weather, from depredations &c. A *baron* is an armed, defenceful, or powerful man. A *barge* is a strong boat. A *bargain* is a confirmed, strengthened agreement . . . A *bark* is a stout vessel. The *bark* of a tree is its defence . . . The *bark* of a dog is that by which we are defended from that animal. (Horne Tooke 1805: 182–3, in Aarsleff 1967: 63–4)

For eighteenth- and early nineteenth-century lexicographers, meaning and etymology were indivisible: Nathaniel Bailey, in his *Universal Etymological English Dictionary* of 1721, attempted to show the 'true' meaning of words through their etymologies, and Samuel Johnson's *Dictionary of the English Language* (1755) followed Bailey's precepts. Johnson defined an etymologist as 'one skilled in searching out the true Interpretation of Words', and saw etymology as exhibiting 'the Original of Words, in order to distinguish their true Meaning and Signification' (1824: 20–1). Charles Richardson wrote in the Preface to his *New Dictionary of the English Language* (1836–7: 41) that 'each one word has one radical meaning, and one only'; that 'in the Etymology of each word must be found this single intrinsic meaning'; and that 'when the intrinsic meaning is fixed, every lexicographical object is firmly secured'.

Considering this legacy of interwoven etymology and meaning, one of the considerable achievements of the *OED* was the separation of etymological research from semantics, as an independent discipline requiring rigorous empirical investigation.[1] Murray was critical of the fanciful etymological constructs of earlier lexicographers such as Noah Webster, who, 'like many other clever men, had the notion that derivations can be elaborated from one's own consciousness as well as definitions' (1900: 118). Despite Murray's claim that defining came 'from one's own consciousness', the defining work of the *OED* editors was more intimately bound up with both etymological research, and with the analysis of quotations excerpted from texts, than any earlier work. Murray described the preparation of the *OED* as characterized by 'original work, patient induction of facts, minute verification of evidence', suited to 'the scientific and historical spirit of the nineteenth century' (1900: 120–1). In the *OED*, although etymology and meaning were indeed bound together, the method of discovery was not through the imaginative metaphysics of Horne Tooke or Webster, but by the careful investigation of etymology, and of each word's forms and uses in excerpted quotations, through time. In Murray's words:

In one sense an investigation of the etymology is a preliminary to the historical treatment of a word within the language; we must know its previous history in order to have a known point from which to start in the development of the forms and senses; in another sense the complete exhibition of the etymology is only possible after we know the history within the language, the decision between two or more *à priori* [*sic*] possible etymologies depending upon the historical forms and senses of the word itself . . . No history of the forms and senses within the language can be exhibited which does not start from an accurate account of the form, sense, and conditions under which the word entered the language.   (1884: 511)

This conscious turning away from eighteenth-century thinking in English lexicographical methodology has been attributed to Liddell and Scott's *Greek–English Lexicon* of 1843—a translation of Franz Passow's 1819 revision of J. G. Schneider's *Kritisches griechisch–deutsches Handwörterbuch*. Passow's principles were evoked by Dean Richard Chenevix Trench in his lectures of 1857, and were reflected in the Philological Society's *Proposal for the Publication of a New English Dictionary*

---

[1] The *OED*'s methodological separation of etymology and semantics is represented in a concrete manner in the editorial process of compiling *OED3*, a project planned for the years 1993–2010. Each existing entry (excluding the etymology) is edited by a general reviser, who incorporates relevant new data and either confirms or emends the definitions and sense-ordering. The entry is subsequently reconsidered by an etymologist, who, after revising the etymology (frequently with considerable amendment), checks that there is a logical development of the senses flowing out of the new etymology, and that the existing sense-ordering holds.

(1859): 'The theory of lexicography we profess is that which Passow was the first to enunciate clearly and put in practice successfully—viz., "that every word should be made to tell its own story" ' (Aarsleff 1967: 255). In other words:

In the treatment of individual words the historical principle will be uniformly adopted;—that is to say, we shall endeavour to show more clearly and fully than has hitherto been done, or even attempted, the development of the sense or various senses of each word from its etymology and from each other, so as to bring into clear light the common thread which unites all together.   ([Philological Society] 1859: 4)

The *Canones Lexicographici; or Rules to be Observed in Editing the New English Dictionary* of 1860 (OED/MISC/89/5: 6–7) reiterated these principles, which, together with the work of John Jamieson (embodied in his *Etymological Dictionary of the Scottish Language* of 1808) provided the theoretical framework for James Murray when he began work on the *OED* in 1878. It was a framework ideally suited to Victorian scholarship, with its Darwinian world view and its commitment to 'scientific' methodology. In the *OED* Murray attempted 'to marry the empiricism of the "new philology" to the rationalism of the Enlightenment' (represented, for instance, in John Locke's theory of language development from concrete to abstract (Zgusta 1991: 599)), and the dictionary reflects 'an implicit theory of language in which reason acts as the guide for the development of word signification' (Hultin 1985: 41). It was within this philosophical scaffolding that the *OED* semantic methodology was crafted—largely Murray's achievement, despite his modest description of the *OED* as the product of an evolutionary process (1900: 119)—as if the dictionary had 'emerged from the invisible forces of differentiation and speciation then triumphing in the biological sciences' (Bailey 1993: 1). It was Murray who, as designer of this complex structure based on historical principles, inherited Trench's blueprint and interpreted it—selecting from it and expanding upon it. In 1915 the Delegates of the Press acknowledged that it was Murray who 'laid the lines and drew the plan of the Dictionary' (*CWW*: 313). Therefore, while the significant contribution of Bradley, Craigie, and Onions is recognized, Murray is the main focus of this chapter.

Earlier dictionaries played an important role in the *OED* defining process, the 'general excellence of their definitions' offering valuable assistance (Murray 1884: 509). Samuel Johnson's style of defining, and his entry layout (which included both sense-numbers and illustrative quotations), influenced the *OED* editors considerably (Simpson 27/12/97).[2] The dictionaries of Johnson and Webster were among those used constantly as reference works in the Scriptorium (*CWW*: 298), and Murray also acknowledged his debt to Bailey, Todd, and other early lexicographers for their 'original work which has become the common property of all

---

[2] The considerable assistance given by John Simpson and Edmund Weiner (respectively Chief Editor and Deputy Chief Editor of *OED3* while this chapter was being written) is gratefully acknowledged. References to 'Simpson' and 'Weiner', followed by a date in the format '27/12/98', indicate personal communications on email.

their successors' (Murray 1888: p. xxi). The *OED* editors excerpted definitions from existing dictionaries and included them verbatim, with acknowledgement—a convention which saved time (*CWW*: 259), showed the modern reader how earlier lexicographers defined words which were contemporaneous with them (Simpson 4/9/98), and reflected rare words not found elsewhere.[3] Johnson's work was a particularly productive mine for the *OED*, his dictionary providing over 1,500 definitions. Murray lauded Johnson as having 'contributed to the evolution of the modern dictionary' by 'the illustration of the use of each word by a selection of literary quotations, and the more delicate appreciation and discrimination of senses which this involved and rendered possible' (1900: 116). Noah Webster, 'a born definer of words' (Murray 1900: 118), was used particularly (but not exclusively) for definitions of American terms. Nathaniel Bailey characteristically provided the sole (or first) example of rare or obsolete words such as *Abregation* ('A separation from the flock', Bailey, vol. II, 1731. App. never used). Sometimes more than one borrowed definition was provided (*Adversable*: 'That is adverse or contrary to.' Bailey, vol. II, 1731. 'Contrary, opposite to.' J[ohnson] 1755. 'Capable of being opposed.' Ash 1775). Borrowed definitions were also used to supplement *OED* defining text (*Abdication*, sense 4: Resignation or abandonment, either formal or virtual, of sovereignty or other high trust. 'It is used when there is only an implicit Renunciation, as when a Person does Actions that are altogether inconsistent with his Trust.' Bailey 1721).

While recognizing the considerable achievements of earlier lexicographers, Murray justly commented that 'for the "history" of words and families of words, and for the changes of form and sense which words had historically passed through, they gave hardly any help whatever. No one could find out from all the dictionaries extant how long any particular word had been in the language, which of the many senses in which words were used was the original, or how or when these many senses had been developed' (1900: 119). In 1857 Trench had similarly elaborated on the shortcomings of the treatment of meaning in English dictionaries, the central issue being that important meanings and uses of words had been missed, leading to a 'maimed and incomplete, or even unintelligible' word-history. 'It is one of the primary demands which we make upon a Dictionary, that it should thus present us with the history of words, the significant phases of meaning through which they have travelled', Trench wrote (1860: 3–4). In this context the specimen entries prepared by Murray for the publisher Macmillan in 1876 were for a number of reasons unlike any of the earlier dictionaries: 'or, perhaps, they were like nearly all of them combined' (Bailey 1993: 7). Murray's specimen entry for *Carriage* prefigured the *OED* tree-structure of senses treated in a combination of historical and logical ordering, a considerable innovation—as would be the great advance in sense-differentiation and inclusiveness. (The word *Cat*, for example,

---

[3] This practice will not be retained in *OED3*: new definitions will be written, and all useful cited definitions will be included among the quotations (Simpson 27/12/97).

defined by Bailey and Johnson in one sense, and by Webster in four, appeared in the OED with eighteen main senses and twenty-six subsenses, including numerous phrases and attributive uses, and fifty-four combinations.) For Murray, defining was the 'real work' (see Chapter 1).

The writing of OED definitions was a process which had always passed through several stages and filters. In 1862 Frederick Furnivall had introduced unqualified, voluntary subeditors to the task of sorting the Philological Society's slips into senses and providing preliminary definitions. Murray found much of this work unusable, and consequently his practice was to restrict these more complex tasks to his experienced subeditors in the Scriptorium (*CWW*: 138, 199–200)—although volunteer readers were asked to note 'a short definition, if convenient' on the slips (*CWW*: 347; see also Chapter 2). In 1880 Murray announced that the OED was 'able to accept offers from those competent to sub-edit portions of the material, i.e. . . . to sub-divide words into their meanings, and determine the order and affiliation of these, and to write trial definitions, to expedite the editor's work' (1880: 130). He later reported that about thirty subeditors had volunteered (Murray 1888: p. vi), and that much of their work, 'so far as the discrimination and arrangement of the senses are concerned', would need little modification (1884: 518). According to Murray's description, a subeditor divided the slips for a large entry into '20, 30 or 40 groups' (with provisional definitions provided). These went to young helpers to sort into chronological order, and subsequently to more experienced assistants to sort into parts of speech and senses. The subeditor then subdivided the senses further (attaching a preliminary definition to each sense), and spread the batches out 'on a table or on the floor where he can obtain a general survey of the whole', and spent many hours 'shifting them about like pieces on a chess-board, striving to find in the fragmentary evidence of an incomplete historical record, such a sequence of meanings as may form a logical chain of development'. No systematic defining methodology was set down for subeditors, but no doubt Aristotle's analysis of defining was familiar to the OED staff, and the technique of defining a word as part of a class (by *genus*) and then distinguishing it from all other members of that class (by *differentiae*), was well known (Landau 1989: 120). As discussed in Chapter 2, a document entitled 'Directions to Sub-Editors' (in several versions) outlined the basic practical steps to be followed in terms of sense-division, definition, and arrangement. 'Directions for Re-Sub-editors' (OED/MISC/91/11) instructed that they 'read through the sub-editor's definitions, and master his plan of the word', warning that there might be reason, 'either from the new slips or from your own observation, to modify the definitions or re-arrange the meanings'. The re-subeditors inserted new quotations and improved both definitions and sense-ordering as necessary. Finally, the editor himself checked the work, subdividing the senses further, improving the definitions as he saw fit, selecting the best quotations, and adding the etymology and pronunciation (Murray 1884: 509–10; *CWW*: 186–7).

Relinquishing editorial control was difficult for Murray, even once Henry Bradley had been appointed as second editor; for while Murray respected Bradley greatly for his etymological skills, he was concerned at his inexperience as a definer:

Dog's Parsley has sent me to see how you have treated *Fool's parsley*, the now usual name. *I* should make it a Main-word . . . I think the explanation ought to be thus 'Fool's Parsley, [the common name of?] a poisonous umbelliferous weed, *Æthusa Cynapium*; also called *Lesser Hemlock* and formerly *Dog's Parsley*. Hence, a book-name of the genus *Æthusa*.' (OED/EP/MURRA/4)

Although in this case Bradley did not follow the proffered advice (leaving *Fool's Parsley* at *Fool sb.*, sense 7c), he initially relied a great deal on Murray, and begged him to check all his proofs—which at first required considerable correcting and redrafting (*CWW*: 262–4). Subsequently, Craigie's treatment of senses also received Murray's editorial attention. 'I see you have had a severe fight with *Run*,' Murray wrote in December 1909: 'There are some points I would like you to consider . . . I see you have found it difficult to mark off the branches', after which his own suggested framework for the entry was offered (OED/EP/MURRA/30.i). His tone was at times imperious: 'I see that you made no mention of Prince Regent under *Regent* sb. or a., not even a cross-reference to Prince, although you use it in one definition. It looks as if you had studied to avoid it. Had you no quotations?' (OED/EP/MURRA/22). Craigie exasperated Murray by exceeding space limits, and Murray appears to have seen his advice as being ignored. In an acerbic communication in December 1902 he wrote: 'No part of my work is so onerous and unpleasant to me as that of looking through your copy, which has consumed many many hours of the year. I should be infinitely glad to have done with it . . . If you would earnestly set yourself to making my work unnecessary, it might soon be done' (OED/MISC/12/24.ii).

Elisabeth Murray described her grandfather's particular skill as being the ability 'to trace the history of a word in its changing usage from century to century and to write, with the utmost economy of words, definitions which summarise the fruits of profound research' (*CWW*: 284). The 'utmost economy' was imposed on Murray by the Delegates: yet it was necessary that definitions should pay each definiendum due regard, and it could be argued that at times economy was carried too far. As Weiner (14/7/98) has observed, Murray tended to compress under one heading many senses which the other editors would have separated out: for example, whereas at *Speak* a sequence of phrasal verb subentries was recognized, the uses of *Talk* v. with adverbs and prepositions were treated as phrases subsumed under main senses.

Predictably, discovering and describing the meanings of words was to present many challenges. For example, defining Middle English senses and uses was itself pioneering territory (Murray 1884: 509). Thousands of other terms were unfamiliar, many being obsolete, or obscure: 'There remains the queried sense 2 of

[*Trance*] sb.[3], which I do not understand at all. Do you? "The trances & the wind-laces of the first Iesuites"', wrote Murray to Craigie in 1913 (OED/MISC/12/86); this sense was finally omitted. Specialized terms from many areas of activity required expert advice: 'Under *amble* . . . I had a great deal of correspondence & help from the Jockey Club through Lord Aldenham, etc., and satisfied all English jockeys with the definition' (OED/EP/MURRA/8). Many words were highly technical in nature: those from the sciences required a distinctive defining vocabulary (*Acetanilide*: A compound of aniline in union with the radical acetyl, forming an acetamide with the radical phenyl. $C_6H_5.NH.C_2H_3O$. Less correctly *acetaniline*). Editors needed assistance with legal terms: Murray wrote to Craigie, 'All your definitions in [*Real*] 6a, b, c, leave much to be desired, and rather fail to seize the point. An advowson is real property, so is a heritable *title* as duke or baronet. A *lease* is real property in Scotl. but not in Eng.' Murray spent four months working on *Personal* and its legal implications, and was relieved when it was finally approved by several consultants (OED/EP/MURRA/16). The extent of Murray's correspondence with experts from many disciplines, and in various parts of the world, in obtaining assistance with technical, archaic, regional, or specialized words, was extraordinary. The definitions of words which might cause offence required particularly careful treatment: sexual and religious terms were always controversial (*CWW*: 195). Craigie's entry for *Roman Catholic* provoked correspondence from Murray because Craigie had 'made *Roman Catholic* a subordinate entry to *Catholic* in one of its senses to most Englishmen a sectarian sense', which Murray's neighbour, Sir John Hawkins, felt would 'provoke an angry outcry from many English churchmen'. 'I do not feel that I could allow it to pass without an appeal to the Delegates', Murray warned:

It might all be avoided by your wording the definitions thus (which are substantially what all Dictionaries have): A. *sb.* A member or adherent of the Roman Church; = CATHOLIC sb.[2]. B. *adj.* Of or belonging to the Church of Rome or Roman Church; = CATHOLIC a[7]. This, I think, is perfectly void of offence . . . and would be approved by all the Delegates before whom I have quite unofficially brought the matter.   (OED/EP/MURRA/27)

Here Murray's advice was followed to the letter.

Yet another challenge was provided by the idiosyncratic or mistaken use of words, and two prominent poets were among the guilty. Murray commented crustily of Robert Browning that he 'constantly used words without regard to their proper meaning', and had 'added greatly to the difficulties of the dictionary'; and the meaning of Tennyson's *balm-cricket* was the subject of correspondence (*CWW*: 201, 235; see also Chapter 1).

Defining is a multi-dimensional discipline, and no defining manual is able to codify all possible features without losing 'the spontaneity of lexicographical creation' (Simpson 27/12/97). However, despite the apparent absence of established rules for defining the various categories of headword, patterns did emerge, and it seems likely that the *OED* editors developed definition prototypes which they used as models for similar headwords without seeing the need to codify the process. Discernible *OED* defining patterns include the following:

1. The *OED* editors observed the basic rule that the form of the definition should reflect the grammatical function of the headword—that grammatically the definition should be able to replace the headword. So while Johnson used the noun-defining convention 'That which . . .' to define adjectives (*Abditive*: That which has the power or quality of hiding), the *OED* substituted the more appropriate present participle construction (Having the power or quality of hiding). At *Abandon, -oun(e)*, sb.¹, sense 2, the confusion caused by the use of verbal and adjectival elements in the strange definition (To do a thing *in* or *at abandoun*: recklessly, impetuously, unreservedly, lavishly) resulted from the not yet mature treatment of the noun occurring in a phrase.

2. In defining verbs, the infinitive form 'To—' was consistently used, and senses were marked as transitive and intransitive—generally at main- or subsense level (see *Rock* v.¹), but also at branch level—a structure frequently chosen by Craigie (see *Smile* v.) despite Murray's disapproval:

> Your separation of the intrans. & trans. senses [of *Run* v.], with the prepl. & advbial senses in between . . . is a new departure in the Dictionary, and one which I think is much to be deprecated for practical reasons . . . There seems to us no historical ground for it: the first of your trans. branches, seems to all of us here, quite to belong in history to the intrans., & naturally to follow on from it.   (OED/EP/MURRA/30.i)

Sense-division by transitivity was indeed counter-historical, as transitivity is not a strongly entrenched feature of English verbs, and semantic change carries on despite—and indeed partly *through*—change in transitivity (Weiner 17/6/98).

3. In defining adjectives, a range of formats was applied: definition by synonym, generally in addition to a defining sentence (*Angry*, sense 1: Full of trouble actively; troublesome, vexatious, annoying, trying, sharp); the wording 'Of', 'Of or like' (*Cordy*: Of or like cord), or variations on the construction 'Of or pertaining to' (also '. . . designating', '. . . belonging to'), which made its appearance early in the text (*Abbatial* provides the first occurrence); 'That' (*Swerving ppl. a.*: That swerves; deviating; making a swerve; diverted from the straight or right path); or introducing the definition with the present participle of an appropriate verb, for example, 'having' or 'being' (*Able*, sense 4: Having the qualifications for, and means of, doing anything; having sufficient *power*). 'Capable of being' was a formula commonly used for adjectives ending in *-able* or *-ible* (see *Saleable*, *Flexible*).

4. Adverb definitions were characteristically introduced by prepositions, for example, 'In a – manner', 'With [+ abstract noun]' (*Angrily*, sense 2: In an angry or wrathful manner, with anger or open resentment), 'By' (*Binocularly*: By the simultaneous employment of both eyes), or defined by synonym (*Angrily*, sense 1: Vexatiously, grievously).

5. Noun definitions varied a great deal in methodology, shape, and range of content, according to both the object being defined, and the judgement of the definer. Both adjectives and clauses were used to qualify the definiendum (*Bedtick*: A large flat quadrangular bag or case, into which feathers, hair, straw, chaff, or other substances are put to form a bed), and quasi-synonyms were added where appropriate to supplement the definition (*Pain, sb.*[1], sense 1: Suffering or loss inflicted for a crime or offence; punishment; penalty; a fine). Frequently-used formulae included 'The action of' (*Swoon*: The action of swooning or the condition of one who has swooned; syncope), 'One who' for agentive nouns (*Abjurer*: One who abjures or forswears), and 'Each of a number' (*Grave, sb.*[3], sense b: In certain parts of Yorkshire and Lincolnshire, each of a number of administrative officials formerly elected by the inhabitants of a township). Several defining formulas were properly part of the metalanguage—'A name for' (*Article, sb.*, sense 16: A name for the adjectives *the* (Definite Article) and *a, an* (Indefinite Article), and their equivalents in other languages), 'A name given to' (*Grimalkin*: A name given to a cat; hence, a cat, *esp.* an old she-cat), and 'Used *attrib*' (*Antagonist*, sense 5: Used *attrib.* as sb. in apposition, or adj.: = ANTAGONISTIC). Regular formats were developed in defining particular lexical sets (such as colours, or the names of peoples, plants, or minerals): for example, definitions for the colours of the rainbow (except for *Violet*) mentioned their place in the spectrum, and (except for *Indigo*) gave examples of objects from nature in which the colours might be observed. Definitions of plants characteristically included many qualifying words, and took the form 'A plant of the genus—', followed by the taxonomic information, and distinguishing details of size, colour, inflorescence, and provenance (*Tamarisk*: A plant of the genus *Tamarix*, esp. *T. gallica*, the Common Tamarisk (called in L. *myrica* . . .), a graceful evergreen shrub or small tree, with slender feathery branches and minute scalelike leaves, growing in sandy places in S. Europe and W. Asia).

These and other defining patterns established a rhythm (by repeated formulas and a consistent, predictable definition 'shape' for each word-category) which was of considerable assistance to the dictionary user. As Simpson (30/12/97) observes, the formulaic nature of definitions and what becomes (to an editor) the sing-song nature of the definition text is crucial to the success of the dictionary entry. The definition has to have one of several rhythms: the rhythm might be complex, but it helps the reader to understand the definition—not as an abstract scientific or strictly logical construct but as something which flows, a suitable substitute for the defined term. If the definition is successful, the rhythm is imperceptible to the reader—see, for example, the definition at *Heaven, sb.*, sense 1 (The expanse in which the sun, moon, and stars, are seen, which has the appearance of a vast vault or canopy overarching the earth, on the 'face' or surface of which the clouds seem to lie or float; the sky, the firmament). The poetic and archaic wording is a separate issue from the rhythm discovered by the definer, for a similar rhythm can be discerned at *Laugh*, *v.*, despite the definition's 'scientific' approach:

To manifest the combination of bodily phenomena (spasmodic utterance of inarticulate sounds, facial distortion, shaking of the sides, etc.) which forms the instinctive expression of mirth or of sense of something ludicrous, and which can also be occasioned by certain physical sensations, esp. that produced by tickling.

If the rhythm is awkward, or atonal, then the definition fails, and needs reworking (Simpson 30/12/97). *Blottesque* (sense a) provides an example of a failed definition (Of painting: Characterized by blotted touches heavily laid on. *fig.* of descriptive writing. (It belongs to the 'phraseology' of Art-Criticism.)). A comparison of the attempted definition of *Comb*, *sb.*[1], sense 3d submitted by a consultant (version *a* below) with the final definition composed by Murray (version *b*) illustrates the difference between successful and unsuccessful defining:

a. A structure found in those mineral veins, which are made up of plates, differing in composition and lying parallel to the walls of the vein (OED/BL/329/70).
b. A comb-like structure found in mineral veins which are made up of plates or layers parallel to their walls.

Another area which depends a great deal upon the sensitivity and judgement of the individual lexicographer is sense-division—what definers term 'lumping' (broad, inclusive defining) and 'splitting' (fine sense-discrimination). Decisions on the distinction between full sense and subsense, on the role played by context in determining sense-division, and indeed on how far the fineness of sense-division should be taken, are open to dispute. Henry Bradley, reviewing the first fascicle of the *OED* before he joined the project, believed that in sense-differentiation the editors had achieved the happy medium between Littré and Grimm (1884: 105). However, Craigie divided senses to a degree which Murray saw as excessive, and in a fierce letter instructing Craigie to reduce the length of his text, Murray demanded 'reduction of the number of senses and sub-senses, esp. by making definitions broad enough to cover the latter, and abandonment as far as possible of the contextual distinctions introduced by "Of persons" "Of animals" "Of qualities", etc. etc.' He continued: 'As Dean Liddell said to me long ago "Everybody can make distinctions: it is the lexicographer's business to make broad definitions which embrace them; the synthetic power is far above the analytic".' (OED/MISC/12/24.ii). Bradley referred to the matter of individual judgement in sense-differentiation while bemoaning the shortage of data. 'Sometimes I am uncertain whether a shade of meaning, represented for us only by a bad quotation, is found in more extended use or not', he wrote: 'In such cases, it is practically a comment on the quotation if we either place it as the sole example of a sense *b* or incorporate the special shade of meaning in the main definition, with a parenthetical reference to the quotation. I have been fearful of leaving any real sense of a word unrepresented in the Dict.' (MP/15/11/1886). Bradley's editorial note at *Grig, sb.*[1] (sense 4) revealed his ambivalence: 'The genuineness of this sense is doubtful, as the dialect glossaries containing it usually quote as their sole example the phrase "merry as a grig" '.

In *OED* defining text there are many examples of sense-division based upon the *function* ascribed to the word, rather than upon the intrinsic *meaning* of the word in the quotation. In his detailed examination of *Back, sb.*[1], Zgusta (1989: 210) suggests that the earliest quotations at sense 2a (The hinder surface of the body, ... turned upon those who are left behind [*c.*885]) and sense 2c (The part of the body which bears burdens [*c.*950]) might be placed under the 'original' sense, sense 1 (The convex surface of the body of man and vertebrated animals which is adjacent to the spinal axis, and opposite to the belly and most of the special organs, [*c.*1000]), thus solving the problem of dislocation in the dates of these senses. However, if the fine sense-distinctions by function are accepted as valid, then the two early quotations do indeed belong at 2a and 2c, and the problem of dates is unsolved unless research discovers new evidence.

The techniques of defining are mastered through practice, and a comparison of the earlier parts of the *OED* with the later bears this out: the letter A may be seen as experimental, embodying features which were subsequently discarded or improved. Indeed, Murray expressed the belief that A and E (the latter being Bradley's first volume) were the two weakest letters in the *OED* (*CWW*: 263). The shape and metalanguage of defining were still evolving, and there is often the impression of an *ad hoc*, disjointed structure (Weiner 1/6/98). This experimental stage of defining was characterized by many oddities. For example, the plural form of a headword was defined when the word was capable of being defined in the singular (*Apostle spoons*: Old-fashioned silver spoons, the handles of which end in figures of the Apostles.). A Biblical or poetic ring is noticeable in some early definitions, for example at *Apple* sense 4 ('The fruit of that forbidden tree, whose mortal taste brought death into the world, and all our woe' (Milton)). There can be a looseness and discursiveness in early defining text, as at *Abaft adv.* sense 2:

Of position: *literally*, back, behind, in the rear. From an early period, it seems to have been confined to a ship (in reference to which its immediate source *baft* is also found in the 14th c.); the bows are the foremost, and the stern the *aft*ermost part, hence *abaft* means 'In the after part or stern half of the ship'.

Prescriptive statements were made, as at *Abthainry* (As the office itself was the Abthaine, the words ABTHAINRY and ABTHANAGE are unnecessary, and should be disused); occasionally explanations of *OED* conventions were inserted into entries, as at *After-*, sense 1 (Words in **clarendon** are treated specially under **II.**, those in SMALL-CAPITALS in their alphabetical order); definitions were treated as adjuncts to a preceding entry rather than as independent entities—for example *ABC sb.* was followed by a small, idiosyncratic entry for the verbal form (**ABC**, or **abee-cee** is even found as a vb. 'to say the alphabet'). In rare cases, there was no definition at all—for example, the entry following *ABC* [v.]: **ABC process** (in making artificial manure). The definition at *Advowry* (A variant of the word more commonly spelt AVOWRY) illustrates a deviation from subsequent methodology in which a variant spelling and its quotations are not entered separately, but subsumed in the main entry. And, as the final illustration, simple derivatives (for example, *Abasedly* from *Abased*, and *Abasing* from *Abase*) were entered and defined as main words in the first fascicle, and into the second. The practice of subsuming derivatives into main entries, using 'Hence' to introduce a final paragraph, was implemented only at *Archbishop*. Until this point—and indeed beyond it—'hence' was used to introduce sense developments (Weiner 1989: 26–7) such as:

• transferred or figurative uses (*Aaron, sb.*,[1]): Proper name of the patriarch of the Jewish priesthood; hence used of a leader of the church.
• new senses—in the following example (*Affect, v.*[1]) the 'hence' phrase falls between two senses (**5.** To show ostentatiously a liking for; to make an ostentatious use or display of; to take upon oneself artificially or for effect, to assume. [quotations] **b.** To assume the character of (a person).[quotations] **c.** with *inf.*: To 'profess' take upon one. [quotations] Hence, by imperceptible gradations, **6.** To put on a pretence of; to assume a false appearance of, to counterfeit or pretend . . .).
• sub-senses (*Abandon, -oun, adv.*, sense 2: At one's own discretion, at one's will, without interference or interruption from others. Hence, **a.** Unrestrictedly, freely, recklessly, with all one's might, in full career. **b.** Unstintedly, entirely, wholly. **c.** Without bounds, to the fullest extent).
• derived phrases (*Aback, adv.*, sense 3: *Naut.* Said of the sails of a ship, when laid back against the mast, with the wind bearing against their front surfaces . . . [quotations] Hence the nautical phrase **To be taken aback** . . .).

Several defining techniques which were applied consistently in the *OED* are no longer accepted practice. For example, the defining text was often made up of more than one sentence, where the modern practice would either create a note (*Angild*: In O.E. law, payment in composition or atonement for injury. (Erroneously taken by later writers as meaning 'single payment', as if OE. were *ángild*)), or include a new sense or subsense (*Abbot*, sense 1: The head or superior of an abbey. After the dissolution of the monasteries, sometimes applied to the layman to whom the revenues of an abbacy were impropriated). Frequently, several senses were listed in a single definition, separated only by semi-colons (as at *Astrobolism*: Sudden paralysis attributed to the malign influence of a planet or star; sunstroke; blasting of plants in the dog-days). Defining text, metalanguage, and labelling were interwoven (*Attorney, sb.*,[1] sense 1: One appointed or ordained to act for another . . . In later times only *fig.* and perhaps with conscious reference to sense 2); other examples are at *Bingo* (A slang term for brandy), and *Bribe, sb.* sense 2a (The earlier sense probably regarded it as a consideration extorted, exacted, or taken by an official, a judge, etc.; i.e. as the act of the receiver). Traces of eighteenth-century semantic thinking lingered on, with etymology being included in the definition, and defining text in etymology, respectively at *Barbadoes* (Name of a British island in the West Indies, believed to be derived from

Pg. *las barbadas* 'bearded'; epithet applied by the Portuguese to the Indian fig-trees growing there; whence formerly 'the Barbadoes') and at *Abanderado* ([Sp. *abanderado* or *banderado*, 'an Ensignes seruant which carrieth the ensigne for his master' Minsheu 1623, fr. *bandera* a banner])—no true definition being provided in the latter entry. Sometimes an initial (unsupported) definition provided the 'original' sense before the documented senses began, as at *Adrink* (*lit.* To swallow too much water; hence . . . To be drowned); and see also *Canaster* (1. A rush basket used to pack tobacco in. 2. A kind of tobacco made of the dried leaves coarsely broken, so called from the rush basket in which it was formerly imported [followed by quotations only for sense 2]). Despite Murray's explanation of the difference between logical and lexical definition (Landau 1989: 120)— that 'the Cyclopaedia *describes things*; the Dictionary *explains words*, and deals with the description of things only so far as is necessary in order to fix the exact significations and uses of words' (Murray 1884: p. vi)—much encyclopaedic information was included in the defining text, for example, *Aleconner* (An examiner or inspector of ale: 'An officer appointed in every court-leet, and sworn to look to the assize and goodness of bread, ale, and beer, sold within the jurisdiction of the leet.' Phillips 1706. 'Four of them are chosen annually by the commonhall of the city; and whatever might be their use formerly, their places are now regarded only as sinecures for decayed citizens.' Johnson 1755. Still a titular office in some burghs). Some defining text was in reality usage-note rather than definition (*Heaven, sb.*, sense 1b: Things of great height are said by hyperbole to reach to heaven; opposite points of the sky are said to be a whole heaven apart). An obsolete sense of *in order to* (meaning 'in regard or respect to') was used in several definitions, as at *Arbitrament, -ement*, sense 3 (The deciding of a dispute by an authority to whom the conflicting parties agree to refer their claims in order to their equitable settlement). Some definitions reveal an endearing editorial parochialism: for example, spring and summer were defined in terms of only the northern hemisphere; oblique references were made to personalities of the time, as at *Aroint, Aroynt* sense 2 (Used by Mr. and Mrs. Browning as a vb.: To drive away with an execration); 'in the Universities' referred only to Oxford and Cambridge (see, for example, *Act, sb.*, sense 8).

It is generally taken as read that quotations play a central role in sense-discovery in historical dictionaries. However, quotations were consistently described in *OED* documentation as *illustrating* meaning, after the fact—echoing Johnson, whose wide reading provided him with materials which would 'ascertain or illustrate' the meanings of words (1755: A1[r]). In the 'Directions to Sub-Editors' (OED/MISC/89/2) 'illustrative quotations' are mentioned, and in the *OED* Preface (Murray 1888: p. vi) Murray explained that the dictionary 'endeavours . . . to illustrate [the history of words] by a series of quotations'. Yet in practice it is almost invariably in the quotations that the historical lexicographer initially seeks and discerns fine sense-divisions and new senses; and, if the etymology is unknown, meaning has of necessity to be interpreted from the quotations (see

Aroint, Aroynt: [Origin unknown. Used by Shakspere, whence by some modern writers.] **1.** *In Aroint thee!* (?verb in the imperative, or interjection) meaning apparently: Avaunt! Begone! [followed by quotations]). The discovery of meaning in the quotations was acknowledged by Murray when he noted that 'the explanations of the meanings have been framed anew upon a study of all the quotations for each word collected for this work' (1888: p. xxi), and explained that it was from the quotations 'and the further researches for which they provide a starting-point', that 'the history of each word is deduced and exhibited' (1900: 119). Murray's evaluation of Richardson's dictionary, which was 'without definitions or explanations of meaning, or at least with the merest rudiments of them', proves the same point: 'His special notion [that definitions were unnecessary] was quite correct *in theory*. Quotations *will* tell the full meaning of the word, *if one has enough of them*; but it takes a great many to be enough, and it takes a reader a long time to weigh all the quotations, and to deduce from them the meanings which might be put before him in a line or two' (1900: 118).

Murray's description of his own work provides a clear picture of the process of discovering meanings in the data: 'You sort your quotations into bundles on your big table, and think you are getting the word's pedigree right, when a new sense, or three or four new senses, start up, which upset all your scheme, and you are obliged to begin afresh' ([Philological Society] 1887: p. x). If a quotation were clear and comprehensive enough, a reference to it, as 'See quot. *x*' (or 'See quots.'), could even replace the definition—a technique frequently resorted to in the *OED* in order to save time and space.[4] Of course quotations do (usually) add to the meaning provided in the definition—as do the etymology and the editorial notes—and Simpson (27/12/97) emphasizes that meaning is found in the entry as a whole: as it is not possible to describe 'every semantic and syntactic nuance' in the definition, the reader is expected to apply his or her judgement to the surrounding text as well.

While synchronic defining presented the editors with a myriad of difficulties, it was the diachronic description of the sense development of the old, polysemous English words which presented the greatest challenge. The history and development of the senses was 'by far the heaviest and hardest part of the work' (Murray 1884: 509). 'Etymologies are nothing like the trouble of chains of meanings', Murray complained ([Philological Society] 1887: pp. ix–x): 'The word *art* baffled me for several days . . . Such is the nature of the task; those who think that such work can be hurried, or that anything can accelerate it, except more brain power brought to bear on it, had better try' (1884: 510). 'The preparation of this volume has taken a much longer time than any of the promoters of the work anticipated', he wrote in the Preface to the first volume of the dictionary: 'The time has been consumed

---

[4] *OED3* has discarded this convention, but will retain the *OED*'s practice of referring to quotations in order to supplement the definition (see *Agnail*, sense 3), or qualify it (see *Felony*, sense 4b) (Simpson 27/5/1998).

... first, with the larger articles, as those of *At, By, But, Be, Bear, Break*, the construction of which has occupied many days, sometimes even weeks. The mere study of the result ... gives little idea of the toil and difficulties encountered in bringing into this condition what was at first a shapeless mass of many thousand quotations' (Murray 1888: p. xi). In correspondence, Murray's tone was less controlled: 'The brain work that is put into *Pass* ... came near to driving me mad, before I could see my way first *through* it; and second to exhibit it clearly & neatly after I saw it. No, the world will *never* know nor realize it ... the work is too high & too intense for anybody to realize who only sees the result' (*CWW*: 302). A visitor to the Scriptorium in 1909 provided a vivid description of Murray's response to the demands made on him by complex entries:

With his fountain-pen in his mouth for safety—he lost it five times a day—Sir James ... was playing chess with the senses ... With one hand he grasped his long white beard, as he always did when every cell of the alert brain beneath the black velvet skull-cap was busy with some great problem. For over an hour he worked in silence not heeding my presence. Then with a gesture as if he had conquered a province, he bundled the little slips into groups and smiled a 'Good morning'.   (*CWW*: 298)

The historical treatment of the sense-development was very difficult to accomplish when there was a lack of sufficient data. This is particularly true of the first few volumes, and especially of early evidence for the common words (*CWW*: 178). 'Much of the slowness of our progress is due to incompleteness of materials', reported Murray (1884: 515). 'The attempt has never been made before to exhibit such a combined logical and historical view of the sense-development of English words', he explained: 'Our own attempts lay no claim to perfection; but they represent the most that could be done in the time and with the data at our command' (Murray 1888: p. xi). The editors' intuition in the logical ordering of senses has often been confirmed by subsequent data. One example is the long and complex entry for *Make v.*, sense 1: although Bradley noted in the etymology, 'Materials are wanting for a genealogical arrangement of the senses; the order of the main branches in the following scheme has been adopted on grounds of convenience', the (provisional) revised entry for *OED3* has retained the original sense ordering of the *OED*, confirmed by new evidence from Old English (Simpson 22/5/1998). The 'combined logical and historical view' was represented in a defining structure (devised by Murray) of levels which were laid over the ordered mass of data, and which enabled the development of the senses to be displayed as clearly as was possible in a two-dimensional format. Complex entries with numerous related senses were accommodated in a 'family tree' which was shaped by both Murray's 'logical' method and the chronology of the illustrative citations. This tree-structure was not explained in detail in the Preface to the *OED*, but during the computerization of the text for the production of *OED2* the structure had to be carefully analysed, and is described in that Preface. Seven different kinds of 'serial symbol' were devised by Murray to mark the sense-divisions of an entry, each usually being identified with particular functions, and an eighth symbol treated form-variations. The first five symbols, from highest to lowest level, were bold capital letters, **A, B, C**, dividing entries which treat words used in more than one 'grammatical relation' (for example, **A.** *n.* . . . **B.** *adj.*); bold arabic numerals, **1, 2, 3**, identifying the main senses of a word; and (for increasingly fine sense-distinction) bold small letters, **a, b, c**, italic letters within parentheses, (*a*), (*b*), (*c*), and (occasionally) lower-case roman numerals in parentheses, (i), (ii), (iii).

The next two series of symbols formed one of the cornerstones of Murray's 'logical' treatment of senses, operating in a different way from the other numbering. They indicated 'parallel branches' in sense-development, providing an extra, horizontal dimension to the characteristically vertical 'tree'-structure, enabling more than one series of senses to begin with an early date. These numerals did not 'interrupt the numerical sequence of the main sense-divisions'. Bold capital roman numerals, **I., II., III.**, were introduced to head groups of senses which had 'developed along several different and parallel branches', and an increasing series of asterisks, *, **, ***, was used to indicate 'a lower level of branching (in the arrangement of a particularly large and complicated word, for example)' (*OED2* I: p. xxxiii).

Neil Hultin (1985: 47) has questioned the *OED*'s claim to be 'historical' in methodology, arguing that although the sense-ordering certainly proved the quotations to be important, there was another process which took precedence—the process of applying the lexicographer's 'logic'—which might overthrow the evidence of the quotations (see *Rock v.*[1]). 'The meanings are (or should be) arranged in logical order, the earliest quotations usually—but not always—containing the original English meaning', Murray explained to re-subeditors (OED/MISC/91/11). 'When the development of the signification of a word has taken place in the language itself, the historical order (if our history is complete) is also a logical one; and in such a case there is no question as to the proper order in which the senses should follow' (Murray 1880: 138). If there were not sufficient evidence, the logical order would have to be 'inferred'. '*Historically*, . . . a word is often a long series of historically and phonetically connected forms, with a long series of logically and historically related senses . . . The various senses will be arranged in the order in which they seemed to have flowed from the primary sense, now often obsolete' (Murray 1880: 135). So when Murray spoke of 'discovering' the historical order of the senses, he was not referring primarily to the dates of quotations. As Hultin (1985: 47) commented, ' "Discovery" is, in essence, the application of principles of "logic" to the various senses which have been revealed by the citations and from these the base significance is discerned as is the sequence which grows from it'. Richardson (1836–7: 44) summarized the 'logical' approach to meaning as follows:

While investigating . . . the meaning and consequent usage or application of words, I have considered it a duty incumbent upon the lexicographer to direct his view,—1st, To the etymology and literal meaning;—2nd, To the metaphorical application of this meaning—

to the mind;—3rd, To the application consequent or inferred from the literal meaning;—and 4th, To the application consequent or inferred from that which is metaphorical.

In discovering the sense-order for an entry, the *OED* editors applied 'logical' yardsticks: for example, concrete precedes abstract; single precedes generalized; religious precedes secular; literal precedes figurative; simple verb precedes phrasal verb. If there were enough evidence, the logical and the historical order would coincide. In Murray's thinking it was necessary to 'give the main place to the logical order of the senses, and never lose sight of it': this often meant that the chronological order of senses was disrupted. He recognized, however, that historical ordering had to take precedence over logical when sense-development had taken place before the word became English: 'In some words the development has taken place in Latin or French, and instead of the primary meaning being first adopted in English, it was with one of the most abstract, dependent, or figurative that the word was first taken, for the obvious reason that this was the only sense in which English needed it' (1880: 138). In the case of such words it was 'necessary to arrange the meanings in historical order'—for example, *Advent*, which entered English in its religious sense. 'To give *Advent* first with the general sense of "Arrival," whence in a special sense "the coming of the Saviour," and by transference, "the season of the nativity," would be for English purely fictitious, and while ostensibly logical, really illogical' (1880: 139).

The *OED* sense-framework, which offered the editor a range of levels—which might or might not be used, depending upon the complexity of the entry—has been described by Zgusta as 'a presentational apparatus so rich that the reader never has the impression of data being forced into a Procrustean bed of a rigidly preconceived structure; on the contrary, the apparatus is so flexible that the specificity of each situation can be captured' (1989: 226). This flexibility has been tested during the preparation of the third edition. John Simpson recalls that at the start of the project there was no certainty that the exercise would be a feasible one, but this is no longer in doubt. With a mass of new data at their disposal, the editors are following the quotation evidence in ordering the senses, applying the historical method more rigorously than is the case in the first edition of the *OED*—but in tandem with the logical approach. The imposition of higher level branch-numbering often maintains the existing entry structure, solving the problem of disrupted date order; and 'when this is not the case, the discipline of maintaining a chronological ordering raises significant issues of semantic development which would otherwise remain unaddressed' (Simpson 27/12/97).

Marghanita Laski warned in 1972 that the *OED* was 'still—just—a working tool' but would soon become 'a magnificent fossil' (*CWW*: 376)—fair comment on the dated attitudes and vocabulary embalmed in the Victorian and Edwardian defining text. However, the rigorous scholarly research, the fine sense-division, and particularly the sense-structure and logical-historical methodology still serve the *OED* well, supporting the necessary changes which the text is undergoing in order to be recreated as a 'moving document' (Simpson 27/12/97). 'The work thus done is done once for all', Murray stated in the Romanes Lecture (1900: 120)—perhaps an exaggerated claim when the *detail* of *OED* definitions is evaluated; but his assessment of the *structure* was accurate: 'The structure now reared will have to be added to, continued, and extended with time, but it will remain, it is believed, the great body of fact on which all future work will be built.'

REFERENCES

Murray Papers

MP/15/11/1886. H. Bradley to J. A. H. Murray.

OED *Archives at OUP*

OED/BL/329/70. A. H. Green to J. A. H. Murray. 17 June 1890.
OED/EP/MURRA/4. J. A. H. Murray to H. Bradley [undated: 189–].
OED/EP/MURRA/8. J. A. H. Murray to W. A. Craigie. 1 May 1903.
OED/EP/MURRA/16. J. A. H. Murray to W. A. Craigie. 20 June 1905.
OED/EP/MURRA/22. J. A. H. Murray to W. A. Craigie. 14 May 1908.
OED/EP/MURRA/27. J. A. H. Murray to W. A. Craigie. 9 March 1909.
OED/EP/MURRA/30.i. J. A. H. Murray to W. A. Craigie. 14 December 1909.
OED/MISC/12/24.ii. J. A. H. Murray to W. A. Craigie. 3 December 1902.
OED/MISC/12/86. J. A. H. Murray to W. A. Craigie. 13 November 1913.
OED/MISC/89/2. Directions to Sub-Editors [undated].
OED/MISC/89/5. *Canones Lexicographici; or Rules to be Observed in Editing the New English Dictionary of the Philological Society.* [1860].
OED/MISC/91/11. Directions to Re-sub-editors [undated].

Published works

Aarsleff, H. (1967). *The Study of Language in England, 1780–1860.* Princeton: Princeton University Press.
Bailey, R. (1993). 'The Prehistory of the *OED*' (unpublished lecture delivered at the annual meeting of the Dictionary Society of North America, Las Vegas, May 1993).
Bradley, H. (1884). 'A New English Dictionary on Historical Principles'. *The Academy*, 615 (16 February): 105–6.
Horne Tooke, J. (1798, 1805). *Diversions of Purley.* London: printed for the author.
Hultin, N. (1985). 'The Web of Significance: Sir James Murray's Theory of Word-Development', in *Proceedings of the First Conference*, 6–7 November 1985. Waterloo: University of Waterloo Centre for the New *OED*, 41–55.
Johnson, S. (1755). *A Dictionary of the English Language.* London: W. Strahan.
—— (1824). *Works*, ii. London: W. Baynes & Son.
Landau, S. I. (1989). *Dictionaries: The Art and Craft of Lexicography.* Cambridge: Cambridge University Press.
Murray, J. A. H. (1880). 'Ninth Annual Address of the President to the Philological Society'. *TPS*, 1880–1: 117–74.
—— (1884). 'Thirteenth Annual Address of the President to the Philological Society'. *TPS*, 1882–4: 501–31.

—— (1888). 'Preface to Volume I.' *NED* Vol. I. A and B. Oxford: Clarendon Press, pp. v–xiv.

—— (1900). 'The Evolution of English Lexicography' [the Romanes Lecture for 1900]. *International Journal of Lexicography*, 6:2 (1993): 100–22.

Murray, K. M. E. (1977). *Caught in the Web of Words: James A. H. Murray and the* Oxford English Dictionary. Oxford: Oxford University Press.

[Philological Society]. (1859). *Proposal for the Publication of a New English Dictionary by the Philological Society*. London: Trübner & Co.

—— (1887). 'Monthly Abstract of Proceedings', 21 January 1887. *Proc. Philol. Soc.* 1885–7: pp. ix–x.

Richardson, C. (1836–7). *A New Dictionary of the English Language*. 2 vols. London: William Pickering.

Trench, R. C. (1860). *On Some Deficiencies in our English Dictionaries*. 2nd edn., revised and enlarged. London: John W. Parker & Son.

[Trench *et al.*]. (1860). *Canones Lexicographici; or Rules to be Observed in Editing the New English Dictionary of the Philological Society*. London: The Philological Society.

Weiner, E. S. C. (1989). 'Editing the *OED* in the Electronic Age', in *Proceedings of the 5th Annual Conference*. Waterloo: University of Waterloo Centre for the New *OED*: 23–9.

Zgusta, L. (1989). 'The *Oxford English Dictionary* and other dictionaries (Aikakośyam)', in *International Journal of Lexicography* 2: 188–230.

—— (1991). 'Jacob Grimm's Deutsches Wörterbuch and Other Historical Dictionaries of the 19th Century: Dvitīyaikakośyam', in A. Kirkness, P. Kuhn, and H. E. Wiegand (eds.), *Studien zum Deutschen Wörterbuch von Jacob Grimm und Wilhelm Grimm*, ii. (Lexicographica: Series Maior; 33 & 34). Tübingen: Niemeyer, 595–626.

6

The Compass of the Vocabulary

ANNE CURZAN

The apparent objectivity of dictionaries rests on an extensive series of subjective editorial decisions. In the seventeenth century, when the aim of dictionaries of English shifted from being collections of 'hard words' to being comprehensive compilations of 'the language', one of the most fundamental decisions in the dictionary-making process became what words should be included as 'English' and what words excluded. Lexicographers came to wield authority not only over how to define words but also over what words merited definition—an authority that belies Samuel Johnson's description of the lexicographer as a 'harmless drudge'. In fact, dictionaries and dictionary makers define what constitutes 'the language' as much as they do any individual word in the lexicon.

In the 'General Explanations' opening the first volume of the *Oxford English Dictionary*, editor James Murray, one of the most accomplished of English lexicographers, describes his image of the English vocabulary and what it contains:

So the English vocabulary contains a nucleus or central mass of many thousand words whose 'Anglicity' is unquestioned; some of them only literary, some of them only colloquial, the great majority at once literary and colloquial—they are the *common words* of the language. But they are linked on every side with other words which are less and less entitled to this appellation, and which pertain ever more and more distinctly to the domain of local dialect, of the slang and cant of 'set' and classes, of the peculiar technicalities of trades and processes, of the scientific terminology common to all civilized nations, and of the actual language of other lands and peoples.   (Murray 1888: p. xxiv)

Below this quotation appears the famous compass-like drawing of the English vocabulary, with *Literary*, *Common*, and *Colloquial* in the well-defined centre, and *Scientific*, *Foreign*, *Technical*, *Slang*, and *Dialectal* pointing out towards the indiscernible periphery. One of the jobs of the lexicographer, as articulated by Murray, is to include in the dictionary all words passing into common use—to determine the scope of the compass of 'New English'. Murray specifically uses the word *compass* to describe the vocabulary in the Preface to Volume I of the *OED*, a word that he defines in the dictionary as both a 'circumscribed area or space; in wider sense, space, area, extent', and as a 'moderate space, moderation, due limits'. With this one descriptive, polysemous word, Murray captures the dilemma of the conscientious lexicographer when confronting peripheral terms: where does moderation lie in drawing the 'due limits' on the wide area covered by the diverse English vocabulary, specifically with respect to foreign, dialectal, slang, technical, and scientific words?

Given its historical purpose and scope, the *OED* was designed to be—and proves to be—more inclusive of early, now obsolete English words than any other dictionary published at the time or since. But Murray's vision for the expansive scope of the dictionary extended beyond obsolete words: 'The Vocabulary will be found to be, even in its modern words, much more extensive than that of any existing Dictionary. And it will be observed that this fullness is not due to a large inclusion of words strictly foreign, or of the Latin or Latinized generic names of Natural History, which are here inserted only when found to be used, more or less, as English words' (Murray 1888: p. vi). This quotation highlights Murray's sense of competitiveness with other dictionaries—as do his public concerns about the plagiarism of his material (see Chapter 12)—which fuelled his ongoing effort to outdo previous lexicographic endeavours, both in quality and quantity. As Elisabeth Murray (*CWW*: 197) comments: 'Never, at any time, did James Murray yield to the temptation of omitting a word because it was difficult or because it would save time: his own criterion for exclusion was that inclusion would not improve the Dictionary and might cumber it needlessly.' And he erred to the side of richness over paucity, a tendency remarked upon and endorsed in an 1886 *Times* review of the early fascicles: 'We feel some hesitation, moreover, about the admission of purely technical words . . . These, however, if faults at all, are faults in the right direction . . . If, as we have ventured to suggest, there are some words admitted to hospitality whose passports are doubtful, there are, so far as we have been able to discover, very few omissions indeed' (Anon. 1886: 13).

In designing his classification system for words in the dictionary, Murray sought to recognize these words with doubtful passports—words that were entering the nucleus of the vocabulary from the periphery: the 'denizens, aliens, and casuals' that were becoming frequent in usage but were not yet fully naturalized. He seems to have known that this endeavour was a questionable one; he writes later in the 'General Explanations':

Opinions will differ as to the claims of some that are included and some that are excluded, and also as to the line dividing denizens from naturals, and the positions assigned to some words on either side of it. If we are to distinguish these classes at all, a line must be drawn somewhere. (Murray 1888: p. xxvi)

Murray, in fact, draws two lines: words excluded from the dictionary for a variety of reasons (for example, foreign and dialectal words, slang), and words included in the dictionary but marked as peripheral. These marks include '||' next to the headword for unnaturalized terms, and parenthetical notations for slang, colloquialisms, dialectal terms, and technical terms. The decisions about these words remained problematic throughout the decades of production, as a comment in the Preface to the 1933 *Supplement* makes clear: 'As in the main work, there has been continually present the problem of the inclusion or omission of the more esoteric scientific terms and of the many foreign words reflecting the widened interest in the conditions and customs of remote countries, and it cannot be hoped or pretended that this problem has been solved in every instance with infallible discretion' (Craigie and Onions 1933: p. v).

All other lexicographers of Murray's time had to draw a similar line between English and non-English words in creating their dictionaries, and others opted for alternative strategies in handling the issue and in creating word labels. William Dwight Whitney, for example, who was editing the *Century Dictionary* during the first few years of the *OED* effort, also recognized the huge influx of foreign and technical terms into English and he decided to include them unremarked. According to Whitney, not to include these peripheral words was 'unduly to restrict the dictionary' as well as 'practically impossible, for this technical language is, in numberless instances, too closely interwoven with common speech to be dissevered from it' (1889: p. vi); implicit in this statement is the practical impossibility of labelling these closely interwoven technical and foreign words once they are included in the dictionary. Whitney takes a more traditional stance, however, with regard to obsolete and dialectal words, slang, and many technical terms; the *Century*, like the *Imperial Dictionary*, as well as the *OED*, employs introductory or parenthetical labels and symbols to identify these words.

This introduction to lexicographic strategies for handling peripheral English words already pits one dictionary against another as a means of determining where various editors drew their lines around the English vocabulary. This kind of retrospective comparison raises the question of how these editorial decisions may have interacted in the creation of the dictionaries. With specific reference to the compilation of the *OED*, what were the possible effects of previous or contemporaneous lexicographers' decisions on the *OED* editors' word inclusion policies? The *OED* editors worked not only among piles of word slips but also among open dictionaries—a growing stack as new dictionaries were published over the decades required to finish the *OED*—which potentially provided a level of legitimacy to the words they contained. Other scholars have noted Murray's strong individuality and independence as a lexicographer (see, for example, the discussion of sources and models for the *OED* in Zgusta 1989), and decisions on word inclusion prove to be no exception: while Murray clearly relied on other dictionaries, particularly the *Century Dictionary*, as sources, they were not determinative in his final decisions on the 'Anglicity' of words. Murray did not sacrifice his editorial principles for the sake of absolute inclusivity: he would not cross the boundary line he envisaged for the vocabulary simply to include words deemed to be English by other lexicographers.

Beginning in the Prefatory Note to *Depravative–Distrustful* which appeared in 1896, Murray himself set up a comparison between the *OED* and a selection of other dictionaries—including Todd's expansion of Johnson's *Dictionary* (Latham 1882), Hunter's *Encyclopaedic Dictionary* (1879–88), the *Century Dictionary*

(1889–91), and Funk and Wagnalls' *Standard Dictionary of the English Language* (1893–5)—recording the number of words included, the number of words illustrated by quotations, and the number of illustrative quotations. In terms of sheer numbers and size (not to mention years in the making), the *OED* outstrips all these other works. But these numbers testify as much, if not more, to the historical scope of the *OED*—the inclusion of obsolete English words—as they do to the dictionary's comprehensiveness with respect to 'peripheral' terms in contemporaneous English. How does the *OED* compare in the inclusion of words 'now in use', such as foreign borrowings, slang, dialectal forms, and scientific language?

The magnitude of this question defies a complete answer; and the nature of lexicography precludes a systematic one. The fact is that Murray and the other editors of the *OED* had to make individual and usually independent decisions on the inclusion or exclusion of every peripheral term, as they describe in their self-perceptive caveats in the prefaces. Absolute consistency in the process was impossible with several editors and many decades of editing, although Murray's tight control over the editing process and the other editors results in no apparent patterns of discrepancy among the word inclusion policies of later fascicles. As Murray writes in an explanation of why he has included *American* in the dictionary and not *African*:

In dealing with so vast a body of words, some inconsistencies, real or apparent, are, from the nature of the subject, inevitable. Thus, in deciding whether a word on or near the frontier line in any direction shall or shall not be included, it is not easy always to be consistent with what has been done in analogous cases; and it is impossible to anticipate what may have been done in other cases which may yet arise.   (Murray 1888: p. ix)

Before reaching *American*, Murray also excluded *Alaskan* and *Albanian*, a decision not concurred with by all lexicographers: both words are included in the *Century Dictionary*, and *Albanian* also appears in Webster's *American Dictionary of the English Language*. The word *Albanian* was added in the 1933 *Supplement* to the *OED* with supporting quotations dating back to 1561, a hint that Murray had rethought his original decision to exclude this word; *Alaskan* was added in *OED2*. As these examples suggest, the path of each peripheral term into the *OED* (or back into its pigeon-hole) has its own story. It is possible, however, to find some general trends, to identify some of the idiosyncratic variation, and to recreate some of the decisions Murray and the other editors faced—as well as the repercussions of these decisions for the scope of the dictionary.

A word-based comparison of the *OED* with other dictionaries of the time, both those that Murray consulted when creating the *OED* and those that were published during relatively the same time-span, helps sketch the line which Murray, as compared with other lexicographers, sought to draw around the English vocabulary. Five segments of approximately fifty consecutive headwords have been selected for close examination, two segments from the first fascicle, *A–Ant,* edited by Murray and published in 1884, and three from later fascicles, published in 1909: *Romanity–Roundness*, edited by Craigie, and 1910: *Sauce–alone–Scouring*, edited by Bradley; and *T–Tealt*, also edited by Murray. These selections are compared with the general dictionaries mentioned above, as well as with Annandale's revised version of Ogilvie's *Imperial Dictionary*, published in 1882. They are also compared with corresponding segments in more specialized dictionaries, including: for dialectal words, Webster's *American Dictionary of the English Language* (1864), Wright's *English Dialect Dictionary* (1898–1905), and Jamieson's *Etymological Dictionary of the Scottish Language* (1879–82); for slang, Ware's *Passing English of the Victorian Era* (1909) and Farmer and Henley's *Slang and its Analogues* (1890–1904); and for technical and scientific vocabulary, Dunglison's *Dictionary of Medical Science* (1893) and Knight's *New Mechanical Dictionary* (1884).

At the most general level, there can be no doubt that the *OED* successfully achieves its goal of immense comprehensiveness. It includes almost all words that appear in the general dictionaries both preceding it and coinciding with it, and it treats these words in a more detailed fashion. The lexical area where these dictionaries and the *OED* do not overlap is small indeed, and consists almost entirely of compound words, derivative forms (often handled under the base headword in the *OED*), and scientific terms. As Murray's comparison statistics in the fascicle prefaces reveal, the *OED* not only overlaps with these dictionaries but it surpasses them, encompassing more headwords. For the most part, the *OED* headwords not in other general dictionaries are almost all marked as obsolete in the *OED*; in other words, the enormous number of entries in the *OED* reflects more on its historical depth than on its contemporary breadth for word inclusion—and the latter proves to be a more difficult area to analyse.

One of the intriguing aspects of the general observations in the paragraph above about the *OED*'s inclusiveness is that they all require the word *almost*. In other words, despite Murray's claims to breadth, there are—not surprisingly—words included as English in other dictionaries that he and the other editors exclude, either by choice or mistake. Words left out of the *OED* by mistake are difficult to discover. Perhaps the best-known anecdotal example is the word *bondmaid*, added in the 1933 *Supplement* with quotations dating back to 1526. Most of the lexical additions in the latter involve words coming into common usage at the end of the nineteenth century or beginning of the twentieth century, but *bondmaid* does not seem to be the only historical addition. The first few pages of the *Supplement* alone include words such as *aasvogel*, *aboulia*, and *adiate*, all with supporting quotations from the first half of the nineteenth century.

Accidental exclusions from the *OED* are far from shocking; in fact, it is surprising not to find more. While the *OED* took decades to complete, the pace of production, given the volume of material, the number of hands, and the level of technology, was staggering. And the state of the slips when Murray collected them at the Scriptorium in Mill Hill was often chaotic, if the slips could be found at all (see *CWW*: 171–88). Murray did not try to hide this fact about the condition of the original material, either before or during his time at the helm. At a dinner in Oxford, Murray spoke about the dictionary's progress, as reported in a local paper:

Dr. Murray began by acknowledging the services rendered by various voluntary workers in the department of research, and explained how the continually accumulating material was being dealt with. Incidentally, he mentioned that the whole of the original MS. for *Pa* and *Pe* was lost for twelve years; but enough remained to show that the whole of it had at one time been lodged in the stable. The section *Hy* was also lost for many years, but that had fortunately been recovered.   (Marshall 1899: 366)

He did not, however, itemize the slips that had simply vanished.

The *OED*'s exclusion of words that appear in other dictionaries as a matter of policy applies particularly to the vocabulary in specialized technical dictionaries (for example, medical and mechanical dictionaries) and in slang and dialectal dictionaries. The *OED* editors also chose to omit foreign terms included in some contemporaneous general dictionaries. On the other hand, they also included some non-obsolete, often foreign terms that appear nowhere else. And it is these non-overlapping areas that illuminate various editors' decisions about the boundaries of English.

Murray pre-empts at least some potential attacks on his dictionary's size and word inclusion policies by stating, as quoted above, that the work's impressive number of headwords is not the result of the overly liberal inclusion of blatantly foreign terms. And, in fact, the selections examined for this study reveal relatively few words marked as alien in the *OED* that appear in no other dictionaries. In the exerpt from *T–Tealt*, of the seven words marked as unnaturalized, only two appear in no other dictionary:

‖**Tanti** (tæn·təi). [L. *tantī* 'of so much (value)', gen. of *tantum*, neut. of *tantus* so much.] Of so much value, worth so much; worth while. Formerly also as an exclamation of contempt or depreciation: So much *for* . . . !

‖**Tant ne quant**, *adv. phr. Obs. rare.* Also 4 **taunt ne caunt**. [OF. (*ne*) *tant ne quant*.] In no wise, not at all.

The quotations under *tanti* date back to Marlowe in 1590; the brief *tant ne quant* entry includes two quotations from the fourteenth century.

The fact that the phrase *tant ne quant* is also obsolete undoubtedly helps explain why it appears in no other dictionary. The reasoning behind Murray's decision to include the romance borrowing *tanti* in the *OED* is more difficult to recreate, especially when coupled with his decision to exclude certain other romance expressions that appear in the *Century Dictionary* and in Funk and Wagnalls, both of which the *OED* editors consulted for the later volumes. In this same early section of T, Whitney uniquely includes in the *Century*:

Tantum Ergo (tan'tum er'go). [So called from these words in the hymn: L. *tantum* (*sacramentum*), so great (a sacrament); *ergo*, therefore: see *ergo*.] 1. In the *Rom. Cath. liturgy*, the last two stanzas of the hymn of Aquinas, beginning 'Pange lingua gloriosi corporis mysterium', which are sung when the eucharist is carried in procession and in the office of benediction.—2. A musical setting of these stanzas.

Murray's reasons for excluding the name of a liturgical hymn are easy enough to fathom, particularly since it also falls under the category of proper names. Two French expressions in Funk and Wagnalls, however, more closely parallel *tant ne quant* and their exclusion from the *OED* seems more idiosyncratic:

TANT MIEUX (tahN myoe) [F.] So much the better.

TANT PIS (tahN pee) [F.] So much the worse.

These two exclamations are based on the same French root as *tant ne quant*, and their use closely parallels that of *tanti*; both phrases are also accepted as English in Fennell's *Stanford Dictionary of Anglicized Words and Phrases* (1892).

In the section excerpted from S, the *OED* again blazes its own trail on the periphery of the vocabulary, uniquely including the following two French words:

||**Saumur** (*somiir*). [The name of a town in the department of Maine-et-Loire in France.] A French white wine resembling champagne.

||**Saupiquet**. *rare*⁻¹. [Fr., f. *saupiquer* = Sp. *salpicar*: see SALPICON.] A piquant sauce.

In the same subsection, Bradley, the editor of this fascicle, omits the word *saum*, defined by the *Century* (the only dictionary in which the word appears) as an 'Austrian unit of weight, formerly used in England for quicksilver'. Perhaps an even more obvious exclusion from the *OED* occurs in the selection from R: the word *Rothoffite*, a variety of garnet found in Sweden, appears not only in the *Century* and *Imperial*, but also in *Webster's*—and not in the *OED* (while the *OED* includes other mineralogical terms such as *leadhillite* and *tantalite*).

These exceptional foreign words stand in contrast to the more general rule: more common borrowed words tend to appear in several dictionaries, almost always including the *OED*; and they are often marked as foreign in the *OED* and not in other dictionaries. For example, *tantra* 'one of a class of Hindu religious works in Sanskrit' appears in the *OED* (as unnaturalized), the *Century*, and the *Imperial*; the musical term *tanto* 'so much, too much' appears in the *OED* (as unnaturalized), the *Century*, and Funk and Wagnalls. This general 'rule', however, is variable, based on the subjective application of editorial policy. For example, with respect to the latter inclusion of *tanto*, it should be noted that in a previous fascicle, the *OED* omits the musical term *rotondo* 'round, full', which appears in the *Imperial* and *Century*.

This anecdotal evidence highlights the fact that the decision about whether or not to include each and every peripheral word has its own story and it would be difficult to assign significance to, for example, the inclusion of one Italian musical term in the *OED* (*tanto*) and the exclusion of another (*rotondo*), especially given that these two fascicles had different editors. The important point is that a peripheral foreign word's inclusion in another dictionary was not sufficient evidence to legitimize it as English in the *OED*. While Murray and the other editors of the *OED* aimed to surpass other dictionaries in breadth and depth, this drive did not result in the wholesale inclusion of what they viewed as unnaturalized words in other dictionaries.

Such editorial independence does not mean, however, that other dictionary editors' decisions had no effect on the *OED*. The *Century Dictionary*, published while the *OED* editors were finishing Volume C, provides an excellent source for comparing the borrowed, non-scientific words that the *OED* editors passed over or missed, before and after the publication of the *Century Dictionary*. And the influence of the *Century* seems to be significant. A comparison of excerpts from A and from the later volumes indicates a notable difference in the non-overlapping lexical area in the early fascicles, before the *Century* was available, and in the later ones. The number of borrowed, potentially peripheral, words included in the *Century* and not in the *OED* in the two selections from A is larger than in the later fascicles, suggesting the importance of the *Century* as an available source for the later fascicles.

In the selections from R and S, the foreign words that appear in the *Century* and not in the *OED* are all scientific. In the selection from T, there are three borrowed, non-scientific terms in the *Century* that are excluded from the *OED*: *Tantum Ergo*; *tanty*, a type of Hindu loom; and *Tanzimat* 'an organic statute for the government of the Turkish empire, issued in 1839', a word also included in the *Imperial*. In A, the words appearing in the *Century* and not in the *OED* show a far greater range. They include the Arabic items *aba* 'a coarse woolen stuff woven of goats', etc. hair in Syria, Arabia; an outer garment made of the above worn by Arabs of the desert', and *albadara* 'the Arabian cabalistic name for the basal or sesamoid joint of the great toes to which extraordinary gifts were anciently ascribed' (which also appears in the *Imperial*), as well as the Asian *alatcha* 'a cotton stuff made in central Asia, dyed in the thread'; the adjectives *Albanian* and *Abanensian* 'one of the sects embraced under the name Cathari' (which also appears in Hunter's); the living creatures *abacay* 'a kind of white parrot; a calangay' and *abalone* 'a general name on the Pacific Coast of the United States for marine shells of the family *Haliotidæ*'; the building material *albarium* 'a stucco or white lime obtained from burnt marble'; and the foreign objects *abadir* 'among the Phenicians, a meteoric stone worshipped as divine', *alb* 'a small Turkish coin, nearly equal in value to a cent' (which also appears in Hunter's), and *abarello* 'an earthen vessel, cylindrical, used in 15th C and later as a drug-pot'. This discrepancy strongly suggests the influence of the publication of the *Century* on the compilation of later fascicles of the *OED*, as well as on the 1933 *Supplement*. In fact, of the foreign words mentioned above, both *aba* (dated back to 1811) and *abalone* (dated back to 1883) are added in the latter, possibly to compensate for earlier erroneous exclusion. In this list of foreign words, it is also interesting to note the number of non-Romance forms that the *Century* includes and the *OED* does not, similar to *tanty* and *Tanzimat* from the later fascicle.

The stated policy of the *OED* for handling dialectal words was to include currently dialectal words only if they had, one point in time, been in common use. To examine the inclusivity of the *OED*'s treatment of dialectal forms, it is enlightening to compare it, as well as other general dictionaries, with Wright's *English Dialect Dictionary (EDD)*, which Murray and the other editors consulted in creating the *OED*, and with Jamieson's *Etymological Dictionary of the Scottish Language*. (Wright's dictionary is more comprehensive than Jamieson's and includes almost all words listed in the latter, so it provides the most useful basis for comparison.) The most obvious conclusion to draw from looking at the *OED* and *EDD* side by side is that most of the dialectal words in the *EDD* are not included in the *OED*. As a result, many wonderfully expressive dialectal words are excluded from the authoritative history of English in the *OED* and left unacknowledged in the periphery. For example, in the early part of T, the *EDD* includes *tannyiks* 'teeth'; *tanracket* and *tantaran* to describe a noise or uproar; *tantaddlement* 'a trifle'; *tant* and *tanter* for 'to argue'; *tanterboming* 'faulty, crooked'; *tantoozle* 'to whip soundly'; and *Tantarbobus*, a name for the devil also applied to a noisy, playful child. These selected dialectal words, preserved by Wright in his dictionary, are excluded not only from the *OED* but also from all the examined general dictionaries of the time.

In contrast, in the excerpts examined for this study, there are a few dialectal words that have clearly gained such common currency that they appear in multiple general dictionaries, as well as the *EDD*: for example, *saulie* 'a hired mourner at a funeral' and *rother* 'an ox or bovine animal' (they are both labelled as dialectal in the general dictionaries). For less common dialectal forms, the editors of the *OED* are generally more accepting than their contemporaries. If the word is to be found in a non-dialectal dictionary, it is most likely the *OED*. For example, again from the section near the beginning of T, under the word *tannage*, the *OED* lists the meaning 'a tannery', noting that this is a Scottish usage—a treatment identical to that in the *EDD*; the *Century* and the *Imperial*, on the other hand, list no dialectal meanings of the word. Similarly, the botanical meanings of *tansy* appear in the *OED*, *Century*, *Imperial*, Todd, Webster's, and the *Dictionary of Medical Science (DMS)*. The *OED*, *Century*, and *Imperial* all include the additional meaning cited in the *EDD* of a pudding or cake flavoured with tansy (the *Century* marks this meaning as obsolete; the *OED* marks it as archaic or dialectal). Only the *OED* also includes the *EDD*'s definition 'a village feast', citing the *EDD* as its source. As a general rule, however, with dialectal words and definitions, the *OED* editors exclude more than they include. For example, while the *OED* is more thorough than any other dictionary in treating the dialectal meanings of *tansy*, it excludes the second dialectal meaning cited in the *EDD*, 'a children's singing game'.

This partial intersection of the *OED* and *EDD* is exemplified again by the word *tantadlin*. The first definition in the *OED*, labelled as slang or dialectal, mirrors the *EDD*: 'a tart or round piece of pastry' (the *EDD* also specifies an apple-dumpling). The second definition in the *OED*, 'a lump of excrement, a turd' (a meaning that stands in stark contrast to the first!) is labelled as obsolete, does not appear in the *EDD*, and reflects the historical scope of the *OED* in comparison to other dictionaries. The second definition in the *EDD*, 'a contemptuous term for anything strange or fanciful', demonstrates the dialectal scope of the *EDD*, legitimizing words and meanings included in no other dictionary.

There are certainly exceptions to the rule that the *OED* includes dialectal forms where other dictionaries do not, and they are striking because they are so exceptional. The verb *tantle* meaning 'to fondle, caress, pet' appears in Webster's as 'Provincial English'; this meaning is listed as the third of three in the *EDD* (the other two being 'to walk slowly and feebly; to loiter' and 'to attend officiously'), and occurs nowhere else. Another 'Provincial English' word in Webster's, *saur* 'soil, dirt' or 'urine from a cow-house', is included in the *EDD* but does not find its way into the *OED*. Interestingly, the *Imperial* also includes the word as 'Provincial', with the meaning 'soil, dirt', although the *Century* does not. A third unique dialectal example is *rotcoll* 'horse-radish', included in the *EDD*, Jamieson, and the *DMS*, but not in the *OED*. These few exceptions, however, are just that—few. While most dialectal words included in the *EDD* are ignored by contemporaneous general dictionaries, the *OED* proves more tolerant in its inclusion policy than other dictionaries (although it consistently marks the words as dialectal), and the *OED* even includes a few Scottish and other dialectal words not in the *EDD* (for example, *rotch* 'a gun or gun-barrel').

The line between dialectal forms and slang or colloquial forms can be a fuzzy one. For the most part, the *OED* editors' use of the labels *slang* and *colloquial* demonstrates striking consistency with the application of these labels in the *Century* and *Imperial*. For example, *rot* 'nonsense' and *tanner* 'a sixpence' are marked as slang in all three dictionaries (the slang status of these two words is confirmed by their appearance in Farmer and Henley's *Slang and Its Analogues*); *saucebox* 'a saucy, impudent person' is labelled as colloquial in all three. The *Century* strays from the others in labelling *rotgut* 'adulterated or bad liquor' as 'colloquial and low' and in not labelling *tantrum* 'an outburst or display of ill-temper' as colloquial, but the similarities far outnumber the differences.

The highly descriptive term *saucebox*, often used to refer to pertinent people, has a second slang meaning, 'the mouth', included only in the *EDD*, Ware's *Passing English of the Victorian Era* (*PE*), and Farmer and Henley. Further comparison of the *OED* and *PE* highlights the *OED* editors' general avoidance policy towards contemporary slang. *PE* includes, for example, *rotfunks* 'panics' (in cricket), *Rothschild* 'a rich man'; *tannery* 'large boots; also absolute reference to feet almost as capacious'; and *tanter go* 'end, finish'. With a very 'passing' word based on a personal name such as *Rothschild*, the *OED* editors' slang policy seems applicable, although the word also appears in Farmer and Henley (with a fairly mysterious cross-reference to *come*). Another word in Farmer and Henley nicely illustrates the *OED*'s well-publicized skittishness with slang words that touch on the obscene. For the word *tantrum*, the *OED* (like several other general dictionaries) provides only the definition of an outburst or display of petulance, followed by the label *colloq*. Nowhere is there mention of the second definition in Farmer and Henley, 'penis', or its supporting quotation.

Analysing the *OED*'s inclusion of technical terms is as difficult a task as defining exactly what constitutes a technical term. The *OED*'s use of abbreviations such as (*Chem.*) 'in Chemistry', (*Arch.*) 'in Architecture', and (*Build.*) 'in building', in keeping with other dictionaries of the time, immediately indicates its consistent inclusion of words specific to these specialized fields. As a general rule, the *OED* editors' policies of inclusion and marking are consistent with the *Century* and *Imperial*, as well as other dictionaries such as Webster's and Todd. A comparison with Knight's *Mechanical Dictionary* (*MD*) reveals little overlap between the two, however, probably in large part because many of the words in Knight are compounds, which the editors of the *OED* tend to include under the base word if they are included at all. For example, in the selection from R, Knight lists: *Rotary-bed Planing Machine, Rotary Mortising Machine, Rotary Plow, Rotary Pump, Rotary Steam Engine, Rotary Tubular Steam Boiler*, and *Rotary Water Engine* (several of which are accompanied by wonderfully detailed illustrations).

The single word *rotator* is also treated in Knight's dictionary, with a very specific technical meaning: 'an apparatus for producing iron by the direct process'. This specialized meaning is included in none of the general dictionaries; on the other hand, the word's specialized medical meaning, defined most generally in *DMS* as the 'name given to several muscles turning the parts to which they are attached upon their axes', is included in the *OED*, *Century*, *Imperial*, and Webster's with very similar definitions.

A lengthier comparison of the *DMS* with the *OED* provides mixed results. There is certainly more overlap than there is between the *OED* and the *MD*. Some medical words are common enough to be in almost all dictionaries, including the *OED*: *rhotacism*,[1] *rot* 'a wasting disease in man or animals' (only the *DMS* specifies *Distoma hepaticum* in the definition), *Rötheln* 'rubella'; *sauce-alone*; *tannate* 'a salt of tannic acid', and *tannin* 'tannic acid'. The *OED*, unlike any other general dictionary, includes *sauriousis* 'a form of ichthyosis in which the skin resembles that of a lizard' (specifying that the term belongs to Pathology), but it excludes *sauriderma*, another term listed in the *DMS* for sauriosis. In this respect, the editors had to make difficult decisions about which medical terms were common for diseases and treatments and which were not; and with rapid progress in science and medicine, these editorial decisions often needed to be revised (for

---

[1] The dictionary definitions of *rhotacism* expose the dialectal prejudices of many of the editors. Dunglison describes this type of pronunciation in the *DMS* as 'vicious', as did Webster before him; the *Imperial* employs the adjective 'faulty'. Murray includes no judgemental adjective in his definition of the '*r*-ful speech' characteristic of his Scots English (he describes it more neutrally as 'excessive use or peculiar pronunciation of *r*'), although later in life he reportedly shifted his speech towards the southern standard (see Bailey 1996: 102–3).

example, *appendicitis* had to be added in the 1933 *Supplement* as it became the common term for the ailment, not simply an esoteric Latinate diagnosis).

The dilemma facing the *OED* editors in deciding whether or not to include medical terminology, which is often highly Latinate, mirrors the dilemma complicating their decisions on other Latinate, scientific vocabulary. This issue is thoroughly treated in Hoare and Salmon's chapter in this volume; a few brief observations based on comparison with other dictionaries, focused specifically on the *OED*'s treatment of genus and species names, will suffice here to provide some insight on how the editors chose to apply the 'alien' label. The typical pattern in the *OED* is to exclude the name of the genus but to include the name of a member of the genus, with no alien word designation: *Rotalian* but not *Rotalia*; *Rotalid* but not *Rotalidea*; *Tanystome* but not *Tanystomata*. In contrast, both forms appear consistently in the *Century*. And the *OED* editors are not entirely consistent in their application of this policy. For example, the *OED* includes both *Sauria* and *Saurian*; and it lists *Rotifera* but not *Rotiferan*. Interestingly, while the genus member names are accepted by the editors as full English words, the genus names, in the rare instances that they are included, appear with the alien symbol.

This alien symbol ('||') is a critical factor in the *OED*'s overall ability to legitimize loanwords. One of the most obvious features of the *OED*'s policy on loanwords in comparison with other dictionaries is its conservativeness in overtly marking peripheral words as foreign or not yet naturalized. In trying to identify this peripheral area of the vocabulary at all, the *OED* deviates from Funk and Wagnalls, Hunter's, the *Imperial*, and the *Century*, all of which mark obsolete forms but not new or borrowed ones. Webster's *American Dictionary* italicizes words considered foreign, and as a general rule, any word italicized in Webster's is similarly identified as not yet naturalized in the *OED* (in fact, there are no exceptions in the selections from A, R, S, and T examined for this study).

The first four words marked as 'alien' in the first fascicle of the *OED*—which happen to occur consecutively—nicely capture many of the ways that the *OED*'s word inclusion and labelling policies compare with those of other dictionaries. The first word, *aal* 'a plant, a species of *Morinda*' and 'the red dye from it'— accompanied by the note that this is the Bengali and Hindi name for the plant— is unique to the *OED*: it does not appear in the *Century*, the *Imperial*, Funk and Wagnalls, Hunter's, Todd, or Webster's. The words *aam* 'A Dutch and German liquid measure (of approximately 37 to 41 gallons)' and *aardvark* appear in all the dictionaries except Todd and both are marked as foreign in the *OED* and Webster's. (The form *aam* also appears in Wright's *English Dialect Dictionary*, but with a very different meaning: it is labelled as an East Anglian form meaning 'the chill', in the phrase *to take the aam off*.) The fourth alien word, the perhaps less familiar *aardwolf*, is omitted from Todd and Webster's, but it appears in the other three newer and more comprehensive dictionaries.

While there are no instances of the *OED* naturalizing a word italicized as foreign in the earlier Webster's, there are examples of the *OED* relegating to alien or denizen status words not identified as foreign in Webster's. For instance, still in the beginning of the first fascicle, the *OED* marks as foreign the word *Ab* 'Fifth month of the Hebrew ancient sacred year', a word included and similarly defined in the *Century*, the *Imperial*, Hunter's, and Webster's with no foreign designation. The words *abaca* 'native name of palm (*Musa textilis*) which furnishes Manilla hemp' and *abaciscus* 'square compartment enclosing part of Mosaic pattern' are also tagged as alien in the *OED* and not in the other four dictionaries. Webster's notes parenthetically that *abaca* is 'the native name' and Hunter's includes in the definition that it is the 'name given in the Philippine Islands'; all five dictionaries specify that *abaciscus* is a term used in (ancient) archaeology, but it is given nativized status.

Inclusion of peripheral words in the dictionary, whether they be foreign, slang, dialectal, or technical, is unquestionably a first step towards legitimization. In this respect, the editors of the *OED* chose to take a step—but not a leap. Their careful use of labels to designate the status of peripheral words precludes absolute legitimization. In many ways, this classification system of alien words parallels the *OED*'s treatment of nonce-words, which are explicitly identified as nonce forms or erroneous uses (in contrast to the often unmarked inclusion of these words in other dictionaries). These words are thereby recognized as having appeared in the history of the English language, but their status as legitimate English words is indelibly questioned. In a similar manner, the *OED* provides many peripheral foreign, dialectal, and slang words with a place and a history—but that place is on the edge rather than in the centre of the vocabulary. Such careful, editorial marginalization, however, may only be a footnote to interested lexicographers and language scholars; for typical users of the *OED*, it may be the symbols and labels— not the words—that are peripheral, more often than not opaque or unnoticed. The *OED*'s inclusion of the words, therefore, expands the compass of the English vocabulary, defining the periphery only for those interested in finding it.

REFERENCES

Anon. (1886). 'The New English Dictionary'. *The Times*, 12 March: 13.

Bailey, R. W. (1996). *Nineteenth-Century English*. Ann Arbor: University of Michigan Press.

Craigie, W. A., and Onions, C. T. (1933). *A New English Dictionary on Historical Principles.* Introduction, Supplement, and Bibliography. Oxford: Clarendon Press.

Dunglison, R. (1893). *A Dictionary of Medical Science* (21st edn.). Philadelphia: Lea Brothers.

Farmer, J. S., and Henley, W. E. (eds) (1970 [1890–1904]). *Slang and Its Analogues.* Reprint. New York: Arno Press.

Fennell, C. A. M. (1892). *The Stanford Dictionary of Anglicised Words and Phrases.* Cambridge: at the University Press.

Funk, I. K. (ed.) (1893–5). *Standard Dictionary of the English Language.* New York, London: Funk & Wagnalls.

Hunter, R. (1879–88). *The Encyclopaedic Dictionary*. London: Cassell, Peter, Galpin & Co.

Jamieson, J. (1879–82). *An Etymological Dictionary of the Scottish Language*. Revised by J. Longmuir and D. Donaldson. Paisley: A. Gardner.

Knight, E. H. (1884). *Knight's New Mechanical Dictionary*. Boston, New York: Houghton Mifflin.

Latham, R. G. (1882). *A Dictionary of the English Language . . . Founded on that of Dr Samual Johnson as edited by the Rev. H. J. Todd*. 2 vols. London: Longmans, Greeen, & Co.

Marshall, E. (1899). 'The "H. E. D." [Historical English Dictionary]'. *Notes and Queries*, 3/11: 366.

Murray, J. (1888). 'Preface to Volume I.' *NED* Vol. I. A and B. Oxford: Clarendon Press, pp. v–xiv.

Murray, K. M. E. (1977). *Caught in the Web of Words: James Murray and the* Oxford English Dictionary. New Haven and London: Yale University Press.

Ogilvie, J. (1882). *The Imperial Dictionary, English, Technological, and Scientific* (new edn.). Edited by Charles Annandale. London: Blackie & Son. (1st edn. 1876.)

Ware, J. R. (1909). *Passing English of the Victorian Era: A Dictionary of Heterodox English, Slang, and Phrase*. London: G. Routledge & Sons.

Webster, N. (1864). *An American Dictionary of the English Language*. Edited by C. A. Gooderich and N. Porter. Springfield, Mass.: G. & C. Merriam.

Whitney, W. D. (ed.) (1889–91). *The Century Dictionary*. New York: The Century Co.

Wright, J. (ed.) (1898–1905). *The English Dialect Dictionary*. London: H. Frowde.

Zgusta, L. (1989). 'The Oxford English Dictionary and Other Dictionaries (Aikakošyam)', *International Journal of Lexicography*, 2: 188–230.

7

Words and Word-Formation: Morphology in *OED*

D I E T E R K A S T O V S K Y

INTRODUCTION

The *Proposal for the Publication of a New English Dictionary by the Philological Society* of 1859 not only formally inaugurated this project, it also laid down the basic principles which should govern the work on the *NED* (later *OED*) itself. Of these, the following two are regarded as the most important ones by Craigie and Onions in their 'Historical Introduction' to the *Supplement* volume of the *OED* (Craigie and Onions 1933: p. viii):

Principle I: The first requirement of every lexicon is that it should contain every word occurring in the literature of the language it professes to illustrate.

Principle IV: In the treatment of individual words the historical principle will be uniformly adopted.

Both principles do not seem to be unreasonable, especially if one takes into account the historical context in which they were formulated. Previous dictionaries had always been relatively restricted in their coverage, and it should therefore come as no surprise that the compilers of the *New English Dictionary* wanted it to be more comprehensive than its predecessors, ideally even all-comprehensive. After all, the number of words listed has always been a major factor in advertising a lexicon until today (Stein 1978a: 103 f.).[1] And the historical dimension was of course regarded as the only truly scientific approach to language in the heydays of Neogrammarian historical-comparative philology, a theoretical framework that continued to dominate language studies until well into the first half of the twentieth century, namely throughout the completion of the first edition of *OED*. Taken

---

[1] This aspect also figures in the Preface to the first volume of the *OED* (Murray 1888: pp. vi–vii), where we are told that 31,254 words are listed in the volume, not including the words with 'obvious meaning', because the 'number of these combinations is practically unlimited, since they can be formed at will; if the examples of the more important of them here given and illustrated by quotations are also reckoned in, the number of words dealt with in this volume exceeds 40,000'. The implications of this statement for the strict application of Principle I will be discussed below. Moreover, it hints at a problem still not really solved even today, namely, what counts as a 'word' in this competition.

to their extremes, however, both principles by themselves, and even more if applied together, cause a number of problems for the lexicographer, which would seem to call for non-extreme compromise solutions. The founding fathers of the *OED* were quite aware of this, although they did not yet have at their disposal the theoretical and terminological apparatus to discuss these problems systematically in a coherent linguistic framework. This was developed only in the course of the twentieth century in connection with the rise of synchronic linguistics, and a more comprehensive and coherent theory of lexicography, lexicology, semantics, and word-formation (derivational morphology[2]). It would be unfair, therefore, to judge the achievements of the founders of the *OED* exclusively by hindsight on the basis of what progress (if any?) linguistics and lexicography have made since the middle of the nineteenth century. Thus, I have tried to discuss my topic as much as possible from the standpoint of the compilers of the *OED* and not from our modern theoretical position. Nevertheless, it is inevitable that someone writing almost a century and a half after the conception of this monumental enterprise cannot totally dissociate himself from his own theoretical position, nor would he want to. It is in this light of critical respect that my remarks on the role of word-formation in the *OED* should be interpreted.

The main topic of this contribution is the question of how complex lexical items resulting from word-formation processes are treated in the *OED*. This involves quite a number of subtopics, out of which I have selected the following: the manner of listing complex lexical items, the role of the category 'word', the inter-action of the diachronic bias with synchronic exigencies, and the handling of non-native lexical material. All this will, at least to some extent, also be related to the conflicting demands of the two principles mentioned above.

THE EXHAUSTIVENESS PRINCIPLE AND THE
OPEN-ENDEDNESS OF THE VOCABULARY

Let me begin with Principle I, the exhaustiveness principle, as it might be called. The most obvious question it poses is whether any lexicon can really satisfy it, and whether it is actually necessary really to satisfy it literally in view of the poten-tial open-endedness of the vocabulary due to the existence of word-formation processes, which allow us to extend the vocabulary almost *ad infinitum*.

It would seem that every language has both simple and complex lexical items, and that a dictionary might want to handle these two sets in different ways on account of their different properties. This is indeed done, at least up to a point, in the *OED*, as has already been indicated in note 1. The basic reason for this is that simple lexical items are usually unmotivated unless they are onomatopoeia,

---

[2] The terms 'word-formation' and 'derivational morphology' are usually used synonymously: the former seems to be preferred in European linguistics; the latter in American linguistics. In the following, I will follow the European tradition.

and therefore require a lexical definition, since their meaning is unpredictable. This is not necessarily true of complex lexical items, whose meanings are usually predictable on the basis of their forms (at least to a certain degree). Moreover, due to the inherent productivity of word-formation processes, their output is non-finite. But simple lexical items by no means belong to a fixed inventory going back to antiquity; rather, items are continuously added to the general vocabulary from various sources (dialects, slang, loans from other languages, etc.), as was pointed out by Murray in connection with reference to words of unknown etymology. These he characterizes as words that 'have no kin in other languages, but stand quite alone in English, and, it cannot be doubted, are more or less recent creations of English itself—instances of *onomatopœia* in its true etymological sense of "name-creation". [. . .] the creative period of language, the "epoch of roots", has never come to an end' (Murray 1888: p. viii). Examples quoted by him are *bam, bamboozle, bang, bash, bilk, blab, blabber, blad, blare, blizzard, blob, blot, blotch, blurt, bluster, bob, bogus, bosh, bother, bounce, bum, bump, bunch, buzz,* etc., for which he could not find any etymological explanation. The source of these words is seen in the expressive, communicative function of everyday spoken language, and especially in dialects or in slang, from where they make their way into the written language. Many of these words were also analysed as onomatopoeic formations by Marchand (1969: 397 ff.) and listed in the chapter 'Phonetic Symbolism' of his book. The recognition of this continuous addition of words to the general vocabulary makes Principle I difficult to attain in practice, since there is never a guarantee that at the moment of the compilation of a lexicon a new word is not in the process of entering the vocabulary, although relative exhaustiveness might be possible at least in theory, and is also desirable.[3]

The exhaustiveness principle and derivational productivity

While the addition of simple lexical items to the vocabulary is primarily a practical problem for Principle I, the existence of word-formation processes of various kinds in every language makes this principle also problematic from a theoretical point of view for the dictionary maker. Such processes allow the almost unlimited production of new lexical items in response to the communicative needs of a speech community. This in fact had already been recognized by Murray. Thus, he characterizes prefixations with *anti-* and *be-* as having 'indefinite capabilities of extension' (Murray 1888: p. viii), and of the so-called 'simple combinations', under which he subsumes fully transparent compounds such as *air-breathing, air-built, air-current, air-passage,* he says that their number 'is practically unlimited, since they can be formed at will' (Murray 1888: p. vii). Recognition of this fact

---

[3] Nevertheless, the compilers of the first edition of the *OED* seem to have taken this principle with a grain of salt, in so far as they were somewhat hesitant to include vulgarisms (for example, *fuck* is not listed in the first edition, although it has been in use since the early sixteenth century), which is of course not really surprising in the age of Queen Victoria.

has, of course, determined the manner in which such complex lexical items have been handled in the *OED*, as will be discussed below. First, however, it might be useful to take a brief look at this problem from the point of view of word-formation theory rather than lexicography in order to see more clearly what is at issue here.

The functions of word-formation processes

The *raison d'être* of word-formation processes is the fact that they produce motivated complex lexical items, that is lexical items which are morphosemantically transparent such that their meanings can be derived from the meanings of their constituents and some underlying pattern that they share with other similarly formed complex items. This means that a nonce-formation can usually be satisfactorily interpreted by the listener when he or she hears it for the first time. Thus, a *history-changer* will, even without context, be automatically interpreted as 'someone who changes / has changed history', or an *order-giver* as 'someone who gives / has given an order' on the basis of the same pattern that underlies more familiar *stone-thrower, wine-drinker, meat-eater, alms-giver*, which is corroborated by the contextualized sources of these compounds:

'So you simply can't **change history** using stasis?' [. . .] 'No. [. . .] One small boy [. . .] is hardly going to be a **history-changer** because we've brought him forward to our era.' (Isaac Asimov and Robert Silverberg, *Child of Time*, 1992)

But why was this **order given** more than once? Why would the **order-giver** need that sort of privacy repeatedly?   (Isaac Asimov and Roger MacBride Allan, *Caliban*, 1993)

Similarly, *to unlose* in

'See how Ender handles it. If we've already **lost** him, if he can't handle this, who next? Who else?'—'I'll make up a list.'—'In the meantime, figure out how to **unlose** Ender.' (Orson Scott Card, *Ender's Game*, 1992)

is easily identifiable as 'to undo the losing of x', on the basis of the pattern that underlies *undo, unscrew, untie*. The recent coinage *zippergate* is easily interpretable as 'some political scandal (= *-gate*) having to do with the zipper of some pair of trousers', formed in analogy with *Watergate, Irangate, nannygate*. The interpretation of *Rolls Royce shares* in the following advertisement is also unproblematic:

If you want **shares in Rolls-Royce** apply now! [. . .] A Public Application Form for **Rolls Royce shares** appears in this newspaper.   (*The Times*)[4]

The existence of such processes, required by the restricted size of human memory and the potentially infinite needs of a speech community to find designations for communicatively salient segments of extralinguistic reality, makes the

---

[4] The text-cohesive function of such *ad hoc* formations is discussed in Kastovsky and Kryk Kastovsky (1997).

vocabulary of every language in principle open-ended. Necessary as this is for the functioning of language, it creates problems for the lexicographer, who has to decide how to handle both the derivational processes and their output in a necessarily finite dictionary. There are several aspects that have to be considered in this connection.

Morphosemantic transparency and lexicalization

Many of these processes, for example, the formation of agent nouns in -*er*, deverbal nouns in -*ing*, deverbal adjectives in -*able*, or the formation of N + N compounds as well as a number of other patterns, are almost unrestricted, that is they are comparable to purely grammatical-syntactic or morphological-inflectional processes, and consequently often lead to *ad hoc* formations like the ones cited above. There is no way for a lexicon to list all these formations because many are virtual and not actual, but can become actualized any time. Moreover, the size of a dictionary would become unmanageable: compare Murray's remark in connection with prefixations such as *anti-slavery, anti-vaccination, anti-Lacrosser, beperiwigged, be-uncled, bebishop, becobweb*: 'if every such combination had been separately set forth in its alphabetical place among the Main words, the size of this volume would have been seriously increased' (Murray 1888: p. ix). A way out is to refer to the word-formation process itself (prefixation, suffixation) in connection with the listing of the respective affixes, a strategy which has also been employed in the *OED*, but not without problems. But such a strategy does not work with compounds of the type *air-bag, bottle-green, icy-cold*, where the semantic patterns underlying the formations are rather diverse, and where we cannot simply refer to an entry 'compound formation'.

While many morphologically complex formations are also fully transparent semantically in the same way as the examples just discussed, this is by no means true of all of them. Total morphosemantic transparency is often impaired by the phenomenon of lexicalization (Kastovsky 1982: 164 ff.; Lipka 1977, 1981), by which complex lexical items, once they have entered the common vocabulary of a speech community, may undergo semantic (and also formal) modifications in the same way as simple lexical items are subject to semantic (and formal) change in the course of time. Thus, to take some standard examples: *blackboards* are no longer black but may also be green or white; *watchmakers* usually no longer make watches but just sell them; a *pushchair* is a chair that can be pushed but not one which pushes, while a *pushboat* is one that pushes, and not one which is pushed; a *call girl* is certainly not any girl that one might call on the phone, while a *call boy* originally was a youth employed to call actors onto the stage, or a hotel page, while he now may perform functions comparable to his female counterpart, etc. Moreover, even in the process of formation itself some semantic specialization may take place. Thus, though *lawn-mower* theoretically might denote a human being, it usually refers only to the gadget, similarly *bread-cutter, can-opener, bottle-opener*, etc., although these might, in an appropriate context, be interpreted as human agents too. Since diachronically lexicalization is a gradual phenomenon, it invariably leads to a synchronic scale of more or less lexicalized complex lexical items. This creates a problem for the lexicographer. He or she might not want to list fully transparent formations individually, but lexicalized formations would have to be given special treatment, because their semantics is not fully predictable. But where is the cut-off point between the totally predictable formations and the more or less lexicalized ones? As far as I can see, no dictionary so far has solved this problem really satisfactorily, and the *OED* is no exception, although its compilers have of course recognized the problem and tried to come to grips with it in various ways.

The organizational principles of the OED: *main words, subordinate words, combinations, and affixes*

The treatment of complex lexical items in a lexicon clearly depends on its internal structure and the structure of the individual entries (articles), on the definition of the basic term 'word', and on the various types of words recognized. In this respect, the *OED* is first of all based on the division of the vocabulary into three basic categories, main words, subordinate words, and combinations, (see the following definitions):

(1) Main words 'comprise (1) all single words, radical or derivative (e.g. *Ant, Amphitheatrically*), (2) all those compound words (and phrases) which, from their meaning, history, or importance claim to be treated in separate articles (e.g. *Afternoon, Almighty, Almsman, Air-pump, Aitch-bone, Ale-house, Forget-me-not, Adam's apple, All fours*). The articles in which these are treated constitute the *Main Articles*' (Murray 1888: p. xviii).

(2) Subordinate words 'include variant and obsolete forms of Main Words, and such words of bad formation, doubtful existence, or alleged use, as it is deemed proper, on any ground, to record' (Murray 1888: p. xviii).

(3) Combinations, 'when so simple as either to require no explanation, or to be capable of being briefly explained in connection with their cognates, are dealt with under the Main Words which form their first element, their treatment forming the concluding part of the Main Article' (Murray 1888: p. xviii).

These subdivisions are based on the following intersecting criteria: (a) the distinction between single words and compound words, (b) the importance and/or age of a lexical item, (c) the degree of semantic transparency of the respective lexical item, (d) the legitimacy of a form.[5]

There is, thus, no uniform way in which complex lexical items are treated in the *OED*. Rather, due to the intersection of these criteria, various classes and

---

[5] The latter criterion concerns only the category of subordinate words and will be disregarded in the following, as well as this category itself. But note that such entries are also used to list irregular inflectional forms of nouns, verbs, and adjectives, with an appropriate cross reference to the main article.

subclasses are created, which are kept apart in terms of the form of their listing, but also typographically (italics, small Clarendon (bold face), small capitals).

Criterion (a) seems to establish a straightforward two-way distinction between so-called single words (both simple and affix-formations) and compound words, where both constituents are words themselves (but see section 'Lexical units: words, phrases, lexemes, compounds, and combinations'). Criteria (b) and (c), on the other hand, establish a hierarchy among compounds, that is, they distinguish between those which are worthy to be treated in a main article, and those that are not, and among the latter, how these are actually handled in the respective main article. Note, incidentally, that the same criteria are applied to the treatment of prefixations and suffixations, which is not mentioned explicitly in the 'General Explanation', but only in the 'Preface' to the first volume (see section 'Morpho-semantic transparency and lexicalization'). Thus, prefix formations 'which appear to demand separate treatment, whether by virtue of their meaning, their long history, or frequent modern use, should be treated in their alphabetical order among other words; the remainder, of rare or unique occurrence, trivial importance, or obvious meaning, being arranged in groups under the various meanings or uses of the prefix, where each can be studied in connexion with words of similar formation' (Murray 1888: p. ix).[6] Thus, criteria (b) and (c) clearly are primary in determining what should figure as a separate entry or lemma in the lexicon, but, as we will see presently, these criteria are subjective and result in some problematic distinctions, which have to do mainly with the demarcation of the categories of 'compound' and 'combination', but also affect the handling of affixations. This, in turn, is related to the somewhat unclear status of the category 'word' in the *OED*.

Lexical units: words, phrases, lexemes, compounds, and combinations

For the compilers of the *OED*, the only cover term for lexical items of all kinds was 'word' as against 'phrase' (as part of grammar, i.e. syntax), and the demarcation between these two as well as the linguistic status of 'word' itself was far from settled. In particular, they did not yet have at their disposal the much more refined terminology current today in the wake of the work of Matthews (1974) and Lyons (1977). Thus they used the term 'word' indiscriminately for what is now neatly kept apart as 'lexeme' or 'lexical item' (= dictionary entry), 'word-form' (inflected form of a lexeme), and 'word' (concrete instantiation of such a form in an utterance). Also note that the meaning of 'lemma' referring to the headword of a dictionary entry, which is in common use today as a lexicographic alternative to 'lexeme', is a twentieth-century innovation, too. The major problem in this

---

[6] The same principle is advocated in the treatment of suffixes, where we also find lists of formations exemplifying the various senses, some of which are then treated in the main body of the lexicon
as main words, some are not. Thus, with the suffix -*age*, we find a sense group 'from verbs expressing
action' exemplified by the English formations *breakage, brewage, cleavage, postage, prunage, steerage,
wreckage*, of which all except *prunage* have a separate entry, while *prunage* is only found under the
suffix. Similar observations hold for other suffixes.

connection is the unclear distinction between 'compounds' and 'combinations', which is not based on a structural but on a usage criterion.

As has been pointed out, a basic distinction is made between 'single words' and 'compound words (and phrases)', the former being either simple words or affix formations, the latter consisting of more than one word. At face value, this distinction seems to be clear and corresponds to what we today call derivation and compounding (leaving aside the thorny problem of separating compounds and phrases, (Marchand 1969: 20 ff.), Bauer (1983: 102 ff.)). But this situation is complicated by the introduction of the category of 'combinations', whose status *vis-à-vis* compounds is not quite clear, although at least partly criteria (b) and (c) seem to play a role in the demarcation.

The nature of these combinations is discussed in greater detail in a separate section (Murray 1888: p. xxiii f.). There, they are defined as 'all collocations of simple words in which the separate spelling of each word is retained, whether they are formally connected by a hyphen, or virtually by the unity of their signification'. Though the hyphen is not regarded as a criterion distinguishing between phrases and compounds, it is interpreted as a signal of closer unity and is said to have a grammatical role: 'it implies either that the syntactic relation between two words is closer than if they stood side by side without it, or that the relation is a *less usual* one than that which would at first sight suggest itself to us' (Murray 1888: p. xxiii). Murray then discusses the difference between the phrase *after consideration* (as a free syntactic construction in *After consideration had been given to the proposal . . .*) and the combination *after-consideration* (as in *After-consideration had shown him his mistake*), pointing out that the relationship between *after* and *consideration* is different in the two examples, namely, it is closer and more unusual in the second. But then he concludes: '. . . *after-consideration* is not really a single word, any more than *subsequent consideration, fuller consideration*; the hyphen being merely a convenient help to the sense, which would be clearly expressed in speech by the different phrase accentuation *a·fter considera·tion* and *a·fter considera·tion.* [. . .] Nevertheless *after-consideration* [. . .] is on the way to become a single word, which *reconsideration* (chiefly because *re-* is not a separate word, but also because we have *reconsider*) is reckoned to be' (Murray 1888: p. xxiii). The apparent equivocation seems to be due to a problem with the use of 'word', or more precisely, 'single word', since a single word obviously cannot in turn be said to consist of words. Thus, the term 'single word' is restricted to simple words and affix formations, leaving compounds in the lurch as to their wordhood. The problem is recognized at least subconsciously, however, since it is admitted that '*after-consideration* [. . .] is on the way to become a single word'. But it is not really solved and eventually related to spelling: '. . . in many combinations the hyphen becomes an expression of this unification of sense. When this unification and specialization has proceeded so far that we no longer analyze the combination into its elements but take it in as a whole, as in *blackberry, postman, newspaper*, pronouncing it in speech with a single accent, the hyphen is usually omitted, and the fully developed compound is written as a single word. But this also is a question of degree . . .' (Murray 1888: p. xxiii). Thus, the fully developed compound (spelled as a single word without a hyphen?) is a single word, and combinations spelled with a hyphen are in principle not single words, but there is a cline between these two. Consequently, the demarcation of lexicalized phrases, combinations that according to our present understanding are compounds, and compounds in the *OED* interpretation remains open, and the hyphen, tentatively introduced as an expression of sense unification, is the weakest of possible criteria in view of its erratic occurrence.

The problem has also to be seen in connection with the historical bias of the *OED*. Historical linguists in those days regarded compounds as the result of an historical process by which the constituents of phrases gradually grew together and finally formed a single lexical item with a homogeneous sense or concept. As a result, semantic unity also figured prominently as a criterion of compound-hood, which, though not explicitly, at least implicitly also plays a role in Murray's argument.

Compounds, combinations, meaning, and article subdivisions

In view of these demarcation difficulties, Murray proposes the following tripartite division of combinations 'for practical purposes', for which he also introduces a typographical differentiation:

(1) Combinations 'in which each word retains its full meaning, the relation between them falling under one or other of the ordinary grammatical categories'[7] (Murray 1888: p. xxiii). These are listed in the form of specimens in italics at the end of each article and are globally illustrated with quotations, for example, *bed-apparel, -blanket, -board, -bolster, -bottom, -bug, -case, -curtain*, etc. (s.v. *bed*);

(2) Combinations 'of which the signification is somewhat specialized, but still capable of being briefly explained in a few words, in connexion with their cognates' (Murray 1888: p. xxiii). These are treated alphabetically at the end of the main article, printed in small Clarendon, (bold face), and illustrated by quotations arranged in the same order, for example *bed-bolster* (in gunnery), *bed-card* 'a card fixed at a hospital patient's bed', *bed-key* 'an iron tool for screwing and unscrewing the nuts and bolts of a bedstead', *bed-litter* 'straw, etc. to make up a bed', *bed-sore* 'a soreness of the skin produced by long lying in bed', etc. (s.v. *bed*);

(3) Combinations 'which attain in specialization of sense to the position of full compounds, or which are used in various senses, or have a long history, and thus require to be dealt with more at large' (Murray 1888: p. xxiv). These are listed in small capitals at the end of the main article, and then dealt with separately as main words, for example, *marriage-bed, state-bed*, or as separate entries after the main article of the first constituent. Thus the following compounds are also treated

---

[7] These, however, are not specified in the dictionary.

as main entries: *bedchamber, bed-clothes, bedfellow, bedgown, bed-head, bed-linen, bed-maker, bed-pan, bed-post*, etc.

This classification is obviously based on the criteria (b) and (c) mentioned above and is rather problematic, since it is hardly possible to objectivize it. Thus, while *marriage-bed* is treated as a main article (perhaps because it contains a hyphen), *wedlock bed* is not (probably because it is spelled without a hyphen), although the two compounds probably have the same degree of specialization. Similarly, it can be doubted that *bed-linen* is more specialized than *bed-case*, although they are treated differently. Examples of this kind can be found for almost every major entry, both in the domain of compounds (combinations) and affixation, where the same principle applies. This subjective classification thus is a major weakness of an otherwise absolutely admirable enterprise.

The criterion of 'importance' in connection with the according of a status different from normal compounds to 'specific names' is also responsible for another problem with the organization of the articles, because firstly these criteria are not applied consistently, and secondly it is not clear what is to be understood by the term 'specific name'. Thus, Murray concludes the section on combinations as follows: 'All compounds and combinations of interest or importance will thus be found either in their alphabetical order, or under the word which constitutes their first element. But phrases are treated under their leading word, as *on account of*, under ACCOUNT; and specific names, like *Sea Anemone, Black Alder*, under their generic names ANEMONE, ALDER, etc. *Sea Anemone* is considered (linguistically) as a kind of *Anemone*, but *Adam's Needle* not as a kind of *Needle*, nor *Mouse-ear* as a kind of *Ear*' (Murray 1888: p. xxiv). Now, linguistically, *sea anemone* is as much a compound as are *sea-adder, sea-angler, sea-bat, sea-bear*, and many others of the same kind, and these latter are as much 'specific names' of animals as is *sea anemone*. It is therefore not quite clear why the latter are treated in separate main articles after the main article dealing with *sea*, while *sea anemone* is relegated to *anemone* as a subsense. But then, in an enterprise of this magnitude, and one that did take almost fifty years to complete, inconsistencies such as these are inevitable.

THE HISTORICAL PRINCIPLE AND WORD-FORMATION:
THE ROLE OF ETYMOLOGY

Let me now turn to Principle IV, the historical orientation of the *OED* and its consequences for the treatment of word-formation. The strict application of this principle was a major innovation in lexicography at the time, and, as has been pointed out above, it was in line with the general linguistic feeling prevalent in the latter half of the nineteenth and the first decades of the twentieth century. It is reflected by the organization of the individual articles, which represent the historical development of the various senses (meanings) of the main words, one of the most important sources of information which the *OED* still provides today.

In the domain under discussion, the historical orientation manifests itself by the dominance of what might be called the 'etymological principle', that is, the all-importance of the etymology or source of a lexical item, cf. the following statement: 'The **Morphology** or *Form-History* [within square brackets] includes:— 1. the *Derivation*, or *Etymology*, showing the actual origin of the word, when ascertained. 2. The *Subsequent Form-history* in English, when this presents special features, as phonetic change, contraction, corruption, perversion by popular etymology or erroneous association' (Murray 1888: p. xx).

Various possibilities are distinguished with regard to 1.: (a) an extant formal representative, or direct phonetic descendant, of an earlier word (usually of Germanic, more precisely OE, origin) has continued until today; (b) adoption (a popular process) from a foreign language, for example, *inch, pound, street, rose, cat, prison, algebra, antic*, etc.; (c) adaptation (a learned or literary process, by which Latin or Greek words were deprived of their terminations, reducing them to their stem form); (d) formation (the 'combination of existing words or part of words with each other, or with *living formatives*, i.e. syllables which no longer exist as separate words, but yet have an appreciable *significance* which they impart to the new product' (Murray 1888: p. xx)). And it is furthermore stated that phonetic descent, adoption, adaptation, and word-formation are 'usually combined under the term *derivation*; but, until we know in which of them, singly or in combination, a word has originated, we do not know its Etymology' (Murray 1888: p. xxi).[8]

Thus, the etymology, the historical origin of a word, was the most important aspect of its morphology. Nevertheless, as aspect (d) above, referring to word-formation, indicated, the fathers of the *OED* were not unaware of the synchronic principle of motivation/analysability as such, but in practice this was sometimes difficult to apply because of the dominant historical perspective, because what had been motivated historically might not be motivated any longer synchronically in the same way. With prefixations and suffixations, there are relatively few problems. Usually the base of a derivative occurs before the derivative itself, so that the historical direction of the derivation (in the sense of note 8) coincides with the synchronic one and vice versa. Thus a strictly historical statement, according to which the derivative (affixation) is formed from the simple word by a word-formation process ('*formed* on or from (f.) native or foreign elements' (Murray 1888: p. xx)), would not in any way be contradicted by the synchronic relationship between the two. This holds for the overwhelming majority of the instances listed in the *OED*. In actual fact, here again it is the most valuable source of information for the gradual growth of the English vocabulary by the activation of word-formation processes.

---

[8] The non-etymological, synchronic sense of 'derivation' is introduced only in *OED2* (1989: p. xxxii), in a separate section entitled 'Derivatives', which are defined as 'any word which has been formed by the addition of a suffix to a main word also treated in this Dictionary (also, more rarely, by the alteration or removal of the suffix of a main word).' This, incidentally, means an indirect renunciation of the strict historical principle.

Back-formation and zero-derivation

There are, however, two special types of word-formation processes, namely back-formation and zero-derivation, where some reservations are indicated.

Back-formation is defined as 'the derivation of such words as are known to have been extracted from longer words which have the formal appearance of bimorphemic, composite signs' (Marchand 1969: 391). The classical examples, also quoted by Marchand, are *pedlar/peddler : to peddle* and *burglar : to burgle*. The noun *pedlar/peddler* was first recorded in 1377, the verb *to peddle* in 1532. The noun *burglar* dates back to the thirteenth century in Latin form (*burglatores*), and is recorded in an English form in the sixteenth century, while the verb occurs first in the nineteenth century as a jocular expression. Historically speaking, the two are parallel: the verb has been extracted from the noun by cutting off what looks like an agent-noun suffix, and the residual verb is defined as 'perform the activity characteristic of N'. But synchronically, there is a difference which cannot be captured by the OED. The derivational relationship between *peddler* and *to peddle* has been reversed, so that today a native speaker will probably interpret *peddler* as 'someone who peddles' rather than *to peddle* as 'act like a peddler', whereas the relationship between *burglar* and *to burgle* is not yet quite the same,[9] although it also seems to move in the same direction. Other examples exhibiting the same kind of switch in the direction of synchronic derivation are *swindler/swindle*, *editor/edit*. This switch cannot be captured in a purely historical account as the one adopted by the OED.

The same problem occurs with zero-derivation. Zero-derivation or conversion is a word-formation process where one lexical item is derived from another without an overt derivational marker (suffix), for example, *look* vb. > *look* sb., *father* sb. > *father* vb., *clean* adj. > *clean* vb. (Marchand 1969: 359 ff.). The problem at issue here is again the direction of derivation. With suffixal derivatives, this is usually clear: the item characterized by a suffix is secondary (derived), the unsuffixed item is primary, except for instances of back-derivation which have not yet been reinterpreted, like *burglar: burgle*. But with zero-derivations, no such formal criterion exists, and one has to fall back on other criteria (Marchand 1963*a*, *b*, 1964). And here again, the only criterion open to the OED is a historical one, namely, chronology. The OED invariably treats that word as basic which is recorded first, regardless of the situation in Modern English. This is of course justified on account of its historical framework and the etymological principle described above. Moreover, in many, if not even in most instances, it also represents the Modern English situation. But, as has been argued by Marchand, from a synchronic point of view the direction of the derivation can be established only on the basis of semantic dependence, namely, that word which is used in a natural definition of the other has to be regarded as basic. And, as with

---

[9] Note that the American verb is *to burglarize* and not *to burgle*.

back-derivations, this direction may change in the course of time due to semantic change or change in the frequency of use, which again cannot be captured by the historical treatment advocated in the *OED* (see the following examples). According to the *OED*, the verb *bore* 'to weary by tedious conversation or simply by the failure to be interesting' (1768) is derived from the noun *bore* 'the malady of *ennui*' (1766), but according to Marchand (1969: 376), the synchronic relationship is verb > noun; similar are *cook* sb. and *cook* vb., *coach* sb. 'a private tutor ...' and *coach* vb. 'to prepare a candidate for an examination'. Somewhat different are the entries for *guide* sb./vb. and *spy* sb./vb. Here, the *OED* merely assumes independent borrowing from Old French, which is certainly historically correct. But this of course does not account for the obvious synchronic derivational relationship that has developed subsequently. Moreover, the ordering of the noun before the verb again seems to give the former priority (it also has the earlier first quotation), although synchronically the relationship is the reverse. Examples of the latter kind are quite numerous and unavoidable, of course, since the historical bias makes a synchronic perspective in the individual articles impossible. This is not intended as a criticism of the *OED* as such; it simply is an automatic consequence of the theoretical framework chosen, of which, however, one has to be aware.

NON-NATIVE WORD-FORMATION PATTERNS

One final aspect, already briefly touched upon in the section 'Back-formation and zero-derivation', that I would like to look at is the handling of non-native lexical items, and in particular of non-native word-formation patterns (prefixations, suffixations). Following the etymological principle, words of foreign origin 'are referred to the foreign word or elements whence they were immediately adopted or formed. In certain cases these foreign words, especially the French, are themselves traced to their antecedent forms or component elements; but these antecedents are considered only with a view to the clearer comprehension of the history and use of the word in English' (Murray 1888: p. xxi). This not only applies to simple lexical items, but also to affixations and compounds, the latter including so-called combining forms such as *astro-* (see *astrography, astrology, astroscope*), *cosmo-* (*cosmocrat, cosmogeny, cosmographer, cosmopolitan*), *tele-* (*telegram, telegraph, telemeter, telephone, telescope*), etc., a still much under-researched area (Stein 1978*b*). Here, the dictionary follows the same principles as with native compounds and affixations: it lists the respective affixes in separate entries with appropriate etymological information, gives definitions of the various senses, and illustrates these with a series of examples and corresponding quotations. These cover the 'less important' instances, whereas the 'more important' items are treated in separate articles, a procedure to which the same criticism applies as that made against the treatment of compounds and combination.

A closer look at the entries for prefixes and suffixes reveals another problem caused by the strict adherence to the etymological principle, which conflicts with the property of transparency/analysability on which modern word-formation theory is based. It is a problem which has by no means gone unnoticed by the compilers of the *OED*, but for which they did not yet have a solution. Take, as a random example, the entry for the prefix *re-*.[10] The article begins with a general etymological statement: '*prefix*, of Latin origin, with the general sense of "back" or "again", occurring in a large number of words directly or indirectly adopted from Latin, or of later Romanic origin, and on the model of these freely employed in English as a prefix to verbs, and to substantives and adjectives derived from these' (s.v. *re-*). This is followed by a section on the use of *re-* in Latin, with ample documentation and the concluding remark: 'Even in Latin the sense of *re-* is not always clear, and in many words the development of secondary meanings tends greatly to obscure its original force. This loss of distinct meaning is naturally increased in English, when the word has been adopted in a sense more or less remote from the strict etymological significance of the two elements which compose it. In many cases the simple word to which the prefix is attached is wanting in English. In others a change of sound or shifting of stress is disguising its original sense' (*ibid.*). This is certainly the case with the first examples of *re-* formations quoted from the twelfth century, namely, *recluse, recoil, record, relief, religion, religious, remission, rebel, receit, relic, relief, repent, restore, revest*. None of these would have been analysable into a prefix and a base at the time of borrowing (nor, incidentally, in the source language), so that it would have been impossible to extract a living prefix from them which could have become productive in English. In fact, this has also been noticed by the compilers of the *OED*, when they make a phonological distinction between such etymological elements and the genuine productive English prefix *re-*: 'In English formations, whether on Latin or English bases, *re-* is almost exclusively employed in the sense of "again". [...] In one or other application of this sense, *re-* may be prefixed to any English verb or verbal derivative, as *rearrange, rearranger, rearrangement; reignite, reignitible, reignition*; [...]. In all words of this type the prefix is pronounced with a clear *e* (ri), and frequently with a certain degree of stress, whereas in words of Latin or Romanic origin, the vowel is usually obscured or shortened, as in *repair* [...], *reparation*' (*ibid.*).[11] The problem thus is to keep apart elements that historically speaking originated as prefixes at some time, but can no longer be regarded as meaningful elements in the lexical item in question, and elements which are meaningful, living, that is, productive elements and as such part of the word-formation system of the English language. As this quotation has shown, the authors of the *OED* were by no means unaware of this problem, but the purely

---

[10] Cf. also the remarks on the treatment of *de-* and *dis-* in Marchand (1969).

[11] For technical reasons, the phonetic transcription of the *OED* cannot be reproduced here, but knowledge of the Modern English pronunciation should make this point clear.

historical-etymological framework underlying the dictionary—and prevalent at the time—did not provide any solution for this problem, which could be solved only by taking into consideration a synchronic approach to the structure of the vocabulary, and the insight that this consists of different levels.

This insight, incidentally, is already present in Murray's 'General Explanations', although it is not applied systematically in the dictionary itself. Thus we find the following statement: 'Formation is the chief natural process by which the vocabulary of a language is increased: it is both popular and learned; in its popular application, it gives such words as *black-bird, shep-herd, work-er, high-ness, grand-ly, a-swim, be-moan, after-noon*; in learned application, such as *con-caten-ation, mono-petal-ous, chloro-phyl, tele-phone*; in a mixture of the two, such as *acknowledge-ment, lion-ize, starv-ation, betroth-al*' (Murray 1888: pp. xx–xxi). Though the division proposed here again is based on etymology and not on synchronic function (the last examples are, despite their non-native ingredients, based on native patterns and therefore from a functional point of view belong to the first group), it foreshadows the division of English word-formation into two layers (word-formation on a native basis of coining and word-formation on a non-native basis of coining) advocated by Marchand (1969: 5 ff.), or the various derivational levels postulated in lexical phonology.

CONCLUSION

The editors and compilers of the *OED* were indeed, as the title of this volume has it, 'pioneers in the untrodden forest'. They did not have a model for what they had planned to do: the history of the English vocabulary. They did not quite formulate their project in this way, though this is what the *OED* eventually turned out to be. What they had in the way of linguistic background was primarily the Neogrammarian way of thinking, and this they applied fairly rigorously in their empirical work. At the same time they noticed its limitations and the problems that a dictionary was facing which not only had to serve historical but also synchronic purposes (though only implicitly, and for practical reasons). The result was a pragmatic compromise, probably more satisfactory for the lexicographer than for the linguist, who tends to be a puritan. But without the *OED*, none of the major contributions to the study of English word-formation in the last sixty years, namely, Koziol (1937), Jespersen (1942), or Marchand (1960, 1969) would have been possible. As I know from the author himself, this is particularly true of Marchand (1960, 1969), the most comprehensive, and most influential synchronic-diachronic description of English word-formation to date. When he was interned in Turkey during the Second World War, he happened to have company: the complete first edition of *OED*, which he read from cover to cover. The result was the first draft of his *Categories and Types of Present-day English Word-Formation*, which would certainly not exist without the *OED*.

REFERENCES

Bauer, L. (1983). *English Word-Formation*. Cambridge: Cambridge University Press.

Craigie, W. A., and Onions, C. T. (1933). 'Historical Introduction', *A New English Dictionary on Historical Principles*. Introduction, Supplement, and Bibliography. Oxford: Clarendon Press, pp. vii–xxvi.

Jespersen, O. (1942). *A Modern English Grammar on Historical Principles*. Part VI. *Morphology*. Copenhagen: Munksgaard.

Kastovsky, D. (1982). *Wortbildung und Semantik*. (Studienreihe Englisch 14). Tübingen /Düsseldorf: Francke/Bagel.

——, and Kryk-Kastovsky, B. (1997). 'Morphological and Pragmatic Factors in Text Cohesion', in H. Ramisch and K. Wynne (eds.), *Language in Time and Space. Studies in Honour of Wolfgang Viereck on the occasion of his 60th birthday*. (*ZDL*-Beiheft 97). Stuttgart: Steiner, 462–75.

Koziol, H. (1937). *Handbuch der englischen Wortbildungslehre*. Heidelberg: Winter.

Lipka, L. (1977). 'Lexikalisierung, Idiomatisierung und Hypostasierung als Problem einer synchronischen Wortbildungslehre', in H. E. Brekle and D. Kastovsky (eds.), *Perspektiven der Wortbildungsforschung. Beiträge zum Wuppertaler Wortbildungskolloquium vom 9.–10. Juli 1975. Anläßlich des 70. Geburtstages von Hans Marchand am 1. Oktober 1977*. (Wuppertaler Schriftenreihe Linguistik 1). Bonn: Bouvier, 155–64.

—— (1981). 'Zur Lexikalisierung im Deutschen und Englischen', in L. Lipka. and H. Günther (eds.), *Wortbildung*. (Wege der Forschung 564). Darmstadt: Wissenschaftliche Buchgesellschaft, 119–32.

Lyons, J. (1977). *Semantics*. 2 vols. Cambridge: Cambridge University Press.

Marchand, H. (1960). *The Categories and Types of Present-Day English Word-Formation*. (1st edn.). Wiesbaden: Harrassowitz.

—— (1963a). 'On Content as a Criterion of Derivational Relationship with Backderived Words', *Indogermanische Forschungen*, 68: 170–5.

—— (1963b). 'On a Question of Contrary Analysis with Derivationally Connected but Morphologically Uncharacterized Words', *English Studies*, 44: 176–87.

—— (1964). 'A Set of Criteria for the Establishing of Derivational Relationship Between Words Unmarked by Derivational Morphemes', *Indogermanische Forschungen*, 69: 10–19.

—— (1969). *The Categories and Types of Present-Day English Word-Formation*. (2nd rev. edn.). München: Beck.

Matthews, P. H. (1974). *Morphology*. London: Cambridge University Press.

Murray, J. A. H. (1888). 'Preface to Volume I'. *NED*. Vol. I. A and B. Oxford: Clarendon Press, pp. v–xxvi.

[Philological Society]. (1859). *Proposal for the Publication of a New English Dictionary by the Philological Society*. London: Trübner and Co.

Stein, G. (1978a). 'The Battle of Words: The Latest 6,000', in C. Gutknecht (ed.), *Contributions to Applied Linguistics*, Vol. 3, Frankfurt: Lang, 103–15.

—— (1978b). 'English Combining-forms', *Tartu Riikli Ülikool. Linguistica*, 9: 140–7.

8

OED and the Earlier History of English

Eric Stanley

THE PHILOLOGICAL SOCIETY'S NEW DICTIONARY
ON HISTORICAL PRINCIPLES

The Oxford English Dictionary, abbreviated *OED*, is the title by which the book that forms the subject of this volume of studies has been known throughout this century, though it appeared on its spines and title-pages only in the twelve-volume reprint of 1933 (see also Chapter 1, note 1). Burchfield (1972–86: i, s.v. *O*) has as the earliest use of the abbreviation *OED* a quotation from E. E. Morris's *Austral English* (1898). The scene for the new name was set by the loyal dedication prefixed to the third volume of the dictionary: 'To the Queen's Most Excellent Majesty this Historical Dictionary of the English Language is by Her Gracious Permission Dutifully Dedicated by the University of Oxford A.D. M DCCC XCVII.' The lexicographers' and the University's pride in a great undertaking of Queen Victoria's reign is evident in that dedication, and it is fully justified by its lexicological planning and lexicographical and typographical execution, clearly to be seen already in the words from A to E that had been published, not quite in alphabetical order, in the fascicles issued by July 1897. A highly significant word in that dedication is 'historical', which answers to the title of the work as used from *A–Ant*, the first fascicle published in January 1884, to the *Supplement* published in 1933: *A New English Dictionary on Historical Principles; founded mainly on materials collected by The Philological Society*, abbreviated in general use to *NED*, an abbreviation first recorded by Burchfield (1972–86: ii, s.v. *N*, II. 1.), who has no use earlier than a quotation of 1904. Other abbreviations in early use include *N.E.Dict.*, thus Triggs (1896: 75), 'See "braid," N. E. Dict.'.

  NED (as it was then called) was not the first English dictionary with citations for each sense and subsense arranged in order of date. The credit for turning that into a lexicographic principle must go to the editor of another dictionary, that by Charles Richardson (1836–7), whose very title proclaims a policy: *A New Dictionary of the English Language, Combining Explanation with Etymology: and Illustrated by Quotations from the best Authorities. The Words—with those of the same family, in German, Dutch and Swedish, or in Italian, French and Spanish,—*

are traced to their Origin. The EXPLANATIONS *are deduced from the primitive* Meaning *through the various* Usages. *The* QUOTATIONS *are arranged Chronologically from the earliest period to the beginning of the present century.* He too called his work 'the New English Dictionary' on the half-title and in Section II of the Preface. His programmatic title might indeed have heralded a new age of English lexicography on historical principles, if only it had been executed with better etymological knowledge. Ominous in the etymological Section II of the Preface is the glowing commendation of John Horne Tooke's *Diversions of Purley* (1798–1805), and the reader's worst fears are realized when, in the same section and more fully in the body of the dictionary, Richardson traces the origin, for example, of *believe* to *live by*, and the origin of *sad* to the past tense *sat* of the verb *to set* from OE *settan*. The earliest of his quotations are of the thirteenth century. Even here, where Richardson comes close in selection of authorities to *OED*, the tone is of another age; he says in Section III (about the quotations adduced by him):

The quotations that have been selected from [Robert of] Gloucester, [Robert Manning of] Brunne, and Peers' Plouhman, always take their place at the head of the array. Then follow, Wiclif, supported, whenever possible, by an early translator of the Bible; next, in rank and order, Chaucer and Gower, free, as the great patriarchs of our speech, from any intermixture with their successors. Chaucer, with whose "ditees and songes glade," his contemporary Gower declared, even then, "the londe to be fulfilled over all;" and Gower himself, so justly named "the Moral Gower," who, he tells us,

> Undertoke
> In Englysshe for to make a boke,
> Which stant betwene ernest and game.
> *Conf. Am.* b. 8.

Here another principle is to be detected, 'rank and order': the order is chronology, and the rank is literary quality. Not that lesser writers are to be neglected by the diligent lexicographer. After his tribute to Chaucer and Gower, the latter honoured by a quotation, *Confessio Amantis*, VIII. 3107–9 (Macaulay 1900–1: ii, 474–5), Richardson goes on:

After these will be found, in due arrangement, a host of writers, whose works have never been before ensearched, for the important service of lexicography: our matchless translator of the Bible, Tindale; Udal, and his associates, the translators of the Commentaries of Erasmus; Berners, of Froissart; Sir Thomas More; the Chronicles of Fabyan, and the Voyages of Hackluyt; with many others, whose compositions, small in size, but of inestimable worth, have hitherto been merely placed upon the shelves of the collector, as rarities to gaze at. In this region of unexplored country, I have travelled with most gratifying success.

DEAN RICHARD CHENEVIX TRENCH

In lexicographical intention, therefore, those members of the Philological Society charged with the task of organizing the compilation of a new English dictionary on historical principles, for the new dictionary was the Philological Society's Dictionary, had a predecessor in Richardson. Unlike him, they, chief among them Herbert Coleridge, F. J. Furnivall, and Richard Chenevix Trench, understood the problems better, and as a result the execution of the Society's Dictionary was vastly superior to the dictionary Richardson achieved.

The 1850s and 1860s are the decades during which the foundations were laid for such a new dictionary on historical principles. Semantic scholarship was promoted by R. C. Trench in a little glossary (1859: p. vii) in the Preface of which he reveals his connection with the proposed new work:

> Seeing that I have had some share, though a small one, in the suggestion of a new English Dictionary to be published by the Philological Society, I may state that I considered it became me to use no portion whatever of the materials which are being collected for it in the composition of this volume—of those contributions for a public object to a private end. Indeed those materials have never so much as come under my eye, except some exceedingly small portions of them, which by accident passed through my hands on their way to those of the Editor; not to say that this little Glossary was in all essential parts completed two years ago, before that great work was so much as contemplated.

Trench's quotations go back no further than Chaucer frequently, the Wycliffite Bible very frequently, and, for no more than the occasional word, *Piers Plowman*, Gower, Lydgate, Capgrave, and *The Storie of Asneth* (Trench 1859: 203 s.v. *specious*). Most are from the sixteenth century onwards, with Shakespeare to the fore in rank and frequency. That Shakespeare occupies a large place in the collection is fully justified by the fact that he was the most widely read early author, and that therefore the semantic difficulties of his works were most in need of explanation for the literary Victorian reader. Chaucer too was widely read, and several editions were available. The Wycliffite Bible was available in a very good edition with a serviceable glossary (Forshall and Madden 1850); and there may have been the further reasons that the Bible was a book with which the intended readership of the *Select Glossary* was very familiar, and that it could be compared with Tyndal's New Testament and the Authorized Version, both quoted frequently by Trench. For him, by then Dean of Westminster (and four years later Archbishop of Dublin), the Bible must have had a special place, and its wording in English a special interest. The use made of *The Storie of Asneth* is puzzling. The poem is given no title and no other identification than 'Metrical Romance of the Fourteenth Century'. It appears not to have been available (other than in MS Ellesmere 26 A 13, at that time still in private ownership and not as readily accessible as it is now in the Huntington Library) before MacCracken's edition (1910). MacCracken says of the author, 'This worthy cleric lived, I suppose, not far from Warwickshire, and not long after the death of Chaucer' (p. 224). One wonders from what (presumably secondary) source Trench drew the quotation. Chaucer's vocabulary had been given glossarial treatment in most of the editions, for example, in the glossary to Urry's edition (1721), compiled by Timothy Thomas (cf.

Hammond 1908: 129). For *The Canterbury Tales* Thomas Tyrwhitt's glossary published 1778 as the last volume of his edition (Tyrwhitt 1775–8) is good. Personal interest and availability inevitably guide the compiler of an unsystematic work of lexicography such as that by Trench, and they guided him. His too was a historical view of the task before those who were undertaking a new English dictionary, and he had better sense than Richardson who had followed Horne Tooke into mistaken semasiology based on often nonsensical etymologies.

-HERBERT COLERIDGE

Availability rather than predilection guided Herbert Coleridge when he produced his slim dictionary of early Middle English, describing this work of only just over a hundred pages, without any false modesty, as 'the foundation-stone of the Historical and Literary portion of the Philological Society's proposed English Dictionary' (1859: p. iii). Coleridge had signed the Preface, 13 June 1859; he died on 23 April 1861, only 30 years old. He knew, of course, that the Philological Society wanted their dictionary to be historical. 'Literary' was not interpreted by him as entirely exclusive of all but literature, for he lists among books and editions referred to (Coleridge 1859: pp. v–vii) '*The Early English Psalter*' (from British Library MS Cotton Vespasian D.vii). The Psalter is, however, an exception; for what might look like a scientific treatise, '*Fragments on Popular Science*, from the Early English Metrical Lives of Saints', is in fact verse (cf. Brown and Robbins 1943: nos 3029 and 3453). Thomas Wright, its editor, describes it (1841: p. xiii): '(MS. Harl., No. 2277, fol. 127, rᵒ, written in the reign of Edward I.). It is curious as being the earliest piece of the kind which we find in the *English* language.' In line with the scholarly usage of the age Wright's use of 'the *English* language' probably meant English as opposed to Anglo-Saxon and Anglo-Norman, rather than English as opposed to Semi-Saxon. Wright attached importance to it for historians of science. A text preserved in a manuscript of the late thirteenth or, as is now thought (Görlach 1974: 84) the early fourteenth century (and Wright's dating is perhaps to be interpreted as 'late in the reign of Edward I'), may be allowed to fall within Coleridge's period of 1250 to 1300.

Coleridge lists the printed sources of his dictionary, and not only in his title but also in his Preface he stresses that his dictionary, like the Philological Society's proposed larger work, is to be based on printed literature. He has dealt with writings assigned by him to the thirteenth century, a period to which he attaches significance in terms now antiquated: 'It is only proper to add that English literature, as distinguished from Semi-Saxon, is assumed to commence about the middle of the 13th century' (Coleridge 1859: p. iii). *OED* itself included the vocabulary of English from the Conquest onwards, that is, it treated what Coleridge called Semi-Saxon as fully as it treated what he called early English. Coleridge's bibliographical introduction to his excerption of words from early texts shows that he was aware of differing versions: for *King Horn* he chose the earlier text from

Cambridge University Library MS Gg. 4. 27. II rather than the later from British Library MS Harley 2253, and for *Poema Morale* he prefers the text from British Library MS Egerton 613 to that in Bodleian MS Digby A. 4. Both versions of each were available in printed editions, *King Horn* (Harley) in Ritson (1802: ii, 91–155) and (Gg. 4. 27) in Michel (1845), and *Poema Morale* (Digby) in Hickes (1705, 1703: i/1, 222–4) and (Egerton) in Furnivall (1858: 22–35), editions of varying reliability. George Hickes had published the Digby version of *Poema Morale* to illustrate what he considers to be the breakdown of Anglo-Saxon, as the first item of chapter xxiv 'De Poetica *Semi-Saxonica*, sive corrupta poesi *Anglo-Saxonum*', with MS Digby A. 4 described as 'Codex *Semi-Saxonicus*'. Hickes's designation of what is now called early Middle English verse as Semi-Saxon or corrupt verse of the Anglo-Saxons influenced scholarly thinking in England about this period of the language: in that view English proper began only when Semi-Saxon was over, a perception still current when the policy for the new dictionary was formulated by members of the Philological Society.

THE SECOND HALF OF THE NINETEENTH CENTURY

The second half of the nineteenth century was a period of very great change in all departments of the historical scholarship of the English language, and by the end of the century the notion of Semi-Saxon had disappeared together with the term. *Old English* was used for Middle English, for example by F. H. Stratmann (1867), who even in his title refers to the writings of the thirteenth, fourteenth, and fifteenth centuries from which he has compiled his dictionary, and he did so still in 1881; or it was used more specifically for early Middle English. From 1871 onwards the term *Old English* began to be used for the language of the Anglo-Saxons, though *Anglo-Saxon* survived and survives. Throughout its long history from 1884 to 1928 and still in the *Supplement* of 1933, *NED* (and so also the reprint of 1933, called *OED*, and the integrated edition of 1989, called *OED* second edition) used the terminology given by Murray (1888: p. xx) in the 'General Explanations' to explain the system of assigning numbers to the spellings listed near the beginning of each entry. *Old English* in the muddled entry published in 1891, s.v. *English*, sb. 1.b., is at variance with the dictionary's own use of '*Old English* or Anglo-Saxon', and was only cleared up by Burchfield (1972–86: i, s.v. *English*, sb. 1.b.), where the credit for the current use of *Old English* is rightly given to Henry Sweet (1871: p. v) in the opening words and first footnote of the Preface to his edition of Alfred's *Pastoral Care*:

Of all the unpublished Old English[1] texts, the present is perhaps the most important.

[1] I use 'Old English' throughout this work to denote the unmixed, inflectional stage of the English language, commonly known by the barbarous and unmeaning title of 'Anglo-Saxon'.

When a few years later Sweet brought out his *History of English Sounds* (1888), reprinting to a great extent his studies on the sounds of Old and Middle English in article form (1874), he throughout used the term *Old English* without explanation, as if the term *Anglo-Saxon* were no longer in his mind and as if it should no longer be in the minds of readers interested in the history of the language, though for the use of students wishing or required to learn Old English he never abandoned 'the barbarous and unmeaning title of "Anglo-Saxon"' in the titles to his elementary books (1876, 1882, 1885*a*, 1887, 1897*a*, and 1897*b*). Henry Bradley, when he published, as *A Middle English Dictionary*, his edition of Stratmann's *A Dictionary of the Old English Language*, has this first footnote to the Preface (1891: p. v):

> In the published editions the work is entitled 'A Dictionary of the Old English Language;' but in revising it for a new edition the author [Stratmann] substituted 'Middle-English' for 'Old English' in the title-page. He also indicated that in the body of the dictionary the abbreviation 'A.-S.' (Anglo-Saxon) should be changed into 'O.E.'

Robert Bridges (1928: 12–17) tells us that Bradley had been working as co-editor since 1885 with Murray, and his concurrence in Stratmann's changes concur also with the practice of *NED*. The term *Middle English* for the language between Old English and Tudor English was derived from Jacob Grimm's use (1819: e.g. 106) of *mittelenglische sprache*; Grimm (1819: e.g. 524) used *altenglisch* for early Middle English. Murray had laid down that the vocabulary of Old English was not included in the dictionary in the same way as that of English after 1150, as he makes clear in the 'General Explanations' (1888: p. xviii):

> [T]he vocabulary of past times is known to us solely from its preservation in written records; the extent of our knowledge of it depends entirely upon the completeness of the records, and the completeness of our acquaintance with them. And the farther back we go, the more imperfect are the records, the smaller is the fragment of the actual vocabulary that we can recover.
>
> Subject to the conditions which thus encompass every attempt to reconstruct a complete English Dictionary, the present work aims at exhibiting the history and signification of the English words now in use, or known to have been in use since the middle of the twelfth century. This date has been adopted as the only natural halting-place, short of going back to the beginning, so as to include the entire Old English or 'Anglo-Saxon' Vocabulary. To do this would have involved the inclusion of an immense number of words, not merely long obsolete but also having obsolete inflexions, and thus requiring, if dealt with at all, a treatment different from that adapted to the words which survived the twelfth century. For not only was the stream of English literature reduced to the tiniest thread (the slender annals of the Old English or Anglo-Saxon Chronicle being for nearly a century its sole representative), but the vast majority of the ancient words that were destined not to live into modern English, comprising the entire scientific, philosophical, and poetical vocabulary of Old English, had already disappeared, and the old inflexional and grammatical system had been levelled to one so essentially modern as to require no special treatment in the Dictionary. Hence we exclude all words that had become obsolete by 1150. But to words actually included this date has no application; their history is exhibited from their first appearance, however early.

This statement explaining the exclusion of Old English from the dictionary (unless required to trace back to the earliest stage words used after 1150) contains exaggerations, both in using 'immense' of the number of words that would have had to be added for total coverage of English from the seventh century onwards, and in averring that for the century from 1050 (perhaps 1066 is meant) to 1150 nothing remains except the later annals in versions of the Anglo-Saxon Chronicle, as well as in ascribing the levelling of inflexions and changes in the grammatical system to that century. The total disappearance of the scientific, philosophical, and poetic vocabulary is a further exaggeration. It is, however, no exaggeration to say that had all of Old English been treated as all of Middle English and Modern English were treated in the dictionary it would certainly have made a large work of reference considerably larger, though probably by no more than about 10 per cent, and would have taken even longer to produce.

THE AVAILABILITY IN PRINT OF OLD AND MIDDLE ENGLISH TEXTS WHEN *OED* BEGAN

A good reason for thinking that the editors were wise not to include all of Old English is that in the 1880s reliable editions of the extant records were simply not sufficiently available. Sound editions of Old English texts began to be produced only very slowly in the nineteenth century; in fact, the Early English Text Society was started so that accurate printed editions of texts should be available for illustrative excerption in the Philological Society's projected dictionary, texts (in early volumes of the Early English Text Society) ranging from the late seventh century (Sweet 1885*b*) to the early seventeenth century (Wheatley 1865). Among editions, especially anthologies, published in the eighteenth century and the beginning of the next, and some of them reprinted (sometimes more than once), the following exemplify good transcriptions mainly of Middle English texts (or relatively good transcriptions compared with other transcriptions of their time): the editions by Thomas Hearne, more often Latin than Old or Middle English texts (1709, 1720, 1723, 1724, 1725), but among them *The Battle of Maldon* (1726: ii, 570–7), all his publications fully listed by himself ([Huddesford and Warton] 1772: i, sigs (E3)-P2^{vo}); editions by Joseph Ritson (1790, 1791, 1793, 1794, 1795*a*, 1795*b*, 1802), more fully listed in Bronson's bibliography (1938: 749–802); editions by George Ellis (1790, in the edition of 1801; as well as in 1805), and his edition of *Sir Launfal* (Way 1796–1800: ii, 296–340); a Scottish anthology by J. Sibbald (1802); and a collection of romances by H. Weber (1810). Many more could be listed. In the eighteenth century Thomas Tyrwhitt's edition of *The Canterbury Tales* (1775–8) marks the beginnings of Middle English textual scholarship, though he did not have access to all the manuscripts on which modern Chaucerians rely. Librarians of the British Museum published significant editions: Sir Henry Ellis (1812), whose interests were historical rather than literary, brought out an edition of Hardyng's Chronicle; Sir Frederic Madden produced excellent editions of Middle English

texts (1828, 1839, 1847, and Forshall and Madden 1850). Societies began their publications as did The Chronicles and Memorials of Great Britain and Ireland During
the Middle Ages (published, from 1858 onwards, by the authority of the Treasury
and under the direction of the Master of the Rolls, and generally known as the
Rolls Series). At about the same time E. V. Utterson (1812, 1814, 1817, and 1839)
published two of Lord Berners's prose translations as well as some verse pieces,
all mainly of the sixteenth century and all mainly from early prints. David Laing
became Secretary of the Bannatyne Club and produced editions for it and for the
Abbotsford Club, as well as for the short-lived Wodrow Society, all principally
Scottish works of the fifteenth and sixteenth centuries. When young, he had a
taste for producing beautifully bound limited editions of fugitive pieces, Scottish
and late medieval or early modern (1822 and 1826), and a little later he edited and
published poems from the Auchinleck MS (1837). Later still he published editions
of the major Scottish writers which were accepted as standard till superseded by
editions in the Early English Text Society and The Scottish Text Society.

On the whole, these early editions, often printed in very small numbers, were
transcriptions of manuscripts or reprints of rare early printed editions. The best
of them were reliably accurate. Unlike French and German editions of works in
French and German of all periods, English and Scottish editions of medieval and
early modern texts were not regularized; often the contractions and suspensions
of the manuscripts and of early prints were reproduced exactly. Except for a very
small number of editors (Thomas Tyrwhitt was the first of them), theirs were
not critical editions of Middle English texts, but they made available more
widely texts that would otherwise have to be read in manuscript, often in a unique
manuscript.

THE USE MADE OF OLD ENGLISH BY LEXICOGRAPHERS
AND ETYMOLOGISTS BEFORE *OED* BEGAN

Old English texts were less well transcribed and edited, and hardly enter the domain
of English lexicography before the end of the nineteenth century, except for etymologies, often mistaken: as we have seen, Anglo-Saxon was treated as the language
preceding English. Joseph Bosworth's *Dictionary of the Anglo-Saxon Language* (1838)
has to be valued as a modest achievement, a better work of lexicography, though
less handsome, than the *Dictionarium* by Edward Lye and Owen Manning (1772),
and an advance on William Somner's dictionary (1659), though that was a learned
compilation considering how limited the printed resources of Anglo-Saxon scholarship then were. Anglo-Saxon lexicography and editions of the texts on which it
was to be based mattered for the Philological Society's new dictionary, once it
had been decided that Anglo-Saxon quotations were to be used to provide evidence for the earliest record of words and meanings surviving into Middle English
or later. Anglo-Saxon words had been adduced for etymologies in dictionaries
of Modern English, but etymologies were often no more than guesses based on

superficial similarities, and too much reliance was placed on Stephen Skinner's *Etymologicon Linguæ Anglicanæ* (1671). German scholars contributed diligently and, on the whole, accurately to Anglo-Saxon lexicography in the second half of the nineteenth century, at least in some measure influenced by the perception of *angelsächsisch* as a part of *deutsch*, the result of a terminological conflation that had received authoritative recognition from Jacob Grimm (1819: p. xxxviii, f.n.):

Ich bediene mich, wie jeder sieht, des Ausdrucks deutsch allgemein, so daß er auch die nordischen Sprachen einbegreift. Viele würden das Wort germanisch vorgezogen und unter seine Allgemeinheit das Deutsche und Nordische als das Besondere gestellt haben. . . . Deutsch bleibt . . . die einzige allgemeine, kein einzelnes Volk bezeichnende Benennung. . . . Daß sich die Norden selbst nicht Deutsche heißen . . . macht keinen gründlichen Einwurf, da sich auch die offenkundig aus {aus} Angeln und Sachsen gewanderten Engländer, weder Deutsche, noch einmal Germanen nennen.

[I make use, as is obvious, of the term *deutsch* in general, so that it also comprehends the Norse languages. Many would have preferred the word *germanisch* and to have placed German and Norse as particulars within its generality. . . . *Deutsch*, however, remains the only general name, designating no single people. That the Norse do not call themselves *Deutsche* is not a well-founded objection since the English too, who have, as is generally known, migrated from Angel and Saxony, do not call themselves *Deutsche* either, not even *Germanen*.]

In the second half of the nineteenth century dictionaries and glossaries of Old English were published in Germany, and they contained improvements on those published in England. Bouterwek (1850–1) published a glossary to his edition (1849–54) of the poems in Bodleian MS Junius 11. Ettmüller (1851) published a glossary to his collection (1850) of Old English verse and prose texts. Grein's *Sprachschatz* (1861–4) is still a very useful dictionary of the verse (as revised by Köhler with addenda by Holthausen, 1912–14); it is a glossary to Grein's excellent edition of almost all the extant Old English verse (1857–8), which remained a standard work in the revision by Wül(c)ker and Assmann (Grein and Wül(c)ker 1883–98). Leo's Anglo-Saxon glossary (1872–7) is based on both verse and prose texts; and, in spite of its inconvenient arrangement, requiring the use of W. Biszegger's alphabetical index appended to it, it was much used in Toller's revised edition (Bosworth and Toller 1882–98) of Bosworth (1838), to which Toller added a *Supplement* (1908–21). The German dictionaries and glossaries were, as a matter of course, consulted and used by the editors of the early fascicles of *NED*, till Bosworth–Toller and *Supplement*—still the standard dictionary of Old English, though now being replaced by the Toronto *Dictionary of Old English* (Cameron *et al.* 1986–)—provided *OED* with most of the lexicographic information needed for such use as was made of Old English. The editions of Old English prose texts, published in Germany in a series founded by Grein and continued by Wül(c)ker and Hecht (1872–1933), constituted a major achievement: its long history coincided in time with the long history of *OED*, from the slow beginnings, leading in the 1870s to J. A. H. Murray's involvement with the Philological Society's Dictionary (Craigie and Onions 1933: pp. xi–xii) to the publication of the first *Supplement* (Craigie and Onions 1933). Like the editions of Old English texts in the Early English Text Society, the editions of the series founded by Grein often came too late for *OED*.

Middle English was less well provided for in dictionaries on which *OED* could draw. Bradley (1891) revised and enlarged the last edition of Stratmann's dictionary (1881); it was a useful but slight work. Mätzner's glossary (Mätzner, Goldbeck, and Bieling 1878–1900, part of 1867–1900) covered only the texts edited by him (Mätzner 1867–9); it went no further in the alphabet than an incomplete entry for *misbileven* 'to hold an erroneous belief, distrust, disbelieve'.

EIGHTEENTH- AND NINETEENTH-CENTURY REPRINTS OF EARLY ENGLISH LITERATURE

The eighteenth and nineteenth centuries saw immense activity in reprinting earlier English literature. The same editors and publishers, many of them scholarly, all of them energetic, figure again and again on numerous title-pages, so many that to list them all in the references appended to this study would take up too much space: Robert Dodsley (1703–64), William Gifford (1756–1826), Sir S. Egerton Brydges (1762–1837), Sir Henry Ellis (1777–1869), Benjamin Thorpe (1782–1870), David Laing (1793–1878), Alexander Dyce (1798–1869), Sir Frederic Madden (1801–73), Joseph Stevenson (1806–95), J. M. Kemble (1807–57), Thomas Wright (1810–77), J. Orchard Halliwell later Halliwell-Phillipps (1820–89) F. J. Furnivall (1825–1910), A. B. Grosart (1827–99), William Aldis Wright (1831–1914), Richard Morris (1833–94), William Carew Hazlitt (1834–1913), W. W. Skeat (1835–1912), Edward Arber (1836–1912), W. E. Henley (1849–1903), A. H. Bullen (1857–1920). The list could be extended easily, and could be continued into the twentieth century, with such editors as J. S. Farmer, who availed himself of facsimiles in one of his several series, The Tudor Facsimile Texts. Concordances are specially useful for lexicography, and some were included in W. Bang's Materialien zur Kunde des älteren englischen Dramas, continued by H. de Vocht as Materials for the Study of the Old English Drama. Up to the First World War impoverished amenuenses were available to transcribe neatly texts from manuscripts and the most valuable of early printed books for the editors to get ready for the printer. Most other printed books were sent to the compositors in the printing houses for setting the reprints. Printing was cheap and accurate, though a little checking was required, and some of the most productive editors, Furnivall and Grosart among them, might with advantage have checked more; Furnivall's many inaccuracies were, however, minor.

The learned societies and clubs of the nineteenth century facilitated the production of a few Old English texts and a very great number of Middle English and early Modern English texts. Many of the societies and clubs were short-lived, but a small number of the best have survived and have been productive to this day. As we have seen, from the second half of the century onwards the Early English Text Society had as its most important aims the editing of Old English texts and, especially, of Middle English texts, sufficient for the new dictionary. To that end its editions usually included glossaries to help the lexicographers. The Chaucer Society made available the variant texts of Chaucer's works from the most important manuscripts. For Chaucer was central in the record of Middle English as perceived by Murray and his colleagues. In several of these societies F. J. Furnivall was the driving force. The Scottish Text Society had aims similar to the Early English Text Society, and produced editions from 1884 onwards, the first of them, *The Kingis Quair*, edited by Skeat (1884), who was as tirelessly active in the Scottish as in the Early English Text Society.

The clubs formed in the early parts of the nineteenth century catered for learned bibliophiles. Fine printing indulged and continues to indulge members of the Roxburghe Club instituted in 1813 (with thirty-one members). In Scotland the Bannatyne Club (limited to one hundred members), the Maitland Club (originally limited to fifty members, subsequently one hundred), both of them the products of Sir Walter Scott's antiquarian bent, and a little later the Abbotsford Club (limited to fifty members) provided books mainly with northern interest. At Durham the Surtees Society followed, among many societies pursuing the history of their locality, and open to a wider membership. The Camden Society and the English Historical Society catered in the first place for historians (the latter producing mainly editions of the Latin chroniclers), as did the Chetham Society centred on Manchester. An excellent account of the publications of the clubs and societies up to *c.*1864—by coincidence, the date of the first publication of the Early English Text Society—is given in Bohn's appendix volume to the last edition of Lowndes (1864). The Master of the Rolls instituted the Rolls Series. The Parker Society and, instituted later, the Henry Bradshaw Society provided texts of ecclesialogical and liturgical interest. The Percy Society, the Spenser Society, the Shakespeare Society and the New Shakespeare Society, and in the twentieth the Malone Society were literary. Reprints of rare tracts, ballads, and broadsheets were produced by several individuals and organizations. Lists of the gentlemen who were members of the societies and clubs were often published after the title-page; they show that the great houses of Great Britain and Ireland had learned libraries. The lists include no women.

At the end of the twentieth century one might well ask, where are the universities in all this learned activity? Some college and university libraries subscribed especially to historical series. English Studies had begun in the University of London, but not at Oxford when *NED* started, and at Oxford even some of those who at that time wondered if English should perhaps be considered for undergraduate study did not think of it as much of a scholarly discipline. Thus, as we learn from a brief account (Palmer 1965: 111) dealing with the beginnings of English studies in England, William Sanday (1843–1920), Dean Ireland Professor of the Exegesis of Holy Scripture, is reported in *The Times*, 6 December 1893, as advocating that English Studies might be pursued at Oxford on the grounds that 'the women should be considered, and the second and third-rate men who were to become schoolmasters'.

OED NOT ONE SINGLE PUBLICATION BUT PRODUCED
SLOWLY OVER THE YEARS IN MANY PARTS, LEADING TO
INCONSISTENCIES AND IMPERFECTIONS

The many volumes of *NED* as originally published in parts and sections—the details are conveniently set out in Raymond (1987),—even greater in number of volumes when they were reprinted as *OED* are not to be judged as a single act of publication, however uniform the volumes may look. The editors learnt and improved as the volumes appeared, and, as important, the texts on which they exercised their lexicographical learning and skill improved as did the tools they used: glossaries, concordances, and dictionaries. At the beginning Murray had to ask scholars on the Continent for help with etymologies more often than he and his fellow editors did later. From the very beginning the dictionary was conceived as a dictionary of English literature in print. An aesthetic literary judgement guided the editors to some extent in their selection of quotations: verse was accorded a higher place than prose. The books read by readers for the dictionary in the early stages of the project do not, however, reflect that bias, as is clearly evident from the 'List of Readers and Books Read by them for the Dictionary' (Murray 1885: 601–42). Murray was well aware of two lines of criticism that could with justice be levelled at the coverage achieved by his dictionary; first, that the dictionary did not pay enough attention to minor users of the English language, and secondly, that it did not give enough quotations from the greatest of the writers in English (1885: 523): 'if human life were longer, and the Dictionary four times the size, it would be well to give both more attention to the minor authors and their curious words, and more weight to Shakspere, and Milton, and Addison, and Burke, and Macaulay, and Matthew Arnold, with their literary authority.'

For Old English the literary bias, both in giving better coverage to verse than prose, and also in letting verse quotations usually precede prose quotations (because most of the extant verse, whatever the date of the manuscripts, is thought to be earlier than most of the extant prose) was enhanced by the excellence of Grein's *Sprachschatz* (1861–4). For early Middle English (at least, in the first fascicles of the dictionary) the literary bias towards verse was reinforced by the selectiveness of Coleridge's *Glossarial Index* (1859) and by the better glossaries available for Chaucer than available for other verse and for prose. For early Modern English Shakespeare was thought to tower above all, except perhaps the Authorized Version of the Bible.

The editors came to each word one by one, though they must have considered similar lexical items together to give some kind of consistency to the dictionary, a consistency that was often abandoned when it was thought necessary to revise the thinking underlying the entries. An obvious example of a lexical set is *east*, *north*, *south*, and *west*. They were edited, respectively, by Bradley, *east* published in 1891; Craigie, *north* published in 1907 and *south* in 1913; and by Bradley, *west* published in 1926 (after his death). The words go back to Old English; Old English had both *east* and *eastan*, *norð* and *norðan*, *suð* and *suðan*, *west* and *westan*. The inconsistencies and weaknesses of *OED*'s handling of Old English have been set forth before (Stanley: 1987), and may be sufficiently exemplified by the entries for this group of words. The details are set out in the standard grammars, such as Sievers (1898: §§ 314, 321), Campbell (1959: §§ 675, 677), and Sievers and Brunner (1965: §§ 314, 321). Old English *east* (and derivative forms) is now available in the Toronto *Dictionary of Old English* (Cameron, *et al.* 1986–: s.v.). *OED* is not a dictionary specializing in Old English; to some extent it distinguishes adjectival from adverbial forms. The extant Old English forms (not all of them recorded or referred to in *OED*) are: *east* 'to(ward) the east'; *eastan* 'from the east'; *east-weard* 'toward the east, eastwards'; *eastan-weard*, *east(e)weard* 'in or toward the east, eastern, easterly'; *easterne* 'in or towards the east, eastern'; *east(e)ra(n*, *easte-meste* comparative and superlative of *east*; *east-norþ* '(to the) north-east'; *east-norþerne* 'from the north-east'; *eastan-norþan* 'from the north-east'; *east-suþ* '(to the) south-east'; *eastan-suþan* 'from the south-east'. The comparative forms listed in the paradigms of the standard grammars show the danger a modern lexico-grapher may be in when relying on grammars instead of texts: the lexicographers' (and grammarians') *easterra*, *suþerra*, and *westerra* are not attested in the texts (cf. Venezky and Healey 1980: s.vv.), and, perhaps to make the paradigms neater, they have been hypothecated from *norþerran* (adj., acc. fem.), in fact, *hapax legomenon* in the Parker Chronicle for the year 918 (see Bately 1986: 68). In the manuscript the word, begun by hand 2e at the foot of fol. 24vo, was completed by hand 2f at the top of fol. 25ro (see Flower and Smith 1941); so even this form is not ideally attested, though better than not at all. Bradley, s.v. *East*, distinguishes as different forms OE *eastan* from *east*, and he traces both forms from the Alfredian period to ME *bi esten* and to MnE *east*. The Old English *Orosius*, which he quotes, is now no longer ascribed to King Alfred (cf. Bately 1980: pp. lxxiii–lxxxi), but Bradley could not have known that. He has a good quota-tion from what he calls Cædmon's *Genesis*, which he dates *a* 1000. It is from *Genesis B*, a distinction well known because of Sievers's study (1875) of the differences between the older and the later Old English *Genesis*, though not yet confirmed, as it was a few years later, by the discovery in the Vatican of the Old Saxon source (cf. Zangemeister and Braune 1894). Bradley's dating is therefore far from ignor-ant, and indeed my impression is that of the four editors of *OED* he was the best Anglo-Saxonist. Like Sievers, Campbell, and Sievers and Brunner, Bradley believed in the existence of an Old English comparative form *éasterra*: 'A trace of the lost OE. **éaster* appears in the adj. (compar.) *éasterra* more easterly.' It follows that absolute reliance is not to be placed on an Old English form given in the list of spellings near the beginning of an entry, unless it is supported by a quotation used to exemplify a sense. Bradley has an entry for *Eastern*, of course, and there he cautiously and correctly traces the suffix to Proto-Germanic (in the terminology of *OED*, O[ld] Teut[onic]) *-ōnjo-* suggesting, also correctly, that a development of that suffix may be found perhaps in cognate Latin *-āneus* (cf. Meid 1967: § 103). Such combinations as *east-south-east* and *East-by-South* are traced no further back than the sixteenth century; the superlative *Eastermost* is not recorded by him before 1555, *Eastmost* not before 1535, and *Easternmost* not before 1830. *Eastward* is traced back to Old English. Bradley's failure to quote uses of OE *eastemest* is easily excused. He knew it from the *Orosius* (cf. Bately 1980: 19 line 32, 132 line 28), available to Bradley in Bosworth's edition (1859: 24 line 27, 115 line 21), and from the more recent edition by Sweet (1883: 34 lines 33–4, 252 line 5); and he referred to it s.v. *Eastmost*: 'OE. had *éastmest* adj., superl. f. EAST *adv.* + *-m-*, *-st*, suffixes (see -MOST); but continuity is not proved, and the word was prob. formed afresh at a later period.' He should, however, have known ME *estmest* adj., as should Coleridge who himself had excerpted this text for his *Glossarial Index* (1859). It is now recorded in the *Middle English Dictionary* (*MED*), (Kurath, Kuhn, Reidy, and Lewis, 1952–) as *hapax legomenon* from 'Robert of Gloucester's *Chronicle*', printed as two words, *est most* by Wright (1887: i, 317 line 4494), and cf. his glossary (Wright 1887: ii, 909): 'EST MOST. Most easterly. 4494.', and as one word, *Estmost* by Hearne (1724: i, 219 bottom line). The details matter for medieval texts: how words are written, by which hands on what folios and with what spacing within the line or split at the end of the line; but even in dictionaries specializing on Old and Middle English, let alone in *OED*, such details are usually subordinated to editorial policy decisions and ignored. It is easy for us to say, 'should have known': we have better research tools than did Bradley in the 1880s. With fuller information ready to hand we forget how each of the editors of *OED* and their subeditors—we learn from the 'Historical Introduction' to *OED* (Craigie and Onions 1933: p. xxiii) that P. W. Jacob was the subeditor for 'portions of D, E, P, Q, R, and S (1881–6)', when the Rolls Series edition was not yet available—must have worked, pen in hand, inkpot and blank paper in front of him, the completed pages, one by one, by his side, and in front of him, pile upon pile, the slips sorted editorially as he surveys the whole of the materials supplied individually by variously diligent readers who had sent in their excerpted quotations, book after book. If the reader had been better in this instance he or she would have transcribed the sentence from 'Robert of Gloucester', and the editor might have written something like: 'OE. had *éastmest* adj., superl. f. EAST *adv.* + *-m-*, *-st*, suffixes (see -MOST), and ME. had *éstmost*; but continuity for the superl. is not proved; the suffix was, however, continuously available for adding to adjectives, and the word was prob. formed afresh at each later period.' That, however, is not what Bradley wrote. If he had known the Middle English form he might well have produced an altogether differently shaped entry, beginning with a quotation from the Old English *Orosius*, continuing with the only quotation from Middle English, and then going on to early Modern English. It is noteworthy that *MED* (at the very beginning of its publishing history, part E 3, published 1952) did not go back to Old English either for ME *ēst-mōst*, but gave this etymological explanation: 'Cp. attrib. use of **ēst** n.'

Bradley's entries for *West* and derivatives are different. They were published after his death by Craigie who had the final responsibility; Bradley's entries *Wavy* to *Weigh* were left unchanged, but Craigie edited *Weighable* to *Wezzon* as he reports in the Preface to the fascicle (Bradley and Craigie 1926: no pagination). The letter W is not yet fully in print in *MED*, nor, of course, in the Toronto *Dictionary of Old English*, but the *Microfiche Concordance* (Venezky and Healey 1980) is available for the whole alphabet, and Bosworth and Toller (1882–98) with *Supplement* (1909–21) and Campbell's addenda (Bosworth and Toller 1972) give excellent information for Old English. For W, unlike for E, Bradley is the donor of information: thus Campbell's entry *wester* is indebted to Bradley's *Wester* in *OED*. Greater philological boldness is shown than under *East*. Quotations of *west* are assigned to adverb, adjective and substantive: 'In OE. *west* occurs only as an adv., the use as noun and adj. being a later development.' It is by implication conceded that attributive *west-* in compounds such as *west-dæl* exists, and that that is close to adjectival usage. In Bradley's analysis the substantival usage defines itself because the definite article *the* (Anglo-Norman *le* in the first quotation) precedes *west*. The difficulty of assigning English usage to Latinate parts of speech is obvious from Bradley's creation of 'B. 1. Quasi-*sb.* = C [*sb.*].' Whether *Paris Psalter* 102.12 (Grein and Wül(c)ker 1883–98: iii, 404 [= iii/2, 158]; Krapp 1932 [London, 1933]: 75) might have been regarded as prototypical of nominal usage rather than as an adverbial use seems arguable: *eastrodor and æfter west* 'eastern heaven and then the west', or, more probably, with -*rodor* understood after *west* 'eastern heaven and then western (heaven)'. Similarly, the second element of a compound is probably to be understood in Byrhtferth's *Manual* (Crawford 1929: 202), less clearly set out in Baker and Lapidge (1995: 200, apparatus), though that edition supersedes Crawford's (cf. Hollis and Wright 1992: 151–2):

east wind   west   norð
Sunt enim *iiii*^{or} principales uenti quorum hec sunt nomina: subsolanus, zephirus, septentrio,
suð   *.i. partes .i. mundi*   *eastdæl*   *west*   *norð*   *suð*
auster . . . sunt quattuor climata cosmi, id est, oriens, occidens, aquilo, meridies.

With winds, however, the same problem of interpretation applies as in Modern English: MnE *the west* for *the west wind* is much like Byrhtferth's use six hundred years earlier: the word *wind* is to be understood because it has been used immediately preceding *west*, etc. Under *West*, C. *sb.* (Usually with *the*), 5., 'the west wind', Bradley (Bradley and Craigie 1926: s.v.) has no quotation earlier than 1604, E. G[rimeston?], translator of Joseph de Acosta's *The Naturall and Morall Historie of the East and West Indies*, III. v. 133, 'They have reckoned two other windes, the East of summer, and the East of winter, and by consequence, two Weasts.' All later quotations are verse. Old English quotations, such as those from the Paris Psalter and Byrhtferth's *Manual*, might have been included, perhaps in square brackets, if only to indicate that comparable problems of analysis are older than early Modern English. Under *Western*, 'Of the wind, a gale, etc.: Blowing from the west', Bradley (Bradley and Craigie 1926: s.v.) has a quotation from Old English, '*c.* 1050 *Bæda's Hist.* v. xix (MS. B.) . . . ða astah westerne wind & bleow.' It shows his skill in presenting the early material. The quotation he gives is longer than that in Bosworth and Toller (1882–98: s.v. *westerne*); he must therefore have consulted the editions, and that in spite of the wrong page number being given by Bosworth and Toller (1882–98: s.v. *westerne*) in citing Smith's edition, the only edition available at that time (Smith 1722: 635, *recte* 639 note to lines 19–20; see Schipper (in Grein and Wül(c)ker 1885–1905, iv 1897–9 [ii/2 1899]: 664 col. 2 lines 2637–8; cf. Miller 1890–8: ii, 575, MS B line 16). Bradley dated MS B, Corpus Christi College Cambridge 41, as of *circa* 1050, and that agrees well enough with current opinion, Ker (1957: 43, no. 32), 's. xi[1]'; cf. Miller (1890–8: i/1, p. xvii), 'the date of the MS. about the time of the Conquest'. Bradley's dating implies that he regards this variant reading (the other manuscripts have *west-wind*) as of the date of the manuscript, and not (about a century and a half earlier) of the date of the Alfredian translation. He gives another quotation from the Old English *Bede* s.v. *West wind*, and he dates it '*c.* 900'. Bradley's lexicographical scholarship was very distinguished. Now and again it is possible to disagree with him, but, if it is borne in mind what editions (with glossaries), concordances, and dictionaries were available to him, it is very rare indeed for someone at the end of the twentieth century to find that he, at the beginning of the century and before, has made a genuine mistake.

Craigie was responsible for *North* (published 1907) and *South* (published 1913). The preface to the relevant fascicle (Craigie 1907: no pagination) gives Mr E. L. Brandreth (London) as the name of the subeditor for *North*; the Preface to the relevant fascicle gives Mr P. W. Jacob as the name of the subeditor for *South*. The entry for *Northmost* goes straight from two Alfredian entries (*Orosius* and *Boethius*) to the sixteenth century, and Craigie was able to refer to Bradley's entry for the suffix *-most* (published half a year later than the fascicle with *North*) in which OE *eastmest*, *westmest* (also *westema*), *norðmest* and *suðmest* are given. It would have been preferable to have mentioned that the reading *þæt norþene mennisc* 'that northern people' of the Ælfric text in Bodleian MS Bodley 343, dated 's. xii[2]' by Ker (1957: 368, no. 310) is corrected from *þæt mennisc norþene*; see Assmann's edition (Grein and Wül(c)ker 1883–98: iii, *Angelsächsische Homilien und Heiligenleben*, 84 line 109 and note). It should have been mentioned that the earlier copy of the same text in Bodleian MS Laud Misc. 509, dated 's. xi[2]' by Ker (1957: 422, no. 344) reads *þæt norþerne mennisc*; see Crawford's parallel-text edition (1922: 27 line 278 and note). The reading *northen* in MS Bodley 343 is suspect as early as Transitional English; it is recorded more commonly from fifteenth-century manuscripts, for example, Bodleian MS e Musaeo 16 (cf. Seymour 1975–88: iii, 15–17) of John Trevisa's translation of Bartholomaeus Anglicus quoted in Craigie's entry, and dated '1398', and British Library MS Harley

7334 of *The Canterbury Tales* quoted in the good entry *northen*, adj., in *MED*. Dan Michel has an earlier use, but <r> is lost or assimilated quite frequently in his spellings (cf. Gradon 1979: 49). *A Microfiche Concordance to Old English* (Venezky and Healey 1980: s.v.) gives a reading of what is clearly an adjective from a fourteenth-century copy of the bounds of an authentic Anglo-Saxon charter, *one ðat norðene stod-dich* 'on to that ditch enclosing horses (?) to the north' (see Kemble 1839–48: iii, 433 bounds of no. ccccxxxv; cf. Sawyer 1968: 217 no. 632), but the spellings in such a late copy may be indicative of nothing other than the scribe's ignorance of Old English. OE *norþan* (in late copies the ending is also found spelt *-en* and *-on*) is adverbial, 'from the north'. Probably the recorded adjectival forms of points of the compass ending in *-en* are common enough to support the view that they are not the result of scribal carelessness or ignorance, but that they either go back (cf. Kluge 1926: §§ 201, 217), or that in late Old English these endings were no longer strictly differentiated, as is known from more northerly texts (cf. Jordan 1906: 105; Gneuss 1968: 167). S.v. *Northward* the Old English evidence is insufficiently dealt with by Craigie: the spelling *norþeweard* is not recorded by him, and under A. b. 'of relative position' no use earlier than Chaucer is given, but see *De Temporibus Anni*, IV. 45, *Ðonne heo norðweard bið* 'when it [the sun] is north'; and similarly in the next sentence *suðweard* 'south', a sense not recorded under *Southward*, A., adv., 1. b., before Gower. Ælfric's next sentence has *suðor* 'further south', but the dictionary has no entry for the comparative adverb (and no quotations in the etymological discussion of the adverb *south* where the 'Common Teut[onic]' comparative is referred to), though the weak adjectival comparative *suðran* is cited s.v. *Souther*, adjective, from this very text in the last of three Old English quotations. S.vv. *Souther* and *Southward* Craigie cites this text from the edition in the Rolls Series (Cockayne 1864–6: iii, 250, 270), at the time the only one, but now superseded by Henel (1942: 38, IV. 45–7; 68, IX. 8). Craigie had not used this piece of what Cockayne called 'starcraft' a few years earlier under the letter N for any of the words derived from *North*. The reason is simple: Bosworth and Toller (1882–98) does not cite the text for points of the compass under N, till Toller's *Supplement* (1908–21) which came too late for Craigie's *North*, but Bosworth and Toller do cite the text under S. As a result Craigie used *suðran* s.v. *Souther* but failed to use *norðran* (on the same page of text) s.v. *Norther*. The experience gained from reading Craigie's entries for the two cardinal points (and their derivatives) under his editorship tends to confirm the impression that he was not as good a lexicographer, especially of Old and Middle English, as Bradley.

It is not surprising that the reader who excerpted Cockayne's *Leechdoms* was not as careful as the readers who excerpted Chaucer and Gower, and that those who undertook the subediting and editing of them were more careful to include Chaucer's and Gower's usage, in Middle English the highest in rank (to use Richardson's term for his literary value-judgement). Dictionary making is a practical activity making the most of limited funding in as short a time as possible.

To have spent greater care on the *Leechdoms* than on Chaucer and Gower would not have pleased the civilized readers for whom the dictionary was intended, though it might have been better lexicographical science and so might have better pleased some who have this in common with Shakespeare's pedants: 'They haue beene at a great feast of Languages, and stolne the scraps.' Craigie's schoolmasterly attitude is revealed s.v. *Southard*, where Caxton is accused of perhaps having been guilty of a 'mere misprint', in the quotation from Caxton (Malory 1485): '**1470–85** MALORY *Arthur* IV. xxv. 153 Now torne we vnto syr Marhaus that rode with the damoysel . . . southard.' The Winchester manuscript (Malory 1976: fol. 66^v lines 17–18), discovered after the completion of *OED*, has: 'Now turne we vnto sir Marhaute that rode w^t þ^e damesel . . . southwarde.' Craigie would have done better to compliment Caxton for having been aurally aware of loss of /w/, a sound-change mentioned in the standard phonology (Sweet 1888: 269 § 921) available to Craigie, and discussed more fully in later phonologies (Luick 1914–40: i/2, § 716 and Anm. 2 and 3; Dobson 1968: ii, § 421 (ii)). Craigie's comments, s.v. *Southen*, adv., on a use of *suðen* in line 1167 of the early Middle English *Genesis and Exodus* (R. Morris 1865: 34; cf. Arngart 1968: 83, and glossary s.vv. *suð*, *suðen*, as well as *est*, *esten* and *west*, *westen*) are even fiercer in their schoolmasterliness, 'Misuse of OE. *sūþan*, or error for *suð*':

> Suðen he wente & wunede in Geraris

Though the metre of this text is far from regular, *suð* would have been a syllable short, and such an irregularity could have been regarded as scribal; *suðe* would have been a possible adverbial form but final *e* would have been elided before *he*. It looks therefore as if *suðen* was used, I presume by the author, to give a disyllabic form that could not suffer elision. Though the collections available to *MED* may hold as yet unpublished evidence for ME *bisouthen* (< OE *besūþan*), as is indicated s.v. *southen*, adv., it seems better to regard the doublet *suð* and *suðen* as a parallel development to the doublets *est* and *esten* and *west* and *westen* recorded in this text.

EARLY MODERN ENGLISH TOO RICHLY PRESERVED FOR A COMPLETE LEXICOGRAPHICAL RECORD TO BE POSSIBLE

When we come to early Modern English difficult choices have to be made. The corpus of Middle English is disproportionately smaller than that of Tudor English, and that of Tudor English is small when compared with seventeenth-century English. In theory, everything printed should have been excerpted for *OED* by an army of readers, most of whom had no training in English linguistics. Though they were alert to new words and perhaps to new senses and uses of words previously attested, they knew little about the complexity of printing. For most of the time during which the readers, subeditors, and editors were producing the dictionary, *STC* (Pollard and Redgrave 1926) had not been published and the compilation of Wing (1945–51) lay in the future. The editors themselves were ill informed about bibliography as is shown by the attempt (included in the *Supplement* of 1933) at listing books used in compiling the dictionary. In fact, the editors often, perhaps usually, did not know which edition had been used and which issue. In checking quotations they were content to use the earliest available to them. The bibliographical list usually gives the date of the first edition of a printed book, but not infrequently a later edition was excerpted, with changes in spelling and punctuation or even more substantial changes. For early printed books the editors often relied on nineteenth- and early twentieth-century reprints. Of course, they knew about variants in Old and Middle English manuscripts; of course, they knew about Shakespeare's and Ben Jonson's quartos and folios, and, no doubt, were aware of some of the complexity in the printing of other major authors. But they seem not to have checked the editions of all authors as an editorial principle; and the dating of the quotation did not necessarily represent the date of the imprint of the book actually cited. Limits of time are set to dictionary making by the funding allocated. The editors tried to record the spellings of the early printers (as well as of Middle English scribes); a glance at, for example, the entries *Stomach* and *Tongue*, shows that care was taken with early spellings. The readers did their work of excerpting one book at a time. The editors put them in order of date one word at a time. They were interested in the earliest use, and they tried by various means to antedate the uses the readers had presented them with. For obsolete words they were also eager to give the last use, and for any obsolescent word they sought to establish whether any writer still used it. They did not limit their searches to works of literary excellence, or theological, historical, or scientific importance. But the quality of the writing remained a major consideration of theirs: for example, they did not excerpt Philemon Holland with the care they bestowed on Shakespeare. It would have shown a sad want of literary taste and lexicographical judgement if they had done so; but it would have made the dictionary a better store of linguistic information for later users. At the end of the twentieth century we are able to gain access easily by means of the electronic version of Simpson and Weiner (1989), and we may use that to ask questions, often statistical questions, to which the dictionary as envisaged by Murray and the other editors, on whose work the CD ROM version depends, can provide no reliable answer.

Let us stay for a few moments with just one book of Holland's, his translation of Livy (Holland 1600); there appear to be no bibliographical complications (see Pollard and Redgrave 1926, and 2nd edn. 1976–91: no. 16613). The title-page has *Doctor in Physicke*, a use of *in* not recorded in *OED* s.v. *Doctor*, sb., 6. a.; the dedication to Queen Elizabeth has 'and consecrate to the happie and immortall memorie of your most sacred Majestie', where, since the queen was alive, *memory* perhaps means 'memorial', cf. *Oxford Latin Dictionary* (Glare 1968–82) s.v. *memoria*, 10, and *OED* s.v. *Memory*, 10, but the sense is not identical. Holland's Preface 'To the Reader' yields: 'Trojanes … who resting seat did want'; the compound *resting-seat* is not in *OED*, cf. Latin *sedes* which it renders here (in a quotation from Virgil); 'Livie, who commended their deeds to everlasting fame' perhaps sufficiently covered by *OED* s.v. *Commend*, 1., 'such phrases as *commend to memory*'; 'their sensible declining and decay' similar to the use quoted in *OED* s.v. *Sensible*, 7. a., from Holland's *Pliny* 1601, with an earlier quotation from Chaucer not identical in sense; '*Livie* enchronicled their acts', some years later than the last use recorded in *OED* s.v. *Enchronicle*; 'no Epitaph nor inscription either enchased in stone or cut in brasse', no quotation in *OED* s.v. *Enchase*, 4., between 1463 and 1682; 'in stately port at home', said by *OED* to be a rare sense s.v. *Port*, sb.[4], 1. d., first quotation 1633; *Aristarches*, first quotation in *OED* some years later s.v. *Aristarchy*; 'Patavinitie', first quotation s.v. *Patavinity* some years later, and that though Livy of Padua is mentioned in the explanation given in *OED*; 'the whole truth & nothing but the truth', the legal phrase, here transferred to historiography, is not in *OED*; 'he hath the pricke and price above all others', with *prick* in the sense of 'the highest point' (well exemplified s.v. *Prick*, sb., 8.—the last quotation from Holland's *Suetonius*), but the alliterative word-pair, *pricke and price,* is not cited; 'The Gauls he may seem to gall', a paronomastic, transitive use meaning 'to scoff at', for which sense *OED*, s.v. *Gall*, v.[1], 6. b., has an intransitive use from Shakespeare; 'love of my countrey language', compounds and attributive use of *country* are not well exemplified in *OED*, s.v., when the sense is 'national, nation's' and not 'rustic', and this combination is not recorded; 'free bourgeoisie', where *bourgeoisie* means 'citizenship', a sense not recorded for *bourgeoisie* in *OED*, which does not record the word in any sense till 1707.

Some four pages folio of Holland's *Livy* have yielded a goodly crop of supplementations of *OED*. There follow 1,450 pages folio, and a glossary is appended 'of those tearmes in Livie which are not yet familiar in English'. The book was to some extent excerpted for the dictionary; thus there are quotations from later in the *Livy* for *dissite* and *ne*, words that occur also in the preliminaries. Any scholar concentrating on the lexis of Philemon Holland may find it disappointing that more use was not made of the *Livy*. Such a specialist may condemn *OED* because it treated Holland less fully than, for example, Shakespeare whose 'rank' (to use Richardson's term again) is higher in the estimation of the editors than Holland's. It is easy to supplement the entries in *OED* by reading Holland with greater care than he was read. Should the editors of *OED* be condemned for some degree of failure with Holland whereas they succeeded with authors that stand higher in general, literary estimation? I think not. It is a common fault of scholarly pedants to bestow as much detailed care on the minor author at the centre of their investigation as on the major author studied by the rest of the world, and in the process they forget the grand sweep by which *A New English Dictionary on Historical Principles* lays before us, word by word, lexical change, both in the admittance of words and of senses of words and in the obsolescence of words. It is easy to antedate and postdate the record given in *OED*, and thus to demonstrate by reading Holland with care that the first and last uses recorded in *OED* are not absolutes.

The late Jürgen Schäfer has compiled lexical information on Thomas Nashe and, comparing his compilation with what *OED* has compiled from Shakespeare, he finds *OED* on Nashe sadly wanting (Schäfer 1980). The opening words of his introduction show lines of inquiry that cannot succeed because the dictionary was not constructed with such objects in mind. It is not that improper questions are asked, but that it is an improper expectation to believe that *OED* can answer them:

> Ever since its publication *The Oxford English Dictionary* has provided the basis for innumerable studies of periods and authors, foreign influences, and native coinages. No matter whether it has been a question of word formations in the seventeenth century, the contributions of Sir Thomas Elyot to the vocabulary, or the cultural relations between England and the Netherlands, the *O.E.D.* entries have been consulted, usually as a court of final appeal. (Schäfer 1980: 1)

For Elyot we might read Holland or Nashe; and if one were to write on the lexis of anyone in print one would be wise to go first to *OED*, to see what happens to be in it on the minor figure who has assumed a major role in one's academic endeavours. But 'as a court of final appeal'? Certainly not. *OED* has some gross omissions because it failed to consult later editions than the one excerpted. Some years ago R. F. Kennedy (1971) exemplified what amounts to a systematic set of imperfections in *OED*, resulting from the failure to excerpt all the editions of the works of Owen Felltham: over seventy-five antedatings and sixty omissions all from Felltham's small canon. Such imperfections in greater number were easily demonstrable from Nashe; an even greater number would be easily demonstrable from Holland. *OED* does not become the competent final authority merely because an investigator, having heard *OED* justly praised, instead of treating it as a good starting-point, elevates it to 'a court of final appeal' to pronounce judgement in some cause of interest to him.

OED'S TREATMENT OF SHAKESPEARE NOT ALTOGETHER BEYOND THE POSSIBILITY OF SUPPLEMENTATION

One can, however, expect *OED* to do well with major Middle English texts (in so far as they, complete with manuscript variants, were available to the editors), and with the great authors of later periods, with Shakespeare first among them. Schäfer (1980: 18) quotes 'John Dover Wilson's dictum that the *O.E.D.* is an "incomparable editorial instrument"'. Dover Wilson published that dictum in 1934, the year after the publication of *OED* was completed. He was right: there is nothing to compare with *OED* when an editor of Shakespeare is considering the poet's lexis. It is better even than Schmidt's *Shakespeare-Lexikon* (1902), fuller than Onions's *Shakespeare Glossary* (1941) derived from *OED*. It is always the first authority to go to; but it is not the last word. The editor's judgement must be that in each case.

One turns to *OED* for every lexical obscurity in Shakespeare. There is room here for only one example, *strip* at *King Lear* IV. vi. 165. The Folio reads: 'Thou,

Rascall Beadle, hold thy bloody hand: why dost thou lash that Whore? Strip thy owne back, thou hotly lusts to vse her in that kind, for which thou whip'st her.' One would expect the editors to have commented on the word: is it *stripe* 'to beat, whip'? That is found in late Middle English and early sixteenth-century English, but was never common. *OED* shows that spelling with *-pp-* occur in forms of *stripe*; and cf. the infinitive *swype* in *MED* s.v. *swippen* (whatever its etymology and history may be). There are such verbal doublets as *shit* (strong and weak) and *shite* (strong), but shortening of ME $\bar{\imath}$ is rare (cf. Dobson 1968: ii, § 32). For some verbs weak and (class I) strong forms exist side by side (cf. Price 1910: § 2). By the end of the sixteenth century *stripe* 'to beat, whip' seems to have been obsolete or obsolescent, and may have been unfamiliar to the printers, who, knowing final *-e* to be labile in their time, may (if *stripe* is what the copy before them had) have substituted their *strip* for an original *stripe*. I am not sure if that is right; and I was disappointed in my expectation that *OED* could resolve my doubts. This famous use was quoted under neither of the relevant verbs, *strip* or *stripe*. I had expected at least some expression that in this use there may be an ambiguity, and would have given a wilderness of words from Nashe, Holland, or Felltham for guidance on one crux in Shakespeare: there is a scale of values in English writings. J. A. H. Murray, Henry Bradley, W. A. Craigie, and C. T. Onions understood that scale well. Trying to be as complete as it was possible to be in the time their funding allowed them, they included much of the lexis of minor authors of the early periods and more of the great authors of all periods. They were particularly interested in the earliest periods. Murray had gladly undertaken to produce a dictionary on the principles envisaged by the Philological Society. Bradley was learned in Comparative Philology. Craigie had been professor of Anglo-Saxon in the University of Oxford; and Onions was till the late 1940s Reader in English Philology there and lectured regularly on early Middle English texts. Bradley, s.v. *Lexicography*, accepted into his definition Dr Johnson's definition of that word: 'The art or practice of writing dictionaries.' As the editors practised English lexicography it remained an art: they excelled when they excerpted and analysed the words used by the authors who excelled in the English language.

REFERENCES

Arngart, O. (ed.) (1968). *The Middle English Genesis and Exodus re-edited from MS. C.C.C.C. 444.* Lund Studies in English, 36.

Baker, P. S., and Lapidge, M. (eds.) (1995). *Byrhtferth's Enchiridion.* EETS, supplementary series 15.

Bately, J. (ed.) (1980). *The Old English Orosius.* EETS, supplementary series 6.

—— (1986). *The Anglo-Saxon Chronicle, MS A.* Cambridge: D. S. Brewer.

Bosworth, J. (ed.) (1838). *A Dictionary of the Anglo-Saxon Language.* London: Longman, Rees, Orme, Brown, Green, and Longman; Oxford: Talboys; Cambridge: Stevenson.

Bosworth, J. (1859). *King Alfred's Anglo-Saxon Version of the Compendious History of the World by Orosius.* London: Longman, Brown, Green, and Longmans.

Bosworth, J., and Toller, T. N. (eds.) (1882–98). *An Anglo-Saxon Dictionary based on the manuscript collections of the late Joseph Bosworth*. Oxford: Clarendon Press. *Supplement*, ed. T. N. Toller. Oxford: Clarendon Press, 1908–21. *Enlarged Addenda and Corrigenda to the Supplement*, ed. A. Campbell. Oxford: Clarendon Press (1972).

Bouterwek, K. W. (ed.) (1849–54). *Cædmon's des Angelsachsen biblische Dichtungen*. i, 2 parts. Part 1, Elberfeld: Julius Bädeker; part 2, Gütersloh: C. Bertelsmann.

—— (1850–1). *Cædmon's des Angelsachsen biblische Dichtungen*. ii, 'Ein angelsächsisches Glossar'. Elberfeld and Iserlohn: Julius Bädeker, 1850; Elberfeld: Julius Bädeker; and London: Dulau & Co., D. Nutt, Williams & Norgate, 1851.

Bradley, H. (ed.) (1891). *A Middle English Dictionary Containing Words Used by English Writers from the Twelfth to the Fifteenth Century by Francis Henry Stratmann*. Oxford: Clarendon Press.

Bradley, H., and Craigie, W. A. (eds.) (1919). *NED*, Volume IX. Part I. SI–ST. Oxford: Clarendon Press.

—— (1926). *NED*, Volume X. Second Half. V–Z. *Wavy–Wezzon*. Oxford: Clarendon Press.

Bridges, R. (1928). 'Henry Bradley Born 3 Dec. 1845 Died 23 May 1923 A Memoir', in R. Bridges (ed.), *The Collected Papers of Henry Bradley*. Oxford: Clarendon Press. 1–56.

Bronson, B. H. (1938). *Joseph Ritson Scholar-at-Arms*. 2 vols. Berkeley, California: University of California Press.

Brown, C., and Robbins, R. H. (eds.) (1943). *The Index of Middle English Verse*. New York (New York): Columbia University Press for The Index Society.

Burchfield, R. W. (ed.) (1972–86). *A Supplement to the Oxford English Dictionary*. 4 vols. Oxford: Clarendon Press.

—— (1987). *Studies in Lexicography*. Oxford: Clarendon Press.

Cameron, A. *et al.* (eds.) (1986–), *Dictionary of Old English*. Toronto: Pontifical Institute of Medieval Studies, for the Dictionary of Old English, Medieval Centre of the University of Toronto.

Campbell, A. (1959). *Old English Grammar*. Oxford: Clarendon Press. Last revision 1968.

Cockayne, O. (ed.) (1864–6). *Leechdoms, Wortcunning, and Starcraft of Early England*. 3 vols. Rolls Series 35.

Coleridge, H. (ed.) (1859). *A Glossarial Index to the Printed English Literature of the 13th Century*. London: Trübner & Co. 2nd edn., *A Dictionary of the First, or Oldest Words in the English Language; from the Semi-Saxon Period of* A.D. *1250 to 1300. Consisting of An Alphabetical Inventory of Every Word Found in the Printed English Literature of the 13th Century. By the Late Herbert Coleridge, Secretary to the Philological Society.* London: John Camden Hotten, 1862.

Craigie, W. A. (ed.) (1907). *A New English Dictionary on Historical Principles; Founded on the Materials Collected by The Philological Society*. (Volume VI. L–N). N. part 2 *Niche–Niwe*. 'Preface to the Letter N.' Oxford: Clarendon Press.

Craigie, W. A., and Onions, C. T. (eds.) (1933). *A New English Dictionary on Historical Principles; Founded on the Materials Collected by The Philological Society. Edited by James A. H. Murray, Henry Bradley, William A. Craigie, C. T. Onions. Introduction, Supplement, and Bibliography.* Oxford: Clarendon Press.

Crawford, S. J. (ed.) (1922). *The Old English Version of The Heptateuch, Aelfric's Treatise on the Old and New Testament and his Preface to Genesis*, EETS, original series 160.

—— (1929). *Byrhtferth's Manual.* EETS, original series 177.

Dobson, E. J. (1968). *English Pronunciation 1500–1700.* 2 vols. 2nd edn. Oxford: Clarendon Press.

Ellis, G. (ed.) (1790). *Specimens of the Early English Poets.* London: for Edwards. 2nd edn. 3 vols. London: for G. and W. Nicol, and J. Wright, 1801.

—— (1805). *Specimens of Early English Metrical Romances, Chiefly Written during the Early Part of the Fourteenth Century.* 3 vols. London: for Longman, Hurst, Rees, and Orme; Edinburgh: A. Constable and Co.

Ellis, H. (ed.) (1812). *The Chronicle of Iohn Hardyng* . . . *together with the Continuation by Richard Grafton.* London: for F. C. and J. Rivington; T. Payne; Wilkie and Robinson; Longman, Hurst, Rees, Orme, and Brown; Cadell and Davies; J. Mawman; and R. H. Evans.

Ettmüller, L. (ed.) (1850). *Engla and Seaxna Scôpas and Bôceras. Anglosaxonum Poëtae atque Scriptores Prosaici.* Bibliothek der gesammten deutschen National-Literatur, xxviii. Quedlinburg and Leipzig: Gottfr. Basse; London: Williams and Norgate.

—— (1851). *Vorda Vealhstôd Engla and Seaxna. Lexicon Anglosaxonicum ex Poëtarum Scriptorumque Prosaicorum Operibus nec non Lexicis Anglosaxonicis Collectum, cum Synopsi Grammatica.* Bibliothek der gesammten deutschen National-Literatur, xxix. Quedlinburg and Leipzig: Gottfr. Basse; London: Williams and Norgate.

Flower, R., and Smith, [A.] H. (eds.) (1941). *The Parker Chronicle and Laws.* EETS, original series 208.

Forshall, J. and Madden, Sir F. (eds.) (1850). *The Holy Bible, Containing the Old and New Testaments, with the Apocryphal Books, in the Earliest English versions made from the Latin Vulgate by John Wycliffe and his Followers.* 4 vols. Oxford: [Oxford] University Press.

Furnivall, F. J. (ed.) (1858). *Early English Poems and Lives of Saints.* Part 1. *TPS.*

Glare, P. G. W. (ed.) (1968–82). *Oxford Latin Dictionary.* Oxford: Clarendon Press.

Gneuss, H. (1968). *Hymnar und Hymnen im englischen Mittelalter.* Buchreihe der Anglia 12. Tübingen: Max Niemeyer.

Görlach, M. (1974). *The Textual Tradition of the South English Legendary,* Leeds Texts and Monographs, new series 6.

Gradon, P. O. E. (ed.) (1979). *Dan Michel's Ayenbite of Inwyt.* ii, Introduction, Notes and Glossary. EETS, original series 278.

Grein, C. W. M. (ed.) (1857–8). *Bibliothek der angelsächsischen Poesie.* 2 vols of texts. Kassel and Göttingen: Georg H. Wigand.

—— (1861–4). *Sprachschatz der angelsächsischen Dichter.* 2 vols. Vols iii and iv of Grein (1857–8). Kassel and Göttingen: Georg H. Wigand.

—— (1872). Bibliothek der angelsächsischen Prosa in kritisch bearbeiteten Texten. i, *Älfrik de vetere et novo testamento, Pentateuch, Iosua, Buch der Richter und Hiob.* Kassel and Göttingen: Georg H. Wigand.

Grein, C. W. M., and Köhler, J. J., with Holthausen, F. (eds.) (1912–14). *Sprachschatz der angelsächsischen Dichter.* Heidelberg: Carl Winter. 2nd edn. of Grein, C. W. M. (ed.) (1861–4).

Grein, C. W. M., and Wül(c)ker, R. P. (eds.) (1883–98). *Bibliothek der angelsächsischen Poesie.* 3 vols, vol. iii/2 (ed.) B. Assmann. i, Kassel: Georg H. Wigand; ii and iii, Leipzig: Georg H. Wigand.

—— (1885–1905). Bibliothek der angelsächsischen Prosa begründet von Christian W. M. Grein. ii. Schröer, A. (ed.), *Die angelsächsischen Prosabearbeitungen der Benedictinerregel.* Kassel: Georg H. Wigand, 1885–8. iii, Assmann, B. (ed.), *Angelsächsische Homilien und*

Heiligenleben. Kassel: Georg H. Wigand, 1889; iv, Schipper, J. (ed.) *König Alfreds Über-setzung von Bedas Kirchengeschichte*. Leipzig: Georg H. Wigand, 1897–9; v, Hecht, H. (ed.), *Bischofs Wærferth von Worcester Übersetzung der Dialoge Gregors des Grossen*; v/1, Leipzig: Georg H. Wigand, 1900; v/2, Hamburg: Henri Grand, 1907; vi, Leonhardi, G. (ed.), *Kleinere angelsächsische Denkmäler*. Hamburg: Henri Grand, 1905.

Grein, C. W. M., Wülker, R. P., and Hecht, H. (eds.) (1910–33). Bibliothek der angelsächsischen Prosa begründet von Ch(r). W. M. Grein fortgesetzt von R. P. Wülker. vii, Wildhagen, K. (ed.), *Der Cambridger Psalter*. Hamburg: Henri Grand, 1910; viii, Schlutter, O. B. (ed.), *Das Epinaler und Erfurter Glossar*, part 1 (no more published) 'Facsimile und Transliteration des Epinaler Glossars'. Hamburg: Henri Grand, 1912; ix, Fehr, B. (ed.), *Die Hirtenbriefe Ælfrics*. Hamburg: Henri Grand, 1914; x, Crawford, S. J. (ed.), *Exameron Anglice or the Old English Hexameron*. Hamburg: Henri Grand, 1921; xi, Endter, W. (ed.), *König Alfreds des Grossen Bearbeitung der Soliloquien des Augustinus*. Hamburg: Henri Grand, 1922; xii/1 (no more published), Förster, M. (ed.), *Die Vercelli-Homilien I.–VIII. Homilie*. Hamburg: Henri Grand, 1932; xiii, Raith, J. (ed.), *Die altenglische Version des Halitgar'schen Bussbuches (sog. Poenitentiale Pseudo-Egberti)*. Hamburg: Henri Grand, 1933.

Grimm, J. (1819). *Deutsche Grammatik*, i. 1st edn. Göttingen: Dieterichsche Buchhandlung.

Hammond, E. P. (ed.) (1908). *Chaucer: A Bibliographical Manual*. New York (New York): Macmillan.

Hearne, T. (ed.) (1709). *The Life of Ælfred the Great, by Sir John Spelman, Kt.* Oxford: at the Theatre.

—— (1720). *Textus Roffensis*. Oxford: at the Theatre.

—— (1723). *Hemingi Chartularium Ecclesiæ Wigorniensis*. Oxford: at the Theatre.

—— (1724). *Robert of Gloucester's Chronicle*. 2 vols. Oxford: at the Theatre.

—— (1725). *Peter Langtoft's Chronicle (as illustrated and improv'd by Robert of Brunne) from the Death of Cadwaladon to the end of K. Edward the First's reign*. 2 vols. Oxford: at the Theatre.

—— (1726). *Joannis Confratris & Monachi Glastoniensis Chronica sive Historia de Rebus Glastoniensibus*. 2 vols. Oxford: at the Theatre.

Henel, H. (ed.) (1942). *Aelfric's De Temporibus Anni*. EETS, original series 213.

Hickes, G. (ed.) (1705, 1703). *Linguarum Vett. Septentrionalium Thesaurus Grammatico-Criticus et Archæologicus*. 3 vols. Oxford: at the Theatre.

Holland, P. (trsl.) (1600). *The Romane Historie Written by T. Liuius of Padua. Also, the Breviaries of L. Florus: with a Chronologie to the whole Historie: and the Topographie of Rome in old time. Translated out of Latine into English, by Philemon Holland, Doctor in Physicke*. London: printed by Adam Islip.

Hollis, S., and Wright, M., with Mills, G. M. D., and Pedder, A. (eds.) (1992). *Old English Prose of Secular Learning*. Annotated Bibliographies of Old and Middle English Literature IV. Cambridge: D. S. Brewer.

[Huddesford, Wm, and Warton, T. (eds.)] (1772), *The Lives Of those eminent Antiquaries John Leland, Thomas Hearne, and Anthony à Wood*. 2 vols. Oxford: printed at the Clarendon Press, For J. and J. Fletcher and J. Pote.

Jordan, R. (1906). *Eigentümlichkeiten des anglischen Wortschatzes*. Anglistische Forschungen 17. Heidelberg: Carl Winter.

Kemble, J. M. (ed.) (1839–48) *Codex Diplomaticus Aevi Saxonici*. 6 vols. London: English Historical Society.

Kennedy, R. F. (1971). 'Words from Owen Felltham'. *Notes and Queries* 216: 4–12.

Ker, N. R. (1957). *Catalogue of Manuscripts Containing Anglo-Saxon.* Oxford: Clarendon Press.

Kluge, F. (1926). *Nominale Stammbildungslehre der altgermanischen Dialekte.* 3rd edn., rev. L. Sütterlin, and E. Ochs. Halle: Max Niemeyer.

Krahe, H., and Meid, W. (1969, 1967). Germanische Sprachwissenschaft, i, *Einleitung und Lautlehre,* Sammlung Göschen 238; ii, *Formenlehre,* Sammlung Göschen 780; iii, *Wortbildungslehre, Sammlung Göschen* 1218, 1218a, 1218b. Berlin: Walter de Gruyter & Co.

Krapp, G. P. (ed.) (New York 1932, London 1933). *The Paris Psalter and the Meters of Boethius.* The Anglo-Saxon Poetic Records A Collective Edition, v. New York (New York): Columbia University Press, 1932; London: George Routledge & Sons, 1933.

Kurath, H., Kuhn, S. M., Reidy, J., and Lewis, R. E. (eds.) (1952–). *Middle English Dictionary.* Parts E 1–3, F 1–4, Plan and Bibliography, A 1, Ann Arbor (Michigan): University of Michigan Press; London: Oxford University Press, Geoffrey Cumberlege, 1952–6; parts A 2–4, B 1–2, Ann Arbor (Michigan): University of Michigan Press; London: Oxford University Press, 1956–7; parts B 3–5 and all subsequent parts, Ann Arbor (Michigan): University of Michigan Press, 1958–.

[Laing, D. (ed.)] (1822). *Select Remains of the Ancient Popular Poetry of Scotland.* Edinburgh.

—— (1826). *Early Metrical Tales; Including the History of Sir Egeir, Sir Grime, and Sir Gray-Steill.* Edinburgh: for W. & D. Laing; London: for J. Duncan.

—— (1837). *Owain Miles, and Other Inedited Fragments of Ancient English Poetry.* Edinburgh.

Leo, H., with Biszegger, W. (eds.) (1872–7). *Angelsächsisches Glossar.* Halle: Buchhandlung des Waisenhauses.

Lowndes, W. T. (ed.), rev. Bohn, H. G. (ed.) (1864), *The Bibliographical Manual of English Literature . . . by William Thomas Lowndes.* New edn. 'with an appendix relating to the books of literary and scientific societies.' viii, Appendix. London: Henry G. Bohn.

Luick, K. (1914–40); i/2 (1929–40) ed. Wild, F., and Koziol, H. *Historische Grammatik der englischen Sprache.* Vol. i, 2 parts, no more published. Leipzig (later Stuttgart): Bernhard Tauchnitz; reprinted (1964) Oxford: Basil Blackwell; and Stuttgart: Tauchnitz.

Lye, E., and Manning, O. (eds.) (1772). *Dictionarium Saxonico et Gothico-Latinum.* 2 vols. London: for Benj. White; Cambridge: J. Woodyer, and T. & J. Meril; Oxford: J. and J. Fletcher, and D. Prince.

Macaulay, G. C. (ed.) (1900–1), *The English Works of John Gower,* 2 vols. EETS, extra series 81–2; also published in Macaulay, G. C. (ed.) (1899–1902), *The Works of John Gower,* 4 vols. Oxford: Clarendon Press, ii–iii (with the same pagination).

MacCracken, H. N. (ed.) (1910). 'The Story of Joseph and Aseneth', *Journal of English and Germanic Philology* 9: 224–64.

Madden, Sir F. (ed.) (1828). *The Ancient English Romance of Havelok the Dane.* London: for the Roxburghe Club.

—— (1832). *The Ancient English Romance of William and the Werwolf.* London: for the Roxburghe Club.

—— (1838). *The Old English Versions of the Gesta Romanorum.* London: for the Roxburghe Club.

Madden, Sir F. (cont.) (1839). *Sir Gawayne, a Collection of Ancient Romance Poems, by Scotish and English Authors, relating to that celebrated Knight of the Round Table.* London: for the Bannatyne Club.

—— (1847). *Layamons Brut, or Chronicle of Britain.* 3 vols. London: for the Society of Antiquaries.

Mätzner, E., Goldbeck, K., and Bieling, H. (eds.) (1867–1900). *Altenglische Sprachproben nebst einem Wörterbuche.* 2 vols. i/1 'Poesie' (1867), i/2 'Prosa' (1869), ii 'Wörterbuch' (1878–1900). Berlin: Weidmann.

Malory, Sir Thomas (1485). *Thys book entytled Le Morte Darthur.* Westminster: Caxton.

—— (1976). *The Winchester Malory: A Facsimile with an introduction by N. R. Ker.* EETS, supplementary series 4.

Meid, W. (1967). *Wortbildungslehre,* in Krahe and Meid (1969, 1967: vol. iii).

Michel, F. (ed.) (1845). *Horn et Rimenhild–Recueil de ce qui reste des poëmes relatifs a leurs aventures composés en françois, en anglois et en écossois dans les treizième, quatorzième, quinzième et seizième siècles.* Paris: for the Bannatyne Club.

Miller, T. (ed.) (1890–8). i/1, *The Old English Version of Bede's Ecclesiastical History of The English People.* EETS, original series 95. ii/2, *A Collation of Four MSS. Of the Old English Version of Bede's Ecclesiastical History of The English People.* EETS, original series 111.

Morris, E. E. (ed.) (1898). *Austral English: A Dictionary of Australasian Words, Phrases and Usages.* London and New York (New York): Macmillan.

Morris, R. (1865). *The Story of Genesis and Exodus, An Early English Song, about A.D. 1250.* EETS, [original series] 7; 2nd edn. 1873.

Murray J. A. H. (1885). 'Thirteenth Address of the President of the Philological Soc.,... 16th May, 1884': Report on the Philological Society's Dictionary, 508–31, List of Readers and Books Read by them for the Dictionary, 1879–84, 601–42. *TPS,* 1882–4.

Murray, J. A. H. (ed.) (1888). *A New English Dictionary on Historical Principles; founded mainly on the materials collected by The Philological Society.* i 'A and B'. Oxford: Clarendon Press.

Onions, C. T. (ed.) (1941). *A Shakespeare Glossary.* Last revision. Oxford: Clarendon Press.

Palmer, D. J. (1965). *The Rise of English Studies.* London, New York (New York), and Toronto: Oxford University Press for the University of Hull.

Pollard, A. W., and Redgrave, G. R. (eds.) (1926). *A Short-Title Catalogue of Books Printed in England, Scotland, & Ireland, and of English Books Printed Abroad, 1475–1640.* 2 vols. London: The Bibliographical Society. 2nd edn., revised and enlarged: begun by Jackson, W. A., and Ferguson, F. S., completed by Pantzer, K. F. 3 vols. London: The Bibliographical Society, 1976–91.

Price, H. T. (1910). *A History of Ablaut in the Strong Verbs from Caxton to the End of the Elizabethan Period.* Bonner Studien zur englischen Philologie III.

Raymond, D. R. (1987). *Dispatches from the Front: The* Prefaces *to the Oxford English Dictionary.* Waterloo, Ontario: Centre for the New Oxford English Dictionary, University of Waterloo. [I am indebted to the UW Centre for the New Oxford English Dictionary for a copy of this very useful publication, and to Professor Antonette diP. Healey of the *Dictionary of Old English,* University of Toronto, for facilitating that gift.]

Richardson, C. (ed.) (1836–7). *A New Dictionary of the English Language, Combining Explanation with Etymology: and Illustrated by Quotations from the best Authorities. The Words—with those of the same family, in German, Dutch and Swedish, or in Italian, French and Spanish,—are traced to their Origin. The* EXPLANATIONS *are deduced from the primit-*

ive Meaning *through the various* Usages. *The* QUOTATIONS *are arranged Chronologically from the earliest period to the beginning of the present century*. 2 vols. London: Wm Pickering; New York (New York): Wm Jackson.

Ritson, J. (ed.) (1790). *Ancient Songs, from the Time of King Henry the Third, to the Revolution*. London: for J. Johnson.

—— (1791). *Pieces of Ancient Popular Poetry: from Authentic Manuscripts and Old Printed Copies*. London: for T. and J. Egerton.

—— (1793). *The Northumberland Garland; or, Newcastle Nightingale: A Matchless Collection of Famous Songs*. Newcastle: Hall and Elliot.

—— (1794). *Scotish Song(s)*. 2 vols. London: for J. Johnson and J. Egerton.

—— (1795*a*). *Poems on Interesting Events in the Reign of King Henry III. Written, in the year* MCCCLII. *By Laurence Minot*. London: for T. Egerton.

—— (1795*b*). *Robin Hood: A Collection of all the Ancient Poems, Songs, and Ballads, Now Extant, Relative to that Celebrated English Outlaw*. 2 vols. London: for J. Johnson and J. Egerton.

—— (1802). *Ancient Engleish Metrical Romanceës*. 3 vols. London: for G. and W. Nichol.

Sawyer, P. H. (ed.) (1968). *Anglo-Saxon Charters*. Royal Historical Society Guides and Handbooks 8. London: The Royal Historical Society.

Schäfer, J. (1980). *Documentation in the O.E.D.: Shakespeare and Nashe as Test Cases*. Oxford: Clarendon Press.

Schmidt, A., and Sarrazin, G. (eds.) (1902). *Shakespeare-Lexikon*. 2 vols. 3rd edn. Berlin: Reimer; New York (New York): G. E. Stechert.

Seymour, M. C. (ed.) (1975–88). *On the Properties of Things: John Trevisa's Translation of Bartholomæus Anglicus De Proprietatibus Rerum, a Critical Text*. 3 vols. Oxford: Clarendon Press.

Sibbald, J. (ed.) (1802). *Chronicle of Scottish Poetry; from the Thirteenth Century, to the Union of the Crowns*. 4 vols. Edinburgh: for J. Sibbald.

Sievers, E. (1875) *Der Heliand und die angelsächsische Genesis*. Halle: Lippert'sche Buchhandlung (Max Niemeyer).

—— (1898). *Angelsächsische Grammatik*. 3rd edn., Halle: Max Niemeyer; 1st edn., Halle: Max Niemeyer, 1882.

Sievers, E., and Brunner, K. (1965). *Altenglische Grammatik nach der angelsächsischen Grammatik von Eduard Sievers*. 3rd edn. Tübingen: Max Niemeyer.

Simpson, J. A., and Weiner, E. S. C., prepared by (1989). *The Oxford English Dictionary First Edited by James A. H. Murray, Henry Bradley, W. A. Craigie and C. T. Onions combined with A Supplement to the Oxford English Dictionary edited by R. W. Burchfield and reset with corrections, revisions and additional vocabulary*. 20 vols. Oxford: Clarendon Press.

Skeat, W. W. (ed.) (1884). *The Kingis Quair: together with A Ballad of Good Counsel: by King James I. of Scotland*. The Scottish Text Society. 2nd and revised edn. The Scottish Text Society, new series 1, 1911.

Skinner, S. (ed.) (1671). *Etymologicon Linguæ Anglicanæ, seu explicatio vocum Anglicarum etymologica ex propriis fontibus, scil. ex linguis duodecim*. London: T. Roycroft for H. Brome, R. Clavel, B. Tooke, T. Sawbridge.

Smith, J. (ed.) (1722), *Historiæ Ecclesiasticæ Gentis Anglorum Libri Quinque, auctore Sancto & Venerabili Bæda Presbytero Anglo-Saxone*. Cambridge: [Cambridge] University Press.

Somner, Wm, (ed.) (1659). *Dictionarium Saxonico-Latino-Anglicum—Voces, Phrasesque Præcipuas Anglo-Saxonicas, e libris, sive manuscriptis, sive typis excusis, aliisque monu-*

mentis tum publicis tum privatis, magna diligentia collectas; cum Latina et Anglica vocum interpretatione complectens. Oxford: printed by William Hall for the author; London: Daniel White.

Stanley, E. G. (1987). 'Old English in *The Oxford English Dictionary*', in Burchfield (1987: 19–35).

Stratmann, F. H. (ed.) (1867). *A Dictionary of the Old English Language compiled from writings of the thirteenth, fourteenth and fifteenth centuries*. Krefeld: Kramer & Baum. 2nd edn. 1873; 3rd edn. 1878; supplement 1881.

Sweet, H. (ed.) (1871). *King Alfred's West-Saxon Version of Gregory's Pastoral Care*, EETS, original series 45.

Sweet, H. (1874). 'A History of English Sounds'. *TPS*, 1873–4: 461–623; also published in English Dialect Society, ix, 1–163.

Sweet, H. (ed.) (1876). *An Anglo-Saxon Reader in Prose and Verse*. Oxford: Clarendon Press.

—— (1882). *An Anglo-Saxon Primer*. Oxford: Clarendon Press.

—— (1883). *King Alfred's Orosius*, part 1 (no more published). EETS, original series 79.

—— (1885a). *Anglo-Saxon Reading Primers*, 2 vols; i, selected homilies of Ælfric; ii, extracts from Alfred's *Orosius*. Oxford: Clarendon Press.

—— (1885b), *The Oldest English Texts*, EETS, original series 83.

—— (1887). *A Second Anglo-Saxon Reader: Archaic and Dialectal*. Oxford: Clarendon Press.

—— (1888). *A History of English Sounds from the Earliest Period*. Oxford: Clarendon Press.

—— (1897a). *First Steps in Anglo-Saxon*. Oxford: Clarendon Press.

—— (1897b). *The Student's Dictionary of Anglo-Saxon*. Oxford: Clarendon Press.

Tooke, J. Horne (1798–1805). *Epea Pteroenta* [Greek]. *Or, The Diversions of Purley*. 2nd edn. 2 vols. London: for the author.

Trench, R. C. (ed.) (1859). *A Select Glossary of English words used formerly in Senses different from their present*. London: John W. Parker.

Triggs, O. L. (ed.) (1896). *The Assembly of Gods*. EETS, extra series 69.

Tyrwhitt, T. (ed.) (1775–8). *The Canterbury Tales of Chaucer. To which are added, An Essay upon his Language and Versification; an Introductory Discourse; and Notes. In Four Volumes.* v, 'Containing a Glossary'. London: for T. Payne and Son.

Urry, J. (ed.) (1721). *The Works of Geoffrey Chaucer, compared with the Former Editions, and many valuable MSS. Out of which, Three Tales are added which were never before Printed: By John Urry, Student of Christ-Church, Oxon. Deceased; Together with a Glossary, By a Student of the same College*. London: B. Lintot.

[Utterson, E. V. (ed.)] (1812). *Sir John Froissart's Chronicles of England, France, Spain, Portugal, Scotland, Brittany, Flanders, and the Adjoining Countries . . . by John Bourchier, Lord Berners. Reprinted from Pynson's Edition of 1523, and 1525*. 2 vols. London: for F. C. and J. Rivington; T. Payne; Wilkie and Robinson; Longman, Hurst, Rees, Orme, and Brown; Cadell and Davies; J. Murray; R. H. Evans; J. Mawman; and R. Baldwin.

—— (1814). *The History of The Valiant Knight Arthur of Little Britain. A Romance of Chivalry. Originally Translated from the French by John Bourchier, Lord Berners. A New Edition.* London: for White, Cochrane, and Co.

—— (1817). *Select Pieces of Early Popular Poetry: Re-Published Principally from Early Printed Copies, in the Black Letter*. 2 vols. London: for Longman, Hurst, Rees, Orme, and Brown.

—— (1839). *Kyng Roberd of Cysylle*. London: for private circulation.

Venezky, R. L., and Healey, A. diP. (eds.) (1980) *A Microfiche Concordance to Old English.* Toronto: Pontifical Institute of Medieval Studies, for the Dictionary of Old English, Medieval Centre of the University of Toronto.

Way, G. L. (ed.) (1796, 1800). *Fabliaux or Tales Abridged from French Manuscripts of the xiith and xiiith Centuries By M. Le Grand.* 2 vols. ii, with a Preface, Notes, and Appendix, by G. Ellis. London: for R. Faulder.

Weber, H. (ed.) (1810). *Metrical Romances of the Thirteenth, Fourteenth, and Fifteenth Centuries: Published from Ancient Manuscripts.* 3 vols. Edinburgh: for A. Constable; London: for J. Murray, and Constable, Hunter, Park, and Hunter.

Wheatley, H. B. (ed.) (1865), *Of the Orthographie and Congruitie of the Britan Tongue; A Treates, noe shorter then necessarie, for the Schooles, Be Alexander Hume,* EETS, original series 5.

Wing, D. G. (ed.) (1945–51). *Short-Title Catalogue of Books Printed in England, Scotland, Ireland, Wales, and British America and of English Books Printed in Other Countries 1641–1700.* 3 vols. New York (New York): The Index Society. Revised edn. (1982–94): Morrison, J. J., Nelson, C. W., and Seccombe, M. (eds.). New York (New York): The Modern Language Association of America.

Wright, T. (ed.) (1841). *Treatises on Science Written During the Middle Ages in Anglo-Saxon, Anglo-Norman and English.* London: for the Historical Society of Science.

Wright, W. A. (ed.) (1887). *The Metrical Chronicle of Robert of Gloucester.* 2 vols. Rolls Series 86.

Zangemeister, K., and Braune, W. (eds.) (1894). 'Bruchstücke der altsächsischen Bibeldichtung', *Neue Heidelberger Jahrbücher,* 4, 205–94.

9

The Vocabulary of Science in the *OED*

MICHAEL RAND HOARE AND VIVIAN SALMON

Méphistophélès: 'Un tas de sciences. Je m'y noie—Géo ceci, géo cela, et des métries, des nomies, des logies, des graphies, des stiques, et des tiques . . .'
Paul Valéry, *Mon Faust*, Act 3, Scene 5

Scientific terminology has always confronted lexicographers with special problems, manifested as early as Cawdrey's monoglot English dictionary of 1604. Most important of these are the criteria for inclusion in a dictionary, namely, which 'hard words', as Cawdrey and several successors described rare or difficult terms, would be of sufficient general interest to be included— a particular problem when those likely to be concerned constituted a small élite group. A second major issue is the extent to which scientific terminology should be glossed; should the definition be sufficiently detailed to make clear to the layman the objects and processes denoted by the word, or should only the briefest of definitions be given which would satisfy the specialist but not necessarily enlighten the layman?

The 'hard words' of the early dictionaries were often derived from Latin, and frequently denoted a technical or scientific concept. At first, lexicographers like Cawdrey, made no attempt to classify 'hard words', but in 1656 Blount grouped them into semantic categories, and shortly after Edward Phillips made use of such classifications as *natural history, chirurgery, chemistry, astronomy*, and *mechanics*, as well as less technical subjects such as *hunting* and *hawking* (1658). Phillips also makes claims for the accuracy of his definitions by naming specialist sources of information, for example 'Dr Sparks' for 'physicks', 'Mr Molins' for 'botanicks', and 'Dr Wybard' for geometry. Later dictionaries increased the number of scientific and technical categories by adding, for example, *husbandry, navigation*, and *mathematics* as in Coles (1676). Kersey (1708) claims to provide a clear explication of the 'liberal and mechanical' terminology of *maritime affairs, military discipline*, and even *cookery*, while Bailey (1730), claiming that his sources are 'several Hands', names two of them as 'G. Gordon' for mathematics and 'P. Miller' for botany. A more professional treatment was already evident in William Johnson's *Lexicon chymicum* (1652) and John Harris's *Lexicon technicum* (1704) and continued into the eighteenth century with further single-subject dictionaries, which began to cite specialist sources as guarantees of the propriety of inclusion and the accuracy of definitions. Among the many specialist dictionaries are Stephen Blanckaert's (1693) of anatomy, Nicholson's (1795) of chemistry, Dunglison's (1842) of medicine, and the great medical lexicon of the Sydenham Society (Power and Sedgwick 1881–9) the Preface of which is dated 1879, just as Murray was setting to work on the dictionary.[1] From such dictionaries the 'pioneers' of the *OED* would have learned the necessity of dealing with technical and scientific vocabulary, so in this respect they were hardly pioneers—though of course they were the first to add a historical dimension.

The second major problem relating to entries on scientific topics is that of the degree of definition and explanation required, and the extent of extraneous material, such as classical myth and geographical information. In short, lexicographers have to decide how far a dictionary should also be an encyclopaedia. John Harris, two centuries earlier, anticipated the problem when, in justifying his *Lexicon Technicum*, he wrote that his aim was: 'to make it a Dictionary not only of bare *Words* but *Things*; and that the Reader may not only find here an Explication of the *Technical* words, or the Terms of Art made use of in all the *Liberal Sciences*, and such as border nearly upon them, but also those *Arts themselves*; and especially *such*, and *such* Parts of them as are most Useful and Advantagious to Mankind' (1704: Preface, 1).

Other early dictionaries inclined towards this position. Bailey (1730), for example, glossed Abacus as follows: 'The ABACUS . . . was originally designed to represent a square Tile laid over an Urn or Basket. The Original or Rise of this first regular Order of Architecture is said to be as follows. An old Woman of *Athens* having placed a Basket covered with a Tile over the root of an Acanthus . . . the plant shooting forth the following Spring, encompassed the Basket all round, till having met the Tile, it curled back in a kind of Scrolls.' Similar examples can be found in Johnson's dictionary.

As a forerunner of the 'pioneers' of the *OED*, Trench sets out his views on these topics in two treatises, *English Past and Present* (1855) and *On Some Deficiencies in our English Dictionaries* (1860). Even before the Philological Society had decided to embark on a totally new dictionary, Trench had considered the question of including scientific terminology, and had expressed a degree of approval. Speaking of the invention of new vocabulary generally, he pointed out that one motivation is the desire to reduce lengthy explanations, a single word often saying at a stroke what it would otherwise have taken sentences to express (1855: 86). He illustrates this with an example: '*Isothermal*', he says, 'is quite of modern invention; but what a long story it would be to tell the meaning of "isothermal lines" which is a phrase summarised in the one word'. *Watershed*, he adds (1855: 87),

---

[1] For full bibliographical details of these and other early dictionaries mentioned see Kennedy (1927).

'has only recently begun to appear in books of geography . . . taking the place of "the line of water parting"; and yet how convenient it must be admitted to be—meaning . . . not merely that which *sheds* the waters, but that which *divides* them ("wasserscheide")'. 'It must be allowed', he claims, 'that not merely geographical terminology, but geography itself, had a benefactor in him who first endowed it with so expressive and comprehensive a word' (1855: 88). However, some terms had never passed the threshold of a scientific treatise, and should not be regarded as words at all; they were, he claimed, merely 'signs' invented as a kind of algebraic notation in the relevant science (1855: 63). They should not find a place in any but a technological lexicon, although 'multitudes' of them had been coined because of the advances of physical science. But others had passed the boundaries of scientific writing: 'photography', he points out (1855: 63), is one such; another was 'stereotype' (1855: 64), being current in a secondary and figurative sense. However, he suspects the motives of some lexicographers in including scientific vocabulary in their work, arguing that they are impelled by 'barren ostentation' (1860: 57) to boast of innumerable additions. 'Nothing is easier', he adds, than to 'turn to modern treatises on chemistry or electricity . . . and to transplant such terms in their hundreds and thousands', thus 'crowding out' and 'deforming' the pages of a dictionary (1860: 57). He admits (1860: 59) that much of such 'rubbish' had already been thrown overboard by Richardson (1836–7), but even so, he was at fault because he had not sufficiently distinguished between the words of 'common English' and those of specific arts and sciences.

In considering the problem of selection, Trench, in 1857, addressing the Philological Society on deficiencies in current English dictionaries, pointed out that all were inadequate, 'inserting some things, and some of them many things, which have properly no claim to find room in their pages' (1860: 3). However, when proposals for a new dictionary, the *Canones Lexicographici*, were published it was laid down that every word, however 'worthless', found in English books should be included except those devoted to purely scientific subjects, such as treatises on electricity or mathematics ([Trench *et al.*] 1860: 3) and when the rules for contributors to the dictionary were published in 1860, further clarification of the role of scientific terminology was provided. There were to be three major parts in the dictionary. The first was to include not only every word in the language 'for which sufficient authority, whether printed or oral, can be adduced' but also those scientific words which 'have passed out of their peculiar province into general use' ([Trench *et al.*] 1860: 4) or were 'such as are found in works of general literature' as opposed to purely technical or scientific treatises. Such terms were the 'heritage of all intelligent men', as were those 'scattered up and down our literature' such as Robert Burton's *elegm* and Jeremy Taylor's *spagyrist* (Trench 1860: 60). Further recommendations included the proposal that 'Where a word, admissible into the Main Dictionary [i.e. Part 1] has, besides its ordinary sense another of a technical nature, which, if it were the only one, would exclude it, the technical sense or senses shall be added for the sake of "completeness"'.

The second part of the proposed dictionary would be dedicated to technical and scientific words, and would be comparable with the supplement to the French Academy's dictionary. Such terminology, it was claimed, had often been incorporated incorrectly into general dictionaries, Johnson's being a prime example. Among his improper inclusions were such words as *aegilops, parotis, striatura, lamellated, striae, polypetalous, quadriphyllos* (Trench 1860: 58). Also criticized were such entries in Webster's dictionary as *zeolitiform, zinkiferous,* and *zygomatic* (Trench 1860: 59). To this dictionary of scientific terms should be added a list of proper names, both personal and geographical, with a final section on etymology, for 'such a work [as the proposed dictionary] ought not to go forth to the public incomplete in any respect' ([Trench *et al.*] 1860: 7).

The degree of detail required for definitions was a second issue addressed by Trench. He was concerned that too much information might be provided to explain scientific terms, arguing that a dictionary 'must everywhere know how to preserve the line firm and distinct between itself and an encyclopaedia' (1860: 60). He gave as an illustration Johnson's definitions of a number of words which were quite unacceptable, for example, *rose* (nineteen lines), *opal* (thirteen lines), and *air-pump* (twenty-one lines) (1860: 61). He also cites Webster, from whom, he says 'we may learn of the camel, that it constitutes the riches of the Arabian', and in all, twenty-five lines of its natural history (1860: 61). In the *Canones*, it is specified that every technical and scientific term should be accompanied with a 'line or two of explanation in the shortest possible form, and a reference to the best treatise known, where fuller information may be found' ([Trench *et al.*] 1860: 8). As Trench succinctly argued, 'Let the quotations yield as much information as they can be made to yield, in subordination to their primary purpose, which is, to illustrate the *word*, and not to tell us about the *thing*' (1860: 60–1). It is 'in the due and happy selection of these, so as, if possible, to combine both objects, [that] the lexicographer may display eminent skill' (Trench 1860: 61). The *Canones* also specified the use of a very brief form of definition, which has survived to the current edition of the dictionary in the labelling of words as members of some specific subject area. Described as 'Technical Marks', for example, *leg.* for 'legal', *her.* for 'heraldic', and *chem.* for 'chemical', no recommendations are made for their number or type ([Trench *et al.*] 1860: 7).

Among reactions to the plan for a dictionary, some influential comments on the proposals came from Derwent Coleridge, who presented his 'Observations on the Plan' to the Philological Society on 10 May 1860. He agrees that 'technical words will of course be marked according to their department in the usual manner', though many have 'found their way into ordinary speech', for example, *zenith, culminate,* and *amalgamate,* but he also postulates a large class of words which 'without being exactly technical, are yet incapable of being used, except on occasions implying scientific research and technical precision'; to use *saponaceous* for 'soapy' and *amygdalaceous* for 'almondy' would be 'intolerably pedantic', except in connection with natural history, physiology, or the like. Other words which should be included in a general dictionary, but distinguished as 'scientific', include *anaesthetic, mephitic, empyromatic, analogue,* and *correlate* (1860: 166).

When, in the 1870s, the publisher Macmillan was proposing to bring out a new dictionary, Murray was an obvious candidate as editor because of his contributions to dialectology, although, as he himself pointed out, he knew nothing of the Philological Society's earlier plans, and had to 'get hold of' material with which to prepare a specimen entry (Timpson 1957: 18). A second qualification was his lifelong interest in science, as he remarked in his autobiography (Timpson 1957: 12). While still at school, he was encouraged by the Revd James Duncan to take an interest in the natural sciences, and Murray's younger brothers recalled how he used to make collections of rocks, flowers, and insects (W. Murray 1943: 26). Murray himself claimed to have made 'incursions' into nearly all the sciences, botany and geology especially, but also entomology, chemistry, and electricity (Timpson 1957: 12) and to know enough of most scientific disciplines to understand their terminology without assistance. As he said, he could write to various specialists—as a geologist to Archibald Geikie, as a botanist to Thistleton Dyer, as an anatomist to Burdon Sanderson, as a chemist to Roscoe and Thorpe, and 'not as the man in the street merely'. 'And I know', he went on, 'when an article I want to quote is wrong' (Timpson 1957: 21). For proof, one need only look at the many letters, preserved in the archives of the Oxford University Press, from distinguished scientists writing to Murray in response to the various enquiries he had sent them. It is clear from the letters that Murray was asking searching questions. One writer, Thistleton Dyer, comments 'As with most of your enquiries, the answer is not easy' (22 August 1907, from the Royal Gardens at Kew). The physicist Silvanus P. Thompson wrote a long and detailed letter about the first use (by Kelvin or Rankin) of the word *thermo-dynamic* (13 October 1911). Occasionally it is the correspondent who is seeking information on a technical matter from Murray, as when Thompson asked whether he had come upon various terms for the compass needle (31 March 1914). Yet another letter, from Henry Roscoe, informed Murray that his explanation of a doubtful chemical compound, was 'what is wanted to make things understood' (10 February 1884). One unusual letter, from the American geologist Albert Chester, reproaches Murray for not making use of the citations he had sent him, since they were earlier than some which Murray had, in fact, used (19 October 1891).[2]

In describing his sources, Murray lists, among others, the technical glosses added to specialist treatises, arguing that 'when a man writes a treatise on Botany and adds a Glossary at the end, it ought to mean that he uses or *would* use the word himself, if he needed it' (1880: 126). Other authorities to which he refers are specialist dictionaries, 'as of Medicine, Architecture, or Mineralogy' (1880: 126). Murray

---

[2] Other eminent persons consulted included Thomas Huxley, Flinders Petrie the archaeologist, and the botanist James Britten. It would seem, however, that Murray's correspondence tended to concern his problems with a word being edited, rather than actively seeking 'feedback' about the latest scientific vocabulary.

accepted that the authority of a specialist gave 'some sort of sanction to the terms which they think fit to include; though too many . . . include terms which are long obsolete' (1880: 126). But to any of his contributors who gives a dictionary as his only source for a word, such as Weale's *Dictionary of Scientific Terms*, Murray replies 'I want proof of the word's use, not of its occurrence in a list' (1880: 127).

When, in 1879, Murray published a list of works to be examined, among them was a number of scientific treatises by, for example, Darwin, Faraday, Huxley, Lyell, and Spencer (see also Chapter 3). It appears, however, that such material was not popular with the readers, since he found himself obliged to issue appeals for special attention to be paid to scientific writings. In his Presidential Address for May 1880 he informed the Philological Society that he needed no further help in collecting the vocabulary of general literature, but he would be glad if readers would 'devote themselves to the examination of scientific and technical books' (1880: 125), admitting a year later that, for scientific material, 'much still remains to be done' (1881: 263).

Between the date of this appeal and his Presidential Address of 1884, contributors responded by undertaking a wide range of reading, though some thought that the line had been drawn 'somewhat too widely in reference to technical terms' (1884: 523), whilst various 'men of science' would have preferred 'rather more indulgence' to have been shown to the vocabulary of their particular departments.[3] But as Murray remarked, the canon proposed by some critics, that no word should be admitted for which a quotation from a non-technical work could not be given, was 'impracticable of application'; it would have meant an attempt to establish a universal negative for tens of thousands of words. He adds (1884: 524): 'the line *may* be drawn more closely than heretofore; but it will still remain as vague as ever'.

In describing the place of scientific terminology in the English language, Murray referred to his well-known 'compass diagram' in the introductory 'General Explanations' to the dictionary. He had already considered this in his Presidential Address of 1880: 'The English language', he said, 'is not a square with definite sides containing its area; it is a circle, but a circle such as Euclid never contemplated . . . clear and definite and unmistakable at the centre, but whose circumference melts marginless into the surrounding nothingness, and seems to have a margin, only till we try to trace it' (1880: 131).

The vagueness of the English vocabulary did not make the problem of selection any easier. As Murray enquired in the same Presidential Address: 'Do we take a series of animals: *Horse* . . . *Amoeba, Agama*; or a series of plants: *Rose, Anemone . . . Geranium, Pelargonium* . . . where do the general words end, and the technical begin? Are *Hippopotamus* and *Geranium* English because known to every

---

[3] The word *scientist* was still not current during the Murray period, though he correctly cites William Whewell's attempts to establish it in the 1830s. Whewell invented the word by analogy with *artist* and not as a conscious back-formation from the much earlier *scientific, scientifical* with sixteenth-century origins. These entries, together with that for *science* in *OED1*, edited by Bradley, show the extraordinary ramifications of the word.

town-arab? . . . Shall we insert *Gold*, and omit *Aluminium*, or insert *Aluminium* . . . but omit *Tellurium* and *Rubidium*?' If the lexicographer inclines to the theoretical (1880: 133–4) 'he will draw his line very close': if he tends to be practical, he will probably say 'For one person that will turn to the dictionary to learn the meaning of *Camel*, ten will turn to learn what an *Agama* is'. Hence the lexicographer, he argues, will be as comprehensive as his limits will allow (1880: 134).

The editors were well aware of the increased problems caused by the burgeoning of new scientific language by the time the complete *OED1* finally went to press. In the Preface to the 1933 reissue, Craigie remarks that a lexicographer must record 'not only the standard language of literature and conversation . . . but also the main technical vocabulary'; and in the Preface to the 1933 *Supplement* he points out the great enlargement of the terminology of the arts and sciences, citing *biochemistry, wireless telegraphy* and *telephony, mechanical transport, aerial locomotion, psychoanalysis,* and the *cinema* as new areas of concern. Such developments, and many more in the meantime, were to be prominent in the rationale for beginning work on the Burchfield supplements forty years later.

Having looked in some detail at the background to *OED1* and the problems at its inception, we must attempt an evaluation of the finished product in terms of its scientific content and utility as a reference source. While this study of 'pioneers' necessarily focuses on the first edition, the even more formidable bulk of *OED2* must also come into consideration for the obvious reason that it provides a ready diagnostic tool for examining the strengths and shortcomings of Murray's original enterprise. Though this may fail to reveal problems endemic in both editions, such comparison is of prime importance when we come to evaluate the scientific content, or the lack of it, in the first edition. Fortunately, this exercise, which thirty years ago would have been a haphazard and thankless task, of sampling and endless searching for non-existent entries, was, in effect, carried out for us with the completion of Burchfield's *Supplements* in the 1980s. These, along with the shorter 1933 *Supplement,* rather than *OED2* itself, are, in fact, the simplest tool for arriving at an estimate of the extent and character of the 'scientific lacuna' in *OED1*, and may well be an equally good guide to other specialized lexis.[4]

By sampling the subset of added entries with first use before, say, 1910 we can obtain a good qualitative idea of what is missing from *OED1* and the kind of fields most neglected.[5] To put it differently, this exercise enables us to

[4] As a caveat, however, we note that Burchfield's team did not read material before 1884, or after 1972, and did not include pre-1820 antedatings. These drawbacks mean that our reasoning here only sets a *lower limit* to the extent of the 'scientific lacuna' in *OED1*, but this is of little consequence for our qualitative conclusions.

[5] Though the figures are not of great importance, this can, with a little statistical work, be made quantitative. A rough estimate by random sampling of all letters leads to a figure of about 8 per cent of *Supplement* headwords (Burchfield 1972–86) that *could have* appeared in *OED1* under the conditions described. This represents about 5,000 items in all.

estimate the number of *scientific* headword additions that might have been expected if 'Murray's algorithm'[6] for discovery and inclusion had been equivalent to 'Burchfield's algorithm' *during the original project*. The cut-off at 1910 would no doubt have been quite exacting for the original team, but the then recent discoveries in wireless telegraphy, radioactivity, atomic physics, aeronautics, quantum theory, genetics, and the like would have amounted to a sub-vocabulary of the greatest importance.

As we know, Murray defended his corner with characteristic stubbornness on the question of the admission of scientific words. He was able to prevail both against philologists such as Trench and against those of the Delegates, like Benjamin Jowett, who for different reasons sought to limit the scope of specialized entries. The end result, in *OED1*, is nevertheless clearly a compromise, reached under a combination of technical and economic pressures. Yet, while the list of works consulted shows that Murray cast his net wide, the competence of the readers would have determined, so to speak, the size of the 'mesh'. 'Editability', a factor still admitted to be important in the ongoing project (Gilliver 1999), must also have played its part after a word had been caught for consideration—later to be 'landed' or 'thrown back' as the case might warrant.

There is abundant evidence that Murray was very conscious of the snares and pitfalls that awaited him in the outer reaches of the compass diagram. These would attend every stage of the production process, with certain problems characteristic of, if not unique to, scientific lexis. In less metaphorical terms the sequence involved can be summarized as follows:

(1) The selection of likely material for 'reading' (primarily technical works, though also works of popular science[7] as well as previous dictionaries).
(2) The 'reading' process itself, that is the 'trawling' of this material for new words, usage, and semantic shifts, while locating apt and historically significant quotations (a task now increasingly focused on 'catching' new coinages, variants, and collocations, but markedly different for the 'pioneers' of *OED1* when the whole language stood before them).
(3) The evaluation of items for inclusion in terms of their role in scientific discourse and its interaction with everyday language (a step requiring both familiarity with the frequency and utility of target words and a certain instinct for

---

[6] Throughout we shall often ascribe decisions to Murray where a term such as 'Murray and co-editors' might be more correct. We use the term *algorithm* to comprise the notional set of rules governing the whole decision process, beginning with instructions for reading, decisions on acceptability, and ending with the approved entry. ('Algorithm': 'the learned *algorism* which passed through many pseudo-etymological perversions including a recent *algorithm* in which it is learnedly confused with Gr.αριθμος "number"'—an illustration of (presumably) Murray at his most querulous. No quotation is given for the 'recent' perversion. The mathematical/linguistic use was given its due in the Burchfield *Supplements* and *OED2*.)

[7] Such works would include, for example, *Scientific American* and *The Penny Cyclopedia*. The periodical *Nature*, much cited, would be borderline in this respect, containing original works along with news and commentary.

what is 'catching-on', ephemeral, obsolescent, and otherwise non-standard —in short a scientifically-informed view of the 'frequency, transparency, and productivity' criterion more generally applied).

(4) The drafting of correct and adequate definitions, the discrimination of subheads, nuances of use, the analysis of combining forms, etc. (a process potentially more liable to serious error where scientific terms are concerned than when ordinary language is glossed).

(5) It was desirable to have input from historians of science—for at no stage could there be any question of science being exempt from fidelity to the *modus operandi* of the dictionary 'on historical principles'.

It will be clear from the most superficial scan of *OED1* that much of the scientific lexis deemed fit for inclusion resides so far out in the 'compass diagram' as to be well beyond the characterization as 'such of the scientific, technical, slang, dialectal and foreign words as are passing into common use and approach the position or standing of "common words"' described by Murray in 1888. Needless to say this is even more markedly the case in *OED2*, where it would seem that any pretence that specialized terms are 'passing into common use' had been effectively abandoned. Nevertheless, in practical terms, the decisions about 'hard words' that Murray faced would not have been essentially different from those made in the production of *OED2* (and indeed the ongoing work on *OED3*); almost all the problems that beset specialized lexicography were there, some accentuated in the scientific context, some of less consequence, and some specific to the more recondite fields, such as mathematics.

Of the age-old problems reappearing in scientific guise we can cite the inclusion of proper nouns, the reception of unnaturalized forms of foreign origin, and, in more recent times, acronyms.[8] To these we may add editorial decisions, such as whether to allow chemical formulae, mathematical equations, and non-alphabetic symbols. The problem, discussed earlier, of 'encyclopaedic' items recurs at almost every turn, and it is clear that Murray struggled with this from the earliest days without achieving more than an uneasy compromise. The example of Webster was before him throughout, and with it, we would imagine, a certain pressure not to emulate the American example too obviously. Clearly, to the many faculties called into play by the lexicographer, there must be added a certain knowing prescience. Murray may be criticized for leaving out *radium* [1899], *chromosome* [1889], and *appendicitis* [1886], yet it is salutary to wonder whether an editor in the 1950s would have given much thought to the obscure compound *desoxyribonucleic acid*, or in the 1970s to the equally obscure disease *bovine spongiform encephalopathy*.

Given the way science develops by unpredictable leaps and bounds, it is inevitable that fresh discoveries should be attended by both a burgeoning of new

---

[8] Acronyms were perhaps the one problem that Murray did not have to deal with. The word does not appear in *OED1* and the 1972 *Supplement* gives a first use as 1943.

vocabulary and a degree of semantic shift—and the latter may be more difficult to catch than the headwords themselves. The examples of *aeroplane* [1873] (originally *aëroplane!*) and *electron* are interesting illustrations. In *OED1* the former is still 'a plane placed in the air for aerostatical experiment' (a usage rightly awarded a † in the 1933 *Supplement*). Likewise, *electron* [1891] appears as || = ELECTRUM 2. 'gold much alloyed with silver'. A user interested in Larmor's electron theory of the atom in the early years of the century would have been mystified by this, if not actually misled. Though these items were brought up to date only with the 1933 and later *Supplements*, where the references of first use given above, as [ ], are to be found, modern usage was certainly current during Murray's editorship. This type of unwitting archaism is perhaps a more serious fault than the better-known omission of headwords.

Though Murray (and the other editors) can be faulted on entries of this kind, nevertheless, we can see in his general approach the beginning of the much more extensive treatment to be found in *OED2*. This is the case, for example, with combining forms. The dictionary makes a good beginning with *aero-*, *electro-*, *radio-*, *thermo- magneto-* and a similar variety in medical terms. Combining forms are at once a problem and a blessing to the lexicographer. W. E. Flood's *Scientific Words, their Structure and Meaning* (1960) lists some 1,200 beginning with: *alpha-*, *a-*, *ab-*, *acanth-*, *-acea*, *aceto-*, *actin-* and ending with *xiph-*, *xyl-*, *-yl*, *zeo-*, *zoo-*, *-zoic*, *zyg-*, *zym-*, and *-zyme*. A good many of these were available to the *OED1* editors, and those found particularly productive were set out in their own right. Lancelot Hogben in his *Vocabulary of Science* (1970) uses the great multiplicity of combining forms to make the point that, on combinatorial grounds alone, they can easily generate a million or two scientific terms, a result which, if nothing else, makes nonsense of any attempt at strict comprehensiveness in scientific vocabulary. Yet the decision, already taken in *OED1*, to treat the commonest combining forms individually reduces the problem to manageable scale. Since, in almost all cases, the meaning of the whole can be deduced unambiguously from the parts, words like *magnetoencephalography* or *thrombocytopenia* should hold no terrors once broken down into components. Common combining forms, for example, *proto-*, *neo-*, *hetero-*, *iso-*, that is to say *concept-indicators*, and those of a descriptive nature, particularly in the fields of anatomy and medicine, in *OED* (*brachy-*, *-blast*, *cephalo-*, *pachy-*, *myelo-*, *teleo-*, *tropho-*, *-zyme*, and suchlike) are distinguished well. Though many are obscure to the ordinary reader, the combining forms of anatomy, morphology, and medicine, logically founded in Greek and Latin, vastly outnumber those found in the physical sciences. However, less self-descriptive forms, such as those of organic chemistry, for example, *amino-*, *phenyl-*, *keto-*, *benzo-*, are as a rule less carefully examined.

Just as the general treatment of combining forms in *OED1* is the model for their handling in the supplements and later editions so it is with collocations, though the number admitted in *OED1* is greatly inferior to that in *OED2*. This was evidently a major growth area for the later edition, but it is understandable that, if Murray were to keep within the 'eight times Webster' length target, collocations would have been among the first classes to be sacrificed. Neither were the pioneers in a position to imagine the later proliferation of what might be called 'pseudo-combining forms' such as the ubiquitous -*on* suffix that, starting from *ion* and *electron* in physics, went on to colonize whole areas of the natural sciences (*proton, neutron, positron, Fermion, polaron, exciton, soliton, amorphon, cistron, codon, operon, taxon* . . .).[9] There are some curiosities among *OED1* combining forms, which occasionally cast doubt on the strictness of Murray's avoidance of normative comment. One is the form *calo-*, with Murray seemingly at pains to promote the term *calogram* to replace the newly-coined *cablegram*, on the strength of a single letter to the *Daily News* complaining of the 'mongrel' character of the latter and proposing the analogically-formed alternative from Greek καλος (kálos) = 'cable'.

Though it is easy to point to Murray's numerous faults of omission and his occasional errors of commission, it remains a difficult problem to decide how well the scientific sub-lexicon in both *OED* editions satisfies the requirements of a 'dictionary on historical principles' set for the general language. Did the notorious 'eighteenth-century gap' have implications for science as well as otherwise? We know that no eighteenth-century reading was done for the *Supplements* and the extent to which a possible gap was repaired in *OED2* remains uncertain. Evidently, many first uses have been 'pushed back' in the new edition, but, as Murray himself emphasized, first use is always likely to antedate the discovery of choice quotations. It is not difficult to find headwords in, for example, Harris's *Lexicon Technicum* (1704), with only a mid-eighteenth-century first-use citation in the *OED* (1 and 2).[10]

The concept of 'ephemeral' scientific language and the onset of obsolescence is especially problematic. It is not uncommon for a scientist, sometimes with more vanity than linguistic sense, to attempt a coinage only to have it ignored by his peers (a phenomenon not unknown in more literary discourse for that matter— Samuel Taylor Coleridge did it all the time). Scientific words may fail to stand the test of time for various reasons. There may be a kind of natural selection between competitors for the same usage; there can be unaccountable shifts of fashion; more importantly, a word can be rendered obsolete by a discovery or a theoretical advance in the subject, or as happens occasionally, through legislation as 'discouraged' by a responsible body.[11] The latter process, where obsolescence is caused by the

---

[9] Though, interestingly, *ion* is much earlier (1834) and, unusually, exists both free-standing and as a suffix (*anion, cation, zwitterion*). The 1976 *Supplement* explanation in terms of the Greek neuter suffix was, for some reason, cut in *OED2*.

[10] Furthermore A. M. Hughes, currently Chief Science Editor at *OED*, has recently appealed to historians of science for help in correcting and backdating existing entries (*British Society for History of Science Newsletter*, n. 55, February 1998).

[11] In particular, the International Union of Pure and Applied Physics (IUPAP) and its analogue for chemistry (IUPAC) which regularly publish lexical standards. Earlier the biological sciences were brought under the International codes for Botanical and Zoological nomenclature, which are taken account of in the Burchfield *Supplements* (1972–86) and *OED2* See Burchfield (1972): Preliminary notes.

subject moving on, is particularly characteristic of science and medicine and has no real analogue in the common language. It presents a challenge to the lexicographer who, however *au fait* with progress, will always find it difficult to distinguish the point at which *current usage* merges into *obsolete*. Moreover, modern science moves quickly relative to human generations; nowadays we would hesitate before Murray's statement in the first volume of the *OED* that 'Our own words never become obsolete: it is always the words of our grandfathers that have died with them.'

There is no shortage of examples in *OED1* of scientific words in the process of transition. In some cases there may be just a simple change of nomenclature, generally agreed as, for example, when *azote* became *nitrogen* in the early nineteenth century, without any real change in its chemical status. Murray, always reluctant, it seems, to apply a '†' or an '*obs.*' to scientific terms, preferred to mark the change in the gloss: '. . . the gas now known as nitrogen'. The obsolescence of physicochemical terms like *phlogiston* or *caloric*, or the biological *protoplasm*, each burdened with a discredited theory, is a different matter. Murray again handles this in the gloss rather than with a label. For the first we have: (*Chem.*) 'A hypothetical substance or "principle" formerly supposed to exist in combination in all combustible substances and to be disengaged in the process of combustion'. No † is given, but in a subhead we do find '† *phlogisticated air* or *gas*. Names for nitrogen in the phlogistic theory'. Similarly with *caloric*, where we find no obsolete mark, but '. . . [now generally abandoned, with the theory to which it belonged]'. *Protoplasm*, to which the same remark might have applied, was in frequent use in the early *OED1* period but effectively dead by the time P was processed (1904–09). No obsolete mark is given either to *protoplasm* or its derivatives; in fact none appears even in *OED2*, which, moreover, fails to find a single 'living' reference after the turn of the century. More gradual changes can go almost unperceived. Norbert Wiener's *cybernetics*, a popular term a generation ago, has long been going out of fashion—leaving only the pernicious legacy of the *cyber-* combining-form.

In terms of scientific language more generally, there is a clear two-way migration of words between what may loosely be termed *Common English* and *Scientific English*. Sometimes a word even returns to general use after altering its flavour in scientific contexts. A good example would be the word *energy* in its progression from a term related to personal demeanour, first to a semi-metaphorical term in science, then losing metaphorical status by precise definition, finally taking on new metaphorical overtones in our own time. Entries in both *OED1* and *OED2* chart this progression, though failing precisely to pin down the crucial nineteenth-century transition to the rigorous thermodynamic quantity. Semantic shifts at the common/scientific borderline were classified by Wright (1974: 41) as involving processes of: Internationalization, Elevation, Degradation, Narrowing, and Extension, or certain combinations of these. Examples of each can be found in *OED1*, for the most part well-examined. But perverse mutations sometimes occur where science meets the common language. We are familiar with modern examples of this, such as *transistor* passing from a solid-state electronic device to become a portable radio, or *diesel* describing the engine invented by Rudolf Diesel to the oil used as fuel for the same. It is interesting to note that *wireless* underwent a similar period of semantic uncertainty. *OED1* has it as adjective and transitive verb, though substantivization seems to have followed quite rapidly. Other scientific terms are assimilated to the common language through figurative use over a period of time, which in notable cases can span the interval between *OED* editions. Terms such as *apogee, focus,* and *catalyse* seem to have lost both scientific and figurative character in present-day English, while others, such as *feedback* and *quantum jump* are at an earlier stage in this process of shedding their metaphoric component. (*Focus*, as '*lit. & fig.*', receives the briefest mention in *OED1*; *catalyst* appears only as the chemical term, still to be verbalized.) That *quantum*, which would have been the talk of the whole physics world in the early years of the twentieth century, is missing in its scientific sense perhaps typifies the editors' inattention to new developments—even, in this case, to one which occurred conveniently late in the alphabet.

A more serious problem for lexicographers arises in the reverse direction with what might be called 'wild strains', that is to say the case of a common, often deceptively everyday term, taken into science or mathematics with a highly technical meaning, and sometimes only the slightest analogical connection with the original. Some, like *accommodation* (Opthalmology), *passivity* (Metalurgy), *dress* (Mineralogy), are simple enough, once explained; others require a degree of familiarity with the subject: *base, derivative, radical, excited* (Chemistry), *express* (Genetics), *robust* (Statistics). Most difficult of all, probably the hardest of all 'hard words', are the simple-sounding *colour, charm* (Particle Physics), or *manifold, basis, degenerate, measure, strange-attractor* (Mathematics), where an adequate gloss would have to be so technical that only users already familiar with the word would be in a position to access it. Resort to the lame formula: 'A term in physics used to describe certain . . .' is clearly unacceptable, and even that would fail with mathematical concepts where the whole context might be shrouded in abstraction.

A final aspect worth distinguishing is that of migration of scientific terms from foreign languages. Though this was never perceived as a problem with the learned languages Latin and Greek (with French often considered under this heading), less congenial aliens, particularly from German, seem to have faced a certain prejudice beyond that already due to their scientific status. In fact the once common import of German words to Physics and Chemistry now seems almost to have ceased, *denizens* such as *Eigenfunction, Ansatz, Zwitterion*, having long passed into the realm of *naturals* within the subjects concerned. In the Earth sciences *tsunami, gyttja,* and *pahoe* have followed a similar course.

The term *jargon*, though happily not part of the lexicographer's metalanguage, nevertheless haunts much of our discussion. In common speech it is virtually a mendicant-word in collocation with *scientific, technical,* and *legal*—with all its negative overtones of verbiage, exclusivity, and pretence. One may wonder why it so easily attaches to scientific terms when other specialized lexis, obscure as it may be, seems to escape. Why, to take just one example, was there such unquestioning and comprehensive inclusion of heraldic terms (*bordure, bendlet, frett, fitchee*, and so on, and most of them barely naturalized at that) in the OED when scientific words far more likely to gain everyday importance were summarily ruled out? No doubt a similar crop of legal and theological obscurities could be cited. Clearly 'passing into common use' was never either a sufficient or a necessary condition for inclusion; scientific words simply faced a prejudice based on little more than their perceived lack of the right pedigree and literary flavour.

The now relatively high proportion of scientific words in OED2 and, if the Addition Volumes are an indication, the still larger component to be expected in OED3, is perhaps bewildering to the general user and interested browser alike, and may still seem an unpleasant necessity to some generalists. Yet scientific words have a life and an aesthetic of their own and the scientific lexicon can be as fascinating as it is informative. Along with the often displeasing variants and back-formations, there are nevertheless forms that tantalize the reader and enrich the general language. There are the near-spoonerisms (*aminate/animate, dielectric/ dialectic, hysteresis/hysteria*), the historical surprises (*theorist* [1594], *adjuvant* [1614]) and the now common-or-garden terms that have a distinguished literary history. (Consider, for example, Coleridge's many contributions, among them *substrate, norm, rationalize, artefact, abstract, relativity*). There are the survivors and adaptations of great beauty (*aliquot, moiety, martingale*), alongside the weird and wonderful (*dy, bort, quark, clast, cephem, spline, smectic*). All add their special testimony to the richness of our language and the diversity of its roots. Could anyone nowadays seriously complain that inclusion of such material was 'barren ostentation' which 'crowded out and deformed' the dictionary? Then there is the colourful vocabulary of traditional arts and industrial practice, words such as *gyle, hackling, sparge, plodding, spangle, gaize, cokey, argol*, etc. These terms, not all of them ancient, seem to be welcomed into the OED corpus with a certain priority over 'scientific' words of equal remoteness, perhaps because they are at least concrete rather than abstract in character, fairly easily glossed, 'rare' rather than 'obscure'. Yet, with whatever justification, they inhabit the outer reaches of the compass diagram in hardy coexistence with their more scientific cousins and in fascinating relationship to dialect.

Throughout the whole of his editorship, Murray faced severe constraints, which continually discouraged excursions far into the outer reaches of the language. Fears of delay and mounting cost appear to have combined with the prejudices of the less visionary pioneers to reduce treatment of science in OED1 to what might seem a tentative and somewhat antiquated component— though, to his credit, far more than a merely token presentation. Murray, with his notorious stubbornness, combined with a curiosity that could not be arbitrarily bounded, can be said to have served science well in the long term and laid the slim, yet firm foundations on which the phenomenal coverage achieved in *OED2* could eventually be based. And the scientific coverage in *OED2* is truly phenomenal, as anyone will soon discover on trying to find fault with the editors by sampling current research periodicals. Their crop of untreated words will prove to be a meagre gleaning over a very well-harvested field.

Things have now come to a very full circle, when the two original 'taboo' subjects, Science and Slang, find themselves side by side in the Addition Volumes and the *OED3* database. Thus *quark* coexists with *nerd* and *eigenfunction* with *gobsmacked* in a grand linguistic unity, the extent of which Murray and his fellow pioneers could scarcely have contemplated achieving, though he, at least, was well aware of its significance.

REFERENCES

Bailey, N. (1730). *Dictionarium Britannicum: or a more compleat universal etymological English dictionary than any extant . . . Collected by several hands, the mathematical part by G. Gordon, the botanical by P. Miller. The whole revis'd and improv'd with many thousand additions, by N. Bailey.* London: T. Cox.

Blanckaert, S. (1693). *A Physical Dictionary. Wherein the terms of anatomy, the names and causes of diseases, chyrurgical instruments and their use, are accurately describ'd.* London: S. Crouch.

Blount, T. (1656). *Glossographia, or a dictionary interpreting all such hard words . . . as are now used in our refined English tongue.* London: Tho. Newcombe.

Burchfield, R. W. (ed.) (1972–86). *A Supplement to the Oxford English Dictionary.* 4 vols. Oxford: Clarendon Press.

Cawdrey, R. (1604). *A Table Alphabeticall, Conteyning and Teaching the True Writing and Understanding of Hard Usuall English wordes.* London: I. R. for Edmund Weaver.

Coleridge, D. (1860). 'Observations on the Plan of the Society's Proposed New English Dictionary'. *TPS*, 1860–1: 152–8.

Coles, E. (1676). *An English Dictionary: explaining the difficult terms that are used in divinity, husbandry, physick . . . Containing many thousands of hard words . . .* London: Samuel Crouch.

Craigie, W. A. and Onions, C. T. (1933). *A New English Dictionary on Historical Principles.* Introduction, Supplement, and Bibliography. Oxford: Clarendon Press.

Dunglison, R. J. (1842). *Medical Lexicon. A New Dictionary of Medical Science, containing a concise account of the various subjects and terms, . . . and formulae for . . . preparations etc.* Philadelphia: Lea and Blanchard.

Flood, W. E. (1960). *Scientific Words; their Structure and Meaning.* London: Oldbourne.

Gilliver, P. (1999). 'Specialized Lexis in the *Oxford English Dictionary*', in *Fachsprachen Languages for Special Purposes. Ein internationales Handbuch zur Fachsprachenforschung und Terminologiewissenschaft. An International Handbook of Special-Language and Terminology Research*, edited by Lothar Hoffman, Hartwig Kelverkämper, Herbert Ernst Wiegard, together with Christian Galinski, 2. Berlin, New York: Walter de Gruyter.

Harris, J. (1704). *Lexicon Technicum: or, an universal English dictionary of arts and sciences, explaining not only the terms of art, but the arts themselves.* London: Dan Brown, Tim Goodwin.

Hogben, L. (1970). *The Vocabulary of Science.* New York: Stein and Day.

Johnson, W. (1652). *Lexicon Chymicum.* London: Impensis Guglielmi Nealand.

Kennedy, A. G. (1927). *A Bibliography of Writings on the English Language, from the Beginning of Printing to the End of 1922.* Cambridge, Mass.: Harvard University Press.

Kersey, J. (1708). *Dictionarium Anglo-Britannicum: or, a general English Dictionary, comprehending a brief . . . explication of all sorts of difficult words etc.* London: J. Phillips, H. Rhodes & J. Taylor.

Murray, J. A. H. (1880). 'Progress of the Dictionary'. *TPS*, 1880–1: 120–39.

—— (1881). 'Report on the Dictionary of the Philological Society'. *TPS*, 1880–1: 260–9.

—— (1884). 'Thirteenth Annual Address of the President to the Philological Society'. *TPS*, 1882–4: 501–31.

Murray, W. (1943). *Murray the Dictionary-maker.* Wynberg: Rustica Press.

Nicholson, W. (1795). *A Dictionary of Chemistry, exhibiting the present state of the theory and practice of that science, its application to natural philosophy, the processes of manufactures . . .* 2 vols. London: G. G. and J. Robinson.

Phillips, E. (1658). *The New World of English Words.* London: Nath. Brooke.

[Philological Society]. (1859). *Proposal for the Publication of a New English Dictionary by the Philological Society.* London: Trübner & Co.

Power, H. and Sedgwick, L. (1881–9). *The New Sydenham Society's Lexicon.* London: The New Sydenham Society.

Richardson, C. (1836–7). *A New Dictionary of the English Language.* 2 vols. London: William Pickering.

Timpson, G. (1957). *Sir James A. H. Murray: a Self-portrait.* Gloucester: Bellows.

Trench, R. C. (1855). *English Past and Present.* London: John W. Parker and Son.

—— (1860). *On Some Deficiencies in our English Dictionaries.* 2nd edn. rev. & enlarged. London: John W. Parker and Son.

[Trench *et al.*]. (1860). *Canones Lexicographici; or Rules to be Observed in Editing the New English Dictionary of the Philological Society.* London: The Philological Society.

Wright, P. (1974). *The Language of British Industry.* London: Macmillan.

10

Pronunciation in the *OED*[1]

MICHAEL K. C. MACMAHON

PLANNING FOR PHONETICS IN THE DICTIONARY

The decision to include pronunciation in the dictionary came about almost by accident. Richard Chenevix Trench, in his paper to the Philological Society in 1857, 'Some Deficiencies in our English Dictionaries', had not even broached the question (Trench 1860: 5); nor had the official *Proposal for the Publication of a New English Dictionary by the Philological Society* of 1859. The first formal mention of it—perhaps as an afterthought—was in the *Canones Lexicographici* of 1860, the set of instructions drawn up by the Society to inform members about the proposed contents of the dictionary. Readers were given guidance on how words were to be 'collected', and were told that 'the Pronunciation and Accent shall be marked; and any changes which the former have undergone shall be briefly pointed out' ([Trench *et al.*] 1860: 5).

Shortly afterwards, Derwent Coleridge (uncle of the dictionary's first editor, Herbert Coleridge) spoke on the question of pronunciation, in a paper read to the Society in 1860. He expressed the view that there would be 'some difficulties' in tackling the orthoepical part of the dictionary, but that 'the standard of pronunciation should be fixed by a comparison with some foreign standard or standards' and that 'varying pronunciations should be given, and where the preference is not decided by custom, then, and then only, it may be given in favour of the spelling or etymology' (Coleridge 1860: 166–7, fn. 1). Members of the Society must have agreed with his views—at least to some extent—because a decision was made that in the 'concise Dictionary' (described as 'a preliminary to the Society's proposed new English Dictionary') the pronunciation would be given for each word (Furnivall 1863: 328; cf. also Onions 1934: 99). Putting such an aim into prac-

---

[1] This chapter is based, unashamedly, on MacMahon (1985) but with additional information drawn from *OED2*. Some of the more technical details about Murray's phonetic notation, however, have been omitted; for these, see MacMahon (1985). The unpublished source-materials include the Murray Papers (MP) and the Hallam Papers ('Hallam's Dialect Collections') in the Bodleian Library, Oxford (Madan and Craster 1924: 123–9), especially MSS. Eng.lang. d. 17, d. 34 (henceforth referred to as HP); and various items in the Archives of the Oxford University Press and the Oxford English Dictionaries.

tice was a different matter. Of the earlier orthoepists who had created a system for marking the pronunciation of individual words in dictionaries, the most successful had been John Walker, whose *Critical Pronouncing Dictionary* of 1791 was to provide a benchmark for many of the later nineteenth-century pronouncing dictionaries.[2]

When James Murray took over as Editor in the late 1870s, he had already had some first-hand experience of the problems involved in dealing with pronunciation. He had worked on pronunciation for the proposed Macmillan's Dictionary, a project which he had been involved with since the autumn of 1876 (*CWW*: 140–2). Earlier still, he had devised a notation for Jamieson's *Etymological Dictionary of the Scottish Language* (*CWW*: 51). By the summer of 1878, he was convinced that a sufficiently solid basis existed to contemporary phonetic practices to make the marking of the pronunciation a realistic undertaking. Thus, for example, he was able to assure Bartholomew Price, the Secretary of the Clarendon Press, who had expressed reservations about indicating pronunciation, that it could all be accomplished 'in some simple and intelligible form', that the notation would be 'permanently intelligible', and that a Key would be provided to explain the values of the symbols and diacritics (MP/14/5/1878, MP/16/5/1878).

From 1879 onwards, however, his faith in the methods he would employ was severely tested, as he gradually appreciated the formidable difficulties associated with treating a whole range of English pronunciations in a systematic way. There would have been relatively little difficulty in describing a specific speaker's pronunciation of thousands of words, but to devise a means of notating scales of variability across a range of accents was a quite different matter. None of his predecessors or contemporaries had attempted it in the way he proposed to.

THE CHOICE OF ACCENT(S)

As work progressed, Murray recognized that there were three key questions he had to address:

(1) which accent or accents should be used as the basis for the pronunciation of each word;

(2) how should differences of pronunciation produced by the same speaker in different contexts be handled; and

(3) which set of phonetic symbols and diacritics should be employed in the notation.

In his 'Introduction' to the dictionary, he made it clear that the vocabulary was to be that of 'English-speaking men'—thus automatically ruling out the possibility of words being included which were restricted to, for example, Scots or

---

[2] See MacMahon (1998) for further details.

American English.[3] Yet a clear distinction between the lexis of English and that of Scots would not have extended a priori to English and Scottish accents of English. Given the wide geographical distribution of accents of English throughout the world at the time, Murray might even have considered not only British Insular accents but also some from further afield, for example, North America, South Africa, and Australasia. Nevertheless, there is no evidence that he ever considered anything other than an accent or accents of mainland British English as the focus for the notation.

Nor, perhaps surprisingly, is there any evidence that he ever considered notating a notional or fictitious 'standard' accent of English. Unlike many of his middle- and upper-class contemporaries in England at this time, he never countenanced the idea of imposing an elocutionary or orthoepical form of English on the population as a whole. His attitude towards accents was, with certain exceptions connected with specialist registers of vocabulary, that of the descriptivist. He was reminded, too, by his Irish phonetician colleague, James Lecky, of the need to notate 'real, living speech', not the 'formal, fictitious or antiquated orthoepy' of earlier dictionaries (MP/27/7/1881).[4] In any case, he was only too well aware that the pronunciations laid down by such orthoepists as Thomas Sheridan (1780), John Walker, and Benjamin Smart (1836) were 'often obsolete in actual London usage' (Murray 1879a: 574).[5]

Only educated pronunciations of English were to be admitted in the dictionary—for reasons connected with the scholarly nature of the work as well as the social class structure of Victorian England. For comparative purposes, however, comments had frequently to be made about 'vulgar' pronunciations. Nevertheless, the restriction to educated speech would not have led Murray to think in terms of only one particular accent of English. Lecky's recommendation was that he should include two regionally distinct forms, since 'educated pronunciation divides itself into two well-marked dialects, the northern and the southern'. By 'northern' was undoubtedly meant a Lowland Scottish accent, because in Lecky's opinion Murray would be able to provide the 'forms' of that accent himself (MP/21/7/1881, MP/27/7/1881). However, Murray never consciously pursued this suggestion of 'northern' and 'southern' accents—however much transcriptions in the dictionary such as *rain* (rē^{i}n) and *bowl* (bō^{u}l), with their diphthongal variants, might be read as representing both Scottish and Southern English forms.[6]

---

[3] There are, nevertheless, numerous examples of Scots words, some of them current in Murray's day, which slipped into the dictionary. See e.g. the entries for *braw, broo, fit* (v.[3]), *fulyie, oy*, and *poind*.

[4] On Lecky, see MacMahon (1979).

[5] For a discussion of the quality of such sources, see MacMahon (1998). *OED2* has continued the tradition of sometimes using late eighteenth- and early nineteenth-century orthoepists as evidence of pronunciations in modern English. A random sample is the entries for *climacteric, contemplate, notable, toward*, and *vertigo*.

[6] *OED2* has continued Murray's policy of quoting Scottish pronunciations—not always successfully. For example, the entry for *sew*, which gives /ʃu/ as the 'mod.Sc. pronunciation', is rarely, if ever, heard.

Murray's only other comment about accents in the dictionary is to be found in a letter to Thomas Hallam. What he was indicating was 'the general outline of recognized pronunciation', or 'pronunciation in the broad sense' (MP/5/10/1882).[7] But even this is ambiguous. 'Recognized' could be a slip for 'received'. And why should there be only a 'general outline'? The available evidence, both published and unpublished, indicates that there is no means of determining precisely how many and precisely which accents of English are subsumed in the notation. One might read Murray's comment to Hallam as referring to those features which characterize *all* educated accents of English. Yet such an interpretation is clearly at variance with what Murray must have known about the phonological and phonetic characteristics of nineteenth-century English, as well as with the types of phonetic distinction that he draws in his inventory of symbols.

Would the solution, then, to his problems have been to specify RP as the model accent, especially in view of the natural connection between RP and the intellectual and cultural milieu in which Murray was working? The answer has to be in the negative, for two reasons. Firstly, because the close association that is often made between 'educated English' and RP is largely a product of twentieth-century attitudes towards language usage. And secondly because in Murray's day the term r.p. (Alexander Ellis's abbreviation)[8] referred to a form of speech that was far less homogeneous than the RP that Daniel Jones was later to describe. In 1869 Ellis had spelt out the contexts in which r.p. could be heard: 'the metropolis, the court, the pulpit and the bar', to which he added, in 1874, 'the stage, the universities, parliament, the lecture room, the hustings and public meetings' (Ellis 1869: 23, 1874: 1216). His transcriptions of r.p. speakers in the 1874 volume of *Early English Pronunciation* (Ellis 1874: 1168 ff.) reveal the wide range of variation to be heard within the accent—Melville Bell's modified, but still rhotic, Scottish pronunciation was just one example he quoted in this regard. Yet despite his use in print of the term 'r.p.', he explained on at least one occasion, in a private letter to Murray, his real feelings about the accent. It was, he said, 'altogether a made language, not a natural growth, constantly made in every individual even now' (MP/26/9/1882). Murray may well, then, have decided not to base the pronunciation on an accent whose very rationale might be considered suspect, but, rather, to attempt to delineate all forms of 'educated' British pronunciation.

Until the publication of Jones's *English Pronouncing Dictionary* in 1917, there was no reliable dictionary that one could turn to for information about RP—let alone any other accent of English. Hence there is a difficulty in trying to make a close comparison of Murray's pronunciations of the 1880s and 1890s with those of a pre-Jonesian form of RP for determining as precisely as possible the nature of the accents in the dictionary. Numerous dictionaries published in the nineteenth century which included pronunciation were coloured by the elocutionary principle

---

[7] For the background to Hallam's work as a phonetician and dialectologist, see MacMahon (1983).
[8] I retain it here to distinguish it from Daniel Jones's RP.

that Murray rightly set his face against. They cannot necessarily, then, provide comparable data with which to compare his pronunciations.

In the area of specialist vocabulary registers, Murray's contacts with a number of scientists showed that variant pronunciations of the same word were rife. He claimed that for *acediamine* '12 or 20 pronunciations can be heard from as many professors' (MP/19/11/1882).[9] To help solve his difficulty, he sought the opinion of Ellis—as much a scientist as a phonetician and philologist. Ellis's reaction seemed to be the most realistic in the circumstances, and Murray appears to have heeded it: 'I'm obliged to give what I feel at a glance I should use because I think that such a first shot is likely to be more analogous', and 'since scientific words have no settled pronunciation I would lay down a consistent and thorough English one' (MP/29/10/1882, MP/31[*sic*]/9/1882).[10]

Henry Sweet was another phonetician whose views Murray sought out on the question of which accent to notate. Ideally, said Sweet, Murray should list 'all existing educated pronunciations' (MP/22/3/1882), quickly adding that this would be obviously impossible in view of the considerable ignorance that existed at the time about the actual state of English pronunciation.[11] Before Murray could even start work on the notation for the dictionary, he would have to undertake a detailed investigation into the many social and stylistic variables at work in English speech (MP/22/3/1882). Murray's reaction was to invite Sweet to take over the work of developing a notation and transcribing the pronunciation of all the words. Not surprisingly, Sweet refused, again quoting the lack of any reliable, objective information about current speech-patterns (MP/27/3/1882). On what grounds, he asked, could Murray reasonably establish a 'standard pronunciation' of unfamiliar technical and obsolete words and phrases—words such as *quoth*? In the opinion of Sweet and certain other members of the Society, the plan to mark pronunciation in the dictionary should be given up. Murray's weary, despondent, and cool response was to ask Sweet whether there was any need to have perfection in the 'phonology', when defects in the 'sematology' and 'etymology' were being condoned (MP/29/3/1882). Sweet was prepared to compromise: he suggested that only the stress-accent of words should be marked. In any 'irregular or doubtful words', however, the vowel could be notated, and, where necessary, special

---

[9] Isaac Pitman too had noticed the extensive range of pronunciations of scientific terms (MP/6/10/1882). See also Chapter 1.

[10] Murray did, nevertheless, try to verify putative pronunciations with colleagues (Murray 1888: xi).

[11] With nearly 35 million people resident in the British Isles in 1881, the task Sweet envisaged as being a prerequisite for any statement about the characteristics of English pronunciation was thoroughly unrealistic. The number of people whose speech would have had to be sampled would have been far beyond the powers of any one individual. In England and Wales, in 1881, there were well over half a million members of the 'Professional Classes' (Registrar-General's Class I). Of these, more than 170,000 were 'Teachers, Professors & Lecturers'. Another 8,000 were engaged in 'Literary & Scientific Work' (*Census of England and Wales 1881*, 1883). Furthermore, Murray did not have any technical devices for making recordings of speech, despite the existence of the phonograph. Unless he had personally heard a person's speech, or could rely on descriptions provided by fellow-phoneticians, he was unable to generalize about what constituted 'educated speech'.

notes could be added to an entry: for example, to explain the change from (o) to (w) in the word *one* (MP/29/3/1882, MP/3/4/1882). Needless to say, Murray did not follow any of Sweet's suggestions.

The evidence is incontrovertible, then, that Murray was unwilling to set up any one idiolect or accent of educated English as his model. In which case, he was compelled to find an appropriate means of categorizing the wide range of phonetic variation that could be heard in English speech. Consequently, he was soon caught in a phonological 'trap', from which, at that time, there seemed no obvious means of escape. None of the phoneticians of his day had begun to think about how accents of a language could be systematically compared. Hence, there was no ready-made procedure for Murray to follow in determining the patterns in the 'great variety of pronunciations'. With hindsight, one can see that his mistake was to believe that it was possible to accommodate several accents, expressed in mainly phonemic terms, within a single notational system, without first setting up a 'base-form' to which all the accents could be related by means of a series of phonological rules. To be fair to Murray, he was being scrupulously accurate and true to his descriptivist instincts in not wishing to give pride of place in his system to any one accent of educated English. Nevertheless, this policy was to lead, inevitably, to considerable practical difficulties.

One of these was unaccented vowels. In the word *brimstone*, for example, he was aware of eight different possibilities for the unaccented vowel, in *propose* seven, and in the second vowel in *aconite* and *acolyte* three. The initial vowel of *authority* could, he said, be pronounced in six different ways (MP/12/10/1883, MP/5/10/1882, MP/19/11/1882). How was he to cope with such a wide range of variation? Two phoneticians came to his assistance. Sweet, despite the differences that existed between him and Murray on the general management of pronunciation in the dictionary, sent him detailed information about the pronunciation of word-initial orthographic <au-> as in *authority* etc. (MP/3/11/1884). And Hallam, who had spent nearly forty years studying a small selection of phonological variants in English, forwarded a large bundle of papers on the use of /ɪ/ and /ə/ in unaccented position (MP/15/1/1883, HP Bod. MSS. Eng. lang. d.17).

STYLE-SHIFTING

Murray was very aware that variation could depend on another factor—the style of speaking used by an individual in a particular context. Initially, he focused on the differences that arose from altering the tempo of an utterance, and at one point apparently considered giving two pronunciations for each word in the dictionary, slow and rapid.[12] Later, he concluded that five speech-styles (in his nomenclature, 'varieties of pronunciation') existed in English, ranging from the 'muzical, or that adopted in singing, in which every unaccented vowel is uttered

---

[12] We have only Lecky's word for this (see MP/27/7/1881).

with the same clearness as an accented one', through the 'rhetorical', the 'cultivated', and the 'familiar' to, lastly, the 'vulgar' ([Philological Society] 1882: 77–9).[13] Most of the older dictionaries of English, he said, used the 'muzical' style, whereas Sweet opted almost consistently for the 'familiar' style in his publications. All of which had convinced Murray that the dictionary should give 'what cultivated English-men aimd at . . . [which] they actualy produced in deliberate speech', rather than 'atempt to fotograf the slurd utterances of the average Londoner' ([Philological Society] 1882: 78). Consequently, the unaccented vowels were to be given their 'full "muzical" value', but transcribed in such a way that their pronunciation in 'ordin-ary "familiar" utterance' could be deduced. Thus, in the dictionary, the so-called 'obscure' vowels are marked with a breve diacritic (˘) above the vowel symbol. This means that in the 'muzical' style (ŭ), for example, is to be read as (u), but, in the 'familiar' style, as a vowel with a quality anywhere between (u) and [ə^w].[14]

Murray's views on style-shifting were not accepted uncritically—at least not by Ellis and Sweet. They both thought that the distinctions he had drawn were 'artificial', and Ellis was quite opposed to notating the 'muzical' values of vowels, on the grounds that singers 'treat the vowels vilely' ([Philological Society] 1882: 78–9; MP/19/9/1882. See also MP/19/11/1882). Nevertheless, the other members of the Society supported Murray, and so his viewpoint prevailed. In *OED2*, how-ever, the policy appears to be to employ, wherever possible, an unambiguous symbol for the pronunciation that is used in educated conversation. With relat-ively few exceptions, the unaccented vowels in *OED2* correspond with those to be found in most twentieth-century pronouncing dictionaries of RP.

CHOOSING A PHONETIC NOTATION

It is now possible to understand what Murray was trying to do in his notation of the pronunciation of each word in the dictionary. Firstly, to take account of as wide a range of educated pronunciations of English on the British mainland as possible; and, secondly, to acknowledge formally those style-based differences between the extremes of 'muzical' and 'familiar'. In short, he was developing a subtle form of diaphonetic notation for educated varieties of British English.

The phonetic theory that underlies the symbols and diacritics is set out variously in the 'Introduction' to the dictionary and, more extensively, in the Prefaces to individual letters of the alphabet and also to CH- and TH-. The inventory of items remained virtually unchanged during the forty-four years in which the dic-tionary was in the process of being published, but, as time passed, a certain amount of inconsistency crept into the descriptions of certain symbols. For example, in 1899 (k) was described as a 'back voiceless stop consonant', but, ten years later (t) was a 'point breath-stop'. In his discussion of the phonetics of Y (a letter for

---

[13] Note the use of the reformed spelling 'aproovd of by the Philological Society'.
[14] This is explained in the dictionary in the first column of A.

which he was the editor, in 1920), Charles Onions referred to 'voiced guttural or palatal stops', but described (z) not in the same conventions as a 'voiced alveolar fricative' but as a 'blade-open voice consonant'. Despite these, and other, examples of changing nomenclature, the classificatory principles remained the same, namely the schema that Murray himself devised, based on the views of Ellis, Melville Bell, and Sweet.

The space allocated to the phonetic description of sounds shows that Murray intended that the dictionary, in its phonetic aspects, should be of use (and value) not only to the educated layperson with minimal acquaintance with phonetic matters but also to those who were proficient in the subject. To accommodate the former category of reader, he sometimes used longer established terminology such as *tenuis, mute, surd,* and *sonant*. Indeed, the arrangement of the subject-matter of articulatory description and classification under the heading of letters of the alphabet rather than specific categories of consonant and vowel is proof of his desire to integrate the discussion of phonetics into the rest of the diction-ary material in the most beneficial way possible for the layperson. For the phon-etician, there are some useful asides on more specialized topics, such as the forms of certain non-RP accents, and the phonetic and orthographic practices of Scots.[15] Later, in 1908, Henry Bradley was to draw attention to some of the finer points in the articulation of /s/ and /ʃ/ (s.v. *S*).

The terminology for places of articulation derives from the work of Ellis, Melville Bell, and Sweet. For manners of articulation, the major source is Sweet's publica-tions. The description and classification of vowels is based on the schema of thirty-six vowels in Melville Bell's 'Visible Speech' system of 1867. (Visible Speech is a general phonetic theory and phonetic alphabet; the latter is quite unlike IPA in its appearance.) The Burchfield *Supplements* (1972–86) and *OED2* have moved over to Jones's Cardinal Vowel schema.

There are, however, a number of important differences between Bell's clas-sification of certain English vowels and Murray's. One example is the interpreta-tion of the /ɛ/ of *head*. For Bell, the vowel is a 'primary' vowel, whereas for Murray it is a 'wide' vowel. In *OED2*, the transition to IPA notation brought in its wake the assumption of twentieth-century IPA nomenclature for phonetic categories. Yet much of the pre-IPA nomenclature has been retained.

To interpret Murray's vowel symbols properly, a two-stage procedure is neces-sary. Firstly, the symbols have to be aligned with the Visible Speech categories; and, secondly, IPA equivalents must be derived for them. By using material in Murray's *Dialect of the Southern Counties of Scotland*, his 1888 'Introduction' to the dictionary, the Prefaces to individual letters of the alphabet, and certain comparative data in works by Bell and Sweet (Bell 1867; Sweet 1877, 1890), it is possible to 'reconstruct' the Visible Speech values of his symbols (see Table 1 in MacMahon (1985: 86) for details).

---

[15] See, for example, the introductions to the letters *H* and *O*.

The second stage of assigning IPA values to Murray's symbols, however, is less straightforward. Murray was utilizing a schema in which thirty-six vowels was the highest possible number that could be classified, but the Cardinal Vowel system, of course, allows for considerably more than thirty-six. A further factor which hinders an accurate transliteration of Murray's symbols into IPA is his use of the wide/narrow (primary) distinction. The nearest one can reasonably come to this in IPA terms is to specify the narrow vowels as being more close, the wide vowels more open. For a proposed IPA interpretation of the symbols, see Table 2 in MacMahon (1985: 88). (It was this table that allowed a computer program to be written for *OED2* to bring Murray's nineteenth-century symbols and diacritics for vowels into line with twentieth-century IPA practices.)

Murray had a choice: he could either use an existing notational system (with or without modifications) or he could devise one of his own, tailor-made for the needs of the dictionary. Eventually he found himself compelled to adopt the latter course, although he did think seriously about using a number of notations already current at the time. (The IPA's notation was not developed until the late 1880s, and so was not an option.) The choice was thus between either reformed-spelling systems or phonetic notations proper.

A system of reformed spelling might seem a somewhat unusual possibility for him to have considered, but, at the time when he was working on the notation, the question of whether or not to alter the spelling of English was of interest to the general public. A dictionary notation of that format would not, then, have been viewed as an unusual choice. In any case, many of the older dictionaries, especially the pronouncing dictionaries, had utilized the principle, often fairly effectively.

In Murray's view, however, a system of reformed spelling was inappropriate for his purposes, mainly because no one particular system had established itself yet as the most acceptable version. If there could be agreement 'upon one system of writing English words, there would be an obvious advantage in adopting this as a pronunciation Key in the dictionary', he told members of the Society (Murray 1879a: 573; see also Murray 1881: 268). Still, during his first two years' work on the dictionary notation, he did attempt to devise a system that would have the dual function of a reformed orthography and a phonetic notation (MP/7/10/1882). People recognized that a reformed orthography which was sanctioned by both the Philological Society and the Clarendon Press at Oxford would be a sufficient guarantee of the system's quality and effectiveness as an instrument of instruction.

There were a number of phonetic notations that Murray considered using. The major systems he considered (and subsequently rejected) were those by Ellis, Melville Bell, and Sweet. Although Murray held Ellis in high regard generally as a phonetician, he was out of sympathy with him on the specific question of phonetic notations, on account of 'his hobby to invent systems and discard them' (MP/15/3/1881). His specific objection to Palaeotype, an alphabet that was based on the principle of 'old type', that is only roman characters, was that it was 'unsuited in many ways for Dictionary purposes', in that it could not handle 'Pronunciation . . . in the broad sense'. It was more efficient, he thought, for the transcription of idiolects (MP/5/10/1882). The objection to Glossic, which was similar in some respects to Palaeotype, was that the 'vowel sounds [were] on a Modern English basis': the dictionary would be notating older as well as contemporary pronunciations.

Even though Bell's phonetic theory provides much of the frame of reference in the presentation and discussion of points of pronunciation in the dictionary, Murray seems to have decided against using Visible Speech as the phonetic notation on the grounds that the general public would very likely have found it off-putting visually as well as hopelessly intricate—despite, of course, the small number of simple principles on which it was based.

The case for Sweet's Narrow Romic was argued in detail and with some passion by Lecky, primarily because 'as an instrument [it] is almost perfect'. It was easier than any other system 'to work with in phonetic study, easier for the printer to reproduce, easier for the public to understand' (MP/11/1/1882, MP/31/7/1881). Murray, on the other hand, objected that, like Palaeotype, it could not notate pronunciation 'in the broad sense'. Yet, in the process of developing his own system, Murray came very close to choosing a mixture of features from both Palaeotype and Narrow Romic.

With hindsight, we can regret his decision not to use one of the Romic systems, especially since the IPA alphabet is partly modelled on Broad Romic. Had he done so, the notations in the dictionary and in works using the IPA conventions would have been that much closer. Ironically, no later lexicographer or phonetician used the dictionary notation: it was strictly an *ad hoc* construction, whereas hundreds of publications have used what, from the mid-1890s onwards, became a fairly standardized IPA system.

Murray approached the question of developing his own phonetic notation with an extensive working knowledge of various types of notation. Two years after starting the study of phonetics with Melville Bell in 1857, he had prepared a phonetic key for Jamieson's *Etymological Dictionary* (*CWW*: 51). Then, for ten years, between 1868 and 1878, he had provided Ellis with material, transcribed in Visible Speech, on various accents and dialects from different parts of the British Isles (Ellis 1874: 1254 *et passim*; 1889: 682 ff.). It was during this period, too, that he gathered together his materials for what was to be his *Dialect of the Southern Counties of Scotland*. The notation he used was Ellis's Palaeotype, with the symbols explicated by reference not to key-words but to Visible Speech.

For the period from 1873 to 1879, there are few extant published examples of his use of phonetic notation. Of those that do exist, one such example calls for comment. In his *Encyclopædia Britannica* article of 1878 on the English language, he notates *bow* (/baʊ/) as (*bow*), *high* as (*hī*) and *dough* as (*dō*) (Murray 1878: 400). Such a notation was to be the first version of what would eventually become the dictionary notation proper.

A few years before taking up the editorship of the dictionary, Murray had been asked if he would become the editor of a new dictionary of English being sponsored by Macmillan's, the publishing house. One result of his association with them was the preparation, in the autumn of 1876, of a typeset proof to illustrate something of the proposed format of the work (unpublished; copy in MP). He used a phonetic notation to indicate the pronunciation of various words, and this reveals the strong influence of Ellis's two notations, Glossic and Palaeotype, especially in the symbolization of vowels. Glossic symbols include, for example, (ee) for /iː/. An example from Palaeotype is the use of the raised period (ˈ) to denote stress—it is also used as such in Glossic, and subsequently became part of the dictionary notation. Nevertheless, he did not slavishly imitate these two notations. From the proof it is clear that he was deliberately experimenting with alternative symbols for the same phonemes. Thus, he transcribes *carpet* as (kaar pet) but *carp* as (kahrp). Also, one sees the conscious symbolization of rhoticity, although at this stage he did not allow for non-rhotic and rhotic forms to be notated simultaneously, as he was later to do in the dictionary with the use of (ɹ) as distinct from (r).

Some two and a half years later, in March 1879, the first proof of three words for the dictionary (*castle, persuade,* and *persuaded*) was made public (loose insert to *TPS* 1877–9). The phonetic notation shows not only a continuation of certain Glossic features from the Macmillan's work, but the emergence of other ideas. The three words appear as (kaaˈsˈl), (peɹ-swaidˈ), and (pĕɹ-swaiˈd-ed). A second specimen page a few weeks later includes the word *address* transcribed as (a-dresˈ) (Murray 1879*b*: 622). In both proofs there is a certain resemblance to Glossic, but where Murray departs from it most radically is in the diacritics for stress, unaccented vowels, and the marking of syllable-boundaries. Numerous examples of what might be called the '1879 notation' can be found amongst the dictionary slips stored in the Bodleian Library in Oxford, and also in an early draft (*c.*1879) of the Introduction.[16] For example, *abiogenesis, alms, alteration,* and *carousingly* appear as (ā-bei-ˈŏ-genˈ-ĕs-is), (ɑhmz), (ɑul-te-raiˈ-shŭn) and (kɑ-row-zing-li). Their relative visual simplicity, as well as their association with traditional orthography, should be compared with the notations of the same words in Murray's dictionary notation and, in IPA format, in *OED*2.

Between 1879 and 1881 Murray was assailed with advice and criticism from well-meaning colleagues on which notation he should be using in the dictionary. The practical result of this was that his 1879 notation, based mainly on Glossic, began to seem increasingly inappropriate for the task he had set himself. As he himself admitted, an Old English base for the representation of the vowels 'would suit best with the scientific character of the Dictionary', yet, on the other hand, it would be 'less popular as a practical guide to the pronunciation'. If he made the base Modern English, 'digraphs for simple vowels [= monophthongs]' would often be 'cumbrous and awkward in the extreme [for words of Romance

---

[16] An unclassified and undated document in the Archives of the Oxford English Dictionaries.

origin]' (Murray 1881: 268). It was this conflict between the need for the system to be capable of notating sounds unambiguously (whatever their nature and current orthographic equivalents), and at the same time to be intelligible to a lay person, that was to compel him to recast his notation in favour of a 'scientific' rather than a more traditional-looking 'orthoepical' format. Thus, in July 1881, he began abandoning the relative simplicity of a Glossic-based notation for something more adventurous. One slip of paper that has survived reveals the extent to which he was experimenting with different notations: in this case, for the /ɛ/, /eɪ/, /ʌ/ and /ɒ/ phonemes (MP/23/7/1881).

At the same time as having to contend with questions of symbol-shapes, Murray was also compelled to take into account an important theoretical matter that Lecky and Isaac Pitman had raised. They objected to the proliferation of symbols for unaccented /ɪ/, for which Murray was using at least three different symbols. Lecky could accept this 'degree of minuteness', as he called it, if equally fine distinctions were made between the different realizations of /aɪ/ and /aʊ/ (MP/27/7/1881). Pitman too pointed out that Murray had 'two notashonz for the same sound in the same pozishon' (MP/29/7/1881). Murray's reaction was simply to disregard the points that his two colleagues were making. Ironically, if he had taken their views into account, a different direction might have been given to the later development of the notation.

By about the end of November 1881 Murray's ideas had evolved to the point at which his notation showed strong resemblances not only to features of Sweet's Revised Romic (1880) but also to what was to be the final phonetic notation used in the dictionary. This included the use of italics to indicate narrow vowels, the diaeresis for front rounded vowels (for French, German, etc.), and a macron for long vowels.

The next few months were critical for the final development of the notation. Although Murray felt that he had produced a notation which was equal to the task, Lecky did not share this view. He thought the notation was full of 'heresies', and would have to be 'learnt as something fresh both by the public and by phonetic students' (MP/11/1/1882; see also MP/1/3/1882). What Murray had done, he said, was to alter the conventions of Narrow Romic, for example by using italics for narrow vowels, by assigning 'totally new values' to eight symbols. In short, he was acting perversely by devising a system of his own, based in part on Romic, when Romic itself would have been perfectly suitable for his purposes. Murray's response, though not directly to Lecky, was that his system had to be seen as a 'compromise, necessary for practical purposes' (MP/11/12/1882).

In May 1882 the Clarendon Press had been asking for a copy of the Key to the Pronunciation—which suggests that Murray had by now either completed his work on the notation, or else was being urged to do so as quickly as possible. He was still at work on it as late as October of that year. One change, which may have resulted from Lecky and Pitman's remarks on the excess of symbols being employed, was for what Murray called 'elastic values' to be assigned to certain symbols. He explained that a symbol had to be read as meaning, for example, any vowel sound between two extremes (MP/5/10/1882). From this we can conclude that the dictionary transcription was meant to be as phonemic as possible, as Lecky and Pitman had implied it should be. Yet, this same principle was never extended formally to the notation of unaccented vowels. Furthermore, Pitman discerned something of the contradiction between phonemic and allophonic criteria when he suggested that Murray should have a convention whereby vowel + (ɪ) sequences could be interpreted in two slightly different ways. In other words, Pitman, ever a pragmatist, wanted to see a 'base-form' notation being used, to avoid the necessity of indicating two or more separate notations (MP/6/10/1882).

The first Part (but not Volume) of the dictionary appeared in January 1884. For eighteen months the printers had been working on setting Murray's copy in type, and, for this reason, any alterations he proposed making to the notation were, to all intents and purposes, out of the question. Still, there is evidence that he had, on reflection, wanted to make further changes. For example, in a letter to Hallam in January 1883, he confided that he wished he had symbolized /eɪ/ and /oʊ/ simply as (e) and (o), 'leaving the tapering [i.e. the diphthongization] to be supplied by the reader where he pleased' (MP/29/1/1883). A further change would have been to symbolize /aɪ/ as (ɑi), not (ai): the latter had been more or less forced on him by Ellis. Another change he had in mind, despite the advice of his colleagues, was to indicate even more precisely the actual qualities of unaccented /ɪ/! Not only did he want to have different symbols for the /ɪ/ of *roomy*, *solid*, and *mid*; he also wanted to show that, in a word like *city*, there could be three phonetically distinct versions of the unaccented vowel, depending on the regional background of the speaker (MP/29/1/1883, MP/12/10/1883).[17]

MURRAY'S ACHIEVEMENTS

A close examination of Murray's symbol repertoire and how it was used in the dictionary, both by Murray and later editors, reveals a number of problematical features. The vowels of *first* and *turn*, for example, are distinguished; in *OED2* they are the same. Murray distinguishes between the vowels of *got* and *watch*; *OED2* does not. There are various possible reasons for such apparent deviations from the expected notations (MacMahon 1985: 97–101). Whatever defects one finds in Murray's notation, it should not be forgotten that he developed it under conditions that were far from ideal. He was never really free from the pressures of being Editor of the dictionary or from a spate of well-intentioned, but sometimes contradictory, advice from his colleagues, to be able to devote his thoughts exclusively to the subject. His integrity as a phonetician is underlined by his decision to persevere with a bespoke system of notation, instead of taking the simpler course

---

[17] See also MacMahon (1998) for further details about this vowel in nineteenth-century pronunciation.

of using one of Sweet's Romic systems. However, if he had thought harder and longer about the nature of the task he had set himself, he might have recognized earlier than he did that to try to devise a system which was partly phonemic, partly allophonic, and partly comparative would be fraught with problems. The concept of the phoneme was understood and used at this time,[18] but no attempt had been made to incorporate it into comparative work—which, essentially, was what Murray was trying to do. In this sense, he was starting to break new ground.

His notation can be seen as being diaphonetic in certain respects. At the level of phonological structure, there is the distinction between rhotic and non-rhotic forms; and between the use of /ɒ/ or /ɔː/ and /æ/ or /ɑː/ in certain contexts. But many other examples of structural variation are overlooked: for example, the use of /iː/ for the unaccented vowel of *city*—despite, as has been indicated, Murray's wish to indicate at least three possible variants of the vowel.[19]

The only examples he gives of variation in the realization of phonemes are the monophthongal and diphthongal forms of /eɪ/ and /oʊ/. Not only does he fail to refer to diphthongal realizations of, for example, /iː/, he also omits any mention of a whole series of other realizational variants: for example, /ɪ/, /ɛ/, and /ʌ/. Perhaps he singled out diphthongization because it could be easily symbolized, and because it was an obvious distinguishing feature of English versus Scottish accents. To have indicated differing qualities of, say, /ɛ/ would have meant, inevitably, a set of additional symbols. Examples of different pronunciations involving the selection of phonemes in particular words (for example, /æ/ or /eɪ/ in *patriot*) were handled not by special diaphonetic symbols, but by listing the pronunciations side by side.

In spite of reservations about the form of the notation and lingering doubts about which accent or accents of educated English Murray was actually attempting to encapsulate in his notation, it seems clear that the dictionary notation reflected a brave attempt, in the face of many theoretical and practical difficulties, to show how individual words were pronounced across the educated spectrum of mainland British or, perhaps more narrowly, English English accents. The task Murray set himself was certainly more ambitious than anything that had been attempted before.

PHONETICS AFTER *OED2*

The editors of *OED2* have tacitly accepted, in the absence of any major re-evaluation of the pronunciation of each headword,[20] that the bulk of Murray's pronunciations reflect late twentieth-century speech, of the type referred to as 'broadly speaking, educated standard southern British', or 'Received Pronunciation'

---

[18] For references, see MacMahon (1985: fn. 106).   [19] See above, fn. 17.

[20] They point out that time restrictions prevented any full-scale reassessment of the entire set of pronunciations (*OED2*: pp. xviii–xix).

(RP)' (*OED2*: p. xix). A few examples, however, from letter A, will suffice to show that the situation is more complex than this.

The first pronunciation that *OED1* and *OED2* give for *absolve* is /æb'sɒlv/. (For ease of comparison, the phonetic transcriptions have been converted into IPA.) Wells (1990) does not list this—nor did Jones (1917)—even as a minority pronunciation; but Jones (1997) allows it. For *accomplish*, *OED2* gives the pronunciation /ə'kɒmplɪʃ/ alongside /ə'kʌmplɪʃ/. Jones (1917) had regarded the /ə'kʌmplɪʃ/ pronunciation as 'rare'. Wells, on the other hand, more than seventy years later, found the reverse to be the case. From a sample survey he conducted, /ə'kɒmplɪʃ/ was restricted to 8 per cent of the informants; the remaining 92 per cent used /ə'kʌmplɪʃ/. Jones (1997), however, gives both pronunciations, just as Murray had done. Murray's (and *OED2*'s) first pronunciation for *angina* is /'ændʒɪnə/, a pronunciation that is not listed in any of the above pronouncing dictionaries.

OED2 contains more than three times as many entries as either Wells (1990) or Jones (1997). The task of a full-scale revision, then, already predicted in *OED2* and which may involve taking into account non-RP forms (both British and non-British), will be a mammoth one. In November 1882 Murray had written gloomily to Hallam that he had 'no definite opinion on the obscure vowels—I've given up the subject in despair. I hear so many different forms of them, and so many different appreciations of the same sound by men who are authorities in phonetics that I feel the ground give way beneath me' (MP/19/11/1882). His fortitude in persevering with pronunciation in the dictionary, when the task seemed unmanageable and hopeless, should be a lodestar in future lexicographical phonetics.

REFERENCES

Murray Papers

MP/14/5/1878. B. Price to J. A. H. Murray.
MP/16/5/1878. J. A. H. Murray to B. Price.
MP/15/3/1881. J. A. H. Murray to J. B. Rundell.
MP/21/7/1881. J. Lecky to J. A. H. Murray.
MP/23/7/1881. W. R. Evans to J. A. H. Murray.
MP/27/7/1881. J. Lecky to J. A. H. Murray.
MP/29/7/1881. I. Pitman to J. A. H. Murray.
MP/31/7/1881. J. Lecky to J. A. H. Murray.
MP/11/1/1882. J. Lecky to J. A. H. Murray.
MP/1/3/1882. F. J. Furnivall to J. A. H. Murray.
MP/22/3/1882. H. Sweet to J. A. H. Murray.
MP/27/3/1882. H. Sweet to J. A. H. Murray.
MP/29/3/1882. J. A. H. Murray to H. Sweet.
MP/3/4/1882. H. Sweet to J. A. H. Murray.
MP/19/9/1882. A. J. Ellis to J. A. H. Murray.
MP/26/9/1882. A. J. Ellis to J. A. H. Murray.

MP/31[*sic*]/9/1882. A. J. Ellis to J. A. H. Murray.
MP/5/10/1882. J. A. H. Murray to T. Hallam.
MP/6/10/1882. I. Pitman to J. A. H. Murray.
MP/7/10/1882. J. A. H. Murray to I. Pitman.
MP/29/10/1882. A. J. Ellis to J. A. H. Murray.
MP/19/11/1882. J. A. H. Murray to T. Hallam.
MP/11/12/1882. J. A. H. Murray to T. Hallam.
MP/15/1/1883. T. Hallam to J. A. H. Murray.
MP/29/1/1883. J. A. H. Murray to T. Hallam
MP/12/10/1883. J. A. H. Murray to T. Hallam.
MP/3/11/1884. H. Sweet to J. A. H. Murray.

Published works

Bell, A. M. (1867). *Visible Speech: The Science of Universal Alphabetics*. London: Simpkin, Marshall; N. Trübner.

Burchfield, R. W. (ed.) (1972–86). *A Supplement to the Oxford English Dictionary*. 4 vols. Oxford: Oxford University Press.

Coleridge, D. (1860). 'Observations on the Plan of the Society's Proposed New English Dictionary'. *TPS*, 1860–1: 152–68.

Ellis, A. J. (1848). *The Essentials of Phonetics*, London: F. Pitman.

—— (1867). 'On Palaeotype; or, the Representation of Spoken Sounds'. *TPS*, 1867–9: 1–52.

—— (1869, 1874, 1889). *On Early English Pronunciation, With Especial Reference to Shakespere and Chaucer* [Parts I & II, IV, V]. London: Asher & Co.

—— (1872). 'On Glosik, a Neu Sistem of Ingglish Speling'. *TPS*: Pt 1, 89–118.

—— (1874). See Ellis, A. J., 1869, 1874, 1889.

—— (1889). See Ellis, A. J., 1869, 1874, 1889.

Furnivall, F. J. (1863). 'On the Next Step in the Dictionary Plan'. *TPS*, 1862–3: 328.

Jamieson, J. (1808 etc.). *Etymological Dictionary of the Scottish Language* [title varies]. Edinburgh: W. Creech.

Jones, D. (1917). *An English Pronouncing Dictionary (on Strictly Phonetic Principles)*. London, Toronto, New York: J. M. Dent, E. P. Dutton.

Jones, D. (in Roach, P., and Hartman, J. eds.) (1997). *English Pronouncing Dictionary*. 15th edn. Cambridge: Cambridge University Press.

MacMahon, M. K. C. (1979). 'British Phonetics in the 1880s: the Work of James Lecky'. *Histor. Ling.*, 6: 47–56.

—— (1983). 'Thomas Hallam and the Study of Dialect and Educated Speech'. *Trans. York. Dial. Soc.*, 15: 19–31.

—— (1985). 'James Murray and the Phonetic Notation in the New English Dictionary'. *TPS*: 72–112.

—— (1998). 'Phonology', in S. Romaine (ed.), *The Cambridge History of the English Language*, IV. Cambridge: Cambridge University Press, 373–535.

Madan, F. and Craster, H. H. E. (1924). *Summary Catalogue of Western MSS in the Bodleian Library*, VI. Oxford: Clarendon Press.

Murray, J. A. H. (1873). *The Dialect of the Southern Counties of Scotland*. London: Asher & Co. (Also as *TPS*, 1870–2, Pt 2: 1–251).

—— (1878). 'English Language', in *Encyclopaedia Britannica* (9th edn.) VII. Edinburgh: A. & C. Black, 390–402.

Murray, J. A. H. (1879*a*). 'Eighth Annual Address of the President to the Philological Society'. *TPS*, 1877–9: 561–621.

—— (1879*b*). 'Specimen of the Dictionary'. *TPS*, 1877–9: 622–4.

—— (1881). 'Report on the Dictionary of the Philological Society'. *TPS*, 1880–1: 260–9.

—— (ed.) (1888). *NED*. Vol. I. A and B. Oxford: Clarendon Press.

Murray, K. M. E. (1977). *Caught in the Web of Words*. New Haven and London: Yale University Press.

*OED*2 (1992). *The Oxford English Dictionary on Compact Disc*, 2nd edn. Oxford: Oxford University Press.

Onions, C. T. (1934). 'Afterthoughts of a Lexicographer'. *TPS*, 1934: 99.

[Philological Society]. (1859). *Proposal for the Publication of a New English Dictionary by the Philological Society*. London: Trübner and Co.

—— (1882). *Monthly Abstract of Proceedings*. [Minute of meeting held on Friday, 17 March 1882]. *Proc. Philol. Soc.*, 1881–2: 77–9.

Sheridan, T. (1780). *A General Dictionary of the English Language*. London: J. Dodsley, C. Dilley, and J. Wilkie.

Smart, B. H. (1836). *Walker Remodelled: A New Critical Pronouncing Dictionary*. London: T. Cadell.

Sweet, H. (1877). *A Handbook of Phonetics*. Oxford: Clarendon Press.

—— (1880). 'Sound Notation'. *TPS*, 1880–1: 177–235.

—— (1890). *A Primer of Phonetics*. Oxford: Clarendon Press.

Trench, R. C. (1860). *On Some Deficiencies in our English Dictionaries* (2nd rev. edn.). London: J. W. Parker & Son.

[Trench *et al*]. (1860). *Canones Lexicographici; or Rules to be Observed in Editing the New English Dictionary of the Philological Society*. London: The Philological Society.

Walker, J. (1791). *A Critical Pronouncing Dictionary and Expositor of the English Language*. London: G. G. & J. Robinson.

Wells, J. C. (1990). *Longman Pronunciation Dictionary*. Harlow: Longman Group.

11

'An Historian not a Critic': The Standard of Usage in the *OED*

Lynda Mugglestone

'Every language has . . . improprieties and absurdities, which it is the duty of the lexicographer to correct or proscribe', declared Samuel Johnson on the opening page of his *Dictionary* (1755: A1ᵛ). The responsibilities accorded to the maker of dictionaries are, in this particular construction, indeed markedly interventionist. 'Adulterations' are 'to be detected, without a settled test of purity', and 'modes of expression . . . rejected or received'; likewise 'confusion' must be regulated, and choice made 'out of boundless variety, without any established principle of selection'. Images of linguistic redemption for a language hitherto neglected and 'suffered to spread, under the direction of chance . . . exposed to the corruptions of ignorance' predominate in Johnson's account of the task which first confronted him.

In Trench's systematic reassessment of lexicographic practice just over a century later, the lexicographer was, however, to assume a somewhat different form. If Johnson was ultimately brought to the recognition that, in his earlier desires to correct and embalm the language, he had 'indulged expectation which neither reason nor experience can satisfy' (1755: C2ᵛ), such expectations undergo a categoric rejection in Trench's text. Descriptive rather than prescriptive imperatives inform his redefinition of the rightful role of the lexicographer. Not the 'slave of science' (Johnson 1755: A1ᵛ) but a scientist of language, his occupation was to be that of neutral observer, a linguistic historian impartial in the face of change and variation, the shifts of sense or spelling. His business, Trench stressed, was simply 'to collect and arrange all the words, whether good or bad, whether they do or do not commend themselves to his judgement' (1860: 5). A role as judge or critic was untenable, not least in the fundamental subjectivities which this revealed towards language and its forms. Indeed 'if [the lexicographer] . . . begins to pick and choose, to leave this and to take that, he will at once go astray' (1860: 4–5). In accordance with the dictates of the new philology, linguistic usage was instead to be registered rather than reformed or purified. Outright incredulity surrounds notions that the dictionary should attempt to enforce linguistic submission in terms of which words are to be preferred and which proscribed. As Trench comments:

I cannot understand how any writer with the smallest confidence in himself, the least measure of that vigour and vitality which would justify him in addressing his country men in written or spoken discourse at all, should consent in this matter to let one self-made dictator, or forty, determine for him what words he should use, and what he should forbear from using.   (1860: 5)

It is in the exercise of democracy rather than dictatorship that the future of lexicography was seen to lie. James Murray was later to agree. 'Happily we are in a free country', he affirmed, explicit in his refusal to engage in the politics of accept-ability with reference to co-existing variants; we are, he insisted, 'allowed some liberty in such matters' (MP/28/3/1884).

Such assumptions were to constitute a fundamental part of that 'revolution in English lexicography' (Craigie and Onions 1933: p. v) manifest in Trench's pioneering vision of a new and ideal dictionary. True to these theoretical founda-tions, the *OED* was—at least intentionally—to cast aside the prescriptive resist-ance to change and variation which had long hallmarked its predecessors. As John Walker had notably proclaimed in his dictionary of 1791, variation was one of the 'evils left by Providence for man to correct', not least since 'a love of order, and the utility of regularity, will always lead him to confine this versatility within as narrow bounds as possible.' (1791: p. iv, fn.). In a similar way, the workings of linguistic change were often dismissed as evidence of an inadequately normat-ive control. In contradistinction, the historical method adopted in the *OED* was to mean that the realities of change were not only impossible to ignore, but salient to its very construction. Convictions of the organic nature of language ('a language has a life, just as really as a man or as a tree' (Trench 1853: 126)) equally served to affirm a commitment to its continued dynamism. The lexicographer was no longer to be depicted as Canute, as in Trench's account of the lexico-graphic ambitions of the members of the Académie Française.[1] With lexicographic precedents resting firmly in Liddel and Scott, in Grimm and in Littré, the dic-tionary was henceforth to deal with facts rather than fictions of usage, with empir-ical evidence above individual prejudices and preconceptions: 'The first aim of the Dictionary . . . is to exhibit the actual variety of usage', Murray proclaimed (1888: p. x). This was part of its distinctive quality, the 'fresh start' and 'ori-ginality' of method which it was to represent (MP/27/11/1883).

Though lexicographic expedients clearly necessitated the selection of one form alone as the lemma (the 'typical form' as Murray termed it, carefully rejecting the use of 'received form' on the grounds of its potentially prescriptive overtones),[2] notions that normative control was intended by means of such selection could not be further from the truth. 'It is a mistake to suppose that there is a "correct"

---

[1] '[They] once sought to exercise . . . domination over their own language . . . But the language recked little of their decrees, as little as the advancing ocean did of those of Canute' (Trench 1853: 126).

[2] See Murray's manuscript draft of 'The English Dictionary of the Philological Society: Explana-tions' (MP/n.d.) in which every instance of 'Received Form' is carefully crossed out and 'Typical' substituted in each case.

spelling of every English word', he asserted in response to a query on whether *licence* or *license* was 'better'. Instead 'there are hundreds of words of which one spelling is historically as good as another, or which have had 2 forms from the beginning' (MP/21/11/1899). Usage, rather than issues of theoretical correctness, habitually governs the choice of 'typical form' so that, as Murray continued, 'there is usually one [variant] more current than the other, tho' this is not always what the scholar would prefer'.[3] True to the descriptive methodologies insisted on by Trench, pronunciation exhibits a similar latitude in terms of the information supplied, so that, as for *vase*, the authority of usage—in all its many shades— decisively triumphs over any authority which, as in Walker's *Critical Pronouncing Dictionary*, might be assumed by the dictates of the individual lexicographer. Though a pronunciation [vāz] accompanies the headword, a variety of others immediately follows:[4]

> The earlier pronunciations (vē's) and (vē'z) are still current in America; the former of these is indicated by the rimes in the following passages. Another variant (vǫz) has still some currency in England.
>
> **1731** SWIFT *Strephon & Chloe* 191 [*rime* face]. **1822** BYRON *Juan* vi. xcvii. [*rimes* place, grace]. **1847** EMERSON *Poems* Wks. . . . I. 425 Cut a bough from my parent stem, And dip it in thy porcelain vase [*rime* grace]. **1857** WHITTIER *Skipper Ireson's Ride* 26 Girls . . . such as chase Bacchus round some antique vase. *c.*1860 LOWELL *Ambrose* x, The water unchanged, in every case, Shall put on the figure of the vase.

This deliberate acknowledgement (and recording) of diversity does not of course imply that the dictionary moves away from the domains of 'standard' English. Indeed, as the *Proposal for . . . A New English Dictionary* had itself asserted, 'As soon as a standard language has been formed, which in England was the case after the Reformation, the lexicographer is bound to deal with that alone' ([Philological Society] 1859: 3), a maxim later used in the *OED* (in *Supplement* IV) to provide one of the first citations for 'standard' in this decisively linguistic sense. There is, however, a clear and significant difference between the normative and deliberately standardizing impulse exhibited by many of the *OED*'s predecessors, and the intended description of the consensus norms of a superordinate variety which is the explicit aim of the *OED*. In terms of lexicography, a concentration on the non-localized is, for example, almost inevitable once a standard variety has appeared. As Zgusta affirms, 'for the lexicographer . . . the most important task is to handle the standard national language . . . It is no undue pedantry if he does this and if he, more than that, concentrates his task and his work around the literary and the cultivated spoken language, and around the colloquial language' (1971: 187). Accordingly, while the English Dialect Society was collecting materials on the regional varieties of English usage for the *EDD*

---

[3] That there are occasional exceptions to this rule merely reveals the complexities of lexicographical principle in its translation into practice. See further pp. 202–3.

[4] The transcriptions given here follow the practice of *OED1*. See further Chapter 10.

(Wright (1898–1905)), it was the national, and supraregional, which was prioritized by the *OED*.[5] This was the 'common language', the 'national tongue' (Murray 1873: p. v), the words of which, as Murray explained, 'belong to all classes of speakers and to all species of composition', shading between the 'literary' and 'colloquial' depending upon context and the educational level of the user. As a result, while coexisting variants are scrupulously acknowledged, popular binarisms of 'good' (and 'bad') English, 'right' and 'wrong', are resolutely distanced. 'The impropriety of applying *right* and *wrong* to mere matters of current usage' is self-evident, Murray stressed (MP/28/3/1884), and the restrictive labels which do appear are characterized by their intended objectivity; *catachr[estic]* indicates, for example, the mistaken use of *aboard* for *abroad*, or of *hardiness* for *hardness*, *observant* for *observable*, signifying cases of genuine communicative conflict rather than the enforcement of a prescriptively imposed norm. The same is generally true of *erroneous*, as in instances where *decussation* is, for example, used instead of *decussion*, *impertinacy* instead of *impertinancy*, or *plentitude* instead of *plenitude*.[6]

Imposing the normative upon the norms observed is, in consequence, an activity intentionally remote from the standards of judgement formally adopted in the *OED*. As Ellis reminded Murray on the subject of *reliable*, a word which regularly provoked the outraged sensibilities of 'educated' users of the language in the late nineteenth century, personal opinions and professional practice must, in this as in other instances, remain distinct: 'you (like myself) may object to the use of the word *reliable*, but there is no doubt it is used' (MP/5/1/1883). As such, it must be recorded. This is the foundation of the ideal standard of usage in the *OED*, one based on the descriptive authority of a linguistic corpus, rather than the authoritarian (but often unfounded) edicts of prescriptivism. As Ellis continued, well aware of the potential for confusion which this particular construction of authority might present for those versed in more normative traditions of the dictionary: 'it might be as well to explain that every quotation you give is *a testimony to the use of the word in such a sense* or *your* authority for saying that it is used, and not generally an authority or permission for people to use it in that way.' Such precepts are firmly adhered to in the entry for *reliable* itself. Though Henry Alford in his highly popular *Plea for the Queen's English* censured its use as 'hardly legitimate' (1864: 253), and complaints about 'that hideous barbarism which is often cropping up' similarly surface in the popular press (*Daily News*, 6 January 1875), the *OED* merely records, with praiseworthy objectivity, that *reliable* has been in 'current use only from about 1850, and at first perhaps more frequent in American works, but from 1855 freely employed by British writers,

---

[5] Murray's own attitude to dialects was both descriptive and scientific, affirming rather than negating their value, and lamenting their gradual demise: 'The local dialects are passing away . . . even when not entirely trampled underfoot by the encroaching language of literature and education, they are corrupted and arrested by its all-pervading influence, and in the same degree rendered valueless as witnesses of the past and the natural tendencies of the present' (1873: p. v).

[6] Though see further pp. 200–2.

though often protested against as an innovation or an Americanism. The formation has been objected to (as by Worcester in 1860) on the ground of irregularity, but has analogies in *available, dependable, dispensable, laughable*'. Citations from Coleridge ('The best means and most reliable pledge of a higher object') and from Gladstone ('He seems to think that the reliable chronology of Greece begins before its reliable history'), among other writers, provide their own refutation for the popular, though unwarranted, prejudices against this form.

Ellis's words of warning were well founded, however. Tensions between prescriptive and descriptive methodologies often underscore the gap between popular language attitudes and the new departures taken in the *OED* with reference to the simple documentation of linguistic usage, and the validity which this may be assumed to have. Reviewers, for example, could clearly be perplexed by the apparent refusal to condemn observable 'errors' in late nineteenth-century English. 'If possible [the dictionary] is too elaborate, and might be the means of preserving words which have no right to a place in a Dictionary, being neither good words nor slang', commented the *Yorkshire Post*: 'For example, what justification is there for "maturish—somewhat mature"?' (OED/MISC/58/8/2). The citational evidence (here from Meredith) is, in a dictionary on historical principles, of course the only justification needed, as indeed it was for the inclusion of the 'abominable word' *leaderette* (censured by a reviewer in *Notes & Queries* (OED/MISC/58/8/1)), or for *referee* as a verb: '[it] has, as might be expected, nothing but journalistic support, and is a contemptible word' as the same journal declared (OED/MISC/58/8/42).

Users of the dictionary were likewise often to evince marked consternation when confronted with the apparent latitude exhibited by the *OED* in these matters. The existing archives provide ample evidence of those who sought further clarification on the nuances of correctness only to be met with a clear rejection of standardization so far as it pertained to the lexicographer's role. A correspondent in 1906 requesting information on 'the correct spelling of words such as fulfil, skilful, whiskey & pygmy' (MP/8/12/1906) was, for example, supplied (by Murray himself) with a full account of co-existing variants, but no definitive solutions, nor indeed any attempt at such:

The ordinary spellings at present are *skilful, fulfil*; these, I think, so predominate that any others would probably excite remark; although the latter is not *etymologically* so defensible as *fulfill* ... As to *pigmy, pygmy*, these are about equally common, the second is etymologically the more regular ... we slightly prefer *pygmy*, tho' we might be outvoted in a plebiscite; *pigmy* is more phonetic ... For *whisky* or *whiskey*, there is no etymological or historical preference, both forms are current and equally correct or incorrect. So, when in a hurry you may save a fraction of time by writing *whisky*, and when lingering over it you may prolong it to *whiskey* ... in matters of taste there is no 'correct' or 'incorrect'; there is the liberty of the subject.   (MP/10/12/1906)

As Murray, echoing Trench, resolutely maintained, 'I am not a *judge* of the language—only its *historian*'. Hence if co-existing variants are supported by usage, then, in the ideal of linguistic democracy formally endorsed by the *OED* and its editors, individuals are unquestionably at liberty to use whichever they please. 'Is not speech as free as dress, when the pronunciations are equally well-grounded', as he responded when similarly asked to prescribe on the nuances of correct enunciation for *laboratory* (MP/21/10/1911).

This refusal to engage in notions of deliberate standardization, or to proscribe where proscription (and prescription) is unwarranted by the actualities of the language, is on many occasions one of the most conspicuous features of the *OED*, especially in the light of the other, more prescriptively inclined, texts which continued to appear during the late nineteenth century (as well as afterwards). What are presented elsewhere as prevalent shibboleths of speech are, in the carefully documented entries of the dictionary, thus often instead revealed as fictions, spurious in their claimed 'incorrectness'. While *decimate* in the sense 'destroyed, annihilated, weakened' is soundly condemned by Alford, the *OED* simply affirms the salience of usage. It is a 'loosely transferred use' but its legitimacy is undoubted, supported by the authority of writers such as Charlotte Brontë and Charles Lyell. *Eventuate*, Alford noted, is 'another horrible word, which is fast getting into our language through the provincial press' (1864: 250). Such preconceptions are countered with admirable impartiality in the relevant fascicle of the dictionary: it was 'first used in U.S., and still regarded as an Americanism, though it has been employed by good writers in England'. Entries for *different to, talented*, and *desirability* (a 'terrible word', Alford opines), all support an adherence to Trench's precepts on the non-normative ideal of the dictionary. As Murray asserted, the dictionary was to be the domain of facts and not phantasms (MP/13/3/1892), a maxim which remains at the heart of its commitment to be a new and entirely descriptive work. Though problems can remain in the real documentation of the language and its range, the main ideological thrust behind the *OED* in this respect is clear. 'There are many who conceive of a Dictionary as though it had this function, to be a standard of the language', Trench had observed. It is, however, as he resolutely averred, 'nothing of the kind' (1860: 5).

Nevertheless, as Trench was also forced to recognize, on this subject 'there is a constant confusion . . . in men's minds' (1860: 5). In spite of the clarity of his own descriptive formulations for the future of English lexicography, and similarly regardless of the ways in which the *OED* itself strove to implement and develop them, it is clear that such confusion was, in a number of ways, almost inevitably to persist, affecting both those who used and those who wrote the dictionary. The separation of descriptivism and prescriptivism was, in particular, often to prove less clear cut, as well as less easy, than either Trench or Murray had envisaged. Misinterpretation of descriptive statements as prescriptive edicts was, for instance, by no means rare, leading Murray to expostulate on the widespread 'delusion . . . that the Dictionary by recording facts as to the use of words, presses readers to use them' (MP/[22]/2/1884). The inclusion of *advertisemental* in the first published fascicle was, he firmly informed one reader, simply the result of descriptive observation, rather than a personal prescription for its general use. In this matter, the personal was irrelevant:

You don't like *advertisemental*: I like it as well as *testamental, monumental, ornamental, governmental, fundamental, instrumental* or any other *-mental*, and it is the distinct increase of power to the language to be able to say 'advertisemental triumphs' instead of 'triumphs in the way of advertising'; but the Dictionary does not advise *you* to say so, it merely records the fact that such has been said.   (MP/[22]/2/1884)

Even where this fact did seem to be appreciated by those who used the dictionary, the exercise of descriptive impartiality could be construed not as a significant and scientific advance in terms of English lexicography but instead as evasiveness, an abdication of the 'proper' authority of the lexicographer whose role was to rule over language, not be ruled by it. 'It is to be regretted that in this country there exists no Philological Academy, with authority to decide on all matters connected with the English language, and from whose judgment there should be no appeal', wrote Heald under the penname 'Anglophil' (1892: 7). In this respect the Philological Society had clearly failed. 'Under present conditions erudite but irresponsible persons issue dictionaries', he continued; 'in many instances expressing views at variance with each other, with the result that frequently, on the particular points on which he desires instruction, the inquirer finds himself left in a state of uncertainty.' Edward Parry, writing to Murray himself, endorsed the perceived problems of descriptivism for the ordinary user of the language. 'The unsophisticated layman longs for an authoritative decision', he lamented; '[he] thinks the important thing is rather that there sh[oul]d be an agreement in pronunciation rather than the pronunciation that is agreed upon' (MP/9/1/1907). The consensus norms of usage can, in these contexts, simply appear suspect. For the ordinary user of the language, the 'uneasy feeling' persists that English and its history should have some rights against 'custom', which, Parry added, is 'often only a name that covers undesirable things like ignorance, mental sloth &c. &c. In other words, that things are what they are is a matter to be faced, yet one feels as if it w[ould] be better if they were what they *ought* to be'.

The very status of the dictionary as a didactic text is, to some extent, at the heart of these problems (Béjoint 1994: 18), not least because, as Parry confirms, the kind of linguistic didacticism expected by users tends to be prescriptive rather than descriptive in nature. Regardless of the formal displacement of prescriptive by descriptive ideologies, it is this that underlies the fact that the normative function of the dictionary was often perceived to continue intact. 'The lexicographer should be aware that all his indications may have some normative influence, because the user may sometimes tend to follow them', states Zgusta (1971: 291). Or, as Murray regretfully explained to Herbert Warren, 'people will not be content to let me be purely historical' but instead prefer to 'make me a king orthographically' with rulings which are taken as law (MP/4/1/1885). In spite of Trench's vision of a brave new world of lexicography, the legacies of the past were, as this suggests, not so easy to dispel. 'I have to consider responsibilities', Murray was forced to acknowledge; 'if I give a preference to Dissyllable [rather than *disyllable*] multitudes will follow the standard.'

If the interface between descriptive and prescriptive was thus, as we have seen, to prove problematic for those who used the dictionary, it is perhaps not surprising it could also give rise to a number of pervasive problems within the making of the dictionary. Data could appear in a variety of normative guises, even when sent in by valued contributors. Alexander Beazeley, for example, provided Murray with a long list of citations for the word *arcade*, as well as with his own opinion on the senses in which it may legitimately be used: 'The meaning—the correct meaning—appears undoubtedly to be "a series of arches". All applications of the word to the *space* or *passage* enclosed by an arcade or wall, or by two arcades, are incorrect' (OED/BL/300/29). The authority of usage is firmly disputed. As Beazeley adds, 'I doubt not, however, that in your slips for the Dictionary you will meet with many examples of this incorrect use'. Such preconceptions are, in this instance, easily transcended. The 'incorrect' sense appears in the dictionary itself as the dominant, and unmarked, meaning. Beazeley's 'correct' use appears as *OED* sense 3, restricted specifically to architectural applications. Henry Hucks Gibbs's censure of *accommodated* ('if you must honour such words . . . by taking notice of them, in case they should ultimately creep into the language . . . you should have a separate limbo to which to relegate them—a hot one, I should suggest' (MP/20/7/1882)) provides a similar example. No trace of such negative sensibilities appears in the dictionary entry, the obligations of the historian rather than the critic again ensuring that the accurate, and impartial, record of the language is sustained.

Elsewhere the critical function could prove more difficult to relinquish, in spite of its potential subjectivity. Bradley's censure of the verb *enthuse*, for example, while appreciated by a number of reviewers,[7] did nevertheless serve in some respects to compromise the objectivity of the descriptive ideal. 'An ignorant back-formation from enthusiasm', he stated, in spite of empirical evidence from Lytton and the *Pall-Mall Gazette*, as well as a variety of American publications. *Back-formation*, having its first citation from the *OED* itself (1889 *N.E.D.* 'Burgle . . . A back-formation from *Burglar*') did not of course either connote, or denote, ignorance: 'The fact or condition of being ignorant; want of knowledge'. Instead, Bradley's choice of words seems informed by his own resistance to the form, irrespective of the descriptive imperatives duly observed in the citations he provides. The entry for *expect* provides a similar opposition between the authority of usage, as represented by the citations, and the authority of the lexicographer as represented by the wording of the entry itself. Its use in the sense 'suppose' is

---

[7] See, for example, the review of *E–Every* in the *Manchester Guardian* 14 July 1891: 'We observe with some regret that the Dictionary recognises the hideous Americanism "enthuse", though it very properly stigmatises it as "an ignorant back-formation from 'enthusiasm'"' (OED/MISC/59/1/11).

categorically given as flawed, regardless of its stated prevalence: 'The misuse of the word as a synonym of *suppose*, without any notion of anticipating or looking for, is often cited as an Americanism, but is very common in dialectal, vulgar or carelessly colloquial speech in England.' Citations from texts such as William Hurrock Mallock's *The New Republic; or, Culture, Faith, and Philosophy in an English Country House* ('Now, I expect, Lady Ambrose, that, in its true sense, you know a good deal more history than you are aware of') serve moreover to dispute the negative social/stylistic restrictions which are theoretically imposed.

Murray too could share in these same susceptibilities so that, with reference to another semantic change in progress, here in *avocation*, he could be downright condemnatory. Sense 3 ('That which has the effect of calling away or withdrawing one from an occupation. *Hence*, A minor or less important occupation, a by-work') is unmarked, and supported by citations from Fuller, Johnson, Godwin, as well as Furnivall. Sense 4 ('Ordinary employment, usual occupation, vocation, calling') in contrast displays a striking resistance to the semantic extension which it attests: 'But as, in many cases, the business which called away was one of equal or greater importance (see quot. in a., where *avocation* is rightly used), the new meaning was improperly foisted upon the word.' *Foist* was, of course, not to be given a formal definition until the fascicle *Flexuosity–Foister*, published in March 1897. When it did appear, the gloss provided was illuminating: 'To palm or put off; to fasten or fix stealthily or unwarrantably *on* or *upon*.' The accompanying citations for *avocation* further support this implicit binarism of 'right' and 'wrong' (in spite of Murray's stringent denial of such terms in his private correspondence). Macauley is 'right' ('Found, even in the midst of his most pressing avocations, time for private prayer'). Later citations from Thomas Moore, Charles Dickens, and Henry Buckle merely attest an 'improper' use, as in Moore's *Lalla Rookh* ('Poetry was by no means his proper avocation') or Buckle's 'War and religion were the only two avocations worthy of being followed' from his *History of Civilization in England* (1873). As Béjoint confirms, 'the difficulty, for lexicographers, is to disentangle themselves from generally accepted prejudices' (1994: 136). In the case of *avocation* such disentangling was evidently less than complete, the *OED* instead coming to manifest a close correlation with the prescriptive (and popular) censure of Alford for whom this particular semantic shift is 'another monster patronised by these writers [of newspapers]', its 'proper' meaning mangled and ignored (1864: 250).

This concord between the *OED* and more prescriptively orientated texts such as those written by Alford or Heald is in fact sustained on a number of occasions. Alford is, for example, firmly condemnatory on the use of *allude* in the sense 'to refer', stigmatizing it as a further instance of the journalistic debasement of language. Such stigmatization is endorsed in the relevant fascicle of the *OED* where the definition given for sense 5 ('To make an indirect or passing reference to, to glance at, to refer indirectly *to*'), is supplemented by the explicitly negative coding of 'Often used ignorantly as = refer to'. The dichotomy between 'often' (attesting the frequency of usage and thereby, of course, according to the formal tenets of the *OED*, its authority), and its accompanying negative gloss, signifying its evident unacceptability, is not resolved. The distinction prescribed (between indirect/direct reference for *allude/refer* respectively) is, for instance, clearly not maintained in practice, in spite of its assumed desirability from a logical point of view. It does, however, emerge as a semantic differentiation which is particularly enduring in prescriptive theory. As Burchfield states in *MEU3* in another attempt to dispel the overtones of notional incorrectness in this context: 'the complexity of the language has ensured that indirection is not always part of the sealed meaning of the two words . . . The reference is sometimes ambiguously direct or indirect or just plainly direct.'

Comments on *literally* display some of the same problems. It is 'improperly used' to signify 'absolutely, actually, really', Heald states. Eleven years later in the fascicle *Lief–Lock* the *OED* entry provides an almost exact correlation: 'Now often improperly used to indicate that some conventional metaphorical or hyperbolical phrase is to be taken in the strongest admissible sense.' From a strictly descriptive point of view, 'often' and 'improperly' again seem to stand at odds. The evidence is provided (as from Frances Kemble's *Journal of a Residence on a Georgian Plantation in 1838–1839*: 'For the last four years . . . I literally coined money', or *A Lady's Ranche Life in Montana* (1887) by I. R.: 'The air is literally scented with them all'), but the refusal to endorse—or condone—its existence within the standard of usage is clear.

Reviewers, who, as we have seen, were often to urge the editors of the *OED* to deploy greater powers of discrimination and judgement towards the words recorded, were quick to seize on such apparent inconsistencies in methodology. The entry for *everybody* provides a particular case in point. Affirming traditional notions of grammatical correctness, it is formally given in the dictionary as used 'sometimes incorrectly' with a plural verb or pronoun. The evidence of the accompanying citations, however, presents a rather different picture, one in which constructions with a plural pronoun predominate, and in which the notionally 'correct' form is in fact non-existent. From the first citation from Lord Berners in *c*.1530 ('Everye bodye was in theyr lodgynges'), to Sidney's *Arcadia* in 1580 ('Now this king did keepe a great house, that euerie body might come and take their meat freely'), Blount in 1620 ('To take vpon him the disciplining of euery body for their errours'), Bishop Warburton in 1759 ('Every body else I meet with are full ready to go of themselves'), Byron in 1820 ('Every body does and says what they please'), or Ruskin in 1866 ('Everybody seems to recover their spirits') the plural pronoun uniformly appears. If fully substantiated in these quotations, the consensus norms of usage which the dictionary aims to record are again apparently absent in the accompanying definition and (mis)usage note, as the *Glasgow Herald* in turn pointed out to its own readers. Aligning the *OED* with the prescriptive tenets of the schoolmaster (' "everybody" is a notoriously difficult word to deal with. The schoolmaster—and the new dictionary follows him—decrees that it is incorrect to use a plural pronoun with it' (OED/MISC/59/2/58)), it made a clear but significant distinction between this theoretical correctness and the actual usage of 'ordinary mortals', including those cited by the dictionary itself:

The ordinary mortal, conscious that a plural idea is involved in the word, and feeling too, that if it can be followed by 'his' only, one half of creation is unfairly excluded, does not hesitate to use 'their'. That same ordinary mortal may derive comfort and courage to face the irate schoolmaster from the quotations given here. Beginning with Lord Berners in 1550, and continuing with Sidney, with De Foe, with Bishop Warburton, with Byron and with Ruskin, we find them all using the plural pronoun . . . In view of this, it is perhaps justifiable to question the schoolmaster's decision on the point. At any rate, it does not seem to be going too far to follow the principle which the quotation from Byron supplies, and according to which 'everybody does and says what they please'.

Like the eighteenth-century rulings on *shall* and *will*, such proscriptions tend 'to support a "standard" that made "normal" usage non-standard' (Arnovick 1997: 135). Such examples clearly remain problematic in the context of a dictionary founded on the tenets of descriptive impartiality, and the unquestioned validity of usage above individual or traditional preconception.

Trench had of course allowed, at least in part, for the needful exercise of lexicographical judgement in terms of the data to be set down within the pages of the dictionary. Though an 'impartial hospitality' was rigorously to be maintained in the interests of a complete record of the language, intimations of linguistic status and register were to be seen not only as permissible but desirable. Hence, while the lexicographer's duty as historian remained paramount, 'where he counts words to be needless, affected, pedantic, ill put together, contrary to the genius of the language, there is no objection to his saying so' (Trench 1860: 6). This aspect of his role was potentially significant: 'he may do real service in this way', Trench added. Terms such as 'affected' or 'pedantic' do indeed form part of that armoury of status labels used throughout the dictionary. *Darling* ('sweetly pretty and charming') is labelled *affected*, *ambilogy* is 'needless' ('A needless hybrid for ambiloquy'), *forfex* is pedantic, if *humorously* so ('*Humorously pedantic. A pair of scissors*'), editorial judgement in each case attempting to convey some sense of the stylistic overtones of particular usages. The range of such labels is extensive; *familiar, colloquial, ludicrous, illiterate, vulgar, improperly, erroneously,* and *low* all appear (among others) to denote further shades of meaning linked to register and context, or to restrict aspects of usage whether in diachronic or stylistic terms. *Codger* ('Fellow, chap') is *low colloq.*, while *chivalry* used to denote 'a team of horses' is *improperly* employed. As in other aspects of the dictionary, the aim was, at least formally, that of descriptive elucidation.[8] 'Be not sparing of marks of condemnation or distinction', as Gibbs had early advised Murray,

---

[8] Though Cassidy (1997: 110) praises the uniformly objective use of labels in the *OED* ('Murray's great *New English Dictionary* . . . followed Johnson in giving illustrative quotations . . . and using such objective labels as "arch, colloq, dial, ellipt, euphem, fig, lit, techn" but avoiding Johnson's "bad, barbarous, corrupt, low, vulgar." The closest Murray comes to these are "error, informal, prop[erly]" '), there are instances where such objectivity can be questioned. *Low* and *vulgar* do in fact appear, and other aspects of labelling also potentially diverge from this objective ideal. See further pp. 204 ff.

making one important proviso: 'make it clear that you don't at all propose that our Dictionary should be held to be an authority as to the significations to be rightly attached to words, but a register of [their] growth and use' (MP/30/7/1882).

Labelling is nevertheless an area which poses significant problems for the lexicographer. Whereas Johnson regularly appended terms such as 'cant', 'low', or simply 'bad' to words which failed to meet his own linguistic preferences, the policy by which the *OED* was to deploy status labels was, at least in theory, to be more stringent, objective rather than subjective, and based on evidence rather than individual assumption. The fact that such labels 'arise from a judgment about usage rather than a judgment about meaning, and hence emerge from the lexicographer's sense of the language', as Richard Bailey has pointed out (Ekbo 1980: 310) was, on the other hand, almost inevitably to mean that here too there was a certain latitude in their deployment within which the potentially normative (as well as the idiosyncratic) could, in a variety of ways, come into play.

Establishing the consensus norms of usage could, for instance, be particularly difficult in this context. To take one particularly marked example, Murray originally defined *huff* sense 10 ('To scare *away* by calling *huff*!') by using the verb *fray* ('To frighten or scare away'), only to find that *fray* had been labelled obsolete by Bradley in the fascicle *Frank-law–Gain-coming*. 'My impression (subject to correction) is that it is the ordinary word for "to frighten away birds by shouting or with a rattle" all over rural England. It is *my* natural word for this', Murray remonstrated; 'I . . . naturally used it to explain *huff*!' (MP/[n.d].1897*a*). In the interests of consistency Murray was here forced to bow to the authority of his own dictionary, rewriting the definition and eliminating *fray* from this conspicuously non-obsolete position within it. Others too experienced similar problems. Gibbs, for instance, 'was distressed to find' the pronunciation of *humour* as /jumə/ given as 'obsolete or at least archaic', not least since this was his own normal mode of articulation for the word (MP/[n.d.]1897*b*).This had also originally been Murray's own pronunciation of the word, a fact which further complicates the rightful allocation of restrictive labels.[9] The proof sheets too record many differences of opinion; 'mark as archaic or *obs*', Furnivall advised for *alms-basket* though the word remains unmarked in the dictionary as published. In a similar way the originally unmarked *glib* ('Smooth and slippery in surface or consistency; moving easily; offering no resistance to motion. Of movement: Easy, unimpeded') has a last minute change to 'Now *rare* exc. *dial.*'. *Gliddery*, likewise originally unmarked, is labelled 'l *dial?*' in proof, the question mark disappearing in the final printed version. *Rare* is added to the *obs.* alongside *tact* sense 3 ('The act of touching or handling'); *artery* sense 1 ('The trachea or wind pipe') has its original catachrestic

[9] 'At school I was taught to say *yūmour*. When I studied under Melville Bell in Edinburgh, I learned that one ought to say *yūmour* in the fig[urative] sense *good yumour, ill yumour*, etc., but *humour* in the physical . . . But this distinction was not permanent; and when I began to teach in England in 1870, I found that *h* had been restored in all senses' (MP/n.d./1897*b*).

label deleted, and replaced by *Obs.*, while *greenable*, originally unmarked, is declared a nonce-word in the first revise.

'Intuition does not extend to a consensus on register labelling among a team of . . . different ages, backgrounds, and speech patterns', Atkins rightly confirms; 'even in a dictionary written over a number of years by a single lexicographer it is impossible to secure consistency in the marking of register' (1992: 27). The occasional lack of consensus in the *OED* is therefore unsurprising. More problematic are, however, those instances where labels appear to be applied which are at odds, not with the opinions of other editors or users of the dictionary, but with the actual evidence supplied. Bradley's entry for sense 3 of *enormity* ('Excess in magnitude; hugeness, vastness') is, for example, labelled obsolete. The fact that he immediately adds that 'recent examples might perh[aps] be found, but the use is now regarded as incorrect' nevertheless already signals the existence of a number of problems within the diachronic restriction formally applied, not least since *enormity* is thereby placed in the paradoxical position of being simultaneously obsolete and current. Nineteenth-century citations from *Fraser's Magazine* and De Quincy further compound this problem, as does the example provided by Bradley himself: ('*Mod.* You have no idea of the enormity of my business transactions, said an eminent Stock Exchange speculator to a friend. He was perhaps nearer the truth than he intended'). The foundations for such marking remain unclear. As Ward-Gilman has commented, Bradley 'may not have liked the sort of tradespeople who used the word, or perhaps it was fashionably condemned by the members of his social circle. We'll never know the reason. But there is no obvious basis for the condemnation' (1990: 84).

Bradley was not alone in such potential misapplications; *cherubim* in the singular is similarly labelled obsolete, in spite of citations from Swift, Addison, and Dickens, though the further addition of the labels *dial.* and *vulgar* makes the basis of judgement clear, if also perhaps still more questionable (*Dombey and Son* (1848), p. xxxi: 'As he looks up at the organ, Miss Tox in the gallery shrinks behind the fat legs of a cherubim on a monument'). *Fault*, sense 5 ('A failure in what is attempted, a slip') appears as *rare*, in spite of the accompanying comment on a suggested gender-specific frequency: 'lady teachers often use it in marking school exercises'. More prevalent are restrictive comments on usage coded into the body of the definition where they operate as ostensibly descriptive glosses. *Fruition* is, for example, fully legitimized in sense 1: 'The action of enjoying; enjoyment, pleasurable possession, the pleasure arising from possession.' Senses such as that attested in *Harper's Magazine* in 1885 ('the greenish nuts, ripened as always from the flowers of the previous year and now in their full fruition') and defined in both the *Century Dictionary* (1889) and the *Standard Dictionary* (1895) without further comment are, however, dually proscribed, first by the appended catachrestic marker ¶, and second, by the comment which accompanies this particular sense development: 'Erroneously associated with FRUIT.' The negative implications are further enhanced by additional information given in parentheses: 'The blunder is somewhat common in both England and in the U.S., but is not countenanced by Dictionaries in this country, nor by Webster or Worcester.' Clearly a change in progress, this shift in the sense of *fruition* was undeniably 'common' in terms of the authority of usage, as Bradley acknowledges. The import of this is nevertheless resolutely denied, as, in an apparent reversal of linguistic priorities, it is denied authoritative status in the dictionary. It is a 'blunder' ('A gross mistake; an error due to stupidity or carelessness') and its negative stigmatization is unmistakable. 'Now a standard usage' states *OED2* for this now acceptable (and accepted) sense, though the emendations made in the accompanying usage note serve merely to underline the problems which had indeed existed (and to some extent continue to exist) in the record of this word, not least in the conspicuous retention of the term 'blunder': 'The blunder was not countenanced by 19th-cent[ury] Dictionaries in this country, nor by Webster or Worcester though it was somewhat common both in England and in the U.S.'

As here, the standard of usage can occasionally appear problematic, clearly being constructed as in need of possible remedy or correction, a manifestation of mass error rather than legitimate semantic change. *Fault*, likewise subject to semantic shift as the *OED* was being written, provides a further example of this potential conflict of linguistic approach. Its 'legitimate' sense in the phrase *at fault* was 'puzzled, at a loss'. Uses in which it came instead to signify either 'not equal to the occasion', 'in the position of having failed', or, alternatively, 'in fault' were, conversely, to be denied such claims. In spite of a citation from Leslie Stephen ('The many difficulties in nature . . . when made the groundwork of an argument . . . imply that the creator has been at fault'), and the admission that the sense 'in fault' is 'frequent' in America and current, if not common, in England too, such deployment is categorically condemned; it is a 'great impropriety', the terms of description here more redolent of Johnson's dicta on the duties of the lexicographer than of Trench's earlier insistence on the scientific rigour of descriptivism. 'Formerly considered an incorrect use', comments *OED2*, again highlighting the tensions between custom and correctness which can at times surface in the dictionary. *Shall*, in constructions such as 'I should have liked to have (seen)' presents similar problems, being both 'sometimes met with' but 'certainly faulty'. *Hideously* offers a further example, as in the identification of its 'misuse' as an intensifier in the manner of *awfully, terribly, dreadfully*, as opposed to its 'proper' adverbial use to signify 'in a hideous manner'—in spite of the marked prevalence of this kind of semantic shift within linguistic history.

Perhaps most explicit is Murray's insistence on forms such as *rime* and *ax* in preference to *rhyme* and *axe* within the dictionary, irrespective of the fact that such forms were demonstrably less common. They were instead 'intrinsically the best', Murray insisted (1888: p. x), an assertion which Craigie was later to find problematic in terms of the guiding principles of the work as a whole. 'Rhyme is, and has been for at least two centuries, the standard spelling', he argued, not least since 'some of the derivatives do not occur at all with the spelling *rim-*, and others very rarely . . . To put these under *rim-* would be awkward, & expose one to a charge of misrepresenting facts' (MP/18/5/1908). Empirical evidence was, in this instance, clearly to be disregarded in favour of the stated norm. 'It was settled long ago, on the very first occasion when a case arose, that the Dictionary spelling should be *rime*', Murray countered; 'I am quite prepared to defend the action publicly, whereas I could offer no defence of the practice [i.e. *rhyme*] which occurs in the made-up sheet' (MP/22/5/1908). Craigie's proofs were duly changed, his own 'defence' drawn from actual linguistic practice clearly having little influence in the face of the norms of correctness advocated by, and insisted upon, by Murray.

Such convictions of linguistic error in the face of usage (and more particularly, change) can, in real terms, be unmistakable in the *OED*, setting up lexicographical constructions of the standard of usage which are clearly less flexible than those which are, in reality, employed. Of course on countless other occasions the *OED* gives evidence of unparalleled objectivity, dispelling prescriptive sensibilities with consummate ease. As in the entry for *different from/to*, we can be informed that a common usage is often 'considered' incorrect without such popular antipathies in any way being endorsed ('The usual construction is now with *from*; that with *to* (after *unlike*, *dissimilar to*) is found in writers of all ages, and is frequent colloquially, but is by many considered incorrect'). *Averse to* reveals a similar balance, as does the entry for *like* as conjunction. The latter constituting a prominent shibboleth in popular manuals of linguistic correctness ('an error which is very common . . . and one of the most repugnant of the many grammatical lapses which abound' (Heald 1892: 49–50)), here the *OED* simply states: 'Now generally condemned as vulgar or slovenly, though examples may be found in many recent writers of standing.' Language attitudes and linguistic facts are both recorded with impartiality. Where such impartiality can be seen to slip, it is therefore all the more striking, though also the more illuminating, revealing the real problems of translating descriptive lexicography from theory into practice where editors are not only impartial lexicographers, but also speakers of the language, embedded, like all other speakers, in its complex matrices of language attitudes and subjective assumptions. Though Murray might, with justice, stress the incompatibility of such considerations with the lexicographer's task ('the history of words . . . ought not be invented to give support to pet prejudices or aversions' (1889: 133)), bias is nevertheless almost inescapable. 'The dictionary is a human product', states Zgusta (1992: 7). In consequence, as Béjoint confirms, citing the cultural bias evident in the *OED*'s definition of *canoe*, 'lexicographers are always, however hard they try, the mouthpieces of a particular social group in the society to which they belong' (1994: 21).[10] In terms of the structuring of Victorian society, this is perhaps more

---

[10] *Canoe*, sense 1, is specified as 'A kind of boat in use among uncivilized nations'. Sense 2 provides the 'civilized use': 'a small light sort of boat or skiff propelled by paddling'. This entry is emended in *OED2*.

pertinently transparent in the images of educated unacceptability in the entries for *pants*, and for *party* (in the sense 'the individual person concerned or in question; more vaguely, the person') where both appear as 'shoppy', a word particularly redolent of 'vulgar' affiliations in nineteenth-century society. *Party*, for example, is accompanied by distinctly negative social coding ('formerly common and in serious use; now shoppy, vulgar, or jocular, the proper word being person') though, in the interests of acceptability, the reader is also informed that 'In the plural, *the parties*, meaning "the persons", is more tolerable'. Stereotypes of gendered use can similarly surface, unsupported by empirical evidence,[11] while popularly proscribed forms such as the use of intrusive /r/ (which, as Sweet (1890) attested, was in fact widespread even in educated speech)[12] were theoretically countenanced in the dictionary only among the 'vulgar': 'in vulgar speech it is even heard in such forms as draw(r)ing'.

It is in this context that the negative coding of change should also be placed. Ellis's reminder to Murray on the necessary disjunction of personal and professional for the lexicographer may well have been heeded in terms of *reliable*, and its own status as neologism. Other new usages, deviating from those traditionally accepted in educated speech, could, as we have seen, clearly be more problematic. Though in theoretical terms 'right' and 'wrong' were untenable in the descriptive recording of usage, in practice, as Murray was forced to admit, there was a sense in which such evaluative criteria could be seen to hold true. 'To be unfashionable or not to know what is good usage, is often as injurious to a man as to be wrong', he acknowledged (MP/28/3/1884), compelled here to distinguish between the descriptive recording of usage *per se* and a potentially more prescriptively orientated 'good' usage. It is in this sense that descriptive and prescriptive may blur, and the standard of usage be constructed in ways which are more normative than were at first intended. Intimations of qualitative norms can as a result intervene in the presentation of usages which are perhaps fully justified by other, quantitative, means. It is this which presumably leads to Bradley's rejection of *enthuse* or *enormity*, or Murray's disavowal of *avocation* in the sense 'ordinary employment, usual occupation, vocation, calling'.[13] The standard of 'good usage' with undeniably prescriptive overtones, one resistant to change and variation,

---

[11] See p. 201. The entry for *horrid*, sense 3 ('Offensive, disagreeable, detested; very bad or objectionable') is similarly illuminating, revealing closer associations with popular folklinguistic belief than scientific lexicography in its statement that *horrid* is 'especially frequent as a feminine term of strong aversion'.

[12] 'I know as a fact that most educated speakers of Southern English insert an r in *idea(r) of*, *India(r) Office* etc. in rapid speech, and I know that this habit, far from dying out, is spreading to the Midlands, and yet they all obstinately deny it' (Sweet 1890: p. viii).

[13] The European dictionaries which served as inspiration for the *OED* provide their own precedents here. Normative judgements can and do appear in the historical record of French provided by Littré, the phrase *remplir le but*, for example, in spite of ample authority for its currency, being categorically proscribed on the logical (rather than linguistic) grounds that a goal is not 'fulfilled' (Zgusta 1991: 7). It is as a result given as both 'frequently used' and 'vicious'.

and committed to the conservative above other forms emerging as current can, inevitably and inextricably, thus on occasion be imposed on the empirical standard of usage which the dictionary is, theoretically, intended to describe.

REFERENCES

Murray Papers

MP/[n.d]. 'The English Dictionary of the Philological Society: Explanations'. Ms draft by J. A. H. Murray.
MP/20/7/1882. H. H. Gibbs to J. A. H. Murray.
MP/30/7/1882. H. H. Gibbs to J. A. H. Murray.
MP/5/1/1883. A. J. Ellis to J. A. H. Murray.
MP/27/11/1883: Proof of 'Preface to Part I', *A–Ant*.
MP/[22]/2/1884. J. A. H. Murray to unnamed correspondent.
MP/28/3/1884. J. A. H. Murray to unnamed correspondent.
MP/4/1/1885. J. A. H. Murray to H. Warren.
MP/13/3/1892. J. A. H. Murray to unnamed correspondent (draft).
MP/[n.d.] 1897*a*. J. A. H. Murray to H. Bradley.
MP/[n.d.]1897*b*. J. A. H. Murray to Mr. Robertson (draft).
MP/21/11/1899. J. A. H. Murray to unnamed correspondent.
MP/8/12/1906. G. Keith Harrison to J. A. H. Murray.
MP/10/12/1906. J. A. H. Murray to G. Keith Harrison.
MP/9/1/1907. E. Parry to J. A. H. Murray.
MP/18/5/1908. W. Craigie to J. A. H. Murray.
MP/22/5/1908. J. A. H. Murray to W. Craigie.
MP/21/10/1911. J. A. H. Murray to unnamed correspondent.

OED *Archives at OUP*

OED/BL/300/29. A. Beazeley to J. A. H. Murray, 8 January 1884.
OED/MISC/58/8/1. Review of *Lap–Leisurely*, *Notes & Queries* (IX), 1902, 58.
OED/MISC/58/8/2. Review of *Matter–Meet*, *The Yorkshire Post*, 9/5/1906.
OED/MISC/58/8/42. Review of *Ree–Reign*, *Notes and Queries* (III), 1905, 297–8.
OED/MISC/59/1/11. Review of *E–Every*, *Manchester Guardian*, 14/7/1891.
OED/MISC/59/2/58. Review of *Everybody–Ezod*, *Glasgow Herald*, 15/3/1894.

Published works

Alford, H. (1864). *A Plea for the Queen's English. Stray Notes on Speaking and Spelling*. London: W. Strahan.
Arnovick, L. (1997). 'Proscribed Collocations with *shall* and *will*: the eighteenth century (non-)standard reassessed', in C. Cheshire and D. Stein (eds.), *Taming the Vernacular. From Dialect to Written Standard Language*. London and New York: Addison Wesley Longman, 135–51.
Atkins, T. S. (1992). 'Theoretical Lexicography and its Relation to Dictionary Making'. *Dictionaries*, 14: 4–43.
Béjoint, H. (1994). *Tradition and Innovation in Modern English Dictionaries*. Oxford: Clarendon Press.

Burchfield, R. W. (ed.) (1972–86). *A Supplement to the Oxford English Dictionary*. 4 vols. Oxford: Clarendon Press.

—— (1996). *The New* Fowler's *Modern English Usage* (3rd edn.). Oxford: Clarendon Press.

Cassidy, F. G. (1997). 'The Rise and Development of Modern Labels in English Dictionaries'. *Dictionaries*, 18: 97–112.

Craigie, W. A. and Onions, C. (1933). 'Historical Introduction', *OED* Vol. I. A–B. Oxford: Clarendon Press, pp. vii–xxvi.

Ekbo, S. (1980). 'Reflections on Some Kinds of Information Given in Historical Dictionaries: Discussion', in W. Pijnenberg and F. de Tollenaere (eds.), *Proceedings of the Second Round Table Conference on Historical Lexicography*. Dordrecht, Holland; Cinnaminson, NJ: Foris Publications, 303–19.

Heald, A. (1892). *The Queen's English (?) Up to Date. An Exposition of the Prevailing Grammatical Errors of the Day, with Numerous Examples. By 'Anglophil'*. London: The Literary Revision and Translation Office.

Johnson, S. (1755). *A Dictionary of the English Language*. London: W. Strahan.

Murray, J. A. H. (1873). *The Dialect of the Southern Counties of Scotland: Its Pronunciation, Grammar, and Historical Relations*. London: Asher & Co.

—— (1888). 'Preface to Volume I'. *NED* Vol. I. A and B. Oxford: Clarendon Press, pp. v–xiv.

—— (1889). 'Words that are not Wanted'. *Notes and Queries*, VIII: 133–4.

[Philological Society]. (1859). *Proposal for the Publication of a New English Dictionary by the Philological Society*. London: Trübner & Co.

Sweet, H. (1890). *A Primer of Spoken English*. Oxford: Clarendon Press.

Trench, R. C. (1853). *On the Study of Words*. 4th (rev.) edn. London: John W. Parker & Son.

—— (1860). *On Some Deficiencies in our English Dictionaries*. (2nd rev. edn.). London: John W. Parker & Son.

Walker, J. (1791). *A Critical Pronouncing Dictionary and Expositor of the English Language*. London: G. G. J. and J. Robinson.

Ward-Gilman, E. (1990). 'Dictionaries as a Source of Usage Controversy'. *Dictionaries*, 12: 75–84.

Wright, J. (1898–1905) (ed.). *The English Dialect Dictionary*. London and Oxford: Froude.

Zgusta, L. (1971). *Manual of Lexicography*. Prague: Academia.

—— (1991). 'The Polysemy of History'. *Lexicographica*, 7: 1–10.

—— (ed.) (1992). *History, Language, and Lexicographers*. Tübingen: Max Niemeyer.

12

'This Unique and Peerless Specimen': The Reputation of the *OED*

RICHARD W. BAILEY

Imperialism, profit, and philology had, by the mid-nineteenth century, become important ingredients of British lexicography—often prioritized in that order. In his *Imperial Lexicon of the English Language* (1852), John Boag made the first of these explicit in describing his two-volume work:

It is called 'the Imperial Lexicon of the English language,' because the Anglo-Saxon speech is not now, as formerly, the instrument of thought and medium of intercourse of the English nation only; it is spoken in every latitude of the globe; it is displacing every older tongue found prevailing in those countries where it has taken root; in a few years it will be the native tongue of more people than the whole of Europe will contain; and whilst, therefore, the complete collection and arrangement of its words becomes truly an English Lexicon, it does so in a sense of prospective usefulness so comprehensive as to be fitly expressed by the word 'Imperial'.   (1852: 3)

Such sentiments had become commonplace. In 1846 an anonymous pamphleteer in Manchester had declared that 'in the literary combat for supremacy, it is, therefore, England against the world'. The following year John Bradshaw was even more convinced of the imperial mission of English: 'it clearly shows the God of providence has a hand in doing it' (quoted with other examples in Bailey 1991: 106–9). Even more gratifying to English sensibilities was the celebration of English presented by the venerable Jakob Grimm to the Royal Academy of Berlin in January 1851; English, he said, 'may be called justly a LANGUAGE OF THE WORLD: and seems, like the English nation, to be destined to reign in the future with still more extensive sway over all parts of the globe' (Bailey 1991: 110).

American English had emerged with distinct, and noticeable, differences from the dialect of educated people in south-eastern England, and so the question of which form of English would hold 'sway' came into the imperial equation. In 1838 W. G. Blackie, the Glaswegian publisher, had contracted with John Ogilvie to produce a dictionary that would appear in parts between 1847 and 1850. This work, too, was 'imperial': The *Imperial Dictionary, English, Technological and Scientific*. In the Preface dated 1860, the publishers explained the reason for reprinting it:

> To bring the Work within the range of a still larger number than heretofore, and to keep the field against American Dictionaries which are introducing into this country vitiated forms of orthography, and many undesirable novelties of speech, the Publishers have resolved to re-issue the IMPERIAL DICTIONARY with the SUPPLEMENT, at a considerable reduction in price.   (1876: p. v)

Here imperialism (in its anti-American form) and commerce joined hands. Among the shrewdest of publishers, W. G. Blackie realized that there would be a profitable market both in Britain and in the colonies, even for a large work based on Noah Webster's long available *American Dictionary*—and even in an edition in which the supplementary material was not distributed in the main alphabet. In re-issuing Ogilvie's *Imperial*, Blackie entered the market in competition with other multi-volume dictionaries, particularly Charles Richardson's *New Dictionary of the English Language* (also published in parts and issued in two volumes in 1836–7) and H. J. Todd's enlargement of Samuel Johnson's *Dictionary of the English Language* in four volumes (1818), and subsequently even further enlarged by Robert Gordon Latham (1866–70). All of these expensive dictionaries competed with one another through the years of preliminary work for the *OED*.

As members of the Philological Society contemplated a new dictionary early in 1857, they found a market-place crowded with large dictionaries and conflicting assumptions about what an ideal dictionary should be. Still, there was much to be done since neither of the two large dictionaries readily in use in Britain— Richardson's and Todd's—'had any claims to be considered as a "Lexicon totius Anglicitatis"' (Trench *et al*. 1857: 944).

In August 1857 an anonymous contributor to *The Athenaeum* made entirely reasonable cautions: 'The very important proposal . . . deserves the goodwill and support of all students; at the same time, a natural anxiety arises lest, in attempting too much, a risk of failure may be incurred' ('Student' 1857: 976). He urged that a series of volumes be produced (and indexed) of materials collected by the members of the Philological Society, and volunteers recruited to assist them, perhaps under some title like 'Contributions to English Lexicography'. Otherwise, 'I feel certain the design will be crushed by its own weight and magnitude' (1857: 976). Undaunted by these cautions, Herbert Coleridge replied that volunteers had taken nearly all the books put on offer and that all that would be needed beyond what was in hand could be gathered in six months—though, he said, it would be wiser to allow the accumulation to proceed over a period of two years. Once the material had been collected, Coleridge declared: 'the difficulty of arranging the crude mass into dictionary order will be comparatively light' (1857: 1007)! During the summer, Richard Chenevix Trench considered the idea that collections be made of 'unregistered words and idioms . . . *primarily* directed to the less-read authors of the sixteenth and seventeenth-centuries' (Trench *et al*. 1857: 944), and he reported his findings to the Society in November. Enthusiasm abounded, and in due course, in January 1858, it was decided to publish not a supplement but 'an entirely new Dictionary': 'no patch upon old garments, but a new garment throughout' (Trench 1860: 1). Still, much would have to be done to create a 'truly national work'. Cautious voices went unheard, including the view expressed in *The Saturday Review* that 'Surplusage is the first and great fault of dictionaries' ('Dictionary-Making' 1858: 183).

In the *Canones Lexicographici* formulated in 1859–60, the dictionary committee of the Philological Society was almost wantonly ambitious, declaring that the dictionary should include '*every* word in the language for which sufficient authority, whether printed or oral, can be adduced' ([Trench *et al.*] 1860: 3). That such a dictionary might be impossible on practical grounds was certainly considered by some. For others, such a broad scope was not even theoretically desirable. Derwent Coleridge, for one, responded to the *Canones* with some scepticism. A unilingual dictionary, he affirmed, 'is eminently regulative—regulative in effect, though declarative in form' (1860: 156). Thus the lexicographer ought to distinguish 'the spurious from the genuine', omit or obloquate certain words, and in everything be 'zealously conservative'. Modern words ought to be admitted very selectively, since most of them would not endure. English, though not an immortal language like Greek or Latin, was, as Coleridge declared, 'still in the flesh'; as a result, 'though too old for much further growth, [it] is very capable of misgrowth' (D. Coleridge 1860: 158).

The imperial impulse, despite Derwent Coleridge's warning, could not be resisted. Herbert Coleridge, 'editor of the literary and historical portion of the Philological Society's New English Dictionary', defended the breadth of inclusion laid out in the *Canones*: that '*Americanisms and Colonialisms . . .* shall be admitted on the same terms as our own words' and that '*Slang Words and Phrases*' should likewise be included if 'the fact of their existence can be vouched for by some creditable authority' ([Trench *et al.*] 1860: 4). Expanding on these and other principles, he laid some of the problems before the Philological Society. In the discussion that followed, as summarized by F. J. Furnivall, the Secretary: 'The Members present thought that the main question was decided by the previous determinations of the Society and its Dictionary-Rules-Committee, that, except in very special cases, *all* words should be admitted into the proposed Dictionary; and though they allowed that a discretion was reserved to the Editor to exclude some words, they desired that it should be exercised sparingly' (H. Coleridge 1860a: 43).

With this most ambitious scheme affirmed, the Society went before the public for help. Even as early as July 1857 the committee of Trench, Furnivall, and Herbert Coleridge had issued a call for readers to gather quotations. Shortly thereafter, the plan was sympathetically reviewed by Georg Büchmann in a German philological journal, announcing to the world of philological professionals the efforts of the British amateurs to compile a dictionary of their own language on a scale approximating that of the *Deutsches Wörterbuch*. Volunteers came forth and by early 1860 there were 147 who had offered their services. Unfortunately, Herbert Coleridge reported, three had died and another forty-three did nothing beyond offering to do the work. Still, there were thirty 'first-rate contributors' and some others of lesser reliability brought the total to fifty, 'a number quite sufficient to do all that yet remains to be done' (1860*b*: 73). In this, as in many other estimates, Coleridge was far short of the mark, but his public enthusiasm (and that of the volunteers) created great hopes for the dictionary.

Then there were setbacks, not least the death of the editor. Writing in *The Athenaeum* on 29 June 1861, John Davis affirmed: 'We are glad to find, contrary to a report which has appeared in some of the newspapers, that the death of Mr. Herbert Coleridge has not interrupted the labours of the Philological Society on their New English Dictionary.' Many eminent writers, he said, remained to be read, and he mentioned some of their works, seeking particularly to draw the attention of 'our educated and intellectual women'. Yet so much more energy was needed: 'Here is temptation to many who may be desirous of aiding in the achievement of a splendid national work' (Davis 1861: 865). In July Thomas Watts, a stalwart member of the Philological Society, reviewed the new American dictionaries published under the names of Noah Webster and Joseph Emerson Worcester. He too praised the Society's scheme and also urged that volunteer readers come forth—'to surround and drive the whole herd of English vocables from their place of resort or concealment to pass before a select band of lexicographers, who are to bring down the game' (1861: 41).

For the next twenty-years, the shooting was not very good. Trench had been appointed to the archiepiscopal see in Dublin and was no longer involved in dictionary work. (Even in his *Select Glossary* of 1859 he had begun to separate himself from the Philological Society's dictionary.) In 1864 John Davis reported: 'The labours of the Philological Society, on behalf of their proposed Dictionary, are suffering from two or three accidents. More than one efficient reader has followed Herbert Coleridge to the grave. One sub-editor has lost his right hand in shooting. Another finds himself overworked. Others have grown either lazy or inefficient' (1864: 638). The hectoring tone continued in the inimitable words of F. J. Furnivall: 'When will the disgraceful apathy of our cultured and moneyed classes in this matter be shaken off!' (1867: 158). Seldom have so many been nagged into scholarship, not only on behalf of the dictionary but in editing early texts for the many societies organized and nurtured by the tireless Furnivall. While the dictionary was seldom mentioned in the annual reports given by the President of the Philological Society, Furnivall did not cease in his efforts. When, at last, an editor was found and a contract signed, he was given due credit: 'Of Mr. Furnivall's services it would be impossible to speak too highly; his zeal for the Dictionary has never flagged for a moment, and it is mainly to his personal influence that the successful issue of a protracted and difficult series of negotiations is due' (Anon. 1879: 413).

Now the work was in the hands of James Murray, and the anonymous writer in *The Academy* for 1879, whose encomium of Furnivall has just been quoted, was unstinting in praising the newly appointed editor:

The editor is Dr. J. A. H. Murray, now president of the society, and author of the *Dialect of the Southern Counties of Scotland*, who, of the various members of the society who have been suggested from time to time, unquestionably possesses in the highest degree that combination of learning, method, energy and power of organisation which his arduous task demands.   (1879: 413)

This author was not as prescient about the time and length of the dictionary—he thought it would be four times the size of Webster's dictionary and likely to be completed in ten years. But he was certainly right in his evaluation of Murray.

In a postcard to Murray in 1890 Furnivall pointed out that 'The Dict[ionary] has to educate folk into wanting it' (quoted in *CWW*: 265); as with much of his advice, Furnivall was urging what James Murray already well knew. As he gathered his spotty and disorganized materials, Murray immediately recognized that he needed to put discoveries before the educated public. In September 1879 he wrote anonymously in *The Athenaeum* to explain how 'Dr. Murray' and his assistants were 'busily engaged' in the work. On 4 June 1880 he presented a paper to the Philological Society: 'On the History of the Word "*Aisle*"'. Now he was ready to display the game so laboriously scouted by the members. In December 1881 he presented another and broader lecture: 'Dr. Murray . . . gave, from his slips of the society's Dictionary, a series of most interesting explanations and histories of the words ammunition, amyl, abnormal, alcohol, antic . . . and antique, antler, anthem, halt, ambush, and animal spirits (the nerves)' (Anon. 1881: 441).[1] As Furnivall had so often done in the past, he asked for help: 'No scientific man could tell him when antennae, antler, aphelion, and perihelion were first used, or what "antimony" came from.' The editor of *The Academy* helpfully appended the invitation: 'Can any of our readers?'

As the publication of the first fascicle approached, Murray cultivated visitors who could appreciate, and approve, his work. Jennett Humphreys came to Mill Hill and wrote breathlessly for *Fraser's Magazine* (1882) about the 'perfect scheme' she found there. Another early enthusiast was Lucy Toulmin Smith who would continue to be a faithful publicist for the dictionary:

The first Part of the Philological Society's *New English Dictionary of the English Language*, which it was hoped would be out in October, is not yet quite ready, owing to the unexpected difficulties attending a work of this magnitude. We have, however, been favoured with a sight of the revised sheets, from which we purpose to give a few gleanings which may show the manner of the fruition of this noble undertaking, for which the world has to thank the spirited Clarendon Press of Oxford. The pages in type on December 1 came down to *Ah*, occupying nearly six hundred columns of print.   (1883: 9)

---

[1] *Halt* was included among these words beginning with *a* because its earliest English form was *alto*.

The sheer size of the work was staggering, and Toulmin Smith was unstinting in her praise of his efforts. Murray, then and subsequently, encouraged visitors to the Scriptorium, especially those who would write about the marvels of scholarship being undertaken there.

A far less happy preview of the dictionary came in July 1883 when Murray was summoned to Oxford to confer with the Vice-Chancellor and Master of Balliol, Benjamin Jowett. On his arrival, he was presented with a document: 'Suggestions for Guidance in Preparing Copy for the Press'. Here were many 'suggestions' highly unwelcome to Murray, and Elisabeth Murray, in her biography, sticks firmly to the side of her ancestor. Like him, she believes these suggestions to have been mostly meddlesome, arising from 'complete ignorance of the Editor's long labour' (*CWW*: 221) and, when the dictionary was completed, entirely forgotten. The differing opinions of Murray and Jowett took some time to resolve, and the publication of the dictionary was hence delayed, an episode which she discusses in detail (*CWW*: 220–34).

In making this dispute a struggle between two titans of nineteenth-century intellectual life, Elisabeth Murray simplifies a rather more complex situation. On 10 May 1883 a committee of the Delegates had discussed the specimens that Murray had provided. Some of the issues raised were certainly those that we value in the finished dictionary: a catholic approach to the vocabulary (including Americanisms, Scotticisms, and 'bad words'); newspapers and 'great authors' treated on an equal footing; many 'scientific words'. In these matters, Murray prevailed to our benefit. But there were other issues that were entirely reasonable concerns if the dictionary were to be completed: that the etymologies ought to be restricted to the immediate sources of English words (namely, that Latin words borrowed from Greek ought not to be pursued to their Greek etymons); that quotations should come from original authors rather from sources quoting those originals; that some date should be set beyond which quotations would not be included (1870 [later 1875] was suggested). There were even more serious issues: that the quotations were unverified against the originals; that some books 'especially seventeenth-century writers, had been inattentively read'; 'that the subdivisions of Articles (e.g., of the word All) were too numerous, and therefore confusing'. And most important of all: the specimens were far more copious than the scale set by the contract (see Committee of the Delegates of the Press 1883).

The Committee also recommended to the Delegates a willingness to have Murray as editor come what might: 'It was agreed to recommend—That Dr. Murray receive an addition to his salary sufficient to enable him to reside in Oxford.' Their report, however painful to his tender feelings, was an endorsement of his work and of the dictionary. But Murray was uncompromising. He could not improve the attention of long-deceased readers of seventeenth-century authors, but he could keep the etymologies of etymologies, Scotticisms, Americanisms, bad words, newspapers, and intricately detailed sense discriminations. And he prevailed.

Finally, in 1884, the first part appeared in print, and the enthusiasm which Murray had so assiduously cultivated poured forth. But there was more criticism too. In

The Athenaeum, an anonymous reviewer, C. A. M. Fennell, looked carefully at what Murray had to say about the span of vocabulary from *A–Ant*. The concluding paragraph must have been gratifying to read:

In conclusion, we must once for all express our general admiration of this unique and peerless specimen of English lexicography, and indulge in a hope that before long we may be able to comment on the beneficial result of attention to our friendly hints in a notice of the whole colossal work. Every Englishman who can possibly afford it ought to do his part in forwarding this great enterprise of national interest by purchasing the parts as they appear.   (Fennell 1884: 178)

The 'friendly hints' were not welcome to Murray, however apt. It would take more time and more pages to complete the dictionary than Murray had claimed; simple multiplication yielded the estimate of the whole at 12,000 pages, and the contract with the Delegates of the Oxford University Press specified no more than 8,400. As Elisabeth Murray notes, 'James was obsessed by self-blame because his underestimate of the size of the work would involve the Delegates in additional cost for paper and printing' (*CWW*: 208–9; see also Chapter 1, n. 21).

Other 'friendly hints' offered by Fennell were similarly unwelcome. Many words were in use before the dates alleged in the dictionary, and many that should have been included were (and still are) not. Murray had treated an 'army of purely technical words', and Trench in his 1857 papers had used this metaphor and warned against their inclusion. Murray did not 'ruthlessly condemn' words that Fennell regarded as 'useless and badly constructed'. Like Trench, he believed that such words should be included but censured; as Trench had stated earlier: 'Where [the lexicographer] counts words to be needless, affected, pedantic, ill put together, contrary to the genius of the language, there is no objection to his saying so; on the contrary, he may do real service in this way' (1860: 6). Fennell even attacked the first part of the dictionary for failing to enumerate sufficiently the words of an era of which Trench had been exceedingly fond: 'we shall make bold to say that the divines of the sixteenth and seventeenth centuries have not been sufficiently laid under consideration' (1884: 178).

'This unique and peerless specimen', in short, was not what Trench had promised. Of course the review did contain many celebratory statements: 'Dr. Murray and his fellow workers are deserving of grateful acknowledgments and cordial encouragement from critics and the public' (Fennell 1884: 177). In many respects, the dictionary was 'immensely superior to all English dictionaries'. What especially pained Murray was that there was even a comparison with another large dictionary: 'We have already mentioned that obsolete words are systematically treated, and in this department . . . the scope of the "New Dictionary" [is] wider than that of any other, except, perhaps, Messrs. Cassell's "Encyclopedic Dictionary" ' (Fennell 1884: 177)! The dictionary might be 'peerless and unique' but it was not the only dictionary to have philological merit.

Cassell's *Encyclopedic Dictionary* was a worthy competitor. In 1872 the publishers had entered into a contract with Robert Hunter for a multi-volume dictionary which had begun to appear in 1879 just as Murray commenced his editorship. Its steady pace continued until the final volume was issued in 1888. Murray's slow progress was as a result especially galling to him and to members of a wider public eager to have a complete dictionary in hand before they followed Herbert Coleridge (and other enthusiasts) to the grave. As others had done, Hunter pointed to 'the rapid growth and spread of living languages', and he noted that his dictionary, at the end, occupied 5,629 pages (compared to 2,922 for Ogilvie's *Imperial*). He too took pride in the 'insertion of American words and phrases' (Hunter 1879–88: 7.2: p. iii), precisely referenced illustrative quotations, scientific words, slang, and provincialisms ('the only surviving remains of good old words' (p. viii)), finely discriminated senses, and—a feature lacking in Murray's more austere work—woodcuts showing various realia and thus adding greatly to the understanding of words. (One would not realize from Murray's scant definition that an *angel-fish* is, as the picture and Hunter's comment reveal, 'the reverse of angelic in its look'). And Hunter took pride in the 'encyclopaedic' character of his work: 'it explains not only words but things: it gives not only the meaning of words but also an explanation of the things to which such words are applied' (p. v). Murray would have nothing to do with an encyclopaedia; his business was words and their philological exegesis. To be compared in any way to Hunter's volumes was, for him, simply to mistake the category to which his dictionary belonged.

Lucy Toulmin Smith gave her views of Hunter's work in a series of reviews in *The Academy*, and she praised the encyclopaedic scope of the dictionary: 'a mass of useful information on a variety of subjects', she wrote as the first volume, *A–Des*, appeared (1883: 207). She could not restrain comparing it to Murray's forthcoming work, and regretted that 'it could not be expected that we should have the full historical method which is so eagerly looked for in Dr Murray's great dictionary' (1883: 207). As Hunter brought his work to a close in 1889, Toulmin Smith hinted that he must have drawn upon the superior scholarship of that 'great dictionary': 'The influence of that monumental work, although still so far from complete, is, no doubt, seen in these pages, and the net result shows a great advance in lexicons of English hitherto available' (1889: 422). But what *was* the 'influence of that monumental work'? By 1888, when Hunter had finished, Murray was still struggling in C. Not a page of Murray's work had been published earlier than the corresponding parts of Hunter. Yet Toulmin Smith's review hinted at indebtedness, even plagiarism, a charge that would soon arise again.

When the first instalment of the dictionary appeared, as Elisabeth Murray points out, the Delegates of the Clarendon Press did not signal their approbation of Murray's work: 'But there was no letter expressing their appreciation, no change of attitude that he could detect. His disappointment, though he did not say much of it at the time, cut very deep and therefore he carried a chip on his shoulder, feeling that his work was inadequately recognized and that he must be satisfied with his own knowledge that it was good' (*CWW*: 234). She goes on to write that most of the reviewers were not competent to form an opinion of the merits of Murray's work, and to complain that timely offers of help would have improved the published fascicles. Both allegations are true, but some reviewers *were* competent, and their observations caused Murray acute pain and profound anger. These feelings were never assuaged by the flood of praise from scholars both foreign and domestic, the honorary degrees and memberships in philological societies, and even, in 1908, a knighthood. Murray was bitter, querulous, combative, and driven. Never in his lifetime did he fully appreciate that his ideas about lexicography would be celebrated worldwide and his practices shape the labours of lexicographers for more than a century.

Even Furnivall, whose efforts to keep the dictionary in the public mind for more than twenty years had made Murray's work possible, did not acclaim the perfect dictionary for which Murray had striven. In his notice of the forthcoming *A–Ant*, he declared that 'only' five words he had collected were not treated in the fascicle and that Murray might make 'a very valuable Appendix' for such omissions. (Of these five, only one, *amorce*, eventually found its way to the *Supplement* of 1933; the others were recent coinages that would never have been considered at all if a *terminus ad quem* of 1870 or 1875 had been adopted as the Committee had recommended.) Furnivall might state that it was 'the duty of the English-speaking public all over the world' to buy the dictionary. He might further declare that what Murray had done was to begin a dictionary 'far and away better than any other of any living language' (Furnivall 1884: 96–7). But even tiny flaws and oversights were intolerable criticisms to the editor.

More acceptable to Murray was the two-part review in *The Academy* written by a philological unknown who had previously been employed in a Sheffield cutlery firm: Henry Bradley. Bradley was deferential and celebratory. He did complain, very slightly, that some compounds (like *able seaman*) and phrases (like *alive and kicking*) were not treated, and he thought that the physical and mental pains described by the word *ache* ought to be distinguished into literal and figurative respectively. But most gratifying to Murray was Bradley's praise of features Murray himself had created and admired: the type faces and page layout ('to render the page eloquent to the eye', as Murray put it in his Preface to the fascicle); the pronunciation scheme (which Bradley said resolved 'the conflicting claims of precision and facility'); the admirable encapsulation of 'all the latest results of etymological research'; the balance between 'historical' and 'logical' order in the presentation of sense evolution. Bradley found the dictionary superior to the works of Littré and the Grimms, and avowed that it 'fully satisfies the high expectations which have been formed respecting it' (1884: 106).

Bradley's and the other reviews taught Murray an important lesson about what appealed to the public. In the Preface to *A–Ant*, he had limited himself to making a few general observations on the plan of the work and to copious (and nuanced) acknowledgements of helpers (for these Prefaces, see Raymond 1987). However, Murray said nothing at all about the words treated in the fascicle. In his Preface to the next instalment, *Ant–Batten*, he drew attention to 'several articles of great length and special difficulty' (for instance, *anti-* and *bank*). For the next, he expanded his list of interesting words of different etymological sources and offered a large view of 'language in its natural state' in dialects, slang, and colloquial speech. Finally, with the Preface to Part III, *Batten–Boz*, Murray hit upon the formula that would continue to the end, giving more and more words of 'particular historical interest'. He also expressed the Victorian enthusiasm for statistics, giving the numbers of 'main words', the 'special combinations', the 'obsolete' and 'alien' words, and other numbers of absorbing interest. By 1897 he was showing comparisons with other dictionaries. In D, for instance, there were 19,051 'total words' treated; this compared favourably with Johnson (2,684 in D), Cassell's *Encyclopedic* (10,089), *Century* (10,705), and Funk's *Standard* (11,181). Murray had discovered the method by which 'to educate folk into wanting it', and most reviews began to follow the Prefaces quite slavishly, giving the numbers (which made 'the big dictionary' obviously better) and turning to the list of words of special interest to create 'stories' just as Bradley (1884: 141) had done in laying out the fact that *hangnail* originally had nothing to do with finger- and toenails. Busy journalists, with no noticeable qualifications for reviewing a dictionary, now had a handy model that made them appear learned, and their reviews and notices followed Murray's Prefaces, and celebrated the dictionary with little or no equivocation.

No one said that the dictionary contained more about words than most people found interesting; many urged, without much optimism, its speedy completion; nearly all conceived it as a great 'national' project. In his 1884 valedictory lecture as president of the Philological Society, Murray summarized the reception of *A–Ant*:

Sixty-one reviews of part i. had appeared, and all approved the work generally. Some reviewers objected to the technical words; but the scientific men each complained how scantily his own science was represented. No hard-and-fast line could possibly be drawn in the matter; the editor must be trusted, and use his own discretion. Other reviewers were distressed at modern newspapers being used as authorities. They did not object to far inferior old newspapers, anonymous Commonwealth daily tracts, being so used; but to-day's journals shocked them. The only rule was to take the best quotation you could get for the meaning you had to illustrate, and not be so silly as to choose a poor quotation because it had a big name tacked on to it. (Anon. 1884: 372)

At the end of Murray's report, Furnivall took the floor and asked for a resolution of thanks to Gladstone, then Prime Minister, who had granted a pension of £250 to Murray. (The reporter for *The Academy* noted that Furnivall had conceived and carried through to completion the idea of a pension for Murray's services to literature.)

In most important respects, the reputation of the dictionary was consolidated in the months after the publication of *A–Ant*, and from our perspective at the end of the twentieth century the enormous influence of the dictionary seems obvious and assured. But it was by no means obvious or assured to Murray, who became deeply depressed that his work was not sufficiently appreciated and sometimes explosively angry when he regarded criticisms as ignorant or unfair. Two instances of Murray's nearly irrational behaviour in defence of his dictionary will illustrate the depths of his rage: his view of the *Century Dictionary*, and the spat over the entry for *couvade*.

A revealing instance of Murray's irrational fears about his dictionary emerges in connection with an American publication, *The Century Dictionary*. Though based on Ogilvie's *Imperial*, the *Century* was a huge and original effort brought out under the editorship of North America's leading philologist, William Dwight Whitney. Public notice of the forthcoming work appeared in 1883, and so Murray commenced publication knowing that yet another large dictionary—in addition to Hunter's *Encyclopedic*—was about to compete with his efforts. Instalments of the *Century* began to be issued in May 1889, and the whole huge work was finished by December 1891: '7,046 large quarto pages including about 5,000 definitions of upwards of 215,000 words, 50,000 defined phrases, 300,000 illustrative quotations, and 8,000 cuts' (according to the calculations of *Publisher's Weekly*). In *The Athenaeum*, Fennell declared: 'The American characteristics of enterprise and thoroughness are conspicuously illustrated by the "Century Dictionary", which bids fair to be far and away the largest and best general and encyclopedic dictionary of the English language' (these quotations from Bailey 1996: 10). In Boston, the *Atlantic Monthly* opined: 'In breadth of selection [from writings by "well-known names of literature"] the "Century Dictionary" seems to rival, if not to surpass, the Oxford' (Anon. 1889: 850). And, the reviewer went on (1889: 855), 'everyone who can afford a high-priced dictionary' should buy the *Century*, which could shortly be had complete while Murray still wrestled with C.[2]

In the Preface, dated 1 May 1889, to the first part of the *Century*, *A–Appet*, Whitney was gracious in invoking Murray's work. For the *Century*, the etymologies that had seemed 'most helpful' (Whitney 1889: p. vii) were those found in the work of Skeat, Eduard Müller, and Murray (the latter available only for A and the first part of B); the collection of citations for the *Century* was larger than any other 'except that accumulated for the Philological Society of London' (Whitney 1889: p. xi). The tone of these acknowledgements was deferential, and Whitney emphasized that 'the conclusions reached are independent' (1889: p. vii). Like Hunter's *Encyclopedic*, Whitney's idea was to produce a work of general reference 'for every literary and practical use'. And he praised the 'unfailing faith and the largest liberality' of his publisher (1889: p. v).

These words must have been poisonous to Murray, who had no confidence in the faith of the Delegates and little experience of their liberality. When in 1890

---

[2] On 11 February 1893 Furnivall reported by postcard to Murray that members of the Philological Society urged him to 'use the Cent. Dict. freely'. Furnivall offered to write to Whitney asking him to use his influence with the Century Company to permit such free use. No letter of this character survives in the Whitney papers archived at Yale University (see Bailey 1996: 13, n. 5).

the next instalment of the *OED* appeared, Murray must have been gratified to read the editorial in *The Times* which declared the work 'simply unrivalled'. The anonymous reviewer went on to slight the transatlantic competitor:

Perhaps the best testimony to its excellence, though one scarcely to the taste of the conductors of the Clarendon Press, is to be found in the copious use—or abuse, as some might be tempted to call it—made of its earlier pages by a recent American publication of greater pretension than merit. The Dictionary cannot hope to escape the fate which sooner or later awaits all books of its class—that, namely, of serving as an inexhaustible reservoir for the supply of later and less original compilations.   (1890: 25)

No one writing for the public disputed this claim, yet it must have been obvious to all that the *Century*, month by month approaching completion, could hardly tap a 'reservoir' from a work whose stately progress through the alphabet had hardly begun.

Privately, however, Murray's reputation was deteriorating among those who dwelt in the inner circle of lexicography. Whitney remained silent, then and thereafter, but others thought that the 'abuse' of which the reviewer spoke might lie elsewhere. (Whitney's quiescence may not have been as tactful as it seemed; as the *Century* began to appear, he was incapacitated by heart trouble. In earlier years he had been a vigorous controversialist, particularly in combat with F. Max Müller, and quick to resent a slight.) Coming forth to prevent the outbreak of another dictionary war was Fennell, author of that 'helpful' review in *The Athenaeum* and editor of the excellent *Stanford Dictionary of Anglicised Words and Phrases* (1892).

Presuming that Whitney followed the reviews of *The Times* as attentively as he himself did, Fennell promptly wrote to Whitney in March 1890 (1890*b*):

In the strictest confidence I think I can explain the disgraceful article on the 'Century' Dictionary in last Saturday's *Times*. I have very good reason to believe that the accusation of excessive use of the New English Dictionary is traceable to Dr. Murray himself. I know he wrote to that effect to one review, and suspect he did so to several papers. Of course a reviewer who has no special qualifications for judging of your work would be almost afraid not to endorse Dr. Murray's opinion. It seems to me that the 'Athenaeum' reviewer has proved what was prima facie obvious, that the 'Century' is thoroughly independent. I know that most competent judges are delighted with the first volume of the 'Century,' and of course the *Times* article will make little impression.

I hope Dr. Murray's absurd vanity will not raise any resentment on your side of the water against the New English Dictionary, as Henry Bradley, the co-editor is quite a different sort of man, and I think you will notice a very great improvement in the editing of his volumes.

I shall be very glad if you could see your way to castigating Dr. Murray without compromising me. If you think it worth while to bring an action, I believe the editors of various papers would have to acknowledge that Dr. Murray had originated the charges against you and your staff. He got hold of a piece of my proof [of the *Stanford*], and without communicating with me, induced the Delegates of the Clarendon Press to charge me with wholesale plagiarism to the Syndics of the Cambridge Press. I proved to the complete satisfaction of the latter that the charge was false, but they felt that it would not do for the two Presses to quarrel, and so put the matter on one side by saying that they would take care that nothing objectionable was published, while they have not asked me to alter a single word of the incriminated articles. This is very satisfactory as far as it goes, but meanwhile Dr. Murray is slandering me without my being able to retort until the 'Stanford' dictionary is published.

This accounts for the tone of the article in the 'Athenaeum', the authorship of which you will have guessed by this time.   (quoted in part by Barnhart 1996: 117–18)[3]

Though this controversy was, at first, concealed from public view, Fennell anonymously reported in *The Athenaeum* that he had conducted a minute examination of the overlapping parts of the two dictionaries and found that 'the "Century" vocabulary is independent of the "New English Dictionary" vocabulary, excepting in the few cases where acknowledgment is made ... A striking proof of independence is shown by the number of cases in which the "New English Dictionary" presents slight faults which are not found in the "Century" ' (1890a: 270). Thus were the rumours allegedly circulated by Murray put to the test. Furnivall, Bradley, and others wrote to calm his rage, but with little success (see *CWW*: 266 and 372, n. 24).

The tenacious Murray could not allow these comparisons to stand, and on 28 April 1890 he drafted a letter to *The Academy* blasting the etymology of *cockney* in the *Century*, declaring that 'I know Somerville Hall girls, perhaps even Extension Students who would irreverently laugh at it as impossible.' Not satisfied with this faint praise of female philological talent, he enlarged his criticism from *cockney* to Whitney, to Yale, and to America:

if a man does not know what is truth and what is error, it is better not to set up as an authority and 'talk tall' like an expert of what is phonetically satisfactory. One can always say 'I don't know.' Especially important is this in America, where in the absence of living English usage, the dictionary occupies a place of authority never conceded to it by educated Englishmen.

Arguments over the origin of *cockney* erupted into print in both Britain and the United States. (These are discussed in detail by Liberman (1996: 40–8), from whom I have drawn these and the following quotations.)

From America, Francis A. March, a philological giant who had recruited readers in the United States, wrote, 'You can not write letters for the public belittling Prof. Whitney, Yale, and Americans and retain this affectionate regard' (*CWW*: 266). Elisabeth Murray alleges that a subsequent letter from March shows him

---

[3] This letter is to be found in the Whitney papers at Yale. In 1882 J. F. Stanford left a bequest to the University of Cambridge of £5,000 for the preparation of this dictionary. In his Preface, Fennell devoted a long paragraph to a comparison between his work and Murray's (pp. vii–viii). He explained his attempt to avoid the 'danger of including words which ought to be excluded because they prove to be, or will eventually prove to be Middle English' and hence the province of Murray's work.

to have been 'convinced' by Murray's argument that failure to denounce the *Century* as inferior would put his arrangements with the Delegates in jeopardy. It is, however, impossible to imagine that March was convinced of the need to sneer at Whitney's scholarship or to deride Americans generally. (Murray had ended his essay with a blast at the hypothetical verb *cockle*: '. . . the fear is that the next poet of the century, freshly inspired by his dictionary, will hear cockles cockling to greet the morn on reeking dung hills of the Bay State, and cockles a-cockling a drowsy response from the chaparrals of New Mexico' (Liberman 1996: 42).)[4]

On Murray's behalf, A. L. Mayhew began to worry the etymologies of the *Century*. He started by generously writing that 'scholars in England . . . are ready to give a hearty welcome to any scholar, coming from any quarter, who promises to add to our knowledge, and to help us in clearing up some of the many doubtful points which have long waited for solution' (1891: 447). That concession, however, was a matter of principle rather than of practice, and Mayhew then opined that 'it would have been a great advantage to the [*Century*] dictionary if all the Comparative Philology had been left out; it takes up an immense amount of room without adding one iota to the scientific value of the book' (1891: 449). Reviewing more than a hundred entries in the first volume, he concluded that the dictionary 'gives ample proof of careless workmanship and inaccurate scholarship' (Mayhew 1891: 457). Anatoly Liberman has recently declared that 'despite his pugnacity and gratuitous rudeness, Mayhew was a first-rate scholar' (1996: 49). Yet here he was solely concerned with destroying the reputation of the *Century* and tried to ensure that no one could dissent from his claim that Murray's dictionary was 'so perfect that there remains nothing to be desired' (Mayhew 1891: 447).

A second instance of Murray's attempt to manipulate the reputation of his dictionary arises in October 1892. Murray published a letter in *The Academy* describing his search for the origin of the term *couvade*. This inquiry began as he tried to elucidate the meaning of a passage in Edward B. Tylor's *Early History of Mankind* (1865). Murray explained that *couvade* 'is now commonly applied by students of anthropology and folklore, i.e., as a general term to comprehend a series of

---

[4] C. P. G. Scott, chief etymologist for the *Century*, wrote a patriotic reply. 'If there were any educated Americans, perhaps we might get along tolerably well, even "in the absence of living English usage"; but "in the absence of" both, we are in a parlous state indeed. Such Americans as have been able to snatch a few hours from their pioneer tasks of fighting the wild Indian and hunting the wild buffalo, in order to read, by the dim flickering light of a pine-knot, a little about the rudiments of language have hitherto supposed that they speak English, and "living English" at that—crude, of course, and incorrect, and with an "American accent", but still a kind of "living English", however different from the clear, delicate, sonorous *r*-less, *h*-less English set forth by Dr. Murray, Dr. Sweet, and other eminent British phoneticians as "living English usage". Americans will be much disappointed to learn from Dr. Murray that "English" means the speech of London, and "living English" the speech of certain persons, "educated Englishmen," now living in or near London; in other words, of educated Scotchmen, who, "if caught young" and careful to avoid pronouncing *r* and *h*, may be allowed admittance into the outer sanctum of "living English usage." But on this point Dr. Murray maintains the traditional reserve of a true-born Englishman' (quoted by Liberman 1996: 44).

customs, according to which, on the birth of a child, the father performs certain acts, or simulates certain states, natural or proper to the mother, or at least acts as an invalid, or abstains from certain foods or actions for a time shorter or longer, as if he were physically afflicted by the birth' (1892a: 389). Tylor had cited an eighteenth-century French author, but in that original source *couvade* was not to be found. Murray discovered that a subsequent editor had amplified the text to include the expression, and from that source an obscure French poet was the origin of the modern usage found in Tylor. At the end of his letter, Murray promised to publish some 'very curious results' of his inquiry in the next number of *The Academy* and to lay out the 'anthropological use (or abuse)' of the term.

In the following week's issue, however, there appeared instead a sharp rebuke from Tylor himself, pointing to two French sources where *couvade* was used exactly in the sense Murray had criticized, one from 1658 and the other from 1724. In his concluding paragraph, Tylor offered a stinging reproof:

> We all trust that Dr. Murray will live to see the completion of the New English Dictionary, at once so great a credit and so great a responsibility to the University of Oxford. May I express a hope that, with his hands already too full, he will not often go out of this way to become, as in this case, a supervisor of new words? He is not the editor of the English language, but of an English dictionary. People who want words will make them in their own way; and if a word gains currency, there is little good in calling its introduction an 'abuse,' seeing that the lexicographer, whether he likes the word or not, has to take it.   (Tylor 1892: 412)

If his original essay had been to display Murray's deep learning and unflagging search for origins, this reply seemed to call both into question. (Murray had not been asking for information about *couvade* but telling a story about the word.) Tylor was an Oxford eminence and an internationally known anthropologist. In two early Prefaces, Murray had written at untypical length about his contribution to the dictionary: 'Dr. E. B. Tylor, Oxford, for help with words from Carib, Brazilian, African, and other savage languages, especially terms connected with native customs, products, weapons', and, later, for Tylor's suggestions for *Boomerang, Boma, Boyuna* (Raymond 1987: 17 and 32)). Now two learned gentlemen of Oxford were engaged in a public debate in a London magazine.

The following week brought still more controversy about *couvade*. Murray wrote that an 'unexpected absence from home and from my books' prevented him from replying to Tylor immediately, but Mayhew wrote vigorously in his defence. Tylor was certainly to be credited with introducing *couvade* into English, and Mayhew reported: 'I have had some talk with the editor of the *New English Dictionary* about this word, and I may truly say that in our familiar converse about Dr Tylor's foster-child I have never heard a word fall from Dr Murray's lips which could hurt the feelings of the most sensitive parent' (1892: 437). This assertion might have prevented the breach that was emerging between the two scholars, but Mayhew, with characteristic combativeness, added more:

Of course if any word has gained currency, he [Murray] will take it, 'liking' having nothing to do with the matter; but in spite of any hopes to the contrary, he will, I expect, go on calling an anthropological use of a word an 'abuse', should he think it a perversion of the original sense of the word. In using the word 'abuse' he would of course employ it in its strict scientific sense without the slightest suspicion of disrespect for any fellow scholar. (1892: 438)

The idea that *abuse* was some 'scientific' term when applied to language fooled no one, not least since, in this great dictionary that promised to give all senses, no such 'strict scientific sense' had been specified in the entry for *abuse*.

Murray would have been wise to have left *couvade* for the portion of the alphabet yet to come, leaving an opening to deny what was apparent to all, that Mayhew was his *agent provocateur*. Instead, two weeks later, he launched even more vigorously into the dispute. Reviewing a string of French authorities, he declared that the idea expressed by *couvade* was a fiction—'a literary or pseudo-scientific myth' (Murray 1892a: 460). In a postscript, he especially urged an essay on 'La Couvade chez les Basques' by a Professor Vinson, a work he thought 'ought to be better known in England'. (Neither the Bodleian nor the Taylorian Institute had a copy, and Murray had been obliged to order one from Paris.) In his final paragraph, he asserted his authority as a lexicographer:

I am not 'the editor of the English language', but I try to be an historian of words that I find used in English; and I sometimes wish that men of science, before making new words or giving new senses to old words, would ask the advice of students of language, who may know the history of the old or have a word of counsel as to the form of the new. (Murray 1892a: 460)

In 1865, when Tylor introduced *couvade* to English, Murray had been an obscure clerk in the Chartered Bank of India, Australia, and China, Threadneedle Street, London, in his spare time toiling away on languages in the British Museum. He was hardly the sort of figure an Oxford don would seek out on a question of vocabulary.

In December Tylor returned to the fray. When he 'looked again' at Vinson's essay, 'I found that Dr Murray has misunderstood him' (Tylor 1892: 542). And there was yet another French author to be discussed. A bigger issue, however, occupied his attention:

This is a matter which touches a far larger public than those who care about the history of a quaint old custom and its name. My own impression, and that of others interested in the New English Dictionary who have spoken to me, is that such extension of its editorial work into independent research is not likely to answer well. If a lexicographer, already overburdened with his duties, hastily takes up outlying philological problems which require for their treatment time and care and knowledge of the subject-matter of each, he will produce work going beyond the needs and possibilities of a dictionary, but not far enough to count for much as research. I do not like having to remonstrate thus with Dr Murray, for whose philological ability I have full respect. But in my former letter I seem not to have spoken plainly enough. When I answered his theory (that the word *couvade* came from a comic poem of 1790) by pointing out that I had long ago given a reference to its occurrence in a French book of 1658, I thought that the matter was settled. Not so; he returns to the fight as if nothing serious had happened, withdraws the comic poet theory, and substitutes a different one, which is another guess. So unconscious is he of the irony of the situation that, at the moment when he is in the act of shifting from one theory disproved to a contradictory one not established, he expresses a wish 'that men of science, before making new words or giving new senses to old words, would ask the advice of students of language who may know the history of the old or have a word of counsel as to the form of the new'. (1892: 542)

Tylor concluded that he 'did not intend to write further on this subject', and he kept that promise. Murray would have done well to content himself with letting the matter drop since he (and Mayhew) were getting the worst of it. But he did not.

A week later Murray fired off another blast to *The Academy*. Far from misunderstanding Vinson, he wrote, it was Tylor who failed to see that all the French authorities regarded the practice of *couvade* as a myth. It angered him that Tylor had 'eagerly borrowed' the very copy of Vinson's essay obtained by the Taylorian Library at Murray's behest; even then, he claimed, Tylor did not understand that *couvade* among the Basques was an imposture foisted upon credulous anthropologists and savants. Yet it was not the issue of the word that enraged him but the matter of the work of the lexicographer:

First, he alleges that I have misrepresented two recent authors whom I incidentally quoted after my summing up, and who have nothing in the world to do with the chain of 'authorities' from whom Dr Tylor's application of *couvade* was taken; and, secondly, he tries to shift the issue into a discussion of my duties as an editor of the New English Dictionary. Into this impertinency I certainly will not follow him. If he likes to appeal to 'a far wider public' on that matter, it must be done as a substantive matter, and not as an amendment to burk the discussion of *couvade*, or to disguise the result of that discussion. I will only say that the way in which I may please to spend the scanty leisure which is left to me after giving sixty hours a week to the Dictionary is entirely a matter for myself. If I choose to spend some of it in probing modern myths, which I come across in the course of my work, it is quite as legitimate a recreation as playing golf or teaching the history of religion to the benighted Christians of Aberdeen. (Murray 1892*b*: 568)

Whether golfing and exhorting Aberdonians were Tylor's special recreations remains mysterious. But the 'far wider public' must have seen Murray's rage over a word that few had ever encountered as irrational and troubling. When the entry for *couvade* appeared in 1893, Murray appended a lengthy note on the etymology in which he said the claim that *couvade* was a practice of the Basques and Béarnese was 'a mistake'. Needless to say, there were no more acknowledgements of Tylor's help in the Prefaces to the subsequent parts of the dictionary,[5] and the grudge thus founded continued until Murray's death in 1915 and Tylor's in 1917.

[5] I am grateful to Jenny McMorris for supplying me with a copy of her index to Murray's Prefaces as compiled by Raymond (1987). Judith C. Avery and Barbara Beaton of the University of Michigan Library provided much help and support. Denise Jennings, Librarian at the City University, London, arranged for me to inspect copies of the volumes of *The Athenaeum* containing annotations identifying authors of anonymous submissions.

These two episodes from the first decade of the dictionary were, to the well-informed, deeply troubling, and Murray's dour nature did not much change as time went on, even though there were no further public spats of the sort illustrated in his reaction to the *Century* and to Tylor's defence of the word *couvade*. Yet there was further corrosion to the reputation of the dictionary. Funding salaries from his own pocket and bedevilled by repeated attempts to limit the scale of the dictionary, Murray regularly threatened to resign his editorship. In April 1896 an anonymous writer in *The Saturday Review*, perhaps stimulated by Murray himself, put these issues again before the public:

Many of our readers will hear with astonishment, and some with indignation, that the Delegates of the Clarendon Press are now considering whether they will continue to defray the expense of carrying on the great English Dictionary except on the condition that its scale be greatly reduced. If these terms be insisted on, we have no hesitation in saying that such a decision will be nothing less than a national calamity and an indelible disgrace to the University. (1896b: 393)

The writer went on to declare that it 'would be very derogatory to England to allow a project of this kind to collapse through want of adequate patronage' (1896b: 394). As Elisabeth Murray explains, however, this crisis of 1896 marked the end of open warfare between the Delegates and their editor. As they had before, they capitulated to Murray's imperious will, even directing Bartholomew Price, their Secretary, to distribute a statement 'correcting' such cries of alarm as had been echoed in the press from the article in *The Saturday Review* (*CWW*: 278).

As the century drew to a close the dictionary continued its slow and steady progress. It was still a financial drain on the resources of the Clarendon Press, but the Delegates increasingly realized that they had entered into a contract that involved more than lexicography and touched on the reputation of Oxford University and even the nation itself. The imperial impulse which had animated the dictionary at the beginnings arose again to sustain the vast labours of editing. Now as each fascicle appeared, the reviews followed a familiar pattern of statistics and stories of words, coupled with a reverential awe for Murray's accomplishment. Though less depressed than before 1896, he was still driven by relentless work and an almost pathological sense of 'duty'. These feelings made him the most severe critic of the dictionary, though he now kept his anguish mostly private.

In April 1904 Murray wrote a letter to Skeat in which he reflected on the entries in A and E. In 1884–5, when the fascicles for A had appeared, Murray was just learning about the 'weakness of the Philological Society slips', and, though he did not put it quite so baldly, it had been his own apprenticeship as a lexicographer. E, appearing in 1891–4, was Bradley's debut. At the time, Murray even contemplated resigning because Bradley's work was 'so bad' that he could not allow it to appear in print without disavowing it. Even in 1904 he judged, 'I have always said that the letter ought to be done again' (*CWW*: 263). Mild and deferential, Bradley had asked Murray to review his copy, and Murray, though still critical of it, believed that no such drastic steps as resigning or repudiating the work were required.

By the twentieth century, the reputation of the dictionary was assured. Murray's Romanes lectures in 1900 were, significantly, titled *The Evolution of English Lexicography*. In them, he displayed the 'progress' that led to his own dictionary, and he redefined dictionary in a way that gave utter primacy to the philological exegesis of words. The *dictionary* as reference work was hardly touched upon, and there was no need to consider the efforts of Robert Hunter or William Dwight Whitney since the books they produced were not really dictionaries but encyclopaedias. The lexicographer—here Murray entirely ignored his own exegesis of the origin of *couvade*—had no business with referents, only with the words that referred to them. He had done a remarkable thing: he had educated people into wanting something from a dictionary that most of them did not want at all—for instance, the historical list of variant spellings—and denying them what they did want—for instance, insight into what an *angel-fish* might look like. Reviewing the dictionary became almost routine and formulaic; in 1896, the *London Quarterly Review* wrote of 'unstinted commendation' (1896a; in 1912, Fennell acknowledged that the reviews constituted 'the monotony of unbroken approbation' (p. 118).

With the rise in the 1920s among some academics of the view that poems (and other 'texts') are autonomous objects, the dictionary had a crucial role to play. History collapsed into simultaneity; a word meant whatever it had ever meant to anybody who had used it, even if those uttering it were innocent of obsolete or irrelevant meanings. Appealing to some vaguely defined cultural memory, critics could draw upon all the definitions and citations provided by the dictionary and allege that all were invoked in the particular usage under scrutiny.[6] 'Texts' acquired a mystery not hitherto suspected by readers. Using the dictionary as a, usually unacknowledged, source, critics have been able to present brilliant and learned exegeses founded on Murray's scholarship. In this way, the dictionary profoundly shaped three-quarters of a century of literary criticism.

The impulses of imperialism, profit, and philology that were important at the beginning have also been important to the present moment, nearly a century and a half later. Recognizing the dictionary as a foundation for vast profits, the Delegates have renewed work upon it while selling an astonishing number and variety of smaller dictionaries allegedly 'based' upon it—in Britain and around the world. As with the name 'Webster' in the United States, 'Oxford' has become a byword for *dictionary*. The 'unique and peerless specimen', conceived by Murray and more than half executed by him personally, thus continues to shape our ideas about dictionaries and about words. In ways still insufficiently understood, it

---

[6] A typical expression of this idea is found in I. A. Richards' early book, *Principles of Literary Criticism* (1924: 90): 'A sign is something which has once been a member of a context or configuration that worked in the mind as a whole. When it reappears its effects are as though the rest of the context were present'. All that was required to make the dictionary an ideal tool for criticism was to expand *mind* from individual to collective unconsciousness.

has been 'regulative in effect, though declarative in form', as Derwent Coleridge
so perceptively recognized in 1860.

REFERENCES

Anon. (1879). 'The Philological Society's English Dictionary'. *The Academy*, 15: 413.

Anon. (1881). Report of the meeting of the Philological Society. *The Academy*, 20: 441.

Anon. (1884). Report of the meeting of the Philological Society. *The Academy*, 25: 372.

Anon. (1889). Review of *The Century Dictionary*. *The Atlantic Monthly*, 64: 846–55.

Anon. (1890). Review of *Cast–Clivy*. *The Times*, 22, 25 March. 1–2.

Anon. (1896a). Review of *Diffluent–Disburden*. *London Quarterly Review*, 87: 197.

Anon. (1896b). 'The English Dictionary and the Clarendon Press'. *The Saturday Review*,
18 April, 81: 393–4.

Bailey, R. W. (1991). *Images of English: A Cultural History of the English Language*. Ann
Arbor: University of Michigan Press.

—— (1996). 'The Century Dictionary: Origins'. *Dictionaries*, 17: 1–16.

Barnhart, R. K. (1996). 'The Century Dictionary: Aftermath'. *Dictionaries*, 17: 116–25.

Boag, J. (1852). *The Imperial Lexicon of the English Language*. 2 vols. Edinburgh, London,
and Glasgow: A. Fullarton & Co.

Bradley, H. (1884). Review of *A–Ant*. *The Academy*, 24: 105–6; 141–2.

Büchmann, G. (1858). 'Lexicalische Pläne der Londoner Philologischen Gesellschaft.'
Archiv, 23: 208–10.

Coleridge, D. (1860). 'Observations on the Plan of the Society's Proposed New English
Dictionary'. *TPS*, 1860–1: 152–68.

Coleridge, H. (1857). 'Collections for a New Dictionary of the English Language'. *The
Athenaeum* (8 August): 1007.

—— (1860a). 'On the Exclusion of Certain Words from the Dictionary' (with an
appendix by F. J. Furnivall). *TPS*, 1860–1: 37–43.

—— (1860b). 'A Letter to the Very Rev. The Dean of Westminster'. Appended to Trench
(1860): 71–8.

Committee of the Delegates of the Press Appointed to Consider the English Dictionary.
(1883). 'Report.' Ms. Bodleian 30254 *c*.2 (41).

[Davis, J.] (1861). Report on the progress of the dictionary. *The Athenaeum* (29 June): 865.

—— (1864). Report on the progress of the dictionary. *The Athenaeum* (12 November): 638.

'Dictionary-Making'. (1858). *The Saturday Review*, 6 (21 August): 183.

[Fennell, C. A. M.] (1884). Review of *A–Ant*. *The Athenaeum* (2 February): 177–8.

—— (1890a). Review of *The Century Dictionary*. *The Athenaeum* (1 March): 269–70.

Fennell, C. A. M. (1890b). Ms. letter to William Dwight Whitney. Yale University Library,
Manuscripts and Archives, 555.40.1225.

—— (1892). *The Stanford Dictionary of Anglicised Words and Phrases*. Cambridge: at the
University Press.

[Fennell, C. A. M.] (1912). Review of *See–Senatory*. *The Athenaeum* (3 Feb.): 118–19.

[Furnivall, F. J.] (1867). Report on the progress of the dictionary. *The Athenaeum* (2 February):
158.

—— (1884). 'The Philological Society's English Dictionary'. *The Academy*, 25: 96–7.

Humphreys, J. (1882). 'English: Its Ancestors, Its Progeny'. *Fraser's Magazine*, 26: 429–57.

Hunter, R. (1879–88). *The Encyclopædic Dictionary*. London: Cassell, Peter, Galpin & Co.

Liberman, A. (1996). '*The Century Dictionary*: Etymology'. *Dictionaries*, 17: 29–54.

Mayhew, A. L. (1891). Review of *The Century Dictionary*. *Englische Studien*, 15: 447–57.

—— (1892). '"Couvade"—The Genesis of an Anthropological Term'. *The Academy*, 42: 437–8.

[Murray, J. A. H.]. (1879). 'The New English Dictionary of the Philological Society'. *The Athenaeum* (13 September): 337–8.

Murray, J. A. H. (1892a). '"Couvade"—the Genesis of an Anthropological Term'. *The Academy*, 42: 389–90; 438; 458–60.

—— (1892b). '"Couvade"—the Genesis of a Modern Myth'. *The Academy*, 42: 567–8.

Murray, K. M. E. (1977). *Caught in the Web of Words: James A. H. Murray and the Oxford English Dictionary*. New Haven and London: Yale University Press.

Ogilvie, J. (1876). *The Imperial Dictionary, English, Technological, and Scientific*. London: Blackie & Son.

Raymond, D. R. (ed.) (1987). *Dispatches from the Front: The Prefaces to the Oxford English Dictionary*. Waterloo, Ontario: UW Centre for the New Oxford English Dictionary.

Richards, I. A. (1961). *Principles of Literary Criticism* (1924). London: Routledge & Kegan Paul.

Smith, L. Toulmin (1883). 'The Forthcoming English Dictionary'. *The Academy*, 23: 9–10.

—— (1883–9). Reviews of Robert Hunter's *Encyclopædic Dictionary*. *The Academy*, 24: 207–8; 28: 406–7; 35: 421–2.

'Student, A.' (1857). Letter to *The Athenaeum* (1 August): 976–7.

Trench, R. C. (1859). *A Select Glossary of English Words Used Formerly in Senses Different from their Present*. London: John W. Parker and Son.

—— (1860). *On Some Deficiencies in our English Dictionaries*. 2nd edn., revised and enlarged. London: John W. Parker and Son.

Trench, R. C., Furnivall, F. J., and Coleridge, H. (1857). 'Collections for a New Dictionary of the English Language.' *The Athenaeum* (25 July): 944.

[Trench, R. C., *et al.*]. (1860). *Canones Lexicographici; or Rules to be Observed in Editing the New English Dictionary of the Phililogical Society*. London: The Philological Society.

Tylor, E. B. (1892). '"Couvade"—The Genesis of an Anthropological Term'. *The Academy*, 42: 412; 542.

[Watts, T.]. (1861). Review of dictionaries by Webster and Worcester. *The Athenaeum* (13 July): 41.

Whitney, W. D. (ed.) (1889–91). *The Century Dictionary*. New York: The Century Co.

Appendix I: *OED* Sections and Parts

JENNY McMORRIS

Publication of the dictionary began with the appearance of parts at intervals of between one and two years. After eight of these had been published—*A–Ant, Ant–Batten, Batter–Boz, Bra–Cass* (also sold in two separate sections *Bra–Byz* and *C–Cass*), *Cast–Clivy, Clo–Consigner, Consignant–Crouching,* and *E–Every*— general dissatisfaction with the rate of publication persuaded the Press to issue more frequent portions in smaller instalments. This became the pattern of future publication; small sections, called at first 'fasciculi', each sixty-four pages in length, were issued quarterly and were then grouped in parts of about five sections and reissued. As an example of this procedure, the three sections *H–Haversian, Haversine–Heel,* and *Heel–Hod* were published separately and then later sold as a single part, *H–Hod,* published in December 1898 at the same time as the last section, *Heel–Hod.* Some double sections with 128 pages were published, such as *Speech–Spring,* and parts might begin in the middle of a double section, for example, *Splenetic–Stillatim.* Triple sections occasionally appeared, for example, *Prophesy–Pyxis.* Subscribers could buy the *OED* in sections, parts, or volumes and were able to return sections or parts for binding when the dictionary was finished. The term 'fascicle' is now used as a general word, referring both to sections and parts.

Dates marked B have been checked in the Oxford University Press Bulletins, first issued in Spring 1912, which give publication dates of all new Press books. All other dates are those given in the Historical Introduction to the *OED* which was published with the 1933 *Supplement.* Dates printed on the covers of most parts and sections are the dates of the quarters for which the parts were published. Considerable confusion about dates has often previously occurred because parts have been used for dating rather than sections, hence, for example, a reference to the section *F–Fang,* published in November 1894, will be dated September 1895 if the part, *Everybody–Field,* has been used for dating. Many extant sets of 'fascicles' are also mixed (including both sections and parts); when completion of a part would be clearly delayed, the earlier section may have been sent out, for example, *XYZ,* published more than six years before the part, *Wise–Wyzen* was issued.

Section	Date	Part
	January 1884	A–Ant
	November 1885	Ant–Batten
	March 1887	Batter–Boz
Bra–Byz	June 1888	
C–Cass	June 1888	Bra–Cass
	November 1889	Cast–Clivy
	October 1891	Clo–Consigner
	May 1893	Consignant–Crouching
Crouchmas–Czech	November 1893	
D–Deceit	November 1894	
Deceit–Deject	December 1894	
Deject–Depravation	July 1895	Crouchmas–Depravation
Depravative–Development	September 1895	
Development–Diffluency	December 1895	
Diffluent–Disburden	June 1896	
Disburdened–Disobservant	September 1896	
Disobstetricate–Distrustful	December 1896	Depravative–Distrustful
Distrustfully–Doom	March 1897	
Doom–Dziggetai	July 1897	Distrustfully–Dziggetai
	July 1891	E–Every
Everybody–Ezod	March 1894	
F–Fang	November 1894	
Fanged–Fee	April 1895	
Fee–Field	September 1895	Everybody–Field
Field–Fish	March 1896	
Fish–Flexuose	September 1896	
Flexuosity–Foister	March 1897	
Foisty–Frankish	October 1897	Field–Frankish
Frank-law–Gain-coming	January 1898	
Gaincope–Germanizing	October 1898	
Germano–Glass-cloth	March 1899	Frank-law–Glass-cloth
Glass-coach–Graded	January 1900	
Gradeley–Greement	July 1900	
Green–Gyzzarn	December 1900	Glass-coach–Gyzzarn
H–Haversian	March 1898	
Haversine–Heel	June 1898	
Heel–Hod	December 1898	H–Hod
Hod–Horizontal	March 1899	
Horizontality–Hywe	June 1899	Hod–Hywe
I–In	October 1899	
In–Inferred	March 1900	
Inferrible–Inpushing	July 1900	I–Inpushing

Section	Date	Part
Input–Invalid	October 1900	
Invalid–Jew	December 1900	
Jew–Kairine	June 1901	*Input–Kairine*
Kaiser–Kyx	October 1901	
L–Lap	March 1901	
Lap–Leisurely	January 1902	*Kaiser–Leisurely*
Leisureness–Lief	March 1902	
Lief–Lock (sb.)	January 1903	
Lock (v.)*–Lyyn*	October 1903	*Leisureness–Lyyn*
M–Mandragon	October 1904	
Mandragora–Matter	July 1905	
Matter–Mesnalty	March 1906	*M–Meet*
Mesne–Misbirth	December 1906	
Misbode–Monopoly	June 1907	*Meet–Monopoly*
Monopoly–Movement	March 1908	
Movement–Myz	September 1908	*Monopoly–Nywe*
N–Niche	September 1906	
Niche–Nywe	September 1907	
O–Onomastic	July 1902	
Onomastical–Outing	March 1903	
Outjet–Ozyat	January 1904	*O–Ozyat*
P–Pargeted	March 1904	
Pargeter–Pennached	December 1904	*P–Pennached*
Pennage–Pfennig	September 1905	
Ph–Piper	June 1906	
Piper- Polygenistic	March 1907	*Pennage–Plat*
Polygenous–Premious	December 1907	*Plat–Premious*
Premisal–Prophesier	December 1908	
Prophesy–Pyxis	September 1909	*Premisal–Pyxis*
Q	October 1902	
R–Reactive	July 1903	
Reactively–Ree	July 1904	*Q–Ree*
Ree–Reign	March 1905	
Reign–Reserve	January 1906	
Reserve–Ribaldously	June 1908	*Ree–Ribaldously*
Ribaldric–Romanite	March 1909	
Romanity–Roundness	December 1909	
Round-nosed–Ryze	March 1910	*Ribaldric–Ryze*
S–Sauce	June 1909	
Sauce-alone–Scouring	June 1910	
Scouring–Sedum	March 1911	*S–Sea-eel*

Section	Date	Part
See–Senatory	December 1911	
Senatory–Several	30 September 1912 B	
Several–Shaster	26 June 1913 B	
Shastri–Shyster	26 March 1914 B	*Sea-egg–Shyster*
Si–Simple	December 1910	
Simple–Sleep	September 1911	
Sleep–Sniggle	27 June 1912 B	*Si–Sniggle*
Sniggle–Sorrow	27 March 1913 B	
Sorrow–Speech	22 December 1913 B	
Speech–Spring	28 September 1914 B	*Sniggle–Splenetic*
Spring–Standard	25 March 1915 B	
Standard–Stead	30 September 1915 B	
Stead–Stillatim	29 June 1916 B	*Splenetic–Stillatim*
Stillation–Stratum	06 December 1917 B	
Stratus–Styx	04 September 1919 B	*Stillation–Styx*
Su–Subterraneous	22 December 1914 B	
Subterraneously–Sullen	21 December 1915 B	
Sullen–Supple	18 January 1917 B	
Supple–Sweep	21 March 1918 B	
Sweep–Szmikite	04 September 1919 B	*Su–Szmikite*
T–Tealt	September 1910	
Team–Tezkere	June 1911	
Th–Thyzle	29 March 1912 B	*T–Thyzle*
Ti–Tombac	23 December 1912 B	
Tombal–Trahysh	25 September 1913 B	
Traik–Trinity	24 June 1914 B	*Ti–Trinity*
Trink–Turn-down	24 June 1915 B	
Turndun–Tzirid	27 March 1916 B	
U–Unforeseeable	06 October 1921 B	*Trink–Unforeseeable*
Unforeseeing–Unright	31 July 1924 B	
Unright–Uzzle	29 July 1926 B	*Unforeseeing–Uzzle*
V–Verificative	26 October 1916 B	
Verificatory–Visor	30 August 1917 B	
Visor–Vywer	01 April 1920 B	*V*
W–Wash	06 October 1921 B	
Wash–Wavy	24 May 1923 B	
Wavy–Wezzon	12 August 1926 B	*W–Wezzon*
Wh–Whisking	17 May 1923 B	
Whisky–Wilfulness	27 November 1924 B	
Wilga–Wise	12 August 1926 B	*Wh–Wise*
Wise–Wyzen	19 April 1928 B	*Wise–Z*
XYZ	06 October 1921 B	

Appendix II: *OED* Personalia

Peter Gilliver

Individuals have been included in this Appendix on the basis of their having actively and directly made a contribution to the content or form of *OED* in the period up to and including publication of the first *Supplement* in 1933. Some of those listed appear because they contributed the ideas and principles from which *OED* eventually emerged; others because they literally created part of the final text, either by editorially shaping the material (like Murray and his assistants), or by making a significant contribution of quotations (like W. C. Minor), or by giving specialist advice (like Alexander Beazeley or Paul Meyer); others, while not actively engaged in editorial or related work, had responsibility for activities and projects without which the dictionary could not have come about. A fourth category, of figures whose impact on *OED* is more indirect, is not included: the compilers of the great dictionaries that *OED* drew on or compared itself with, and other scholars whose work was drawn on by the editors. There are, of course, many such known or likely influences, but rather than take a subjective decision about which of these were most significant, it has seemed simpler to include only those individuals for whom there is clear evidence that they *actively* contributed to the dictionary in some way.

Even when confined to the three categories mentioned, the list of potential names is still huge: for example, approximately 2,000 people are known to have provided quotations for *OED*, either by supplying examples of particular words in response to specific requests (hereafter 'desiderata') or by systematically reading and excerpting particular sources. Therefore only a small, and to some extent arbitrary, selection can be included; I have done my best to include those individuals whose contribution was most substantial, together with a selection of those whose contribution was less substantial but who are nevertheless of some interest.

Biographical resources for many of those listed are extremely scarce. A few individuals have been the subject of biographies in their own right, such as Furnivall (Benzie, W., *Dr F. J. Furnivall: Victorian Scholar Adventurer* (Norman, Okla.: Pilgrim Books, 1983)) and Minor (Winchester, S., *The Surgeon of Crowthorne* (London: Viking, 1998)); and of course many more are mentioned, sometimes at some length, in *CWW*. For many individuals, unless I was able to locate an obituary notice, the only readily available biographical information is that given in the Prefaces which were published with the individual fascicles and volumes of *OED* as they appeared (and which were republished in facsimile by Darrell Raymond in 1987 under the title *Dispatches from the Front*). My main published source, apart from these Prefaces, has been the *Dictionary of National Biography*. Where an individual appears in the *DNB* or its supplementary volumes I have marked the entry with an asterisk; in such cases, the reader is referred to the *DNB* for information beyond that given in the entry. I have also drawn on unpublished material in the archives of OUP and in the papers of the Murray family.

Amours, François (Francis) Joseph (1841–1910). Schoolmaster (at Glasgow Academy and Glasgow High School) and man of letters. Edited texts for the Scottish Text Society. Read and annotated *OED* proofs from C onwards; also contributed a collection of early instances of French loanwords in English.

Anderson, W. J. (*d.* 1900). Of Markinch, Fife. Reader for *OED*; subedited in M and P.

*Anson, William Reynell** (1843–1914). Jurist, and warden of All Souls College, Oxford. Acted as consultant to *OED* on many legal terms.

Apperson, George Latimer (1857–1937). School inspector and man of letters; editor of the *Antiquary* 1899–1915. Reader for *OED* (credited with 11,000 quotations in 1888); subedited in B and C; later drew heavily on *OED* in compiling his historical dictionary *English Proverbs and Proverbial Phrases* (1929); also produced *A Jane Austen Dictionary* (1932).

*Arber, Edward** (1836–1912). English scholar; professor of English language and literature at Birmingham from 1881 (professor emeritus 1894). Edited many early modern texts for publication or reprinting. Friend of Murray, whom he supplied with copies of his 'English Reprints' series for reading, and with whom he corresponded on many specific points.

Austin, Thomas, jun. Of Oxford, Hornsey, and elsewhere. Possibly the most prolific contributor of quotations to *OED* (already credited with 165,000 in 1888), both as a reader and as a supplier of desiderata. Subsequently prepared glossaries to several EETS texts for Furnivall, and edited *Two Fifteenth-Century Cookery Books* (1888) for publication.

Balk, Charles Godfrey (1857–1915). Member of Murray's editorial staff 1885–1913. Also wrote a meditation on the meaning of life, posthumously published as *Life is Growth* (1922).

Bartlett, James (*d.* 1908). Of Bramley, near Guildford. Subedited in G, M, O, R, and S.

Bayliss, Henry James (*b.* 1868). Son of an Oxford gardener. Joined the staff of the Bodleian Library in Oxford in 1884; member of Bradley's, and later Craigie's, editorial staff, 1891–1932 (including work on the 1933 *Supplement*).

Beazeley, Alexander (1830–1905). Civil engineer, involved especially in lighthouse construction; librarian of the Royal Institute of British Architects. 'A devoted friend of the Dictionary from its very commencement' (according to Murray in his 1907 Preface to the section *Pennage–Plat*); read for *OED* (ultimately credited with more than 30,000 quotations), and contributed many desiderata; consulted on terms in architecture, engineering, and associated subjects.

Beckett, William Henry (*d.* 1901). Minister of the Congregational Church of Stebbing, near Chelmsford, and writer on the English Reformation. Reader for *OED*; subedited in W.

Birt, John Wixon (*b.* 1890). Joined Onions's editorial staff in 1906, and continued (with a gap for war service 1914–19) until 1933, including work on the *Supplement*. Assisted Onions with various other lexicographical projects, including the *Shorter Oxford English Dictionary*.

Bousfield, George Benjamin Richings (1824/5–97). Clergyman; curate of Carleton Rode, Norfolk, 1847–52, and of Swaffham 1852–3. Reader for *OED* (credited with 10,000 quotations in 1888); subedited in F, G, R, and W; also read proofs.

Brackebusch, W. Schoolmaster (of the High School for Boys, Finchley Road, London). Subedited in B.

Bradley, Eleanor S. Daughter of Henry Bradley. Member of Bradley's, and later Onions's editorial staff, 1897–1932 (including work on the 1933 *Supplement*).

*Bradley, Henry** (1845–1923). After twenty years working as a clerk to a Sheffield cutlery firm, during which he acquired a knowledge of many languages through private study, he was appointed in 1886 to assist Murray with the letter B, having demonstrated his considerable philological acumen in a review of *OED*'s first fascicle (in the *Academy* in 1884); became second editor in 1888 (initially working from London, but moving to Oxford in 1896), with overall responsibility for E–G, L–M, and parts of S and W; senior editor following Murray's death in 1915. Also prepared a revised edition of Stratmann's *Middle English Dictionary* (published by OUP in 1891). President of the Philological Society 1890–3, 1900–3, and 1909–10.

Brandreth, Edward Lyall (1823–1907). Barrister. Joined the Philological Society in 1872, and regularly served on its Council. Subedited in G, H, K, and N; also read for *OED*, supplied many quotation desiderata, and assisted for many years by reading proofs and by verifying references at the British Museum.

Britten, James (1846–1924). Botanist, working first at Kew and later in the British Museum, where he was Senior Assistant when he retired in 1909; co-author (with Robert Holland) of *A Dictionary of English Plant-Names* (1886). Consulted as an authority on botanical terms; also contributed quotations, and did some subediting in P.

Brown, Janet E. A. (*d.* 1907). Of Further Barton, Cirencester; published some religious writings, including a collection of sonnets *Thoughts through the Year* (1873). Reader for *OED*, and from 1882 one of its most indefatigable subeditors, working on B, C, D, I, and P; close friend of Murray.

Brown, Joseph. Schoolmaster at Kendal Grammar School. The longest-serving of Furnivall's original subeditors; he worked on *OED* for over fifty years from 1860, subediting in M, S, and U.

Browne, Walter Raleigh (1842–84). Civil engineer, and writer on mechanics; also one of the founders of the Society for Psychical Research in 1882. Subedited in S. His wife Effie also read for *OED*.

***Brushfield, Thomas Nadauld** (1828–1910). Physician (a pioneer of humane methods of treating the insane) and antiquarian. A prolific contributor of quotations to *OED* (credited with 50,000 in 1888), including many desiderata.

Bumby, Frederic Edward (1859/60–1918). Member of Murray's editorial staff 1885–7; also did some subediting in N; later read and annotated proofs. From 1897 taught at University College, Nottingham.

***Bywater, Ingram** (1840–1914). Greek scholar; regius professor of Greek at Oxford 1893–1908. Delegate of the OUP from 1879 until his death; was associated with *OED* for longer than any other Delegate. Member (with York Powell) of a subcommittee appointed in 1896 by the Delegates which considered the issue of the scale of *OED* as compared to Webster's Dictionary; supplied information on particular words for many years.

Caland, A. (*c.*1854/5–1910). Dutch schoolmaster; from 1893 *Leerar* of English in the State High School and Royal Agricultural College, Wageningen. Reader for *OED*; read proofs from G onwards; also verified quotations, and supplied many desiderata. Became a close friend of Murray who, like him, was a keen philatelist.

Carline, George Reginald (*b.* 1885). Member of Bradley's editorial staff *c.*1908–1914; later read and annotated proofs; assistant curator at museums in London and Oxford, 1914–25, and thereafter Keeper of the Halifax County Borough Museums.

***Chapman, Robert William** (1881–1960). Secretary to the Delegates of the OUP 1920–42; made many small contributions to the dictionary and 1933 *Supplement*. Also an authority on, and editor of, Johnson and Jane Austen, and a writer on lexicographical matters, including some tracts for the Society for Pure English.

Chester, Albert Huntington (1843–1903). American chemist and mineralogist; consulted as an authority on mineralogical terms; later went on to compile *A Dictionary of Names of Minerals* (1896).

***Coleridge, Derwent** (1800–83). Divine, educationist, and linguist. Son of Samuel Taylor Coleridge the poet. Took a keen interest in the Philological Society's plans for *OED*; spoke in favour of generous inclusion of dialect, and of a regulative function for the dictionary, in a paper given to the Society in 1860.

***Coleridge, Herbert** (1830–61). Grandson of Samuel Coleridge; his mother Sara was Derwent Coleridge's sister, and his father was also a nephew of the poet. Appointed in 1857 to the Philological Society's 'Unregistered Words' Committee; in 1859 was appointed editor of the Society's proposed dictionary, and drafted the 'Canones Lexicographici' (closely following the principles of Trench's papers 'On Some Deficiencies'), a revised version of which was published in 1860; this became the basis, albeit with modifications, of *OED*'s editorial policy, although

Coleridge himself died from consumption before he had prepared more than a few entries.

*Craigie, William Alexander (1867–1957). Philologist. Studied classics and philosophy at St Andrews, and Icelandic, Scandinavian, Celtic, and Germanic languages at Oxford; held a succession of professorial posts in Latin, Scandinavian languages, and Anglo-Saxon at St Andrews and Oxford; published widely on Scottish language and literature and Icelandic; in 1897 was invited to join Bradley's staff working on *OED*; became third editor in 1901, with overall responsibility for N, Q, R, U, V, and parts of S and W, and co-edited (with Onions) the 1933 *Supplement*. In 1919 he proposed to the Philological Society a series of dictionaries treating the English of particular periods and regions according to the same principles as *OED* but in greater depth, two of which (the *Dictionary of the Older Scottish Tongue* (1931–) and the *Dictionary of American English* (1936–44)) he worked on simultaneously with *OED*; accepted an English Chair at Chicago University in 1925 as an American base for his editorship of the *Dictionary of American English*; edited the Supplement to the second edition (1957) of Cleasby and Vigfusson's *Icelandic–English Dictionary*. His wife Jessie (*d.* 1947) also worked on the arrangement of U in 1917–18.

Davies, Thomas Lewis Owen (*b.* 1833/4). Clergyman; vicar of St Mary extra Southampton from 1860. Author of *Bible English* (1875) and *A Supplementary English Glossary* (1881); placed quotations from the latter, and further quotations collected by him, at the disposal of *OED*; also gave advice on particular words.

Dawson, Benjamin. Philologist and man of letters. Joined the Philological Society in 1867, and served as its Treasurer for many years. Reader for *OED*; took on some of the unfinished reading left by Fitzedward Hall and W. C. Minor. Also published *A Terminational Dictionary of Latin Substantives* (1850).

Dixon, James (1813–96). Ophthalmic surgeon; author of *Diseases of the Eye* (1855). In 1870, because of his wife's illness, he gave up his London practice and retired to Dorking, Surrey, taking up literary and historical interests. Contributed quotations to *OED*, including many desiderata; in the help he gave with the history of medical terms he was second only to William Sykes (q.v.), according to Murray's affectionate obituary in *Notes and Queries*.

Dormer, John. Of London, Horsham, Eastbourne, and elsewhere. Subedited or arranged material in C, D, and S; contributed many quotations for scientific terms; also compiled many of the 'Lists of Special Wants', which listed words for which earlier or later quotations were wanted. In 1907 was apparently institutionalized because of mental illness.

Douglas, William. Of London. One of the most productive readers for *OED*; credited with 136,000 quotations in 1888, including many from biological and medical texts but also much from Dickens, Lytton, and other contemporary novelists.

***Dowden, Edward** (1843–1913). Critic. Reader for *OED*; also alphabetized the materials for O prior to subediting, and gave advice on specific points.

***Ellis, Alexander John** (1814–90). Philologist and mathematician. Met Murray in 1868 and became a close friend. President of the Philological Society in 1872–4 and 1880–2; was in the chair, and spoke in favour, at the meeting in 1879 when the Society resolved to accept the proposed agreement with the OUP to publish *OED*. Continued to provide advice on phonological matters.

***Ellis, Robinson** (1834–1913). Classical scholar, perhaps best known for his edition of Catullus. Close friend of Murray, whom he often accompanied on holidays abroad; regularly consulted for advice on particular words; also read for *OED*.

***Elworthy, Frederick (Fred) Thomas** (1830–1907). Philologist and antiquarian. Wrote extensively on Somerset and Devon, including *The West Somerset Word-Book* (1886). Close friend of Murray. He and his family read for *OED* (credited with 10,000 quotations in 1888); he also subedited part of D.

Erlebach, Alfred (*d.* 1899). Schoolmaster; sometime assistant master at Mill Hill. Reader for *OED*; subedited part of A; engaged by Murray in 1881 to work with him in the Scriptorium; left in 1885 to become joint principal (with his brother) of Woodford House School in Kent, but remained deeply interested in the dictionary until his death, reading and revising proofs for Murray and Bradley, and sometimes returning to the Scriptorium to deputize for Murray.

***Evans, Daniel Silvan** (1818–1903). Welsh scholar; compiler of *An English and Welsh Dictionary* (1852–8) and an incomplete *Dictionary of the Welsh Language* (A–E, 1887–1906). Advised *OED* on many points of Welsh philology.

Fayers, Arthur P. Clergyman of Rawdon, near Leeds. Subedited in B and N.

Fennell, Charles Augustus Maude (1843–1916). Classicist and lexicographer; editor of the *Stanford Dictionary of Anglicised Words and Phrases* (1892), for which reading was carried out on a basis similar to that for *OED*, and by many of the same readers. Wrote an important (anonymous) early review of *OED*. Made some of his quotations available to *OED*, and gave advice on specific points.

Fowler, Joseph Thomas (1833–1924). Surgeon, divine, antiquarian, and naturalist; vice-principal of Bishop Hatfield's Hall, Durham, 1870–1917; Hebrew lecturer at Durham University; honorary canon of Durham Cathedral from 1897. Edited several texts for the Surtees Society. Reader for *OED*; supplied many desiderata; read and revised proofs from C onwards.

Friedrichsen, George Washington Salisbury. Member of Murray's editorial staff 1909–14; later read and annotated proofs. Went on to assist Onions in the compilation of the *Oxford Dictionary of English Etymology* (1966), which he saw through to publication after Onions's death (in collaboration with Robert Burchfield, editor of the 4-volume *Supplement* (1972–86)), and revised the etymologies in the third edition of the *Shorter Oxford English Dictionary*.

***Furnivall, Frederick James** (1825–1910). Scholar and editor. Read mathematics at Cambridge and studied law at Lincoln's Inn; joined the Philological Society in 1847, and was its sole Secretary from 1862 until his death; appointed in 1857 to the Society's 'Unregistered Words' Committee; took over the editorship of *OED* in 1861 on the death of Coleridge, in which capacity he organized the work of readers and subeditors; his energies became increasingly diverted from work on *OED* by other literary activities, including the founding of the EETS (1864), the Chaucer Society (1868), the New Shakspere Society (1873), and numerous other literary societies, and the editing of many texts for publication by these societies; nevertheless remained actively involved with the dictionary until his death, as an advocate of the project, as a constant source of advice, by research in the British Museum, and as a tireless contributor of quotations (already credited with 'about 30,000' in 1888), including a great many taken from his ordinary daily reading of newspapers and magazines.

Gee, W. Of Boston, Lincolnshire. Subedited in B (his list of headwords for B was printed as a pamphlet in 1863).

Gell, Philip Lyttelton (1852–1926). Secretary to the Delegates of the OUP 1884–98, during which time he appointed Henry Bradley to assist Murray; constantly sought to improve the rate of production.

Gerrans, Henry Tresawna (1858–1921). Mathematician; vice-provost of Worcester College, Oxford. Gave advice on mathematical words. Was also briefly appointed to act as Secretary to the Delegates of the OUP when Gell fell ill in 1897.

***Gibbs, Henry Hucks, first Baron Aldenham** (1819–1907). Businessman (director of the Bank of England 1853–1901; Governor 1875–7) and man of letters. Joined the Philological Society in 1859, and remained closely involved with *OED* for the rest of his life; became a close friend of Murray, whom he advised and helped in respect of both editorial and practical aspects of the work. Reader for *OED*; subedited in C, K, and Q; read and annotated the proofs of the first fascicle, and continued to help in this way for many years; consulted as an authority on financial terms. Also edited texts for the EETS and other societies.

Gray, Charles. Physician, of Wimbledon. Prolific reader for *OED* (credited with 29,000 quotations in 1888); did research on quotations at the British Museum from 1879; supplied further quotation desiderata, and many eighteenth-century examples of function words; subedited in S; gave help on specific points, particularly in relation to military and naval terms. His wife also read for *OED*.

Green, Robert Frederick. Of Liverpool. Subedited in N. Also wrote books on chess and whist.

Gregor, Walter (1825–97). Clergyman and Scots scholar; minister of Pitsligo, Banffshire, from 1863 until his death. Wrote on Scottish matters, including *The Dialect of Banffshire* (1866), and edited texts for the Scottish Text Society. Subedited in J; also read for *OED*.

Gunthorpe, Edward. Of Sheffield. Subedited in A and B; later worked as Bradley's assistant, verifying quotations in the British Museum.

Haig, Margaret (later Mrs Alexander Stuart). Of Blairhill, Perthshire, later of Edinburgh. Reader for *OED*; subedited in O.

Hailstone, Arthur. Of Cheetham Hill, Manchester. Subedited in C and N; also read for *OED*, and supplied quotation desiderata.

*****Hall, Fitzedward** (1825–1901). Sanskrit scholar and philologist. Born and educated in America (originally as an engineer), he studied Indian languages in India after being shipwrecked there in 1846; professor of Sanskrit at Benares Government College from 1853, and at King's College, London from 1862; edited many Sanskrit and Hindi texts for publication. Also showed an interest in English philology from an early age, and published widely in the field, including *Modern English* (1873). Largely withdrew from public life after being the subject of various accusations, beginning in 1869 with his expulsion from the Philological Society; was, however, persuaded by Skeat to assist with *OED*, and became one of Murray's closest friends and advisers (although the two men never met) and one of the most important contributors to the dictionary, devoting over four hours every day from 1881 until his death to 'the critical examination of the proof-sheets and the filling up of deficiencies whether in the vocabulary or the quotations: there is scarcely a page which he has not thus enriched by his contributions' (according to Murray in his 1887 Preface to Part III; his services are acknowledged in similar terms in many later Prefaces).

Hallam, Thomas (1819–95). Phonetician. Active linguistic fieldworker on behalf of Alexander Ellis and Murray, and writer on dialect and educated speech. Consulted by Murray during preparatory work on phonetic notation for *OED*.

*****Harraden, Beatrice** (1864–1936), novelist (author of the bestselling *Ships that Pass in the Night*, 1893) and suffragette. Friend of Furnivall, who arranged for her to visit the offices of the dictionary; she subsequently wrote a novel, *The Scholar's Daughter* (1906), whose principal characters are at work on or connected with 'a dictionary which was to be the abiding pride of the Anglo-Saxon race'.

Hart, Henry Chichester (1847–1908). Shakespeare scholar. Read and annotated *OED* proofs, supplying many additional quotations from sixteenth- and seventeenth-century dramatists. Also wrote on the dialect and flora of County Donegal.

*****Hazlitt, William Carew** (1834–1913). Bibliographer; author of a *Hand-Book to the Popular Poetical and Dramatic Literature of Great Britain* (1867). Prepared editions of many early modern English texts, and also compiled a book of English proverbs (1869). Reader for *OED*.

Helwich, Hartwig Richard (*d.* 1900). Philologist of Vienna. Prolific reader for *OED*; credited with 50,000 quotations in 1888, including the bulk of the quotations taken from the most frequently cited work in the dictionary, the medieval poem *Cursor Mundi*. Also gave advice on specific points.

Henderson, Thomas (*b.* 1852). Headmaster of Bedford County School 1881–1900. A prolific contributor of quotations to *OED* (credited with 48,000 in 1888), including many desiderata; also subedited in B and C.

Herrtage, Sidney John Hervon. English scholar; edited several texts for the EETS, including the late fifteenth-century glossary *Catholicon Anglicum* (published 1881), and for the English Dialect Society. Reader for *OED*; appointed by Murray as his first assistant in the Scriptorium in 1879, but was dismissed in 1882 for stealing. Subsequently prepared many of the entries in Robert Hunter's *Encyclopaedic Dictionary* (1879–88).

Heslop, Richard Oliver (1842–1916). Of Corbridge, Northumberland; iron and steel merchant and antiquarian. Published several works on Northumberland dialect, including an important glossary (1892). Supplied quotations; gave advice to *OED* on dialect words, and also on terms in mining and engineering.

Hulme, Edward Charles (1821/2–1900). Of South Kensington. 'One of the best workers for the Dictionary' (according to Murray's 1885 Preface to Part II); subedited in C and L; also read for *OED*. His son Edward Wyndham Hulme, librarian of the Patent Office, also supplied information on specific points.

Humphreys, Jennett. Writer of books for children. Prolific reader for *OED* (credited with 18,700 quotations in 1888); also wrote a lengthy article on the dictionary for *Fraser's Magazine* in 1882, and continued to send in quotations and information on particular words, in some cases relating to her collection of materials for a book on early cookery (never published).

Jackson, Benjamin Daydon (1846–1927). Botanist; secretary of the Linnean Society for many years. Compiler of the *Index Kewensis* (published 1892–5 after ten years of preparation), and author of a *Glossary of Botanic Terms* (1900). Gave advice on botanical terms.

Jackson, E. S. Of Plymouth. Reader for *OED* (credited with 10,000 quotations in 1888); helped to replace the quotations for *Pa-* after the original materials were largely lost.

Jacob, Philip Whittington (1805–89). Alderman (later mayor) of Guildford, and author of *Hindoo Tales* (1873), a translation from Sanskrit. Subedited in D, E, P, Q, R, and S (including the famously large entry for *Set*); also read for *OED*.

Jenkinson, Wilberforce W. Of London. Reader for *OED*; also verified quotations in the British Museum, and read proofs.

Johnston, James Brown (1862–1953). Minister of Falkirk Free Church 1888–1928. Author of many works on place-names, including *Place-Names of Scotland* (1892) and *The Place-Names of England and Wales* (1915). Reader for *OED*; after a brief period in the Scriptorium as Murray's assistant in 1883, continued to help by reading and annotating proofs until 1927; joined the staff of the *Scottish National Dictionary* in 1931.

*Jowett, Benjamin (1817–93). Classicist and educationist; regius professor of Greek at Oxford from 1855 until his death, and master of Balliol College from 1870. While Vice-Chancellor of the University (1882–6) he took a particular interest in the OUP; in 1883, after studying the proofs of the first fascicle of *OED*, he suggested a number of changes in editorial policy which brought him into conflict with Murray; later, however, he became a close friend of Murray, who was made an honorary fellow of Balliol in 1885 and who even christened one of his sons Jowett. Supplied advice on specific words.

*Key, Thomas Hewitt (1799–1875). Latin scholar; professor of Latin at London University 1828–42, and headmaster of University College School 1832–75 (jointly until 1842). Founder member of the Philological Society, and its joint secretary (with Furnivall) 1853–62; member of the Committee set up by the Society in 1859 to formulate *OED*'s editorial policy. His (incomplete) *Latin–English Dictionary* was published in 1888.

Kluge, Friedrich (1856–1926). Germanic philologist; *Ordinarius* in German language and literature at Freiburg from 1893. Compiler of the important *Etymologisches Wörterbuch der Deutschen Sprache* (1883); also published widely on English and Anglo-Saxon. Gave etymological advice on particular words.

*Laughton, John Knox (1830–1915). Naval historian; professor of history at King's College, London, 1885–1914. Gave advice on nautical and naval terms; also read for *OED*.

Lecky, James (1855–90). Phonetician. Offered advice on phonetic notation to Murray during preparatory work for *OED*; continued to correspond about particular words, and also did some reading.

Lees, William (1827–94). Rector of Sidlow Bridge, Surrey, 1861–94. Prolific contributor of quotations for *OED* (credited with 18,500 in 1888), including many desiderata.

Lewis, Wilfrid James (*b*. 1868). Son of an Oxford college servant. Member of Bradley's, and later Onions's editorial staff, 1889–1933 (including work on the 1933 *Supplement*). Also compiled a historical dictionary of cricket (*The Language of Cricket*, 1934).

*Liddell, Henry George (1811–98). Greek scholar and lexicographer; dean of Christ Church, Oxford, 1855–91. With Robert Scott he published *A Greek–English Lexicon* (1843), which was originally based on a Greek–German dictionary by Franz Passow and which familiarized English readers with Passow's historical approach to lexicography, an approach closely followed by Trench in his papers 'On Some Deficiencies' and hence having considerable influence on *OED*. As a Delegate of the OUP he took an interest in *OED*, and was a member (with Max Müller and Mark Pattison) of the literary committee set up at Murray's request in 1879; collaborated with Jowett in studying Murray's proofs in 1883.

Lloyd, Richard John (*d. c.*1906). Phonetician; sometime honorary reader in phonetics at University College, Liverpool. Reader for *OED*; subedited in H. Also wrote a book on Northern English (1899).

*Love, Augustus Edward Hough** (1863–1940). Mathematician and geophysicist; Sedleian professor of natural philosophy at Oxford from 1898 until his death. Gave help on specific points, particularly in relation to mathematical and physical terms.

Löwenberg, William Joseph (*d.* 1899). Rector of Bury, Lancashire. Subedited in O and P; also read for *OED*, and supplied quotation desiderata.

Lyall, A. Of Manchester. Reader for *OED*; subedited in T; also supplied quotation desiderata.

Madan, Falconer (1851–1935). Librarian and palaeographer; Bodley's Librarian 1912–19 (Sub-Librarian 1880–1912). Published widely on bibliographical and literary matters, including a history of the OUP (1908). Read many seventeenth-century texts for *OED*, and gave help on other specific points.

*Maitland, Frederic William** (1850–1906). Jurist and legal historian. Gave advice on many legal and historical terms.

Maling, Arthur Thomas (*b.* 1858). Member of Murray's, and later Onions's editorial staff, 1886–1927 (including work on the *Supplement*). Was also a keen Esperantist.

March, Francis Andrew (1825–1911). Philologist; professor of English Language and Comparative Philology at Lafayette College, Pennsylvania (the first chair of its kind in the United States), from 1857. Published an important *Comparative Grammar of the Anglo-Saxon Language* in 1870. From 1879 co-ordinated the work of American readers for the dictionary. Later collaborated with Isaac Funk on his *Standard Dictionary* of 1895, whose definitions were occasionally made use of by *OED* in the same way, though less frequently, as those of the *Century Dictionary* (regarding which *see* Whitney, William Dwight).

*Margoliouth, David Samuel** (1858–1940). Orientalist; Laudian professor of Arabic at Oxford 1889–1937. Gave advice on points of Semitic philology.

Marsh, George Perkins (1801–82). Diplomat and man of letters; United States minister to Turkey, 1849–54, and to Italy from 1861 until his death. Published books in a wide range of fields, including the popular *Lectures on the English Language* (1860), the important ecological text *Man and Nature* (1864), a grammar of Icelandic, and a treatise on the camel. Responsible for co-ordinating the American component of the early phase (from 1859) of reading for *OED*, before this task was taken over by Francis March.

*Martineau, Russell** (1831–98). Orientalist; assistant keeper of the British Museum Library 1884–96. Nephew of the writer Harriet Martineau, who was an early supporter of *OED*. Member of Philological Society from 1867. Read and annotated proofs; gave advice on specific points.

Matthews, Albert (1860–1946). Massachusetts historian. Reader for *OED* (credited with 28,000 quotations in 1897); investigated the history of many American words and meanings (publishing many of his findings in *Notes and Queries*).

*Max Müller, Friedrich (1823–1900). Orientalist and philologist; Taylorian professor of modern European languages at Oxford 1854–68, and professor of comparative philology (first occupant of the chair) from 1868 until his death. His popular lectures at the Royal Institution in 1861 and 1863 were later published as *The Science of Language*. As a Delegate of the OUP, he was closely involved in negotiations with Murray in 1877; subsequently gave advice on specific points.

Mayhew, Anthony Lawson (1842–1916). Philologist; chaplain of Wadham College, 1880–1912. Close friend of the diarist Francis Kilvert. Reader for *OED*; also gave etymological advice on particular words. Published various glossaries, including an edition of *Promptorium Parvulorum* for the EETS; collaborated with Skeat on *A Concise Dictionary of Middle English* (1888), and contributed to his *Etymological Dictionary*; also prepared his *A Glossary of Tudor and Stuart Words* for posthumous publication (1914).

Meyer, Marie-Paul-Hyacinthe (1840–1917). French palaeographer (who was called upon to examine documents in connection with the Dreyfus affair in 1898) and Romance philologist; member of the Institut de France. Published widely on medieval French. Principal adviser to *OED* on matters of Romance philology; read proofs and supplied comprehensive notes, especially of an etymological nature.

Minor, William Chester (1834–1920). American surgeon and soldier; served with the Union forces during the Civil War. Acquired lexicographical experience by contributing to the 1864 edition of Webster's dictionary (working with James D. Dana on the vocabulary of geology and natural history). Suffered from a form of schizophrenia, which led to his killing a man while on a visit to England in 1872; was consigned to Broadmoor for life; became one of the most valued contributors of quotations to *OED*, concentrating on the sixteenth and seventeenth centuries and lending many rare books of his own; kept in close touch with Murray (who became a friend and sometimes visited him) and Bradley so as to be able to look out specifically for words currently being worked on; by 1902 obliged by failing health to cut back on his work; in 1910 was permitted to return to America, where he remained in custody until his death.

Mitchell, John (*c.*1858/9–1894). A valued member of Murray's editorial staff from 1883; also read and commented on Bradley's proofs. His death in a climbing accident affected his colleagues deeply: Murray wrote of their 'unspeakable grief' in his 1895 Preface to the section *D–Depravation*.

*Morfill, William Richard (1834–1909). Slavonic scholar; professor of Russian and Slavonic languages at Oxford from 1900. Gave advice on points of Slavonic philology.

Morris, Edward Ellis (1843–1902). Headmaster of Melbourne Church of England Grammar School 1875–82; professor of modern languages and literature at Melbourne from 1884. Compiled a dictionary of Australian words, *Austral English* (1898); made duplicates of the quotations he collected for this work available to *OED*.

*****Morris, Richard** (1833–94). English scholar and philologist. Close friend of Furnivall; published widely on English and Pali. In 1876, while President of the Philological Society, approached the publisher Alexander Macmillan about the possibility of publishing the Society's dictionary, and suggested Murray as editor; also read for *OED*.

Morris, Rupert Hugh (1844–1918). Schoolmaster (headmaster of Godolphin School, Hammersmith, 1876–84), clergyman (vicar of St Gabriel's, Pimlico, from 1894), and antiquarian. Author of several works on the history of Chester. Subedited in I, and gave advice on particular words.

Moule, Horatio (Horace) Mosley (1832–73). Classical scholar and close friend of Thomas Hardy. Did some subediting in H; also read for *OED*.

Mount, Charles Bridges (*b.* 1827). Clergyman; rector of Heyford Warren, Oxfordshire, 1865–78. Reader for *OED* (credited with 10,000 quotations in 1888); subedited in A–D, J, P, and V; also researched many specific points in the Bodleian Library and elsewhere, and read proofs.

*****Murray, James Augustus Henry** (1837–1915). Principal editor of *OED* from 1879 until his death. Studied for an external B.A. from London University, but did not take any formal philological qualification; spent some years as a schoolmaster (he was on the staff of Mill Hill School, 1870–85) and bank clerk; joined the Philological Society in 1868 (president 1878–80, 1882–4, and 1907–9); edited many texts for the EETS; published *The Dialect of the Southern Counties of Scotland* in 1873. Originally approached by Macmillan about the possibility of editing their proposed new dictionary; subsequently the Philological Society turned to the OUP and Murray's name was again put forward. Edited those volumes of the *OED* containing the letters A–D, H–K, O, P, and T.

Murray's eleven children all assisted their father in his work on the dictionary, if only by sorting quotation slips; the most substantial contributions were made by Hilda (1875–1951), Elsie (1882–1952) (later Mrs R. A. Barling), and Rosfrith (1884–1973), who all worked on the editorial staff as Assistants (for over twenty years in the case of Elsie and Rosfrith), and by Harold (1868–1955), who was a prolific reader for the dictionary (credited with 27,000 quotations by 1888), and was consulted as an authority on chess terms. Hilda also revised her father's article on the English Language for the 1910 edition of the *Encyclopaedia Britannica*. *See also* Ruthven, Ada Agnes.

Napier, Arthur Sampson (1853–1916). Philologist; Merton professor of English language and literature at Oxford from 1885, and later also Rawlinsonian professor of Anglo-Saxon. Gave advice on many points of Germanic philology.

*Newton, Alfred (1829–1907). Zoologist; professor of zoology and comparative anatomy at Cambridge from 1866 until his death. Published widely on ornithology, including *A Dictionary of Birds* (1893–6). Consulted as an authority on bird names.

*Nicholson, Edward Williams Byron (1849–1912). Bodley's librarian 1882–1912. He and his successors, Falconer Madan (q.v.) and Arthur Cowley, co-operated with *OED* by allowing staff to research in the Bodleian Library, as well as by supplying information themselves on particular points.

Nicol, Henry (*c.*1845–80). Philologist, specializing in French phonology. Cousin of Sweet. Persuaded in 1871 by Furnivall to undertake the editorship of *OED*, but prevented by ill-health and other projects from taking up work.

*Onions, Charles Talbut (1873–1965). Grammarian and lexicographer. In 1895, while in his final year at Mason College, Birmingham, he was introduced by Edward Arber to Murray, who invited him to join his staff; between 1906 and 1913 he also worked under Bradley and Craigie, with special responsibility for parts of M, N, R, and S, and in 1914 he became fourth editor, with overall responsibility for parts of S and W and for X–Z (and was thus responsible for 'the last word', *Zyxt*, although the last fascicle to be published was *Wise–Wyzen* in 1928); also co-edited (with Craigie) the 1933 *Supplement*. His editorship was interrupted in 1918 by military service in naval intelligence. Also took over the editorship of the *Shorter Oxford English Dictionary* from William Little on the latter's death in 1922 (first published 1933; 3rd edn. 1944) and edited the *Oxford Dictionary of English Etymology* (published posthumously, 1966; *see also* Friedrichsen, George Washington Salisbury); published many other books and articles on lexicographical and grammatical matters, including *An Advanced English Syntax* (1904) and *A Shakespeare Glossary* (1911).

Peacock, Edward (1831–1915). Antiquarian; published widely on local history, archaeology, and dialect, including a glossary of Lincolnshire dialect and many articles in *Notes and Queries*; also wrote several novels. Reader for *OED*; also supplied many quotation desiderata, and gave help on other specific points.

Peto, John (*d.* 1892). Of London. Subedited in C, F, and H; also read for *OED*.

Pierson, Job (*b.* 1824). Presbyterian minister of Ionia, Michigan; librarian of Alma College, Michigan. Prolific reader for *OED* (credited with 46,000 quotations in 1888).

Platt, James (1861–1910). Linguist. Showed an extraordinary facility with languages from an early age; a prolific contributor of articles to the *Athenaeum* and *Notes and Queries*; also wrote fiction (his *Tales of the Supernatural* were published in 1894). Corresponded occasionally with Murray at least from 1882, but from 1899 became *OED*'s most important consultant on the more obscure languages of Africa, America, and Asia.

*Platts, John Thompson (1830–1904). Persian scholar and lexicographer; compiler of a *Hindustani–English Dictionary* (1881). Regularly gave advice to *OED* on the etymology of words of Persian and Indian origin.

***Pollock, Frederick** (1845–1937). Jurist; author of several classic law textbooks. Gave advice on a great many specific points, particularly in relation to legal terms.

Potts, C. Y. Clergyman, of Ledbury. Subedited in L; also read for *OED*.

***Powell, Frederick York** (1850–1904). Historian and Icelandic scholar; regius professor of modern history at Oxford, 1894–1904. Published widely on history and Scandinavian literature. Member (with Ingram Bywater) of a subcommittee appointed in 1896 by the Delegates which considered the issue of the scale of *OED* as compared to Webster's Dictionary; was instrumental in the appointment of Craigie as third Editor. Gave advice on specific historical matters.

***Powell, Lawrenceson (Lawrence) Fitzroy** (1881–1975). Literary scholar and librarian. Despite having no academic qualifications, was taken on as a boy helper in the library of Brasenose College, Oxford; joined the staff of the Bodleian Library in 1895. Joined Craigie's editorial staff in 1901. Left in 1921 to take up the librarianship of the Taylorian Institution; became an authority on Boswell and Johnson. *See also* Steane, Ethelwyn Rebecca.

Poynter, H. May. Of Oxford. Reader for *OED* (taking on some of the unfinished reading left by Fitzedward Hall and W. C. Minor); she also helped in other ways, including the arrangement of materials into alphabetical order. Also wrote a romantic novel, *Madamscourt* (1902), and other fiction.

***Price, Bartholomew** (1818–98). Mathematician; Sedleian professor of natural philosophy at Oxford, 1853–98, and master of Pembroke College, Oxford, 1891–8. Secretary to the Delegates of the OUP 1868–84, during which time he negotiated the terms of the Press's agreements with Murray and the Philological Society regarding *OED*.

Price, Hereward Thimbleby (1880–1964). Philologist and English scholar. Member of Murray's editorial staff 1896–1904; subsequently studied at Bonn University; became a German citizen after marrying a German in 1911; conscripted into the German army in 1915; recounted his war experiences, including capture by the Russians, imprisonment in Siberia, and escape to China, in his memoir *Boche and Bolshevik* (1919). Appointed to an English professorship at the University of Michigan in 1929, and published widely on Shakespeare; also served as Associate Editor of the *Dictionary of Early Modern English* (one of the series of dictionaries proposed by Craigie (q.v.), which however was abandoned before much had been published), and was for some time in informal charge of the *Middle English Dictionary*.

Prosser, Richard Bissell (1838–1908). Patent officer and industrial historian; Chief Examiner of Patents at the Patent Office 1883–8. Gave help on many points relating to scientific and technical words, including searching in patent specifications for early quotations. Also wrote many articles on figures in science and industry for the *DNB*.

Pye-Smith, Philip Henry (1839–1914). Physician, long connected with Guy's Hospital. Gave advice on medical and biological words.

*Rhŷs, John** (1840–1915). Celtic scholar; Jesus professor of Celtic at Oxford (first occupant of the chair) from 1877, and principal of Jesus College from 1895. Principal adviser to *OED* on matters of Celtic philology.

*Rieu, Charles Pierre Henri** (1820–1902). Orientalist; professor of Arabic and Persian at University College, London, and Adams professor of Arabic at Cambridge, 1894–1902. Gave advice on points of Semitic philology.

Rope, Henry Edward George (1880–1978). Member of Murray's and, from 1905, of Craigie's editorial staff. Later became a Catholic priest, with missions at Morley Hall, Shropshire, and elsewhere; continued for the rest of his life to contribute quotations for the dictionary and its Supplements. Also published poetry, and wrote on topography and Catholic history.

*Roscoe, Henry Enfield** (1833–1915). Chemist; professor of chemistry at Owens College, Manchester, 1857–85 (and subsequently MP for South Manchester). Gave advice to *OED* on specific chemical terms.

*Rossetti, William Michael** (1829–1919). Art critic and man of letters. Reader for *OED*; subedited in B and L; also gave advice on art terms and other specific points.

Ruthven, Ada Agnes (later Mrs James Murray) (1845–1936). Of Kendal. Married James Murray in 1867, and became closely involved with many of her husband's scholarly projects (assisting, for example, in the compilation of the glossary to his edition of *The Complaynt of Scotlande* for the EETS in 1872); was instrumental in his decision to accept the editorship of *OED*, and acted as his unpaid secretary for many years; the first Scriptorium at Mill Hill was built following her suggestion. Read for *OED*, sought out quotation desiderata, and assisted in many other ways.

Ruthven, Herbert F. P. Brother-in-law of James Murray, and his second assistant (with Herrtage) in the Scriptorium. He and his wife also read for *OED*.

Schrumpf, Gustavus Adolphus (d. 1892). Schoolmaster (at University College School from 1884; before that at Tettenhall College, near Wolverhampton) and philologist. Subedited in A and H; also read for *OED*, and carried out research in the British Museum.

Sheppard, Thomas Henry (1814–88). Chaplain of Exeter College from 1851. Subedited in M, U, and V (his list of headwords for U–V was printed as a pamphlet in 1865); also read for *OED*.

Sievers, Eduard (1850–1932). Phonetician and Germanic philologist; holder of professorships at Jena, Tübingen, Halle, and Leipzig. Published widely on phonetics and Germanic philology, including the important *Angelsächsische Grammatik* (1882; Eng. transl. 1885). Principal adviser to *OED* for many years on the etymology of words of Germanic origin.

Sisam, Kenneth (1887–1971). English scholar and publisher. Worked briefly with Bradley on *OED* before embarking on his anthology *Fourteenth Century Verse and Prose* (1921; separate Glossary provided by J. R. R. Tolkien 1922); gave advice on particular words. Worked closely with Chapman at OUP (appointed Junior Assistant Secretary to the Delegates in 1922; Secretary 1942–8).

***Skeat, Walter William** (1835–1912). Philologist and editor. Read mathematics and theology at Cambridge; returned there to lecture in mathematics, but took up Anglo-Saxon, and became skilled enough to be elected in 1878 as the first Elrington and Bosworth professor of Anglo-Saxon, a post he held until his death. Published many important works in English philology, perhaps most notably the *Etymological Dictionary of the English Language* (1882). Joined the Philological Society in 1863, and took an early interest in *OED*; subedited in R. Founded the English Dialect Society in 1873, through which he encountered Murray and became a close friend and adviser; collaborated with Murray during his approach to Macmillan about publishing *OED*, and subsequently gave him constant support (memorably in the form of humorous poems celebrating Murray's completing particular letters), as well as practical help, by seeking out quotations, giving etymological advice on particular words, and reading proofs.

Smallpeice, John (1830/1–1900). Schoolmaster (at St Bees College, 1858–96) and clergyman. Subedited in M, X, Y, and Z; also read for *OED*.

***Smith, Lucy Toulmin** (1838–1911). Scholar; librarian of Manchester College, Oxford, 1894–1911. Edited many texts for the EETS and other societies. Gave advice on specific points; also read for *OED*, and collated quotations in the British Museum. Was also a regular reviewer of *OED* fascicles.

***Stainer, John** (1840–1901). Organist and composer; professor of music at Oxford, 1889–99. Consulted as an authority on musical terms.

Steane, Ethelwyn Rebecca (later Mrs L. F. Powell) (*d.* 1941). Daughter of an Oxford wine merchant. Member of the editorial staff of the dictionary 1901–32 (including work on the *Supplement*); she married a fellow assistant, L. F. Powell, in 1909.

***Stephens, George** (1813–95). Runic archaeologist; also professor of English and Anglo-Saxon in the University of Copenhagen from 1855. Placed his own collection of quotations at the disposal of *OED*.

***Stevenson, William Henry** (1858–1924). Historian, antiquarian, and place-name scholar. Edited many historical manuscripts for publication; also published an important edition (1904) of Asser's *Life of King Alfred*. Read and annotated proofs for many years; also gave advice on specific points.

***Stubbs, William** (1825–1901). Historian (regius professor of history at Oxford, 1866–84), and bishop successively of Chester and (from 1888) Oxford. Gave advice on many historical terms.

Sugden, Edward Holdsworth (1854–1935). Methodist minister and educationist. Reader for *OED*; subedited in I; continued to send in quotations after moving from Bradford to Melbourne in 1887 to become master of the new Queen's College. Later published a *Topographical Dictionary to the Works of Shakespeare and his Contemporaries* (1925).

Sweatman, Frederick John (1873–1936). Son of an Oxford printer-foreman. Joined the staff of the Bodleian Library in Oxford in 1888; member of Murray's, and later Onions's editorial staff, 1890–1933 (including work on the *Supplement*). Also assisted Onions with the *Shorter Oxford English Dictionary*.

*****Sweet, Henry** (1845–1912). Phonetician and philologist; author of many important texts in these fields, including the *History of English Sounds* (1874) and the *Anglo-Saxon Reader* (1876). In 1877, as President of the Philological Society, he wrote to Bartholomew Price with the proposal which later formed the basis of the agreement between the OUP, the Philological Society, and James Murray regarding *OED*; gave advice on etymology, pronunciation, and other editorial matters.

Sykes, George Frederic Holley (1829/30–1910). Member of Murray's, and later (from 1887) Bradley's editorial staff, 1885–1903. Also edited *The Owl and the Nightingale* for the EETS (published posthumously in 1935), and published school English and Latin grammars and translations of Thucydides and Euripides.

Sykes, William (1851/2–1906). Physician (practising at Mexborough, Yorkshire, and later at Gosport) and antiquarian. After being an early critic of *OED* in *Notes and Queries*, became an enthusiastic and valued helper; a prolific contributor of quotations and supplier of information on specific points, especially in relation to medical words; also read proofs.

*****Thiselton-Dyer, William Turner** (1843–1928). Botanist; director of the Royal Botanic Gardens, Kew, 1885–1905. Regularly consulted as an authority on botanical terms.

Thomas, Edward Joseph (1869–1958). Son of a Yorkshire gardener. Became a student gardener at Kew in 1894; gained a place at St Andrews to read Classics; member of Murray's, later Craigie's, editorial staff, from 1900; resumed his classical studies at Cambridge in 1903; subsequently joined the staff of the Cambridge University Library, where he continued to give help by verifying quotations and by providing advice on specific points. Became a leading authority on Buddhism, known especially through *The Life of Buddha as Legend and History* (1927) and *The History of Buddhist Thought* (1933).

Thompson, Edith (1848–1929). Historian. Wrote a popular *History of England* (1873) for schools. Gave advice to *OED* on historical terms, and sought out quotations for particular words. She and her sister Elizabeth Perronet Thompson (who also wrote *A Dragoon's Wife* (1907), subtitled 'a romance of the 17th century') were readers for *OED* (credited with 15,000 quotations in 1888), and gave help throughout its period of publication, including subediting in C, and reading proofs from D onwards.

Thompson, John J. Of London. Reader for *OED*; took on some of the unfinished reading left by Fitzedward Hall and W. C. Minor.

***Tolkien, John Ronald Reuel** (1892–1973). Fantasy writer and philologist. Member of Bradley's editorial staff 1919–20. Went on to publish *A Middle English Vocabulary* (1922) and much else on Old and Middle English; later Rawlinson and Bosworth professor of Anglo-Saxon, then Merton professor of English language and literature, at Oxford.

***Trench, Richard Chenevix** (1807–86). Philologist, churchman, and man of letters. Dean of Westminster, later archbishop of Dublin. Important popularizer of the scientific study of language, especially through his books *On the Study of Words* (1851) and *English Past and Present* (1855). Joined the Philological Society in 1857, and was appointed to its Unregistered Words Committee; later that year he read two papers 'On some Deficiencies in our English Dictionaries', which were published, with a revised and enlarged edition appearing in 1860. These are now generally recognized as having both provided the inspiration for the Philological Society's decision to launch its proposal for a new English Dictionary (published in 1859), and also set out the principles on which such a dictionary should be based. Subsequently appointed member (with Coleridge and Furnivall) of the Literary and Historical Committee set up to advise on editorial policy, although he had ceased to play an active role by the time Murray became editor.

***Turle, Henry Frederic** (1835–83). Editor of *Notes and Queries* 1878–83, which under his editorship (and that of his successor Joseph Knight) became an important forum for discussion of matters relating to *OED*, notably through publication of lists of words for which additional quotations were sought.

***Tylor, Edward Burnett** (1832–1917). Anthropologist; keeper of the University Museum at Oxford from 1883, and professor of anthropology there (the first to occupy the chair) 1896–1909. Author of the classic study *Primitive Culture* (1871). Consulted for advice on the meaning and origin of numerous loanwords relating to indigenous cultures he had studied.

Walkey, Mrs L. J. Of Leamington, later of Bridport and Chipping Camden. Subedited in D and W; also read for *OED*, and gave help in arranging materials in alphabetical order for many years.

***Warren, Thomas Herbert** (1853–1930). Classicist, man of letters, and educationist; president of Magdalen College, Oxford, 1885–1928, and professor of poetry 1911–16 (published volumes of poetry in 1897 and 1907). Influential, like his mentor Jowett, in many aspects of Oxford life; University correspondent of *The Times* (for which he wrote Murray's obituary in 1915, from notes made in personal interviews). Consulted by Murray for advice on many matters, including particular words.

Watson, George Marr (1876–1950). Member of Craigie's editorial staff 1907–27 (including work on the 1933 *Supplement*), with special responsibility for part of

U. Moved to Chicago in 1927 to join Craigie on the staff of the *Dictionary of American English*. Also wrote on Scottish dialect (his *Roxburghshire Word-Book* was published in 1923), and was a keen local historian (member of the Hawick Archaeological Society from 1900).

***Wedgwood, Hensleigh** (1803–91). Grandson of Josiah Wedgwood. Founder member of the Philological Society; published an important *Dictionary of English Etymology* in 1857; member of the Committee set up by the Society in 1859 to formulate *OED*'s etymological policy; continued to give etymological advice to the dictionary's editors for many years.

***Weymouth, Richard Francis** (1822–1902), philologist and New Testament scholar. Headmaster of Mill Hill School, 1869–86. Met Murray at a Philological Society meeting in 1870 and subsequently invited him to join his staff; arranged for him to be partially released from his school duties to work on *OED*; gave advice on many specific points.

Wheelwright, George (1813/14–1875). Vicar of Crowhurst, Sussex. Reader and subeditor for *OED* under Furnivall. In 1875, concerned at the apparent stagnation of the project, he published his pamphlet 'An appeal to the English-speaking public on behalf of a new English dictionary', together with a specimen of his own subedited material for part of the letter F; the pamphlet's title was echoed in that of the title of the *Appeal* issued in 1879 on behalf of the Philological Society asking for volunteers to read books for the dictionary.

White, George Henry (1817–89). Banking official; travelled worldwide as a representative of Barings before retiring to Torquay. Reader for *OED*; also subedited part of C.

Whitney, William Dwight (1827–94). Philologist and lexicographer; professor of Sanskrit at Yale from 1854, and first president of the American Philological Association. Well-known through his critiques of Max Müller's theories and his book *Language and the Study of Language* (1867); elected an honorary member of the Philological Society in 1874. Assisted in preparation of the 1864 edition of Webster's dictionary; editor-in-chief of the *Century Dictionary* (1889–91), which from the appearance of its first fascicles was scrutinized carefully by the *OED* editors, and drawn upon for vocabulary for which quotations were lacking; its definitions were from time to time quoted verbatim (correctly attributed, but without other published acknowledgement) in *OED* entries. The 'List of Spurious Words' published at the end of *OED*, whose compilation was announced by Murray in 1891, includes a high proportion of words found in the *Century Dictionary*, and may have been prompted by it.

Whitwell, Robert Jowitt (1859–1928). Medievalist. A prolific contributor of quotations to *OED* (credited with 33,000 in 1888), including many in response to particular requests; researched in the Bodleian and other libraries and in the Public Record Office, verifying quotations, advising on legal and historical terms, and proofreading. In 1913 he proposed, at the Historical Congress held in London, that a dictionary of medieval Latin be compiled on a similar basis to *OED*; this initiative was later taken up by the British Academy, and eventually bore fruit in the form of the one-volume *Medieval Latin Word-List from British and Irish Sources* (1934) and the more extensive *Dictionary of Medieval Latin* (1975–), to which he was a prolific contributor of quotations.

Wilson, William Bruce Robertson (*b.* 1843). Presbyterian minister of Dollar, Clackmannanshire. Reader for *OED*; was also a most durable subeditor, working in C, T, V, and W; also read proofs for Bradley, and contributed many quotations to the 1933 *Supplement*.

Winchester, Charles Blake (1850/1–1908). Subedited in P, S, and V; also read for *OED*, and verified quotations in the British Museum.

Woods, William Noel (1856–92). Of Blackheath, later of Addiscombe, Surrey. With his wife he subedited in B, C, and H; also read for *OED*.

Worrall, Walter (1862–1943). Member of Murray's, and later Bradley's and Onions's, editorial staff, 1885–1933 (including work on the 1933 *Supplement*); took special responsibility for parts of W after the death of Bradley. Also published editions of Bacon's *Essayes or Counsels* and Milton's sonnets, and some articles of textual criticism.

*****Wright, Joseph** (1855–1930). Philologist; Corpus Christi professor of comparative philology at Oxford, 1901–24. Despite starting work in a Bradford quarry at the age of 6, he managed to acquire sufficient education to study comparative philology at Heidelberg; came to Oxford at the instigation of Max Müller in 1888; editor and publisher of the *English Dialect Dictionary* (1896–1905). Became a close friend of Murray; gave occasional advice on etymological matters.

Yockney, F. A. Member of Murray's editorial staff 1906–15.

*****Yonge, Charlotte Mary** (1823–1901). Novelist; also wrote a *History of Christian Names* (1863). Subedited part of N, in collaboration with her cousin Henry Hucks Gibbs.

*****Yule, Henry** (1820–89). Engineer, Indian administrator, and writer on Asia. Made available to *OED* the proofs of his well-known glossary of Anglo-Indian, *Hobson–Jobson* (1886), and gave advice on matters of Oriental philology, and on Indian English.

Appendix III: The *OED* and the Public

R I C H A R D   W.   B A I L E Y

From the very beginnings, members of the Philological Society worked assiduously to bring their plan to a large public, partly in the hope of gaining volunteer readers and partly (especially through Furnivall's vigorous advocacy) to have their dictionary recognized as a great national effort. Magazines read by the learned (like *The Athenaeum*) and newspapers read by the powerful (especially *The Times*) were regular vehicles for conveying these two messages.

A complete bibliography of notices and reviews of the dictionary would be nearly impossible to compile. The OED archives contain scattered clippings from provincial newspapers (many of them undated) that reveal Murray's effort to persuade readers even in the remotest districts that something important was afoot, but there was no systematic effort in Oxford to gather all the reviews that appeared. In 1980 Leslie Bivens began the job of collecting some of the major notices (her essay concludes the present list). That remarkable scholar Arthur G. Kennedy gathered masses of them in his wonderful bibliography (1927), still a major resource for historical studies of the language, but even his list is not complete. What follows is an attempt to extend their efforts.

Librarians have made this work possible, particularly those at the University of Michigan. I wish also to thank Denise Jennings of the City University of London, where I was enabled to inspect the office copy of *The Athenaeum* with its notations of authorship. It reveals for the first time that C. A. M. Fennell was one of the principal and persevering reviewers of the work, and however critical he was of Murray the man he was consistently celebratory of Murray the lexicographer. In the United States, James M. Garnett and in Germany Max Friedrich Mann wrote careful and thoughtful accounts of the dictionary over many years. (Fennell wrote seventy-five times, Garnett sixteen, and Mann forty-five according to my computation.)

Naturally the first reviews were the most important ones, but, even after the dictionary was well established and making steady progress, editors of both popular and scholarly publications saw fit to tell the story again and again. In many ways, it was the same story year after year: a triumph of scholarship, a testimonial to the antiquity of the language, a tribute to the value of those who had written in it. But if each word told its own story, each part of the dictionary told a new episode in the evolution of English and the sources of its expressiveness. It was thus a slightly different story each time, one that reviewers and readers loved to have told.

CONTEMPORARY PUBLICATION ILLUMINATING THE
HISTORY OF THE *OED* (IN CHRONOLOGICAL ORDER)

Garnett, Richard. 'English Lexicography'. *Quarterly* 54 (1835): 295–330. Repr. in his *Philological Essays* (London: Williams and Norgate, 1859): 1–40.

'Proposal for the Publication of a New English Dictionary by the Philological Society'. *TPS* (1857): 36.

Büchmann, Georg. 'Beiträge zur englischen Lexikographie'. *Archiv für das Studium der neueren Sprachen und Literaturen* 21 (1857): 153–68.

Trench, Richard Chenevix, Furnivall F. J., and Coleridge, Herbert. 'Collections for a New Dictionary of the English Language'. *Athenaeum* (25 July 1857): 944–5.

Student, A. [*pseud.*]. 'Note on the Proposed Dictionary'. *Athenaeum* (1 August 1857): 976–7.

Trench, Richard Chenevix, Furnivall, F. J., and Coleridge, Herbert. 'Proposals for a Complete Dictionary of the English Language'. *Notes & Queries* 4, ser. 2 (1857): 81–4.

Coleridge, Herbert. 'Collections for a New English Dictionary of the English Language'. *Athenaeum* (8 Aug. 1857): 1007.

—— 'Invitation to Readers'. *Notes & Queries* 4, ser. 2 (1857): 138.

R., E. G. ' "Teed", "Tidd".' *Notes & Queries* 4, ser. 2 (1857): 216–17.

T., T. A. 'Collections for a New Dictionary of the English Language'. *Athenaeum* (12 Sept. 1857): 1160.

Büchmann, Georg. 'Lexicalische Pläne der Londoner philologischen Gesellschaft'. *Archiv für das Studium der neueren Sprachen und Literaturen* 23 (1858): 208–10.

'Review of Trench's *On Some Deficiencies*'. *The Times* (19 Jan. 1858): 12a–b.

'Philological Society (7 Jan., 21 Jan.)'. *Athenaeum* (13 Feb. 1858): 212.

'Philological Society (4 Feb., 18 Feb.)'. *Athenaeum* (20 Mar. 1858): 374.

'Philological Society (1 Mar.)'. *Athenaeum* (27 Mar. 1858): 406.

'Philological Society (6 May)'. *Athenaeum* (29 May 1858): 691.

'Dictionary-Making'. *Saturday Review* 6 (1858): 183.

[Fitch, Joshua.] 'English Dictionaries'. *London Quarterly Review* 11 (1858): 71–111.

Coleridge, Herbert. 'Hints Towards the Explanation of Some Hard Words and Passages in English Writers'. *TPS* (1859): 67–74.

Fry, Danby P. 'On Some English Dictionaries, Especially One Proposed by the Late Augus Fry'. *TPS* (1859): 257–72.

[Marsden, John Howard.] 'Dr. Trench on English Dictionaries'. *Edinburgh Review* 109 (1859): 365–86.

Stratmann, Franz H. 'Reply to Büchmann's Review of His *Beiträge*'. *Archiv für das Studium der neueren Sprachen und Literaturen* 26 (1859): 107.

Wedgwood, Hensleigh. 'On English Etymologies'. *TPS* (1859): 125–6.

'Proposed New English Dictionary'. *New Englander* 17 (1859): 288–90.

Eirionnach [*pseud.*]. 'Dr. Johnson's MS. Collections for His Dictionary'. *Notes & Queries* 7, ser. 2 (1859): 256–7.

Coleridge, Herbert. 'Scope of the Dictionary'. *Notes & Queries* 7, ser. 2 (1859): 299.

[Davies, John.] 'Review of Trench's *Select Glossary* and Coleridge's *Glossarial Index*'. *Athenaeum* (2 July 1859): 10–12.

Büchmann, Georg. 'Review of Stratmann, *Beiträge zu einen Wörterbuche der englischen Sprache*'. *Archiv für das Studium der neueren Sprachen und Literaturen* 25 (1859a): 440–4.

—— 'Reply to Stratmann's Response to B's Review of His Book'. *Archiv für das Studium der neueren Sprachen und Literaturen* 26 (1859b): 108.

Coleridge, Derwent. 'Observations on the Plan of the Society's Proposed New English Dictionary'. *TPS* (1860–1): 152–68.

Coleridge, Herbert, and Furnivall F. J. 'On the Exclusion of Certain Words from a Dictionary'. *TPS* (1860–1): 37–44.

'Proposed New English Dictionary'. *New Englander* 18 (1860): 224–9.

Coleridge, Herbert. 'On the Canones Lexicographica and the New Dictionary'. *TPS* (1860).

B., H. 'Das neue englische Lexikon'. *Jahrbuch für romanische und englische Literatur* 3 (1861): 241–4.

Kennedy, James. 'Hints on the Formation of a New English Dictionary. Read Before the Philological Society, May 20, 1858'. *Essays Ethnological and Linguistic*, ed. C. M. Kennedy. London: Williams & Norgate, 1861: 153–63.

[Davies, John.] 'Invitation to Readers'. *Athenaeum* (29 Jun. 1861): 865.

[Watts, Thomas.] 'Review of Webster's *American Dictionary* and Worcester's *Dictionary*'. *Athenaeum* (13 July 1861): 41–3.

S., S. M. 'New English Dictionary'. *Notes & Queries* 12, ser. 2 (1861): 312.

An Alphabetical List of English Words Occurring in the Literature of the 18th and 19th Centuries, and Forming a Basis of Comparison for the Use of Contributors to the New English Dictionary of the Philological Society. Hertford, 1862.

Porter, Noah. 'English Lexicography'. *Bibliotheca Sacra* 20 (1863): 78–123.

'A Word for the New Dictionary'. *The Times* (25 Jan. 1864): 9d.

[Watts, Thomas.] 'Review of Ogilvie's *Comprehensive Dictionary*'. *Athenaeum* (5 Mar. 1864): 333.

[Davies, John] 'Note on the Philological Society's *Dictionary*'. *Athenaeum* (12 Nov. 1864): 638.

Furnivall, F. J. 'Philological Society's Dictionary'. *Athenaeum* (3 Dec. 1864): 749.

Sheppard, Thomas. *Vocabulary of Words Beginning With the Letters U and V for Which Extracts Are Wanted for the Concise Dictionary (Preparatory to the Philological Society's New English Dictionary).* Hertford, 1865.

Irvine, Aiken. 'Philological Society's English Dictionary'. *Notes & Queries* 8, ser. 8 (1865): 352.

[Furnivall, F. J.] 'Note on the Progress of the *NED*'. *Athenaeum* (2 Feb. 1867): 158.
K., G. R. 'Early English Text Society'. *Notes & Queries* 11, ser. 3 (1867): 232.
Skeat, Walter W. 'Early English Text Society'. *Notes & Queries* 11, ser. 3 (1867): 264.
[Furnivall, F. J.] 'Notice of Stratmann's *Dictionary* (Part 5)'. *Athenaeum* (1 June 1867): 730.
'Bishop Percy's Folio Manuscript'. *The Spectator* 40 (1867): 724–5.
L. L. L. 'The Philological Society's "English Dictionary"'. *Notes & Queries* 12, ser. 3 (1867): 169.
Skeat, Walter W. 'The Philological Society's Dictionary'. *Notes & Queries* 12, ser. 3 (1867): 256.
D. 'The Philological Society's Dictionary'. *Notes & Queries* 12, ser. 3 (1867): 296.
Skeat, Walter W. 'Philological Society's Dictionary'. *Notes & Queries* 12, ser. 3 (1867): 358.

White, Richard Grant. 'A Desultory Denunciation of English Dictionaries'. *Galaxy* 6 (1869): 55–68.
'Publications of the Chaucer Society'. *The Spectator* 42 (1869): 1369.

'Philological Society (4. Nov.)'. *Athenaeum* (12 Nov. 1870): 630.
'Philological Society (18. Nov.)'. *Athenaeum* (26 Nov. 1870): 693.

Sweet, Henry. 'Review of Stratmann's *Dictionary of the Old English Language*'. *The Academy* (1874): 492–3.
'Philological Society (16 May)'. *The Academy* 4 (1874): 582.

'Philological Society (5 Feb.)'. *The Academy* 7 (1875): 173.
'Philological Society (10 Feb.)'. *The Academy* 7 (1875): 226.
'Philological Society (10 Apr.)'. *The Academy* 7 (1875): 433.
'Philological Society (29 May)'. *The Academy* 7 (1875): 562–3.

'An English Dictionary'. *Dublin University Magazine* 93 (1879): 393–403.
'The Philological Society's English Dictionary'. *The Academy* 15 (1879): 413.
March, Francis A. 'The Present State of Spelling Reform in America'. *The National Baptist* (USA) (1879): 4.
'The Philological Society's New English Dictionary'. *The Academy* 16 (1879): 194–5.

[Murray, J. A. H.] 'The New English Dictionary of the Philological Society'. *Athenaeum* (13 Sept. 1879): 337–8.

The Nation (New York) 29 (1879): 158.

Smith, Lucy Toulmin. 'The New English Dictionary of the London Philological Society'. *Anglia* 3 (1880): 413–14.

Murray, J. A. H. 'Word Lists'. *Notes & Queries* 1, ser. 6 (1880): 33.

The Nation (New York) 30 (1880): 99.

Murray, J. A. H. 'Word Lists'. *Notes & Queries* 1, ser. 6 (1880): 173.

'Philological Society (21 May)'. *The Academy* 17 (1880): 406.

Skeat, Walter W. 'The Philological Society's New English Dictionary'. *Notes & Queries* 1, ser. 6 (1880): 451–2.

'Philological Society (4 June)'. *The Academy* 17 (1880): 442.

V. 'The Philological Society's Dictionary'. *The Nation* (New York) 31 (1880): 44.

Curiosus [*pseud.*]. 'A Literary Workshop'. *Notes & Queries* 2, ser. 6 (1880): 261–3.

Murray, J. A. H. 'Word Lists'. *Notes & Queries* 2, ser. 6 (1880): 366–7.

—— 'Word Lists'. *Notes & Queries* 2, ser. 6 (1880): 466.

Cook, Albert S. 'The Philological Society's English Dictionary'. *American Journal of Philology* 2 (1881): 550–4.

March, Francis A. 'Recent Philological Works'. *North American Review* 133 (1881): 99–106.

Murray, J. A. H. 'Shakesperian Illustrations and the Philological Society's Dictionary'. *The Academy* 19 (1881): 9.

'Philological Society'. *The Academy* 20 (1881): 441.

Murray, J. A. H. 'Report on the Present State of the Dictionary of the Philological Society'. *TPS* (1882–4): 5–6.

—— 'Word Lists'. *Notes & Queries* 5, ser. 6 (1882): 26.

—— 'Word Lists'. *Notes & Queries* 5, ser. 6 (1882): 47.

'The Philological Society's New Dictionary'. *The Times* (25 Jan. 1882): 10d.

Murray, J. A. H. 'Word Lists'. *Notes & Queries* 5, ser. 6 (1882): 66.

'The Philological Society's Dictionary'. *The Times* (31 Jan. 1882): 4 f.

Reade, A. A. 'Three Great Dictionaries'. *Temple Bar* 64 (1882): 238–49.

'Literary and Other Notes'. *The Times* (3 Feb. 1882): 9f.

'Philological Society ([1882] 20 Jan.)'. *The Academy* 21 (1882): 87–8.

Murray, J. A. H. 'Abacot: The Story of a Spurious Word'. *Athenaeum* (4 Feb. 1882): 157.

—— 'Word Lists'. *Notes & Queries* 5, ser. 6 (1882): 86.

—— 'Word Lists'. *Notes & Queries* 5, ser. 6 (1882): 107.

—— 'Word Lists'. *Notes & Queries* 5, ser. 6 (1882): 146.

—— 'Word Lists'. *Notes & Queries* 5, ser. 6 (1882): 167.

'Philological Society ([1882] 7 Mar.)'. *The Academy* 21 (1882): 217.

Woolrych, H. F. 'Jennetting'. *Notes & Queries* 6, ser. 6 (1882): 65–6.

Allsopp, A. P. 'Jenneting'. *Notes & Queries* 6, ser. 6 (1882): 176.

Humphreys, Jennett. 'English: Its Ancestors, Its Progeny'. *Fraser's Magazine* 26 (1882): 429–57.

Skeat, Walter W. 'Jenneting'. *Notes & Queries* 6, ser. 6 (1882): 457.

'Dictionary Making'. *Leisure Hour* 32 (1883): 362–6.

Stoffel, Cornelis. 'Review of *NED*, A–Ant'. *Taalstudie* 5 (1883): 297–308.

Smith, Lucy Toulmin. 'The Forthcoming English Dictionary'. *The Academy* 23 (1883): 9–10.

'Philological Society (10 Jan.)'. *The Academy* 23 (1883): 65–6.

Mount, C. B. 'Word Lists'. *Notes & Queries* 7, ser. 6 (1883): 183–4.

'Review of *NED*, A–Ant'. *Scottish Review* 3 (1883): 394–6.

Wells, W. H. 'Review of Ogilvie's *Imperial Dictionary*'. *The Dial* 4 (1883): 1–4.

Britten, James. 'Plant Names'. *Notes & Queries* 7, ser. 6 (1883): 353.

'Philological Society (18 May.)'. *The Academy* 23 (1883): 371.

'The New English Dictionary'. *Literary News* 5 (1884): 70–1.

'Review of *NED*, A–Ant'. *Dublin Review* 94 (1884): 486.

'Review of *NED*, A–Ant'. *The Antiquary* 9 (1884): 178–9.

'Review of *NED*, A–Ant'. *Walford's Antiquarian Magazine* 5 (1884): 198–9.

'Review of *NED*, A–Ant'. *London Quarterly Review* 62 (1884): 195–6.

Garnett, James M. 'Review of Bosworth–Toller *An Anglo-Saxon Dictionary*, Parts 1 and 2; and of the *NED*, Part 1'. *American Journal of Philology* 5 (1884): 359–66.

Lovett, Richard. 'Dictionary Making, Past and Present'. *British Quarterly Review* 79 (1884): 336–54.

Stratmann, Franz H. 'Review of *NED*, A–Ant'. *Anglia* 7 (1884): 1–2.

Zupitza, Julius. 'Review of *NED*, A–Ant'. *Deutsche Literaturzeitung* 5 (1884): 691–3.

'Review of *NED*, A–Ant'. *The Antiquarian Magazine* 5 (1884): 198–9.

'A New English Dictionary'. *The Times* (26 Jan. 1884): 6a.

'Philological Society (13 Jan.)'. *The Academy* 25 (1884): 66.

'Philological Society (18 Jan.)'. *Athenaeum* (26 Jan. 1884): 124.

[Fennell, C. A. M.] 'Review of *NED*, A–Ant (First Notice)'. *Athenaeum* (9 Feb. 1884): 177–8.

Furnivall, F. J. 'The Philological Society's English Dictionary'. *The Academy* 25 (1884): 96–7.

'The New English Dictionary'. *The Saturday Review* 57 (1884): 226–7.

'Review of *NED*, A–Ant'. *The Spectator* 57 (1884): 221–2.

Bradley, Henry. 'A New English Dictionary on Historical Principles (First Notice)'. *The Academy* 25 (1884): 105–6.

[Fennell, C. A. M.] 'Review of *NED*, A–Ant (Second Notice)'. *Athenaeum* (16 Feb. 1884): 211–12.

'The New English Dictionary'. *Literary World* (Boston) 15 (1884): 56–7.

'Review of *NED*, A–Ant'. *The Dial* 4 (1884): 292.

Bradley, Henry. 'A New English Dictionary on Historical Principles (Second Notice)'. *The Academy* 25 (1884): 141–2.

'The New English Dictionary (Second Notice)'. *Literary World (Boston)* 15 (1884): 77–8.

'Review of *NED*, A–Ant'. *The Critic* 1 [new ser.] (1884): 110.

Marshall, John. 'Words, or Meanings of Words, for the "New English Dictionary"'. *The Academy* 25 (1884): 185–6.

B., W. C. 'Abaptate, Addubitation, Alligated, Amicableness, Angried, Admeasure'. *Notes & Queries* 9, ser. 6 (1884): 224.

Buckley, W. E. 'Ænographies, Anaragonick'. *Notes & Queries* 9, ser. 6 (1884): 224.

Palmer, A. Smythe. 'Aberuncate, Alcatras'. *Notes & Queries* 9, ser. 6 (1884): 224.

Randall, John. 'Alcalious'. *Notes & Queries* 9, ser. 6 (1884): 224–5.

Wülcker, Richard Paul. 'Review of *NED*, A–Ant'. *Literarisches Centralblatt* (1884): 492–3.

Wells, W. H. 'Review of *NED*, A–Ant'. *The Dial* 4 (1884): 301–4.

Buckley, W. E. 'Alcalious'. *Notes & Queries* 9, ser. 6 (1884): 277.

Marshall, F. A. 'Allycholly or Allicholy'. *Notes & Queries* 9, ser. 6 (1884): 267.

'Review of *NED*, A–Ant'. *The Nation* (New York) 38 (1884): 347–8.

Haig, Margaret. 'Allycholly'. *Notes & Queries* 9, ser. 6 (1884): 314.

Murray, J. A. H. 'Allicholy'. *Notes & Queries* 9, ser. 6 (1884): 313–14.

Tancock, O. W. 'Notes for the *NED*'. *Notes & Queries* 9, ser. 6 (1884): 310.

'Review of *NED*, A–Ant'. *The Nation* (New York) 38 (1884): 367–8.

'The New English Dictionary (Second Notice)'. *The Saturday Review* 57 (1884): 547–8.

Webb, T. W. 'The New English Dictionary'. *Notes & Queries* 9, ser. 6 (1884): 376.

'Philological Society (Anniversary Meeting, Friday, 16 May)'. *The Academy* 25 (1884): 372.

'Philological Society (16 May)'. *Athenaeum* (24 May 1884): 666.

Smith, Lucy Toulmin. 'Review of *NED*, A–Ant'. *The Bibliographer* 6 (1884): 1–4.

'Philological Society (7 Nov.)'. *The Academy* 26 (1884): 344–5.

'Review of *NED*, A–Ant'. *London Quarterly Review* 63 (1885): 279–91.

'Review of *NED*, Ant–Batten'. *The Critic* 4 [new ser.] (1885): 300.

Helwich, H. R. 'Review of *NED*, A–Ant'. *Anglia: Zeitschrift für englische Philologie* 8 (1885): 8–18.

Sattler, W. 'Review of *NED*, A–Ant'. *Englische Studien* 8 (1885): 120–3.

'Philological Society (23 Jan.)'. *The Academy* 27 (1885): 84.

'Review of *NED*, A–Ant'. *New York Evening Post* (1885).

Bradley, Henry. 'Review of *NED*, Ant–Batten'. *The Academy* 28 (1885): 349–50.

'Review of *NED*, A–Batten'. *Journal of Education* 8 (1886): 124–5.

'Review of *NED*, Ant–Batten'. *The Antiquary* 13 (1886): 124.

'Review of *NED*, Ant–Batten'. *Walford's Antiquarian Magazine* 9 (1886): 266–7.

'Review of *NED*, Ant–Batten'. *London Quarterly Review* 65 (1886): 390.

Garnett, James M. 'Review of *NED*, Ant–Batten'. *American Journal of Philology* 7 (1886): 514–17.

Sattler, W. 'Review of *NED*, Ant–Batten'. *Englische Studien* 9 (1886): 466–8.

Zupitza, Julius. 'Review of *NED*, Ant-Batten'. *Deutsche Literaturzeitung* 7 (1886): 370.

'Review of *NED*, Ant–Batten'. *Scottish Review* 7 (1886): 183–5.

'Review of *NED*, Ant–Batten'. *Saturday Review* 61 (1886): 168–9.

Lounsbury, Thomas R. 'Review of *NED*, Ant–Batten'. *The Nation* (New York) 42 (1886): 103–5.

'Review of *NED*, A–Ant, Ant–Batten'. *The Times* (12 Mar. 1886): 13a–c.

Murray, J. A. H. 'The New English Dictionary'. *The Academy* 29 (1886): 184.

Sykes, William. 'The New English Dictionary'. *Notes & Queries* 1, ser. 7 (1886): 430–2.

—— 'The New English Dictionary'. *Notes & Queries* 1, ser. 7 (1886): 303–4.

Dixon, J. 'Achritochromancy'. *Notes & Queries* 1, ser. 7 (1886): 336–7.

Murray, J. A. H. 'The New English Dictionary'. *Notes & Queries* 1, ser. 7 (1886): 370–1.

—— 'The New English Dictionary'. *Notes & Queries* 1, ser. 7 (1886): 471.

Bradley, Henry. 'Word Lists'. *Notes & Queries* 2, ser. 7 (1886): 47.

Sykes, William. 'New English Dictionary'. *Notes & Queries* 2, ser. 7 (1886): 53.

Toy, C. H. 'A New English Dictionary'. *Science* 7 (1886): 557–8.

Bradley, Henry. 'Word Lists'. *Notes & Queries* 2, ser. 7 (1886): 88.

Randall, John. 'New English Dictionary'. *Notes & Queries* 2, ser. 7 (1886): 116–17.

Reader, A. [*pseud.*] 'On Word Lists'. *Notes & Queries* 2, ser. 7 (1886): 117.

Sykes, William. 'Additions and Emendations to "New English Dictionary"'. *Notes & Queries* 2, ser. 7 (1886): 185.

LeM., H. P. 'Brahminee'. *Notes & Queries* 2, ser. 7 (1886): 238.

Sykes, William. 'Additions and Emendations to "New English Dictionary"'. *Notes & Queries* 2, ser. 7 (1886): 225–6.

Chance, F. 'Amyloid'. *Notes & Queries* 2, ser. 7 (1886): 283.

Sykes, William. 'Additions and Emendations to "New English Dictionary"'. *Notes & Queries* 2, ser. 7 (1886): 282–3.

—— 'Additions and Emendations to "New English Dictionary"'. *Notes & Queries* 2, ser. 7 (1886): 343–4.

Dixon, J. 'Astigmatism'. *Notes & Queries* 2, ser. 7 (1886): 464.

Sykes, William. 'Additions and Emendations to the "New English Dictionary"'. *Notes & Queries* 2, ser. 7 (1886): 463–4.

'Review of *NED*, Batter–Boz'. *Walford's Antiquarian Magazine* 12 (1887): 46–9.

'Review of *NED*, Batter–Boz'. *The Antiquary* 15 (1887): 181–2.

'Review of *NED*, Batter–Boz'. *London Quarterly Review* 68 (1887): 389–90.

'Philological Society ([1887] 21 Jan.)'. *The Academy* 31 (1887): 80.

'Additions and Emendations to "New English Dictionary"'. *Notes & Queries* 3, ser. 7 (1887): 104.

Fowler, J. T. 'Additions and Emendations to "New English Dictionary"'. *Notes & Queries* 3, ser. 7 (1887): 173–4.

Wülcker, Richard Paul. 'Review of *NED*, Ant–Batten'. *Literarisches Centralblatt* (1887): 282.

Murray, J. A. H. 'Seeking Reader for Barker's *Art of Angling*'. *Notes & Queries* 3, ser. 7 (1887): 228–9.

'Review of *NED*, Batter–Boz'. *Notes & Queries* 3, ser. 7 (1887): 259–60.

F. [Furnivall, F. J.] 'Behind, Noun'. *Notes & Queries* 3, ser. 7 (1887): 286.

Skeat, Walter W. 'Review of *NED*, Batter–Boz'. *The Academy* 31 (1887): 247–8.

Bradley, Henry. 'Word Lists'. *Notes & Queries* 3, ser. 7 (1887): 307.

Randall, John. 'Additions to the "New English Dictionary"'. *Notes & Queries* 3, ser. 7 (1887): 302–3.

Wilson, W. Ephanius. 'Review of *NED*, A–Boz'. *Church Review* 49 (1887): 465–73.

[Fennell, C. A. M.] 'Review of *NED*, Ant–Boz'. *Athenaeum* (21 May 1887): 666–7.

'Review of *NED*, Batter–Boz'. *Saturday Review* 63 (1887): 775–6.

V., Q. 'Vade-Mecum'. *Notes & Queries* 3, ser. 7 (1887): 512.

'Review of *NED*, Batter–Boz'. *Scottish Review* 10 (1887): 186–7.

'Review of *NED*, Batter–Boz'. *The Nation* (New York) 45 (1887): 137–8.

Nelson, C. K. 'Murray's New English Dictionary'. *Writer* 1 (1887): 112–13.

Bradley, Henry. 'Soul Above Buttons'. *Notes & Queries* 4, ser. 7 (1887): 227.

Palmer, A. Smythe. 'The "New English Dictionary"'. *Notes & Queries* 4, ser. 7 (1887): 285–6.

Bradley, Henry. 'Soul Above Buttons'. *Notes & Queries* 4, ser. 7 (1887): 333.

Marshall, Edward B. 'Soul Above Buttons'. *Notes & Queries* 4, ser. 7 (1887): 333.

'Review of *NED*, Bra-Byz'. *Saturday Review* 66 (1888): 268–9.

Garnett, James M. 'Review of Bosworth–Toller *An Anglo-Saxon Dictionary*, Part 3; and of *NED*, Part 3'. *American Journal of Philology* 9 (1888): 227–9.

Schröer, Arnold. 'Review of *NED*, A–Ant, Batter–Boz'. *Literaturblatt für germanische und romanische Philologie* 9 (1888): 391–400.

Zupitza, Julius. 'Review of *NED*, Batter–Boz'. *Deutsche Literaturzeitung* (1888): 57–8.

March, Francis A. 'Review of *NED*, Batter–Boz'. *Presbyterian Review* 9 (1888): 173–5.

Furnivall, F. J. 'New English Dictionary'. *Notes & Queries* 5, ser. 7 (1888): 504.

Toynbee, Paget. '"Bull-Fight" in the New English Dictionary'. *The Academy* 34 (1888): 11.

'Review of *NED*, Bra–Byz, C–Cass'. *Notes & Queries* 6, ser. 7 (1888): 39.

Furnivall, F. J. 'Arbolettys, Bawde'. *Notes & Queries* 6, ser. 7 (1888): 38–9.

J., M. J. 'Butter-Scotch'. *Notes & Queries* 6, ser. 7 (1888): 89.

Skeat, Walter W. 'Review of *NED*, Bra–Cass'. *The Academy* 34 (1888): 63–4.

Murray, J. A. H. 'Butter–Scotch'. *Notes & Queries* 6, ser. 7 (1888): 137.

'Review of *NED*, Bra–Byz'. *Scottish Review* 12 (1888): 410–11.

[Fennell, C. A. M.] 'Review of *NED*, Bra–Byz; C–Cass'. *Athenaeum* (6 Oct. 1888): 441–2.

Bradley, Henry. 'Word Lists'. *Notes & Queries* 6, ser. 7 (1888): 347.

Wülcker, Richard Paul. 'Review of *NED*, Bra–Cass'. *Literarisches Centralblatt* (1888): 1750.

'Review of *The Century Dictionary*, A–Cono'. *The Atlantic* 64 (1889): 846–55.

Garnett, James M. 'Review of *NED*, Bra–Byz'. *American Journal of Philology* 10 (1889): 94–7.

McLintock, R. 'The New English Dictionary and Some of Its Predecessors'. *Proceedings of the Literature and Philosophical Society of Liverpool* (1889): 151–66.

Phelps, E. J. 'The Age of Words'. *Scribner's Magazine* 6 (1889): 760–8.

Sattler, W. 'Review of *NED*, Batter–Boz'. *Englische Studien* 12 (1889): 296–8.

March, Francis A. 'Review of *NED*, Bra–Byz, C–Cass'. *Presbyterian Review* 10 (1889): 169–70.

Birkbeck Terry, F. C. 'Elect'. *Notes & Queries* 7, ser. 7 (1889): 12.

'Philological Society (18 Jan.)'. *Athenaeum* (26 Jan. 1889): 120.

'Review of *NED*, Batter–Boz, Bra–Byz, C–Cass'. *The Times* (26 Jan. 1889): 4a–c.

'Philological Society (7 Mar.)'. *Athenaeum* (23 Mar. 1889): 380.

[Reeve, Henry]. 'The Literature and Language of the Age'. *Edinburgh Review* 169 (1889): 339–50.

Lounsbury, Thomas R. 'Review of *NED*, Bra–Byz, C–Cass'. *The Nation* (New York) 48 (1889): 287–9.

—— 'Review of *NED*, Bra–Byz, C–Cass'. *The Nation* (New York) 48 (1889): 309–10.

March, F. A. 'Review of the *Century Dictionary*'. *The Nation* (New York) 48 (1889): 450–1.

[Fosse, E.] 'Review of *The Century Dictionary*'. *Athenaeum* (22 June 1889): 793.

Wilson, R. D. 'The "New English Dictionary": Addenda and Corrigenda'. *Notes & Queries* 8, ser. 7 (1889): 4–5.

Nicholson, Br. 'Angler'. *Notes & Queries* 8, ser. 7 (1889): 114.

'Review of *NED*, Cast–Clivy'. *London Quarterly Review* 74 (1890): 197–8.

'Review of *NED*, Cost–Clivy'. *American Catholic Quarterly* 15 (1890): 185–6.

Garnett, James M. 'Review of *NED*, Cast–Clivy'. *American Journal of Philology* 11 (1890): 229–31.

'Lounger'. *The Critic* 13 (1890): 169–70.

Smith, Lucy Toulmin. 'Review of *NED*, C–Clivy'. *The Antiquary* 21 (1890): 131–3.

—— 'Review of *NED*, C–Clivy'. *The Library* 2, ser. 1 (1890): 220–3.

Williams, R. O. *Our Dictionaries, and Other English Language Topics*. New York: Henry Holt, 1890.

'Review of *NED*, Cast–Clivy'. *Scottish Review* 15 (1890): 225–6.

'Review of *NED*, Cast–Clivy'. *Saturday Review* 69 (1890): 20–1.

[Fennell, C. A. M.] 'Review of *NED*, Cast–Clivy'. *Athenaeum* (15 Feb. 1890): 207–8.

'Review of *NED*, Cast–Clivy'. *The Critic* 13 (1890): 101.

'Review of *The Century Dictionary*'. *Athenaeum* (1 Mar. 1890): 270–1.

Hall, Fitzedward. 'Letter to the Editor'. *The Nation* (New York) (1890): 200–1.

'Review of *NED*, Cast–Clivy'. *The Times* (22 Mar. 1890): 15a–b.

Dormer, J. 'The "New English Dictionary": Addenda and Corrigenda'. *Notes & Queries* 9, ser. 7 (1890): 225–6.

Wilson, R. D. 'The "New English Dictionary": Addenda and Corrigenda'. *Notes & Queries* 9, ser. 7 (1890): 224–5.

Frowde, Henry. Letter on a Mistake in Binding. *The Times* (27 Mar. 1890): 13e.

Murray, J. A. H. 'Cockney'. *The Academy* 37 (1890): 320–1.

'Review of *NED*, Cast–Clivy, and *The Century Dictionary*, Vol. 1'. *The Spectator* 64 (1890): 767.

'Review of *NED*, Cast–Clivy'. *The Nation* (New York) 50 (1890): 453–4.

Wilson, R. D. 'The "New English Dictionary": Addenda and Corrigenda'. *Notes & Queries* 10, ser. 7 (1890): 3.

—— 'The "New English Dictionary": Addenda and Corrigenda'. *Notes & Queries* 10, ser. 7 (1890): 183.

Murray, J. A. H. 'Word Lists'. *Notes & Queries* 10, ser. 7 (1890): 407.

Garnett, James M. 'Review of Stratmann–Bradley *Middle English Dictionary*'. *American Journal of Philology* 12 (1891): 90–2.

Bradley, Henry. 'Report on the Progress of Volume III of the Society's Dictionary (19 Feb. 1892)'. *TPS* (1891–4): 261–7.

Murray, J. A. H. 'Report on the Progress of the Philological Society's New English Dictionary (4 Mar. 1892)'. *TPS* (1891–4): 268–87.

[Fennell, C. A. M.] 'Review of *The Century Dictionary*, Cono–L'. *Athenaeum* (20 Jan. 1891): 48–9.

W., C. W. ' "Guarantee" '. *Notes & Queries* 1, ser. 8 (1891): 46.

Skeat, Walter W. ' "Fester", "Glamour" '. *Athenaeum* (17 Jan. 1891): 98.

Toynbee, Paget. ' "Arerage" in the New English Dictionary'. *The Academy* 39 (1891): 91.

Notice of *NED*, E–Every. *The Academy* 40 (1891): 34.

Appleby. 'Baccarat'. *Notes & Queries* 12, ser. 7 (1891): 76.

Busk, R. H. 'Baccarat'. *Notes & Queries* 12, ser. 7 (1891): 75–6.

O'C., T. 'Baccarat'. *Notes & Queries* 12, ser. 7 (1891): 76.

Skeat, Walter W. 'Esquire'. *Notes & Queries* 12, ser. 7 (1891): 77.

V., Q. 'Esquire'. *Notes & Queries* 12, ser. 7 (1891): 77.

'Review of *NED*, Clo–Cosigner'. *The Nation* (New York) 53 (1891): 104.

'Review of *NED*, E–Every'. *The Spectator* 67 (1891): 266.

Gibbs, Henry Hucks. 'Baccarat'. *Notes & Queries* 12, ser. 7 (1891): 152.

Murray, J. A. H. 'Baccarat'. *Notes & Queries* 12, ser. 7 (1891): 151–2.

Skeat, Walter W. 'Review of *NED*, E–Every'. *The Academy* 40 (1891): 167–8.

Hunt, T. W. 'English Lexicography'. *New Englander* 55 (1891): 193–210.

Garrison, W. P. 'Review of *NED*, E–Every'. *The Nation* (New York) 53 (1891): 181–2.

Busk, R. H. 'Baccarat'. *Notes & Queries* 12, ser. 7 (1891): 191–3.

Randall, John. 'Additions to the "New English Dictionary"'. *Notes & Queries* 12, ser. 7 (1891): 201–2.

Mount, C. B. 'The New English Dictionary'. *Notes & Queries* 12, ser. 7 (1891): 246.

Randall, John. 'Additions to the "New English Dictionary"'. *Notes & Queries* 12, ser. 7 (1891): 242–3.

'Review of *NED*, E–Everybody'. *Scottish Review* 18 (1891): 471–2.

Busk, R. H. 'The New English Dictionary'. *Notes & Queries* 12, ser. 7 (1891): 351.

Hartland, E. Sidney. 'Cag'. *Notes & Queries* 7, ser. 7 (1891): 362.

Ingleby, Holcombe. 'The New English Dictionary'. *Notes & Queries* 12, ser. 7 (1891): 361–2.

Mount, C. B. 'The New English Dictionary'. *Notes & Queries* 7, ser. 7 (1891): 398.

The Church Times (1891): 272.

Logeman, H. 'Review of *NED*, Clo–Cosigner'. *The Academy* 40 (1891): 590–2.

Garnett, James M. 'Review of *NED*, Clo–Consigner, E–Every; Bosworth–Toller *An Anglo-Saxon Dictionary*'. *American Journal of Philology* 13 (1892): 492–3.

Murray, J. A. H. '"Cooper"'. *Notes & Queries* 1, ser. 8 (1892): 32.

—— '"Corduroy"'. *Notes & Queries* 1, ser. 8 (1892): 27.

B., W. C. '"The New English Dictionary"'. *Notes & Queries* 1, ser. 8 (1892): 50.

F., J. T. 'The New English Dictionary'. *Notes & Queries* 1, ser. 8 (1892): 50.

[Fennell, C. A. M.] 'Review of *NED*, E–Every; *Century Dictionary*, M–P, Q–Stroyl; *Webster's New International Dictionary*; Stratmann–Bradley, *Middle English Dictionary*; Cassell's *English Dictionary*'. *Athenaeum* (16 Jan. 1892): 78–81.

Ingleby, Holcombe. '"The New English Dictionary"'. *Notes & Queries* 1, ser. 8 (1892): 49–50.

Lysart. '"The New English Dictionary"'. *Notes & Queries* 1, ser. 8 (1892): 50.

Murray, J. A. H. '"An Historical": A Disclaimer'. *Notes & Queries* 1, ser. 8 (1892): 41.

Peacock, Edward. 'The New English Dictionary'. *Notes & Queries* 1, ser. 8 (1892): 50.

S., H. H. '"Cash" = Fund'. *Notes & Queries* 2, ser. 8 (1892): 46.

Anderson, Melivlle B. 'Review of the *Century Dictionary*'. *The Dial* 12 (1892): 348–9.

'Review of *NED*, Clo–Cosigner'. *The Nation* (New York) 54 (1892): 91–2.

Logeman, H. 'Inquiry About Robert Hunter's *Encyclopedic Dictionary* (1887–88)'. *Notes & Queries* 1, ser. 8 (1892): 314.

Murray, J. A. H. '"Cotswold"'. *Notes & Queries* 1, ser. 8 (1892): 315.

—— '"Cottar-Bank"'. *Notes & Queries* 1, ser. 8 (1892): 315.

—— ' "Corroboree" '. *Notes & Queries* 2, ser. 8 (1892): 353.

—— ' "Costermonger" '. *Notes & Queries* 1, ser. 8 (1892): 373.

'Review of *NED*, Clo–Cosigner, E–Every'. *The Guardian* (1892): 703–4.

Murray, J. A. H. ' "Couple, Warp" '. *Notes & Queries* 1, ser. 8 (1892): 514.

—— 'Courage of One's Opinions'. *Notes & Queries* 1, ser. 8 (1892): 514.

—— ' "Couvade" ': The Genesis of An Anthropological Term'. *The Academy* 42 (1892): 389–90.

Tylor, Edward B. ' "Couvade": The Genesis of an Anthropological Term'. *The Academy* 42 (1892): 412.

Mayhew, A. L. ' "Couvade": The Genesis of an Anthropological Term'. *The Academy* 42 (1892): 437–8.

Murray, J. A. H. ' "Couvade": The Genesis of a Modern Myth'. *The Academy* 42 (1892): 458–60.

Tylor, Edward B. ' "Couvade": The Genesis of an Anthropological Term'. *The Academy* 42 (1892): 542.

Murray, J. A. H. ' "Couvade": The Genesis of a Modern Myth'. *The Academy* 42 (1892): 567–8.

Mann, Max Friedrich. 'Review of *NED*, Clo–Consigner'. *Anglia Bleiblatt* 4 (1893): 169–70.

Mayhew, A. L. 'Review of *NED*, Clo–Consigner'. *Englische Studien* 17 (1893): 265–71.

—— 'Review of *NED*, E–Every'. *Englische Studien* 17 (1893): 271–7.

'A Few Words About the New English Dictionary'. *Newbery House Magazine* 8 (1893): 8–13.

'The Stanford Dictionary'. *The Nation* (New York) 56 (1893): 14–15.

Garrison, W. P. 'The Great Dictionary'. *The Nation* (New York) 56 (1893): 230–1.

'Review of *NED*, Consignificant–Crouching'. *The Nation* (New York) 56 (1893): 332.

'Review of *NED*, Consignificant–Crouching'. *The Times* (9 June 1893): 3c.

Owen, J. P. 'The "New English Dictionary" '. *Athenaeum* (1 July 1893): 35.

Murray, J. A. H. 'The Word "Cram" in the "New English Dictionary" '. *Athenaeum* (15 July 1893): 96–7.

Garrison, W. P. 'Review of *NED*, Consignificant–Crouching'. *The Nation* (New York) 57 (1893): 67–8.

Owen, J. P. 'The Word "Cram" in the New English Dictionary'. *Athenaeum* (29 July 1893): 161.

'Review of *NED*, Clo–Crouching, E–Every'. *The Critic* 20 (1893): 118–19.

T., H. 'Lines on "New English Dictionary" '. *Notes & Queries* 4, ser. 8 (1893): 206.

Randall, John. 'Additions to the New English Dictionary'. *Notes & Queries* 4, ser. 8 (1893): 363–4.

[Fennell, C. A. M.] 'Review of *NED*, Clo–Cosigner; Consignificant–Crouching'. *Athenaeum* (2 Dec. 1893): 765–6.

'Review of *NED*, Crouchmas–Czech'. *The Times* (8 Dec. 1893): 4a.

Skeat, Walter W. 'Wherever the English Speech Has Spread' (Poem). *The Critic* 20 (1893): 419.

Garnett, James M. 'Review of *NED*, Consignificant–Crouching'. *American Journal of Philology* 15 (1894): 82–5.

Mann, Max Friedrich. 'Review of *NED*, Consignificant–Crouching'. *Anglia Bleiblatt* 4 (1894): 293–4.

—— 'Review of *NED*, Everybody–Ezod'. *Anglia Bleiblatt* 5 (1894): 10–11.

Garrison, W. P. 'Review of *NED*, Crouchmas–Czech'. *The Nation* (New York) 58 (1894): 35–6.

'Philological Society (12 Jan.)'. *Athenaeum* (27 Jan. 1894): 117.

'Review of *NED*, Crouchmas–Czech'. *The Dial* 16 (1894): 117.

'Review of *NED*, Everybody–Ezod'. *The Times* (16 Mar. 1894): 13a.

'Review of *NED*, Everybody–Ezod'. *The Nation* (New York) 58 (1894): 274.

'Philological Society (13 Apr.)'. *Athenaeum* (21 Apr. 1894): 514–15.

Murray, J. A. H. ' "Delve" '. *Notes & Queries* 5, ser. 8 (1894): 389.

—— ' "Dene-Holes" '. *Notes & Queries* 5, ser. 8 (1894): 427.

—— ' "Demi-Pique" '. *Notes & Queries* 5, ser. 8 (1894): 447.

Schröer, Arnold. 'Über Neuere Englische Lexicographie'. *Die neueren Sprachen* 2 (1894): 193–210.

'Review of *NED*, E–Every, Everybody–Ezod'. *The Critic* 25 (1894): 268.

'Review of *NED*, D–Deceit, F–Fang'. *The Times* (29 Nov. 1894): 4e–f.

Garnett, James M. 'Review of *NED*, Everybody–Ezod'. *American Journal of Philology* 16 (1895): 97–9.

Mann, Max Friedrich. 'Review of *NED*, D–Deject, F–Fang'. *Anglia Bleiblatt* 5 (1895): 291–2.

Murray, J. A. H. ' "Digby Chicks" Digby Herrings'. *Notes & Queries* 7, ser. 8 (1895): 247.

'Notice of *NED*, D–Deceit, F–Fang'. *The Dial* 16 (1895): 277.

'Notice of New Fascicles'. *The Dial* 18 (1895): 90.

Garrison, W. P. 'Review of *NED*, D–Deceit, Deceit–Deject, F–Fang'. *The Nation* (New York) 60 (1895): 167–8.

Murray, J. A. H. ' "Dictate" '. *Notes & Queries* 7, ser. 8 (1895): 247.

'Review of *NED*, Fanged–Fee'. *The Times* (5 Apr. 1895): 13e.

Bradley, Henry. ' "Flash" '. *Notes & Queries* 7, ser. 8 (1895): 287.

Murray, J. A. H. ' "Dike-Grave" and "Dike-Reeve" '. *Notes & Queries* 7, ser. 8 (1895): 287.

'Review of *NED*, Fanged–Fee'. *The Nation* (New York) 60 (1895): 302.

Murray, J. A. H. ' "Dilligront" '. *Notes & Queries* 7, ser. 8 (1895): 327.

'Review of *NED*, Fanged–Fee'. *Notes & Queries* 7, ser. 8 (1895): 359.

Murray, J. A. H. ' "Dimpsy" '. *Notes & Queries* 7, ser. 8 (1895): 367.

—— ' "Dinge" '. *Notes & Queries* 7, ser. 8 (1895): 367.

'Review of *NED*, D–Deceit, Deceit–Deject, F–Fang, Fanged–Fee'. *Literary World* (Boston) 26 (1895): 149.

Mayhew, A. L. ' "Barth" '. *Notes & Queries* 7, ser. 8 (1895): 407–8.

Murray, J. A. H. ' "Dip" '. *Notes & Queries* 7, ser. 8 (1895): 407.

'An Exemplary Work'. *Commerce* (1895).

Murray, J. A. H. ' "Dilligrout" '. *Notes & Queries* 7, ser. 8 (1895): 427.

'Notice of *NED*, Deject–Depravation'. *The Times* (5 July 1895): 13d.

'Review of *NED*, Deject–Depravation'. *The Academy* 48 (1895): 14.

[Fennell, C. A. M.] 'Review of *NED*, Crouchmas–Czech, D–Deject; Everybody–Ezod; F–Fee'. *Athenaeum* (14 Sept. 1895): 347–8.

'Review of *NED*, Depravative–Develolpment, Fee–Field'. *The Times* (4 Oct. 1895): 4.

'Review of *NED*, Depravative–Development'. *The Academy* 48 (1895): 14.

'Notice of *NED*, Depravative–Development, Fee–Field'. *The Dial* 19 (1895): 261.

'Review of *NED*, D–Depravation; F–Fee'. *The Critic* 28 (1896): 1–2.

'Review of *NED*, Depravative–Development, Development–Difficulty'. *London Quarterly Review* 86 (1896): 190–1

'Review of *NED*, Diffluent–Disburden'. *London Quarterly Review* 87 (1896): 197.

Weiner, Leo. 'English Lexicography'. *Modern Language Notes* 11 (1896): 351–66.

'Review of *NED*, Development–Diffluency'. *The Times* (3 Jan. 1896): 3c.

'Philological Society ([1896] 10 Jan.)'. *Athenaeum* (18 Jan. 1896): 91.

Murray, J. A. H. 'An Unrecorded English Verb'. *The Academy* 49 (1896): 138–9.

Napier, A. S. 'An Unrecorded English Verb'. *The Academy* 49 (1896): 158.

Sweet, Henry. 'An Unrecorded English Verb'. *The Academy* 49 (1896): 158.

Liddell, Mark H. 'The Verb "Deech" '. *The Academy* 49 (1896): 178.

McLintock, R. 'The Verb "Deech" '. *The Academy* 49 (1896): 178.

Murray, J. A. H. 'The Verb "Deech" '. *The Academy* 49 (1896): 178.

Toynbee, Helen. ' "Caroon" in the New English Dictionary'. *The Academy* 49 (1896): 201.

Randall, John. 'Additions to the "New English Dictionary" '. *Notes & Queries* 9, ser. 8 (1896): 221–3.

'Review of *NED*, Field–Fish'. *The Academy* 49 (1896): 287–8.

'The English Dictionary and the Clarendon Press'. *The Saturday Review* (1896): 393–4.

'Review of *NED*, Field–Fish'. *Notes & Queries* 9, ser. 8 (1896): 320.

Warren, C. F. S. 'Additions to the "New English Dictionary" '. *Notes & Queries* 9, ser. 8 (1896): 318.

'Review of *NED*, Diffluent–Disburden'. *The Academy* 50 (1896): 13.

'Review of *NED*, Disburdened–Disobservant; Fish–Flexuose'. *The Academy* 50 (1896): 225–6.

[Fennell, C. A. M.] 'Review of *NED*, Disburden–Disobedient, Fish–Flexuose'. *Athenaeum* (26 Sept. 1896): 420.

'Review of *NED*, Disburdened–Disobservant, Fish–Flexuose'. *The Times* (10 Oct. 1896): 12.

'Review of *NED*, Disburdened–Disobservant'. *The Manchester Guardian* (1896).

'Review of *NED*, Disburdened–Disobservant , Fish–Flexuose'. *London Quarterly Review* 28 (1897): 184.

'Review of *NED*, Distrustfully–Doom, Flexuosity–Foster'. *London Quarterly Review* 28 (1897): 393–4.

March, Francis A. 'The Enlargement of the English Dictionary'. *Transactions of the American Philological Society* 28 (1897): 88–91.

Schröer, Arnold. 'Review of *NED*, Consignificant–Field'. *Englische Studien* 23 (1897): 171–83.

'Review of *NED*, Disburdened–Disobservant'. *The Times* (15 Jan. 1897): 7d.

Notice of *NED*, Disobstetricate–Distrustful. *The Dial* 22 (1897): 97.

[Skeat, Walter W. *pseud.* 'Sequin'.] 'The Oxford English Dictionary'. *Notes & Queries* 11, ser. 8 (1897): 107.

Murray, J. A. H. ' "Handmaid" '. *Notes & Queries* 11, ser. 8 (1897): 167.

L., R. M. 'The Oxford English Dictionary'. *Notes & Queries* 11, ser. 8 (1897): 206.

Murray, J. A. H. ' "Hamel–Tree" '. *Notes & Queries* 22, ser. 8 (1897): 207.

'Review of *NED*, Distrustfully–Doom; Flexuosity–Foister'. *Scottish Review* 29 (1897): 410–11.

Murray, J. A. H. ' "Handicap" '. *Notes & Queries* 11, ser. 8 (1897): 270.

'The Oxford English Dictionary'. *The Times* (10 Apr. 1897): 5b–c.

Murray, J. A. H. ' "Hake" '. *Notes & Queries* 11, ser. 8 (1897): 287.

—— 'The Longest Words in the English Language'. *Notes & Queries* 11, ser. 8 (1897): 297.

—— ' "Ha'porth of Tar" '. *Notes & Queries* 11, ser. 8 (1897): 307.

Maxwell, Patrick. 'Pronunciation and the 'New English Dictionary" '. *Notes & Queries* 11, ser. 8 (1897): 325.

Murray, J. A. H. ' "The Greatest Happiness of the Greatest Number" '. *Notes & Queries* 11, ser. 8 (1897): 347.

'Review of *NED*, Flexuosity–Foister'. *The Nation* (New York) 64 (1897): 341.

'Review of *NED*, F–Foister'. *The Critic* 30 (1897): 332–3.

Ingleby, Holcombe. 'Pronunciation and the "New English Dictionary" '. *Notes & Queries* 11, ser. 8 (1897): 410.

'Notice of *NED*, Flexuosity–Foister'. *The Dial* 22 (1897): 331.

Skeat, Walter W. ' "I'm Glad You've Done . . . With Words That Begin With D" (Poem)'. *The Dial* 22 (1897): 339.

Murray, J. A. H. ' "Dick's Hatband" '. *Notes & Queries* 11, ser. 8 (1897): 467.

Palmer, A. Smythe. ' "Callow" '. *Notes & Queries* 11, ser. 8 (1897): 466.

Murray, J. A. H. ' "Harvestry", "Harveyized" '. *Notes & Queries* 11, ser. 8 (1897): 487.

'Review of *NED*, Doom–Dziggetai'. *Scottish Review* 30 (1897): 417–18.

'Review of *NED*, Doom–Dziggetai'. *London Quarterly Review* 29 (1897): 183–4.

[Fennell, C. A. M.] 'Review of *NED*, Development–Dziggetai; Field–Foister'. *Athenaeum* (9 Oct. 1897): 484.

'The Historical English Dictionary'. *The Times* (13 Oct. 1897): 10b; (14 Oct. 1897): 7d–f.

Knight, James. 'The Historical Dictionary of the English Language'. *Notes & Queries* 12, ser. 8 (1897): 321–2.

'Review of *NED*, D–E'. *The Times* (29 Oct. 1897): 13f.

B., W. C. 'The Historical Dictionary of the English Language'. *Notes & Queries* 12, ser. 8 (1897): 370.

'Review of *NED*, Distrust–Doom, Flexuosity–Foister'. *Zeitschrift für Bücherfreunde* 1 (1898): 440.

'Review of *NED*, Foisty–Frankish'. *Imperial and Asiatic Quarterly Review* 5 (1898): 191–3.

'Review of *NED*, Foisty–Frankish, Vol. 4'. *London Quarterly Review* 29 (1898): 396–7.

'Review of *NED*, Vol. 4'. *Imperial and Asiatic Quarterly Review* 5 (1898): 435.

'Words, Words, Words'. *The Academy* 55 (1898): 250–1.

'Review of *NED*, Foisty–Frankish, Frank-law–Gain-Coming'. *Scottish Review* 31 (1898): 211–12.

'Review of *NED*, Frank-law–Fyz'. *The Times* (7 Jan. 1898): 7c–d.

D[avis], N. D. 'The Making of the Oxford Dictionary'. *The Nation* (New York) 66 (1898): 144–6.

Notice of *NED*, Frank-Law–Gaincoming. *The Dial* 24 (1898): 155.

'Review of *NED*, H–Haversian'. *The Times* (7 Apr. 1898): 8c–d.

'Review of *NED*, H–Haversian'. *Scottish Review* 32 (1898): 201–2.

'Review of *NED*, H–Haversian'. *London Quarterly Review* 30 (1898): 395.

'Review of *NED*, Haversine–Heel'. *The Times* (11 July 1898): 15c–d.

Todhunter, John. 'Reading a Dictionary'. *Cornhill Magazine* 78 (1898): 207–17.

'Review of *NED*, Gaincope–Germanizing'. *The Times* (15 Oct. 1898): 9a.

'Review of *NED*, H–Hod'. *The Academy* 55 (1898): 250–1.

'Review of *NED*, Gaincope–Germanizing'. *Imperial and Asiatic Quarterly Review* 7 (1899): 191.

'Review of *NED*, Germano–Glasscloth, Hod–Horizontal'. *London Quarterly Review* 90 (1899): 205.

'Review of *NED*, Gradely–Greement, Inforcible–Inpushing'. *Imperial and Asiatic Quarterly Review* 8 (1899): 419–20.

Lillingston, Leonard W. 'The Making of the Dictionary'. *Eclectic Magazine* 132 (1899): 762–6.

March, Francis A. ' "Uses of the Oxford Historical English Dictionary" (Abstract)'. *Proceedings of the American Philological Association* (1899): xxxiii.

Thomas, Ralph. *Some Words in* 'A New English Dictionary on Historical Principles'. London: By the Author, 1899.

'The New English Dictionary'. *The Times* (14 Jan. 1899): 8e.

Murray, J. A. H. 'Report of a "Dictionary Evening" '. *Literature* 4 (1899): 55.

'Review of *NED*, Gaincope–Germanizing, Heel–Hod'. *Literature* 4 (1899): 88.

Murray, J. A. H. 'Letter'. *Literature* 4 (1899): 150.

'Review of *NED*, Heel–Hod'. *The Times* (24 Feb. 1899): 13c.

'The Great Oxford Dictionary: A National Undertaking'. *The Academy* 56 (1899): 361–2.

[Fennell, C. A. M.] 'Review of *NED*, Frank-law–Germanizing; H–Hod'. *Athenaeum* (25 Mar. 1899): 365.

'Review of *NED*, Germano–Glass-Cloth; Hod–Horizontal'. *Scottish Review* 33 (1899): 423–4.

Skeat, Walter W. 'Dr Murray and the New English Dictionary'. *Modern Language Quarterly* 2 (1899): 257–9.

Whiteway, R. S. 'Note on "Hog Deer" '. *Athenaeum* (15 Apr. 1899): 472.

'Review of *NED*, Germano–Glass-cloth, Hod–Horizontal'. *The Academy* 56 (1899): 453–4.

Marshall, Edward B. 'The "H. E. D." '. *Notes & Queries* 3, ser. 9 (1899): 366.

'Review of *NED*, Germano–Glasscloth, Hod–Horizontal'. *Literature* 4 (1899): 623.

'Review of *NED*, Horizontality–Hywe'. *Scottish Review* 34 (1899): 209.

'Review of *NED*, Horizontality–Hywe'. *The Times* (1 Aug. 1899): 13c.

'Review of *NED*, Horizontality–Hywe'. *The Academy* 57 (1899): 178–9.

'Review of *NED*, Horizontality–Hywe'. *The Nation* (New York) 69 (1899): 133.

[Fennell, C. A. M.] 'Review of *NED*, Horizontality–Hywe'. *Athenaeum* (23 Sept. 1899): 412.

'Review of *NED*, I–In'. *Scottish Review* 34 (1899): 408–9.

Notice of Re-Issue of Earlier Parts. *The Dial* 27 (1899): 248.

'Review of *NED*, I–In'. *The Times* (28 Oct. 1899): 15a–b.

'Review of *NED*, I–In'. *The Nation* (New York) 69 (1899): 354.

'Note on the Oxford English Dictionary'. *The Dial* 29 (1900): 182–3.

'Review of *NED*, I–In'. *Imperial and Asiatic Quarterly Review* 9 (1900): 198.

'Review of *NED*, In–Infer'. *Saturday Review* 89 (1900): 497–8.

'Review of *NED*, Glass-Coach–Graded'. *The Academy* 58 (1900): 48.

'Review of *NED*, Haversine–Heel'. *Scottish Review* 35 (1900): 424.

'Review of *NED*, In–Infer'. *Scottish Review* 35 (1900): 424.

Dyer, Louis. 'A Lexicographer on Lexicography'. *The Nation* (New York) 71 (1900): 28–30.

[Fennell, C. A. M.] 'Review of *The Evolution of English Lexicography*'. *Athenaeum* (21 July 1900): 83–4.

'Some Statistics Relating to the Oxford English Dictionary'. *The Academy* 59 (1900): 84.

'Review of *NED*, Gradely–Greement; Inferable–Inpushing'. *The Nation* (New York) 71 (1900): 152–3.

[Fennell, C. A. M.] 'Review of *NED*, Gradely–Greement; Inferable–Inpushing'. *Athenaeum* (25 Aug. 1900): 242–3.

'Review of *NED*, Gradely–Greement; Inferable–Inpushing, Input–Invalid'. *Saturday Review* 90 (1900): 557–8.

'Review of *NED*, Input–Invalid'. *The Nation* (New York) 71 (1900): 367.

[Fennell, C. A. M.] 'Review of *NED*, Input–Invalid'. *Athenaeum* (29 Dec. 1900): 850–1.

'Review of *NED*, Green–Gyzzarn, Invalid–Jew'. *London Quarterly Review* 95 (1901): 409.

'Review of *NED*, Input–Invalid'. *Imperial and Asiatic Quarterly Review* 22 (1901): 196.

'Review of *NED*, Invalid–Jew'. *Imperial and Asiatic Quarterly Review* 22 (1901): 408–9.

'Review of *NED*, L–Lap'. *Anglia Bleiblatt* 16 (1901): 63–4.

'Review of *NED*, Green–Gyzzern, Invalid–Jew'. *Notes & Queries* 7, ser. 9 (1901).

'Review of *NED*, Green–Gyzzarn'. *The Academy* 60 (1901): 120–1.

[Fennell, C. A. M.] 'Review of *NED*, Green–Gyzzarn; Invalid–Jew'. *Athenaeum* (9 Feb. 1901): 167.

'Review of *NED*, Green–Gyzzarn; Invalid–Jew'. *The Nation* (New York) 72 (1901): 137–8.

'Review of *NED*, L–Lap'. *Glasgow Herald* (1901).

'Review of *NED*, L–Lap'. *The Nation* (New York) 72 (1901): 339.

[Fennell, C. A. M.] 'Review of *NED*, L–Lap'. *Athenaeum* (9 Feb. 1901): 588.

'Review of *NED*, J'. *The Academy* 61 (1901): 7–8.

'Review of *NED*, Jew–Kairine'. *Notes & Queries* 8, ser. 9 (1901): 54–5.

[Fennell, C. A. M.] 'Review of *NED*, Jew–Kairine'. *Athenaeum* (27 July 1901): 115.

'Review of *NED*, Green–Gyzzarn, Invalid–Jew, Jew–Kairine, L–Lap'. *Saturday Review* 92 (1901): 302–3.

[Fennell, C. A. M.] 'Review of *NED*, Kaiser–Kyx'. *Athenaeum* (9 Nov. 1901): 626.

'Review of *NED*, Kaiser–Kyx'. *The Nation* (New York) 73 (1901): 378.

Platt, James Jun. 'Etymology of "Nark"'. *Athenaeum* (16 Nov. 1901): 664.

'Review of *NED*, Kaiser–Kyx'. *Notes & Queries* 8, ser. 9 (1901): 434.

'Review of *NED*, Kaiser–Kyx'. *Saturday Review* 92 (1901): 810–11.

'Review of *NED*, Leisureness–Lief, O–Onomastic'. *London Quarterly Review* 98 (1902): 409.

Mann, Max Friedrich. 'Review of *NED*, H–K'. *Anglia Bleiblatt* 13 (1902): 255–6.

'Some Sense Histories'. *The Academy* (1902): 648.

W. W. 'The Poetic Leg'. *The Academy* 62 (1902): 677.

'Review of *NED*, Lap–Leisurely'. *Notes & Queries* 9, ser. 9 (1902): 58.

'Review of *NED*, Lap–Leisurely'. *The Nation* (New York) 74 (1902): 72.

'Review of *NED*, Lap–Leisurely'. *Nottingham Guardian* (1902).

[Fennell, C. A. M.] 'Review of *NED*, Lap–Leisurely'. *Athenaeum* (15 Feb. 1902): 199–200.

'Review of *NED*, Leisureness–Lief'. *Notes & Queries* 9, ser. 9 (1902): 298–9.

Luick, Karl. 'Review of *NED*, F–K'. *Deutsche Literaturzeitung* 23 (1902): 1188–90.

[Fennell, C. A. M.] 'Review of *NED*, Leisureness–Lief'. *Athenaeum* (14 June 1902): 743–4.

'Review of *NED*, O–Onomastic'. *Notes & Queries* 10, ser. 9 (1902): 79.

[Fennell, C. A. M.] 'Review of *NED*, O–Onomastic'. *Athenaeum* (26 July 1902): 115–16.

'Review of *NED*, Lap–Leisurely, O–Onomastic'. *Saturday Review* 94 (1902): 146–7.

'Review of *NED*, O–Onomastic'. *The Nation* (New York) 75 (1902): 151–2.

'Review of *NED*, Q'. *The Nation* (New York) 75 (1902): 307.

'Review of *NED*, Q'. *Notes & Queries* 10, ser. 9 (1902): 339.

'Philological Society ([1902] 7 Nov.)'. *Athenaeum* (15 Nov. 1902): 656.

'Review of *NED*, Q'. *Athenaeum* (29 Nov. 1902): 715–16.

Garnett, James M. 'Review of *NED*, Vols. 3–5'. *American Journal of Philology* 24 (1903): 85–9.

Luick, Karl. 'Review of *NED*, L'. *Deutsche Literaturzeitung* 24 (1903): 2945–6.

'Review of *NED*, Lief–Lock'. *Notes & Queries* 11, ser. 9 (1903): 60.

'Review of *NED*, Lief–Lock'. *The Nation* (New York) 76 (1903): 95–6.

Murray, J. A. H. 'Note on "Appendicitis"'. *The Academy* 64 (1903): 120.

C., B. C. '"Rose" in the "N. E. D."'. *Notes & Queries* 1, ser. 11 (1903): 205–6.

'Notice of *NED*, Onomastical–Outing'. *The Academy* 64 (1903): 268.

[Fennell, C. A. M.] 'Review of *NED*, Lief–Lock'. *Athenaeum* (21 Mar. 1903): 362–3.

'Review of *NED*, Onomastical–Outing'. *The Academy* 64 (1903): 385–6.

'Review of *NED*, Onomastical–Outing'. *Notes & Queries* 11, ser. 9 (1903): 339.

Dodgson, E. S. '"H. E. D." Jottings'. *Notes & Queries* 11, ser. 9 (1903): 387–8.

'Review of *NED*, R–Reactive'. *Notes & Queries* 12, ser. 9 (1903): 37–8.

'Review of *NED*, R–Reactive'. *The Academy* 65 (1903): 53–4.

[Fennell, C. A. M.] 'Review of *NED*, Onomastical–Outing'. *Athenaeum* (1 Aug. 1903): 149–50.

'Review of *NED*, Lief–Lock, Onomastical–Outing, Q'. *Saturday Review* 96 (1903): 238–9.

Gill, Theo. 'O-Words in the "New English Dictionary"'. *Notes & Queries* 12, ser. 9 (1903): 165–6.

Murray, J. A. H. 'O-Words in the "New English Dictionary"'. *Notes & Queries* 12, ser. 9 (1903): 209–10.

Platt, James Jun. 'O-Words in the "New English Dictionary"'. *Notes & Queries* 12, ser. 9 (1903): 210.

'Review of *NED*, Lock–Lyyn'. *Notes & Queries* 12, ser. 9 (1903): 338.

K., L. L. 'O-Words in the "New English Dictionary"'. *Notes & Queries* 12, ser. 9 (1903): 330–1.

[Fennell, C. A. M.] 'Review of *NED*, R–Reactive'. *Athenaeum* (19 Dec. 1903): 821–2.

Garnett, James M. 'Review of *NED*, Lock–Lyyn, M–Mandragora, Onomastical–Outing, Outjet–Ozyat, P–Pargeted, R–Reactive, Reactively–Rhee'. *American Journal of Philology* 25 (1904): 463–7.

Schröer, Arnold. 'Review of *NED*, D–S'. *Englische Studien* 34 (1904): 260–7.

'Review of *NED*, Outjet–Ozyat'. *Notes & Queries* 1, ser. 10 (1904): 78.

[Fennell, C. A. M.] 'Review of *NED*, Lock–Lyyn'. *Athenaeum* (30 Jan. 1904): 136–7.

Thomas, Ralph. '"The Oxford English Dictionary"'. *Notes & Queries* 1, ser. 10 (1904): 146–7.

B., W. C. '"The Oxford English Dictionary"'. *Notes & Queries* 1, ser. 10 (1904): 193.

Graves, C. L. and E. V. Lucas. 'The Limits of Invective'. *Punch* 126 (1904): 215.

Thomas, Ralph. '"The Oxford English Dictionary"'. *Notes & Queries* 1, ser. 10 (1904): 255–6.

'Review of *NED*, P–Pargeted'. *Notes & Queries* 1, ser. 10 (1904): 338–9.

Graves, C. L. and E. V. Lucas. 'Should We Not Strain Every Nerve to Enlarge the Language?' *Punch* 126 (1904): 367–8.

[Fennell, C. A. M.] 'Review of *NED*, Outjet–Ozyat'. *Athenaeum* (28 May 1904): 684–5.

—— 'Review of *NED*, P–Pargeted'. *Athenaeum* (13 Aug. 1904): 200.

—— 'Review of *NED*, Reactively–Ree'. *Athenaeum* (17 Sept. 1904): 374–5.

'Review of *NED*, M–Mandragon'. *Notes & Queries* 2, ser. 10 (1904): 337.

Mann, Max Friedrich. 'Review of *NED*, L–Lap'. *Bleiblatt zur Anglia* 16 (1905): 63–4.

—— 'Review of *NED*, Lap–Leisurely'. *Bleiblatt zur Anglia* 16 (1905): 95–6.

—— 'Review of *NED*, Leisureness–Leif'. *Bleiblatt zur Anglia* 16 (1905): 127.

—— 'Review of *NED*, O–Onomastic'. *Bleiblatt zur Anglia* 16 (1905): 255–6.

—— 'Review of *NED*, Onomastical–Outing'. *Bleiblatt zur Anglia* 16 (1905): 319–20.

—— 'Review of *NED*, Outjet–Ozyat'. *Bleiblatt zur Anglia* 16 (1905): 350–1.

'Review of *NED*, Pargeter–Pennached'. *Notes & Queries* 3, ser. 10 (1905): 38–9.

Nicholson, Edward. 'The Nail and the Clove'. *Notes & Queries* 3, ser. 10 (1905): 41–3, 231.

[Fennell, C. A. M.] 'Review of *NED*, M–Mandragon'. *Athenaeum* (18 Feb. 1905): 200–1.

V., Q. 'The Nail and the Clove'. *Notes & Queries* 3, ser. 10 (1905): 134.

Baldock, G. Yarrow. 'The Nail and the Clove'. *Notes & Queries* 3, ser. 20 (1905): 231–2.

'Medical Terms in the *New English Dictionary*'. *British Medical Journal* (1905): 842.

'Review of *NED*, Ree–Reign'. *Notes & Queries* 3, ser. 10 (1905): 297–8.

[Fennell, C. A. M.] 'Review of *NED*, Pargeter–Pennached'. *Athenaeum* (13 May 1905): 586–7.

'Review of *NED*, M–Mandragon, Mandragora–Matter'. *TLS* (4 July 1905): 223.

'Review of *NED*, Mandragora–Matter'. *Notes & Queries* 4, ser. 10 (1905): 58.

[Fennell, C. A. M.] 'Review of *NED*, Ree–Reign'. *Athenaeum* (5 Aug. 1905): 166–7.

'Review of *NED*, Pennage–Pfennig'. *Notes & Queries* 4, ser. 10 (1905): 358–9.

[Fennell, C. A. M.] 'Review of *NED*, Mandragora–Matter'. *Athenaeum* (28 Oct. 1905): 570–1.

Bayley, Harold. *The Shakespeare Symphony*. London: Chapman and Hall, 1906.

Bradley, Henry. 'The Oxford English Dictionary'. *Zeitschrift für deutsche Wortforschung* 7 (1906): 311–18.

Leonard, William Ellery. 'Corrections to the *NED*'. *Modern Language Notes* 21 (1906): 63–4.

Mann, Max Friedrich. 'Review of *NED*, Mandragora–Matter'. *Bleiblatt zur Anglia* 17 (1906): 191–2.

—— 'Review of *NED*, P–Pargeted'. *Bleiblatt zur Anglia* 17 (1906): 95–6.

—— 'Review of *NED*, Pargeter–Pennached'. *Bleiblatt zur Anglia* 17 (1906): 126–8.

—— 'Review of *NED*, Pennage–PF'. *Bleiblatt zur Anglia* 17 (1906): 159–60.

—— 'Review of *NED*, Q'. *Bleiblatt zur Anglia* 17 (1906): 255–6.

—— 'Review of *NED*, R–Reactive'. *Bleiblatt zur Anglia* 17 (1906): 286–7.

—— 'Review of *NED*, Reigh–Reserve'. *Bleiblatt zur Anglia* 17 (1906): 383–4.

'Review of *NED*, Reign-Reserve'. *Notes & Queries* 5, ser. 10 (1906): 57–8.

Notes & Queries, ser. 5 (1906): 265.

[Fennell, C. A. M.] 'Review of *NED*, Pennage–Pfennig; Reign–Reserve'. *Athenaeum* (24 Mar. 1906): 353–5.

'Review of *NED*, Matter–Mesnalty'. *The Newcastle Daily Journal* (1906).

'Review of *NED*, Matter–Mesnalty'. *Notes & Queries* (1906).

'Review of *NED*, Matter–Mesnalty'. *Notes & Queries* (1906).

[Fennell, C. A. M.] 'Review of *NED*, Matter–Mesnalty'. *Athenaeum* (16 June 1906): 724–5.

Morton, Wallace. ' "Dictionary" Murray'. *Caledonian* 6 (1906): 380–3.

[Fennell, C. A. M.] 'Review of *NED*, Ph–Piper'. *Athenaeum* (1 Sept. 1906): 234–5.

'Review of *NED*, Matter–Mesnalty, Pennage–Pfennig, Ph–Piper, Reign–Reserve'. *TLS* (21 Dec. 1906): 423.

Conrad, Hermann. 'Murray's New English Dictionary und de Shakespeare-Interpretation'. *Zeitschrift für französiche und englische Unterricht* 6 (1907): 193–220.

Derocquigny, Jules. 'Review of *NED*, Piper–Polygenistic'. *Revue Germanique* 3 (1907): 642–3.

Garnett, James M. 'Review of *NED*, 12 Parts From 1905–1907'. *American Journal of Philology* 28 (1907): 456–60.

Mann, Max Friedrich. 'Review of *NED*, Mense–Misbirth'. *Bleiblatt zur Anglia* 18 (1907): 95–6.

—— 'Review of *NED*, Misbode–Monopoly'. *Bleiblatt zur Anglia* 18 (1907): 287–8.

—— 'Review of *NED*, N–Niche'. *Bleiblatt zur Anglia* 18 (1907): 62–3.

—— 'Review of *NED*, Niche–Nywe'. *Bleiblatt zur Anglia* 18 (1907): 383–4.

—— 'Review of *NED*, Ph–Piper'. *Bleiblatt zur Anglia* 18 (1907): 30–2.

—— 'Review of *NED*, Piper–Polygenistic'. *Bleiblatt zur Anglia* 18 (1907): 101–2.

Toynbee, Paget. ' "Connoissance" in the New English Dictionary'. *Modern Language Review* 2 (1907): 166.

[Fennell, C. A. M.] 'Review of *NED*, N–Niche'. *Athenaeum* (5 Jan. 1907): 7–8.

'Review of *NED*, Mesne–Misbirth'. *The Tribune* (1907).

'Review of *NED*, Mesne–Misbirth'. *The Spectator* (1907): 221.

[Fennell, C. A. M.] 'Review of *NED*, Mense–Misbirth'. *Athenaeum* (30 Mar. 1907): 373–4.

'Review of *NED*, Green–Gyzzern'. *Manchester Guardian* (1907).

'Review of *NED*, Piper–Polygenistic'. *The Spectator* 98 (1907): 580.

B, C. C. ' "Drug" and "Pharmacopœia" in the "N. E. D" '. *Notes & Queries* 7, ser. 10 (1907): 347.

Stachan, L. R. M. ' "N. E. D": A Wrong Reference'. *Notes & Queries* 7, ser. 10 (1907): 367.

[Fennell, C. A. M.] 'Review of *NED*, Piper–Polygenistic'. *Athenaeum* (25 May 1907): 626–8.

'Review of *NED*, Misbode–Monopoly'. *Notes & Queries* 8, ser. 10 (1907): 97–8.

[Fennell, C. A. M.] 'Review of *NED*, Misbode–Monopoly'. *Athenaeum* (10 Aug. 1907): 146–7.

—— 'Review of *NED*, Niche–Nywe'. *Athenaeum* (2 Nov. 1907): 543–4.

'Review of *NED*, Niche–Nywe'. *Notes & Queries* 8, ser. 10 (1907): 397–8.

Thomas, Ralph. 'The Oxford English Dictionary'. *Notes & Queries* 8, ser. 10 (1907): 482–3.

Derocquigny, Jules. 'Review of *NED*, Polygenous–Premious'. *Revue Germanique* 4 (1908): 353–5.

Mann, Max Friedrich. 'Review of *NED*, Monopoly–Movement'. *Bleiblatt zur Anglia* 19 (1908): 159–60.

—— 'Review of *NED*, Movement–Myzostomous'. *Bleiblatt zur Anglia* 19 (1908): 351–2.

—— 'Review of *NED*, Polygenous–Premious'. *Bleiblatt zur Anglia* 19 (1908): 62–4.

[Fennell, C. A. M.] 'Review of *NED*, Polygenous–Premious'. *Athenaeum* (25 Feb. 1908): 184–5.

Murray, J. A. H. ' "Overlay" and "Overlie" '. *The Times* (12 May 1908): 10.

[Fennell, C. A. M.] 'Review of *NED*, Monopoly–Movement'. *Athenaeum* (6 June 1908): 692–3.

—— 'Review of *NED*, Reserve–Ribaldously'. *Athenaeum* (8 Aug. 1908): 145–6.

—— 'Review of *NED*, Movement–Myz'. *Athenaeum* (21 Nov. 1908): 638–9.

'Review of *NED*, Movement–Myz'. *Notes & Queries* 10, ser. 10 (1908): 478–9.

Craigie, W. A. 'A Correction'. *Englische Studien* 40 (1909): 475.

Derocquigny, Jules. 'Review of *NED*, Monopoly–Movement, Movement–Myz, Reserve–Ribaldously'. *Revue Germanique* 5 (1909): 489–92.

Fehr, Bernhard. 'Ergänzungen zum *New English Dictionary*'. *Englische Studien* 40 (1909): 200–7.

Jantzen, Hermann. 'Review of Max Born, *Nachträge zu [J.] A. H. Murray*, Part 1'. *Zeitschrift für französische und englische Unterricht* 8 (1909): 566.

Mann, Max Friedrich. 'Review of *NED*, Premisal–Prophesier'. *Bleiblatt zur Anglia* 20 (1909): 287–8.

—— 'Review of *NED*, Prophesy–Pyxis'. *Bleiblatt zur Anglia* 20 (1909): 383–4.

—— 'Review of *NED*, Ribaldric–Romanite'. *Bleiblatt zur Anglia* 20 (1909): 319–20.

—— 'Review of *NED*, S–Sauce'. *Bleiblatt zur Anglia* 20 (1909): 351–2.

Schröer, Arnold. 'Englische Lexicographie'. *Germanisch–Romanische Monatsschrift* 1 (1909): 550–67.

—— 'Erklärung zu W. A. Craigie's "Correction" '. *Englische Studien* 40 (1909): 476–7.

—— 'Review of *NED*, M, N, P–Premious, Reactively–Ribaldously'. *Englische Studien* 40 (1909): 253–7.

Born, Max. *Nachträge zu [J.] A. H. Murray: A New English Dictionary on Historical Principles*. Berlin: Wissenschaftliche Beilange zum Jaresbericht der Chamisso-Schule in Schöneberg, Ostern, 1909.

Allen, Edward. 'The First Folio of Shakespeare and the "New English Dictionary" '. *Modern Language Notes* 24 (1909): 38–43.

[Fennell, C. A. M.] 'Review of *NED*, Premisal–Prophesier'. *Athenaeum* (20 Feb. 1909): 218–9.

'Review of *NED*, Premisal–Prophesier'. *Notes & Queries* 11, ser. 10 (1909): 179–80.

[Fennell, C. A. M.] 'Review of *NED*, Ribaldric–Romanite'. *Athenaeum* (17 July 1909): 61–2.

'Review of *NED*, Polygenous–Premious, Premisal–Prophesier, Ribaldric–Romanite'. *TLS* (5 Aug. 1909): 286.

'Review of *NED*, Ribaldric–Romanite'. *Notes & Queries* 12, ser. 10 (1909): 179–80.

[Fennell, C. A. M.] 'Review of *NED*, S–Sauce'. *Athenaeum* (28 Aug. 1909): 229–30.

'Review of *NED*, S–Sauce'. *Notes & Queries* 12, ser. 10 (1909): 359–60.

[Fennell, C. A. M.] 'Review of *NED*, Prophesy–Pyxis'. *Athenaeum* (18 Dec. 1909): 756–7.

Derocquigny, Jules. 'Review of *NED*, Premisal–Prophesier, Prophesy–Pyxie, Romanity–Roundness, S–Sauce'. *Revue Germanique* 6 (1910): 219–21.

Garnett, James M. 'Review of *NED*, 12 Parts From 1908–1910'. *American Journal of Philology* 31 (1910): 460–7.

Luick, Karl. 'Review of Max Born, Nachträge Zu [J.] A. H. Murray, Part 1'. *Deutsche Literaturzeitung* 31 (1910): 487.

—— 'Review of *NED*, L–Sa'. *Deutsche Literaturzeitung* 31 (1910): 1323–5.

Mann, Max Friedrich. 'Review of *NED*, Romanity–Roundless'. *Bleiblatt zur Anglia* 21 (1910): 63–4.

—— 'Review of *NED*, Round-Nosed–Ryze'. *Bleiblatt zur Anglia* 21 (1910): 255–6.

—— 'Review of *NED*, Sauce-alone–Scouring'. *Bleiblatt zur Anglia* 21 (1910): 383–4.

Skeat, Walter W. 'Review of *NED*, Prophesy–Pyxis'. *Modern Language Review* 5 (1910): 241–4.

[Fennell, C. A. M.] 'Review of *NED*, Romanity–Roundness'. *Athenaeum* (5 Feb. 1910): 149–50.

Krebs, H. ' "Heortology" '. *Notes & Queries* 1, ser. 11 (1910): 185.

Nicholson, Edward. ' "Pein of the Harte" = Halter'. *Notes & Queries* 1, ser. 11 (1910): 185.

B, C. C. ' "Rose" in the "N. E. D." '. *Notes & Queries* 1, ser. 11 (1910): 205–6.

Williams, J. B. ' "Cleric" and the "N. E. D." '. *Notes & Queries* 1, ser. 11 (1910): 205.

[Fennell, C. A. M.] 'Review of *NED*, Round-nosed–Ryze'. *Athenaeum* (14 May 1910): 574–5.

Murray, J. A. H. ' "Tatting" '. *Notes & Queries* 1, ser. 11 (1910): 426.

Sarum, Old [*pseud.*] ' "Clob"—The "N. E. D." '. *Notes & Queries* 1, ser. 11 (1910): 426.

Skeat, Walter W. ' "Bullion" '. *Notes & Queries* 9, ser. 11 (1910): 6.

V., Q. ' "Portable Railway" '. *Notes & Queries* 2, ser. 11 (1910): 6.

[Fennell, C. A. M.] 'Review of *NED*, Sauce-alone–Scouring'. *Athenaeum* (6 Aug. 1910): 145–6.

—— 'Review of *NED*, T–Tealt'. *Athenaeum* (29 Oct. 1910): 515–16.

Murray, J. A. H. 'The Making of a Dictionary'. *The Times* (1 Nov. 1910): 12.

Jantzen, Hermann. 'Review of Max Born, *Nachträge zu The Oxford English Dictionary*, Part 2'. *Zeitschrift für französiche und englische Unterricht* 10 (1911): 479–80.

Luick, Karl. 'Review of Max Born, *Nachträge Zu [J.] A. H. Murray, Parts 1–2*'. *Deutsche Literaturzeitung* 32 (1911): 3237–8.

Mann, Max Friedrich. 'Review of *NED*, T–Tealt'. *Bleiblatt Zur Anglia* 22 (1911): 30–2.

Munro, John. *Frederick James Furnivall: A Volume of Personal Record*. London: H. Frowde, 1911.

[Fennell, C. A. M.] 'Review of *NED*, Si–Simple'. *Athenaeum* (28 Jan. 1911): 89–90.

'Review of *NED*, T–Tealt'. *Notes & Queries* 3, ser. 11 (1911): 98–9.

[Fennell, C. A. M.] 'Review of *NED*, Scouring–Sedum'. *Athenaeum* (13 May 1911): 532–3.

—— 'Review of *NED*, Team–Tezkere'. *Athenaeum* (29 July 1911): 121–2.

'Review of *NED*, Scouring–Sedum; Si–Simple'. *Notes & Queries* 4, ser. 11 (1911): 159–60.

[Fennell, C. A. M.] 'Review of *NED*, Simple–Sleep'. *Athenaeum* (4 Nov. 1911): 550–1.

'New English Dictionary: Additions and Corrections'. *Notes & Queries* 2, ser. 11 (1912): 29, 63, 138, 265, 267, 308, 327, 376, 409, 427, 446, 470, 494, 508.

Garnett, James M. 'Review of *NED*, Scouring–Sedum, Si–Simple, Simple–Sleep, Team–Tezkere'. *American Journal of Philology* 33 (1912): 83–6.

McKnight, George H. 'Contributions to the *NED*'. *Modern Language Notes* 27 (1912): 112.

Preussner, R. 'Review of Max Born, *Nachträge zu [J.] A. H. Murray*'. *Monatschrift für höhere Schulen* 10 (1912): 38.

Schlutter, Otto B. 'Vier weitere Irrtümer im NED'. *Englische Studien* 46 (1912): 160–3.

[Fennell, C. A. M.] 'Review of *NED*, See–Senatory'. *Athenaeum* (3 Feb. 1912): 118–9.

'Review of *NED*, Simple-Sleep'. *Notes & Queries* 5, ser. 11 (1912): 118–19.

[Fennell, C. A. M.] 'Review of *NED*, Th–Thyzle'. *Athenaeum* (11 May 1912): 524–5.

'Review of *NED*, Th–Thyzle'. *Notes & Queries* 6, ser 11 (1912): 78–9.

'Review of *NED*, Sleep–Sniggle'. *Notes & Queries* 6, ser. 11 (1912): 118–19.

[Fennell, C. A. M.] 'Review of *NED*, Sleep–Sniggle'. *Athenaeum* (10 Aug. 1912): 135–6.

Mayhew, A. L. 'The Word "Broker"'. *Notes & Queries* 6, ser. 11 (1912): 126.

'"Dictograph"'. *Notes & Queries* 6, ser. 11 (1912): 147.

G. '"Nevermass"'. *Notes & Queries* 6, ser. 11 (1912): 170.

Jones, Tom. '"Nevermass"'. *Notes & Queries* 6, ser. 11 (1912): 217.

M., P. K. '"Nevermass"'. *Notes & Queries* 6, ser. 11 (1912): 217.

Thornton, Richard H. '"Like a Thousand of Brick"'. *Notes & Queries* 6, ser. 11 (1912): 209.

Breslar, M. L. R. 'The Word "Broker"'. *Notes & Queries* 6, ser. 11 (1912): 233–4.

Prideaux, W. F. 'The Word "Broker"'. *Notes & Queries* 6, ser. 11 (1912): 233.

Lucas, P. 'The London "Bricklayer"'. *Notes & Queries* 6, ser. 11 (1912): 275.

Robbins, Alfred F. '"Musette"'. *Notes & Queries* 6, ser. 11 (1912): 306.

'Review of *NED*, Senatory–Several'. *Notes & Queries* 6, ser. 11 (1912): 339–40.

'"Geotroposcope"'. *Notes & Queries* 6, ser. 11 (1912): 345.

Mayhew, A. L. '"Notch"'. *Notes & Queries* 6, ser. 11 (1912): 366.

'"Nevermass"'. *Notes & Queries* 6, ser. 11 (1912): 397.

Krueger, G. '"To Be "Out" for a Thing = To Do a Thing"'. *Notes & Queries* 6, ser. 11 (1912): 409.

Bolland, W. C. '"Notch"'. *Notes & Queries* 6, ser. 11 (1912): 427.

H., S. H. A. ' "Cheev, Cheever" '. *Notes & Queries* 6, ser. 11 (1912): 446.

[Fennell, C. A. M.] 'Review of *NED*, Senatory–Several'. *Athenaeum* (4 Dec. 1912): 723–4.

Nicholson, Edward. ' "Notch" '. *Notes & Queries* 6, ser. 11 (1912): 470.

'To Be "Out" for a Thing'. *Notes & Queries* 6, ser. 11 (1912): 494–5.

Parry, G. S. ' "Oake, Oke" '. *Notes & Queries* 6, ser. 11 (1912): 508.

Notice of Vol. 10. *Zeitschrift für Bücherfreunde* 4 (1913): 494.

Garnett, James M. 'Review of *NED*, Parts for 1912'. *American Journal of Philology* 34 (1913): 214–20.

Preussner, R. 'Review of Max Born, *Nachträge zu The Oxford English Dictionary*'. *Monatschrift für höhere Schulen* 11 (1913): 669–70.

Hathaway, Charles M. Jun. 'Notes to the New English Dictionary'. *Englische Studien* 47 (1913): 473–5.

'Review of *NED*, Romanity–Ryze, Si–Sniggle, Sauce-Alone–Several, T–Thyzle'. *TLS* (2 Jan. 1913): 1–2.

[Rendell, Vernon.] 'Review of *NED*, Ti–Tombac'. *Athenaeum* (11 Jan. 1913): 33.

'Review of *NED*, Ti–Tombac'. *Notes & Queries* 7, ser. 11 (1913): 78–9.

'Review of *NED*, Senatory–Several'. *The Nation* (New York) 96 (1913): 133–4.

[Fennell, C. A. M.] 'Review of *NED*, Sniggle–Sorrow'. *Athenaeum* (19 Apr. 1913): 421–2.

'Review of *NED*, Sniggle–Sorrow'. *Notes & Queries* 7, ser. 11 (1913): 399–400.

Allen, F. Sturges. 'News for Bibliophiles'. *The Nation* (New York) 97 (1913): 10.

[Fennell, C. A. M.] 'Review of *NED*, Several–Shaster'. *Athenaeum* (12 July 1913): 30–1.

'Review of *NED*, Several–Shaster'. *Notes & Queries* 8, ser. 11 (1913): 78–9.

'Review of *NED*, Tombal–Trahysh'. *Notes & Queries* 8, ser. 11 (1913): 358–60.

[Fennell, C. A. M.] 'Review of *NED*, Tombal–Trahysh'. *Athenaeum* (13 Nov. 1913): 483.

'Review of *NED*, Several–Shaster, Sniggle–Sorrow, Ti–Traysh'. *TLS* (11 Dec. 1913): 593–4.

'Review of *NED*, Several–Shaster'. *The Nation* (New York) 97 (1913): 622.

'Review of *NED*, Shastri-Shyster'. *Saturday Review* 117 (1914): 736–7.

Garnett, James M. 'Review of *NED*, Parts for 1913'. *American Journal of Philology* 35 (1914): 475–81.

[Fennell, C. A. M.] 'Review of *NED*, Sorrow–Speech'. *Athenaeum* (17 Jan. 1914): 83.

'Review of *NED*, Sorrow–Speech'. *Notes & Queries* 9, ser. 11 (1914): 79–80.

C., B. C. ' "Species" in the "N. E. D." '. *Notes & Queries* 9, ser. 11 (1914): 127.

'Review of *NED*, Tombal–Trahysh'. *The Nation* (New York) 98 (1914): 271–2.

Hoops, Johannes. ' "Oxford Dictionary" '. *Edinburgh Review* 219 (1914): 307–26.

[Fennell, C. A. M.] 'Review of *NED*, Shastri–Shyster'. *Athenaeum* (18 Apr. 1914): 550.

'Review of *NED*, Shastri–Shyster'. *Notes & Queries* 9, ser. 11 (1914): 338–9.

'Review of *NED*, Shastri–Shyster'. *Saturday Review* 117 (1914): 604–5.

Ritchie, R. L. G. 'Early Instances of Words for the "N. E. D." '. *Notes & Queries* 9, ser. 11 (1914): 387.

Woodcock, Herbert De Carle. 'The English Tongue'. *Saturday Review* 117 (1914): 736–7.

'Review of *NED*, Traik–Trinity'. *Notes & Queries* 10, ser. 11 (1914): 59.

[Fennell, C. A. M.] 'Review of *NED*, Traik–Trinity'. *Athenaeum* (18 July 1914): 69–70.

Ritchie, R. L. G. 'Early Instances of Words for the "N. E. D." '. *Notes & Queries* 11, ser. 10 (1914): 127–8.

'Review of *NED*, Speech–Spring'. *Notes & Queries* 10, ser. 11 (1914): 319–20.

[Fennell, C. A. M.] 'Review of *NED*, Speech–Spring'. *Athenaeum* (24 Oct. 1914): 416–17.

'How A Dictionary Grew'. *The Periodical* (1915): 198–201.

Jantzen, Hermann. 'Review of Max Born, *Nachträge zu The Oxford English Dictionary*, Part 3'. *Zeitschrift für französiche und englische Unterricht* 14 (1915): 473.

Mann, Max Friedrich. 'Review of *NED*, Scouring–Sedum'. *Bleiblatt zur Anglia* 26 (1915): 95.

—— 'Review of *NED*, See–Senatory'. *Bleiblatt zur Anglia* 26 (1915): 127–8.

—— 'Review of *NED*, Several–Shaster'. *Bleiblatt zur Anglia* 26 (1915): 191–2.

—— 'Review of *NED*, Shastri–Shyster'. *Bleiblatt zur Anglia* 26 (1915): 223–4.

Vizetelly, Frank H. 'The Story of the Oxford English Dictionary of the English Language'. *Educational Review* 50 (1915): 308–13.

'Review of *NED*, Su–Subterraneous'. *Notes & Queries* 11, ser. 11 (1915): 59.

[Fennell, C. A. M.] 'Review of *NED*, Su–Subterraneous'. *Athenaeum* (23 Jan. 1915): 65.

'Review of *NED*, Su–Subterraneous; the *Century Dictionary*'. *TLS* (4 Mar. 1915): 77.

[Fennell, C. A. M.] 'Review of *NED*, Spring–Squoyle; St–Standard'. *Athenaeum* (17 Apr. 1915): 353–4.

'Review of *NED*, Spring–Squoyle, St–Standard'. *Notes & Queries* 11, ser. 11 (1915): 351.

'Review of *NED*, Trink–Turn-Down'. *Notes & Queries* 12, ser. 11 (1915): 79.

[Fennell, C. A. M.] 'Review of *NED*, Trink–Turn-down'. *Athenaeum* (31 July 1915): 71–2.

'How a Dictionary Grew'. *Literary Digest* 51 (1915): 351–2.

'Review of *NED*, Standard–Stead'. *Notes & Queries* 12, ser. 11 (1915): 331.

[Fennell, C. A. M.] 'Review of *NED*, Standard–Stead'. *Athenaeum* (24 Oct. 1915): 309.

The Oxford Dictionary: A Brief Account. Sir James Murray In Memoriam. Oxford: Clarendon Press, 1916.

Mann, Max Friedrich. 'Review of *NED*, Simple–Sleep'. *Bleiblatt zur Anglia* 27 (1916): 187–8.

—— 'Review of *NED*, Sleep–Sniggle'. *Bleiblatt zur Anglia* 27 (1916): 214–16.

—— 'Review of *NED*, Sorrow–Speech'. *Bleiblatt Zur Anglia* 27 (1916): 270–2.

—— 'Review of *NED*, Team–Tezkere'. *Bleiblatt zur Anglia* 27 (1916): 327–8.

—— 'Review of *NED*, Th–Thyzle'. *Bleiblatt zur Anglia* 27 (1916): 359–60.

Schlutter, Otto B. 'Sind die Angaben des NED durchaus Verlässlich?' *Anglia* 40 (1916): 509–11.

'Review of *NED*, Subterraneously–Sullen'. *Notes & Queries* 1, ser. 12 (1916): 119–20.

'Review of *NED*, Turndun–Tzirid'. *Notes & Queries* 1, ser. 12 (1916): 319–20.

'The Oxford English Dictionary'. *Journal of Education* 38 (1916): 210.

[Rendell, Vernon.] 'Review of *NED*, Subterraneously–Sullen, Turndun–Tzirid'. *Athenaeum* (June 1916): 273–4.

'Review of *NED*, Si–Th, Stead–Stillatim'. *Saturday Review* 122 (1916): 65–6.

'Review of *NED*, Stead–Stillatim'. *Notes & Queries* 2, ser. 12 (1916): 78–9.

'Review of *NED*, V–Verificative'. *Notes & Queries* 2, ser. 12 (1916): 499–500.

Mann, Max Friedrich. 'Review of *NED*, Tombal–Trahysh'. *Bleiblatt Zur Anglia* 28 (1917): 31–2.

Mason, Lawrence. 'Bishop Henry King and the *Oxford Dictionary*'. *Modern Language Notes* 32 (1917): 55–7.

Mutschmann, Heinrich. 'Review of Max Born, *Nachträge zu "The Oxford English Dictionary"*'. *Die neueren Sprachen* 24 (1917): 118.

Bradley, Henry. 'Sir James Murray'. *Proceedings of the British Academy* (1917): 545–51.

'Review of *NED*, Sullen–Supple'. *Athenaeum* (Feb. 1917): 98.

'Review of *NED*, Sullen–Supple'. *Notes & Queries* 3, ser. 12 (1917): 179–80.

'Review of *NED*, Si–Th, Sullen–Supple, Ti–Z'. *TLS* (31 May 1917): 260.

'Review of *NED*, Verificatory–Visor'. *Athenaeum* (Oct. 1917): 523.

'An Oxford English Dictionary'. *Bodleian Quarterly Record* 2 (1918): 156.

'Review of *NED*, Stillation–Siratum'. *Notes & Queries* 4, ser. 12 (1918): 90–1.

'Review of *NED*, Supple–Sweep'. *Athenaeum* (May 1918): 243.

'Review of *NED*, Supple–Sweep'. *Notes & Queries* 4, ser. 12 (1918): 230.

Bradley, Henry. '[Report to the Philological Society]'. *Athenaeum* (1919): 560.

Fischer, Walther. 'Review of Max Born, *Nachträge zu The Oxford English Dictionary*'. *Bleiblatt zur Anglia* 30 (1919): 60–3.

Gilbert, Allen A. 'Words Omitted from the "New English Dictionary"'. *Modern Language Notes* 34 (1919): 121.

Schlutter, Otto B. 'Notes on the New English Dictionary'. *Journal of English and Germanic Philology* 18 (1919): 575–7.

'Philological Society (6 June)'. *Athenaeum* (4 July 1919): 560.

Erlebach, Alfred. 'In the Dictionary Margin: A Sub-Editor's Notes'. *The Times* (25 Oct. 1919): 17e.

'Lexicography for the Ambitious' (Leading Article). *The Times* (30 Oct. 1919): 9d.

'Review of *NED*, Stratus–Styx, Sweep–Szmitike'. *Saturday Review* 128 (1919): 488–9.

'Review of *NED*, Stratus–Styx'. *Notes & Queries* 5, ser. 12 (1919): 334–5.

Loane, George G. *A Thousand and One Notes on 'A New English Dictionary'*. London: Surbiton, Philpott & Co., 1920.

'Review of *NED*, Visor–Vywor'. *Athenaeum* (16 Apr. 1920): 526.

'Review of *NED*, Visor–Vywer'. *Notes & Queries* 6, ser. 12 (1920): 159–60.

'Review of *NED*, Visor–Vywer'. *Saturday Review* 129 (1920): 542–3.

'Review of *A Thousand and One Notes on "A New English Dictionary"'*. *Athenaeum* (19 Nov. 1920): 696.

'Review of *A Thousand and One Notes on "A New English Dictionary"* by George G. Loane'. *Notes & Queries* 7, ser. 12 (1920): 439.

Loane, G[eorge] G. 'More Notes on the "N. E. D."'. *TLS* (11 Aug. 1921): 516.

'Review of *NED*, U–Unforseeable'. *Notes & Queries* 9, ser. 12 (1921): 520.

Luick, Karl. 'Zum Abschluss des Oxforder Wörterbuches'. *Deutsche Literaturzeitung* 43 (1922): 145–8.

B, R. L. 'Notes on the N. E. D.[: "Relax"]'. *TLS* (5 Jan. 1922): 13.

'Review of *NED*, W–Wash'. *Notes & Queries* 10, ser. 12 (1922): 18–19.

'Review of *NED*, Ti–Z, X–Zyxt'. *Notes & Queries* 10, ser. 12 (1922): 159–60.

'Review of *NED*, W–Wash, X–Zyxt'. *TLS* (8 June 1922): 374.

'Review of *NED*, Wash–Wavy, Wh–Whisking'. *Saturday Review* 136 (1923): 109–10.

'Review of *NED*, Ti–Z'. *Notes & Queries* 1, ser. 13 (1923): 100.

Chapman, R. W. 'The Oxford Dictionary'. *TLS* (29 Nov. 1923): 836.

Weekley, Ernest. 'On Dictionaries'. *Atlantic Monthly* 133 (1924): 782–91.

Faverty, Frederick E. 'The Rolls of Parliament and the New English Dictionary'. *Modern Language Notes* 41 (1926): 375–8.

'Notices'. *Catholic Historical Review* 7 (1927): 725.

'The "N. E. D."'. *The Nation* (New York) 124 (1927): 660.

'Notice of the Completion of the *OED*'. *Scribner's Magazine* 83 (1928): 361.

Oxford English Dictionary, 1884–1928: Speeches Delivered in the Goldsmith's Hall. Oxford, 1928.

H[ill], R. H. 'The Dictionary Exhibition'. *Bodleian Quarterly Record* 5 (1928): 221–2.

Onions, C. T. 'The New English Dictionary and the Bodleian'. *Bodleian Quarterly Record* 5 (1928): 220–1.

Wardale, E[dith] E[lizabeth]. 'The "New English Dictionary"'. *Nineteenth Century* 103 (1928): 97–110.

'A Triumph of Lexicography'. *School and Society* 27 (1928): 364–5.

McKnight, Floyd. 'The Greatest of Dictionaries'. *The Bookman* 67 (1928): 141–4.

Weekley, Ernest. 'The Oxford Dictionary'. *Quarterly Review* 250 (1928): 238–43.

'Review of *NED*, Wise–Wyzen'. *TLS* (19 Apr. 1928): 277–8.

Craigie, William A. 'Making of a Dictionary: Oxford English Dictionary'. *Saturday Review of Literature* 4 (1928): 792.

'From A to Zyxt: Oxford English Dictionary'. *The Mentor* 16 (1928): 63.

'Monument to Words: Oxford English Dictionary'. *Wilson Library Bulletin* 3 (1928): 264–5.

—— 'The Oxford English Dictionary'. *Libraries* 33 (1928): 310–13.

Williams, I. A. 'The *New English Dictionary* Completed'. *London Mercury* 18 (1928): 178–85.

'Celebrating a Great Achievement'. *Living Age* 334 (1928): 1057–61.

Beard, Charles Relly. 'Armour, and the "New English Dictionary"'. *The Connoisseur* 81 (1928): 235–7.

Mann, James Gow. 'Armour, and the "New English Dictionary"'. *The Connoisseur* 82 (1928): 121–2.

Emery, H. G. 'Dictionaries: The Race Between the Language and the Lexicographer'. *Century Magazine* 117 (1928): 108–16.

'The Oxford English Dictionary'. *Bulletin of the John Rylands Library* 13 (1929): 9–11.

Erlebach, D. E. 'In the Dictionary Margin'. *The Times* (25 Oct. 1929): 15e.

Craigie, William A. 'New Dictionary Schemes Presented to the Philological Society, 4th Apr. 1919'. *TPS* (1931): 6–11.

Chapple, Joe Mitchell. 'A Century of Dictionary Progress'. *National Magazine* 59 (1931): 249–52.

Dike, Edwin Berck. 'The *NED*: Additions and Corrections'. *Modern Language Notes* 47 (1932): 249–54.

—— '"The *NED*: Words of Divination and Onomatopoeic Terms'. *Modern Language Notes* 48 (1933): 521–5.

Ross, A. S. C. 'Review'. *Neuphilologische Mitteilungen* 35 (1934): 128.

Zandvoort, R. W. 'Review of *A New English Dictionary on Historical Principles. Introduction, Supplement, and Bibliography*'. *English Studies* 16 (1934): 101–5.

Delcourt, Joseph. 'Review of *NED*'. *Revue Anglo-Américaine* 12 (1934–5): 52–3.

Hulbert, J. R. 'Review of *A New English Dictionary on Historical Principles: Introduction, Supplement, and Bibliography*'. *Modern Philology* 32 (1935): 205–7.

Mackie, W. S. 'Shakespeare's English and How Far It Can Be Investigated With the Help of the *New English Dictionary*'. *Modern Language Review* 31 (1936): 1–10.

Murray, Wilfred G. R. *Murray The Dictionary Maker: A Brief Account of Sir James A. H. Murray*. Cape Town: The Rustica Press, Ltd., 1943.

Butt, John. 'A Plea for More English Dictionaries'. *Durham University Journal* 11 (1951): 95–102.

Bivens, Leslie. 'Nineteenth Century Reactions to the *O. E. D.*: An Annotated Bibliography'. *Dictionaries* 2–3 (1980–1): 146–52.

Index